ADVANCED EDUCATIONAL TECHNOLOGY

Advanced Educational Technology

Seema Sharma

ANMOL PUBLICATIONS PVT. LTD.
NEW DELHI - 110 002 (INDIA)

ANMOL PUBLICATIONS PVT. LTD.
4374/4B, Ansari Road, Daryaganj
New Delhi - 110 002
Ph.: 23261597, 23278000
Visit us at: www.anmolpublications.com

Advanced Educational Technology

First Published, 2005

ISBN 81-261-2410-5

PRINTED IN INDIA

Published by J.L. Kumar for Anmol Publications Pvt. Ltd., New Delhi - 110 002 and Printed at Mehra Offset Press, Delhi.

Contents

Preface

Since the origin of mankind, due to his power of thinking and analysing, the man has felt need to communicate and for communicating, he invented a language. But it was only verbal communication. Then, the man devised sketches, figures, and signs to interpret his feeling or thinking and presenting his ideas. But the limitation of this system was that he failed to depict the real picture of his thoughts.

The Early men were nomadic or seminomadic barbarians and they used to make hutments and lived in groups. Then they felt need to know about other people, their culture, the way of living for improving their own living conditions. Only, then there arised the need for education.

The Education, as a discipline and as a science has undergone a long journey, spanned over centuries. Nowadays computers and other advanced teaching devices are being used for improving the quality of education. Yet there is room for other advanced technologies in the area. Due to the advancement and complexity in man's life. He needs more and demands more and more. So that the future and present generation could improve, and could cope with new situations.

Though there is no dearth for books on the subject, yet, this book has its own features. The Editor has liberally drawn upon from the works of other authors and research papers, and he owes, debt and gratitude to all of them.

In the present work, the Editor has suggested a framework and a few advanced techniques for the further advancement of technology of education. The undersigned is hopeful enough that the present work would be of immense help to the present day teachers and students, alike.

Editor

1

Introduction

The use of Educational Technology has been emphasised in both the National Policy of Education, 1986 and revised NPE, 1992, to improve both the quality and quantity of education for the first time in the history of Indian Education. No earlier document of national significance had pointed out the importance of educational technology so clearly and so strongly as it has been done by the NPE, 1986. Spelling out its deployment, the NPE, 1986 (p. 22) has observed, "Educational Technology will be employed in the spread of useful information, the training and retraining of teachers, to improve the quality, sharpen awareness of art and culture, inculcate abiding values etc., both in the formal and non-formal sections."

According to Eric Asbhy (1967), mankind is now in the midst of the Fourth Revolution in Education - the Age of Electronic Media which comprises radio, television, audio/video recorder, computer, and so on. The NPE '86 has therefore added (p. 22): "In the villages without electricity batteries or solar packs will be utilised to run the programme." It has also suggested that in order to avoid structural dualism, modern educational technology must reach out to the most distant areas and the most deprived sections of beneficiaries simultaneously with the areas of comparative affluence and availability.

The Programme of Action (POA), 1986 (p. 180) has rightly pointed out that several efforts have been made in the past to use technological aids for improving the quality of education. Audio visual units and film libraries were set up at the Centre and in States for promoting the use of educational films and projection aids. Educational Technology Centres and Cells were established at the national and state levels respectively for facilitating the use of various media, particularly radio and television. Although School Broadcast programme has been in vogue for more than four decades, it has not yet been accepted whole-heartedly and in massive scale throughout the country. Educational Television Programme, in spite of its glamour and potentiality, has not yet been popular in the educational institutions.

In many States and Union territories, State Institutes of Educational Technology (SIETs) and at the national level the Central Institute of Educational Technology have been producing, utilising, monitoring and following up the television and radio programmes for improving the quantity and quality of education. Under the project "INSAT for EDUCATION" launched in 1982, the SIETs have been generating educational software for children. The Audio Visual Research Centres (AVRCs) and Educational Media Research Centres (EMRCs) have been producing Educational TV Programmes for college/university students. Some Technical Teacher Training Institutions (TTTIs) have also been developing facilities for production of TV as well as other media programmes.

Video Technology has made a headway in the field of education. The Electronic Trade and Technology Development Corporation (ET & TDC) has formulated a TELETEACH Project to prepare software on videotape. A good number of secondary schools have been selected by the Ministry of Education for equipping them with VCRs and viewing equipment to work as viewing centres.

Computer Education has been popular in the country at various stages of education. The Computer Literacy and Studies in Schools (CLASS) Project has been implemented in hundreds of Schools and with availability of microcomputers there, the students have been familiarised with the application and potentiality of computer as learning medium. Computer education courses are now available in many universities besides Ph. D., M. Tech., and B. Tech Programmes conducted by the IITs and other technological institutions. Diploma level courses are being offered by a few dozens of polytechnics.

Although educational broadcasting has the inherent advantages of greater reach, management, convenience and cost effectiveness, the non-broadcast/non-project media and materials are more oriented to individual learning and more appropriate to the indigenous clientele and developing economy. These media would also help in enriching the learning process. Large scale use of audio and video programmes in broadcast and non-broadcast modes would generate enormous demand for qualified manpower to work in educational media set-ups. It would be necessary to develop maintenance structure and train "technician entrepreneurs" for taking up such responsibilities. As enunciated in the POA (1986) "Education requires media support which is related to the curriculum as well as enrichment. Curriculum-based education also requires materials which the teacher can draw upon in the course of this teaching. This could be provided in the form of charts, slides, transparencies, etc. Video technology offers considerable potential for improving the quality of education especially at higher levels."

Similarly computer technology is likely to influence education enormously and can play an important role in enhancing the efficiency of the teaching-learning process, making children more creative and providing them with an individualised learning environment. Computer literacy would be crucial in preparing children to cope with microcomputer explosion which has the same potential for social change as the Industrial Revolution. It is essential to integrate the same progressively with the school curriculum.

The modem world is confronting two general problems which are not only affecting the pattern of human life, but also inflicting their full impact on education. These two problems are called "information explosion" and the "population explosion." They are like two horns of dilemma in education-more things to learn and more people to be taught.

The term "information explosion" really means an explosion of knowledge. We all know, new frontiers of knowledge are opening day by day and the horizon of human knowledge and understanding is expanding very fast. In most of the subjects, moreover, knowledge is cumulative, so that every now and then, there is more to be learnt. Especially in arts subjects, new facts and figures take their place along with the old. In sciences although new knowledge or information often supersedes the old, the students and scientists have to learn both. Besides, closer relations among countries of the world resulting from wide international communications make information explosion more acute and complicated.

The second problem is "Population Explosion" which is immensely affecting traditional pattern of education. The problem of population explosion is more serious in the developing countries than the developed ones. For example, in India population has been increasing in geometrical progression. India now has more than 1000 million people.

Michael J. Apter (1968 p. 10) has rightly observed, "The increase in population has of course tended to occur fastest in the developing countries. For this reason the problem it poses for education is the greatest in these countries. Conversely, the information explosion has the greatest immediate effect on the technologically advanced countries. Fortunately, no country has experienced the full effects of both at the same time. Nevertheless, there is a fair degree of overlap between the effects of the two." The developing countries like India, however, are facing serious difficulties both from population as well as information explosion. Because they have to provide education for a larger population year by year and cover more and more technical and scientific ground for making up the deficiency. Since most of the countries are confronted more or less with the problem of more persons to be taught and more information to be learnt, this general problem is called "Education Explosion."

The problem of "Education Explosion" has both positive and negative aspects. On the positive side the problem has unprecedented record to its credit. The bright features are -

1. Most countries of the world have spent more on education during the last fifty five years than we have in recorded history.
2. More enrolment of pupils than any time in the past has been made during the last three decades. It has more than doubled in most countries since 1950.
3. The educational systems of the world have produced 90% of all the writers, artists, scientists and technologists who have even lived during this time.
4. The products of our educational systems are so creative that they are making the quantum of knowledge double in scientific and technological fields.
5. The youths educated by the modern educational system during the last five decades have published more books and magazines both regards the number of copies as well as that of titles.

Seth Spaulding (1970 p. 9) Director of UNESCO's Department of School and H. E. has thus aptly remarked, "The record is, then impressive. We are, in essence, providing more education than ever before in history and the products of our systems are apparently more creative than all our forefathers put together."

The other side of the coin is however as follows:

1. Although in most of the countries educational expenditure has been enormous, it is estimated that as many as one third of the children of school-going age have not yet seen the inside of a school. If at all they enter the schools, less than one third of them are able to complete lower elementary education. As many as 50% of the pupils' are only repeaters. The wastage and stagnation in many educational systems thus make cost of schooling spectacular and increase the number of illiterates and semiliterates.
2. In spite of the phenomenal quantitative expansion of education the world has still an army of illiterate adults.
3. Almost all governments of the world now recognise education more as an investiment rather than as a social

expenditure. Accordingly the so-called "investment" has been expanded enormously. But many countries are still finding it difficult to reach the quantitative targets like physical facilities and material resources suggested by various international conferences on education.

4. Grave doubts are expressed as to the relevance and effectiveness of education in the modern society not only in India, but also in most of the developed and developing countries of the world. Education cannot serve its purpose unless it is relevant to contemporary and future problems of the community and of the world. For example, education should deal with the pollution problems, population problems, agricultural problems, technological problems and war and peace. If succeeding generations are not able to tackle these problems successfully, education will be deemed to be a failure.
5. Although education has promoted the growth and development of science and technology, education itself has not yet been able to utilise their traits for being more effective and relevant. Seth Spaulding has rightly said, "The way we manage and administer our educational enterprises would probably bankrupt any other kind of business. Although education has shared in the creation of technological age, education itself has not learnt how to use the fruits of technology to improve the efficiency and the quality of its own institutions. In attempts to 'catch up' quantitatively education has usually attempted to multiply what has gone in a pre-technology system of schooling."

In essence, Mr. Spaulding (1970 p. 10) has said that we have provided more and more money to more and more of that we may be doing poorly. We hope that we could do it better. Educationists of international distinction have suggested that it will be possible only by developing suitable curriculum and applying educational technologies to make the curriculum more effective and the school more efficient.

Educational technology, in its global sense, includes the entire process of the setting of goals, the continuous reforms of curriculum, the tryout of new methods and materials, the evaluation of the system as an integrated whole and resetting of goals on the basis of the findings of evaluation and innovations. But it is often identified as pointed out by Spaulding, with various devices and processes which make possible the recording, storage, manipulation, retrieval, transmission and display of data, information and printed and photographed materials with an efficiency and speed unheard of, even 20 years ago. If these capabilities are considered as part of a broad curriculum for research and development design, they have tremendous potential in education.

Technological materials and methods useful in the teaching-learning process range from chalkboards to television sets. Technology of education involves books and blackboards, paper and pencils, models and maps, charts and globes, tapes and slides, radios and televisions, projectors and computers. It comprises both "hardware" and "software" and both audio and visual materials. It also includes decisions about the educational objectives to be achieved and decisions about the size of the learning group, the learning sequence, teaching methods and selection of media.

In its wider perspective, therefore, educational technology deals with the systematic application of the resources of scientific knowledge to the process that each individual has to pass through in order to acquire and use knowledge. "Educational Technology" writes Geoffrey Hubbard (1974), Director of the National Council for Educational Technology, England "is the complement of curriculum reform concerned with the Method where curriculum reform is concerned with the content... Given an acceptance of the concept of educational technology as the process of improving learning method, we are faced with the problems of encouraging innovation in an educational system whose greatest strength is in decentralisation and autonomy. Certainly nothing will be achieved by elaborating authoritarian solutions. What is needed is more discussion of the contribution the different elements of the system can make to the problems facing education. Widespread dissemination of experience (both successful and unsuccessful) of innovations and supporting services, including training, consultancy and information activities are necessary to assist the teacher in the selection and introduction of the new methods appropriate to his own particular situation."

According to GOM Leith "Educational Technology is the application of scientific knowledge about learning and the conditions of learning to improve the effectiveness and efficiency of teaching and training. In the absence of scientifically established principles, educational technology implements techniques of empirical testing to improve learning situations." Hence educational technology seeks to apply scientific knowledge about learning and the conditions of learning for improving its effectiveness.

We find that a large number of new methods and media constitute educational technology. But there is no proper co-ordination and articulation in their use. That is why, no satisfactory results are achieved by such a wide range of materials due to lack of a systematic planning and organisation. Henri Dieuzeide (1970), Director of UNESCO's Division of Methods, Materials and Techniques has aptly remarked, "The new techniques do in fact offer a vast range of possibilities, but their field of application often seems to be a wasteland scattered with spare parts which no one knows how to put together to form an efficient system. Here it is useful to discuss the difference between technology in education and technology of education. We have to move from one to the other, i. e. from the former to the latter. Technology in education is concerned with equipment, preparation of adhoc messages and integration with traditional teacher-centered activities. But as discussed earlier, technology of education deals with the active use of mass media and computer science for the individual pupils learning process under the teacher's supervision. Hence the latter one i. e. educational technology is more scientific, more psychological and more pedagogical than the former one i.e. technology in education."

With the advance of science and technology there are new learning aids which have revolutionized the learning process, in particular and education as a whole. In modern society with its emphasis on mass education and successful citizenship training, the requirement is for efficient learning. Education has now become an assembly-line like mass production factories. A nation can prosper if its education can be made effective. Education can be made efficient, if it uses modern technology. Technology in education will be useful, if it is properly planned and organised on psychological and pedagogical principles. Henri Dieuzeide has rightly observed, "The transition from technology in education to the technology of education involves a thorough appraisal of the existing educational system, of its objectives and of the means used to attain them, before any decision is reached to employ these new techniques for specific teaching purposes. The teacher-turned technologist can then gradually assume the functions of an 'educational engineer' whose job is to increase the output of the entire scholastic machine."

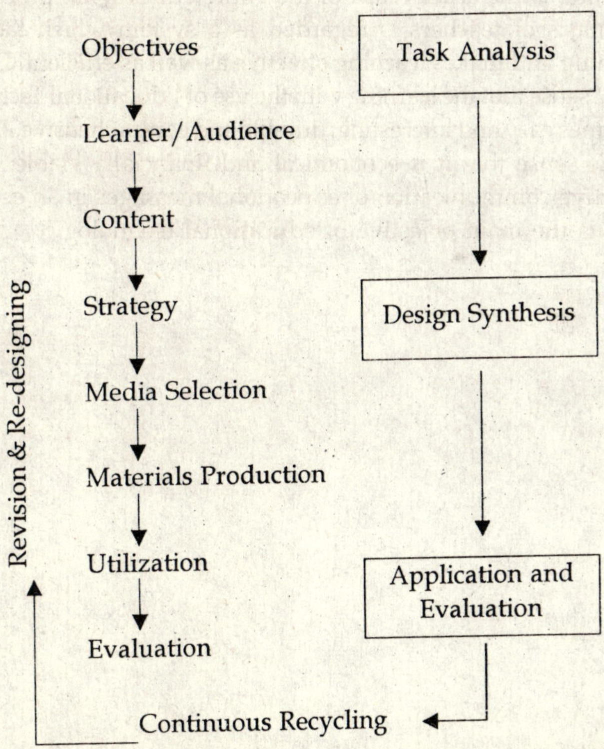

Although educational technology can be interpreted in a rather narrow sense as the use of sophisticated hardware in teaching or in a broad sense as the use of any new educational technique, in fact the concept means more than the sum total of all the media and methods, materials and techniques used for better teaching and learning. It involves or should involve greater psychological and pedagogical preparedness, a scientific attitude and a coordinated approach to the educational process as a whole. It should reflect one's professional interest and zeal for making experiments and innovations for development and success of education.

Educational Technology implies the use of all educational resources—men and materials, methods and techniques, means and media in an integrated and systematic manner for optimizing learning. According to the modern educationists, learning not teaching is the crucial task of the entire educational process and emphasis of teachers is regarded as a system which facilitates learning and makes learning effective as well as efficient. Efficient in the sense that the learning with the use of Educational Technology becomes easy and interesting, durable and comprehensive. Efficient in the sense that it is economical and financially viable. In fact, effective communication of educational messages in an economic way is the main objective of educational technology.

2

The Fundamentals

Before, five centuries, when the first book was printed, no longer did students need to cluster at the feet of their teachers to listen and memorise what was read to them from a precious, laboriously produced hand-written manuscript. The printed book was a form of automation, a kind of teaching machine. Each student could have his own copy of the text to study. It seemed that the teacher has been permanently replaced, but the teacher increased in importance. His function changed. Relieved of the chore of reading to his students, now he had time to counsel and to explain and expound, to interpret and correlate the mass of information and knowledge that books made available to all.

For centuries the teacher's chief job has been that of presenting information and testing students to see whether they can remember it on cue or not. But now it is clear that assignment of lists of non-functional facts to be studied and remembered is out of place. Changes in a society usually bring changes to its institutions including education. The educational institutions are also affected by rapid increase in number of students, increased mobility of students, increased range of students' abilities and broadend backgrounds. Opinions as to what should be done often contradict each other, but there is a clear demand for action that will enhance the learning of the individual students, the effectiveness of schools and colleges and ultimately the quality of the nation's life.

Today we are seeing the beginning of another forward surge that may prove even greater. The electronic age is changing our traditional notion of education. Since last few decades innovations of all kinds are being experimented and the education has come more and more to understand that learning is an active process. The role of teacher, the role of the classroom, as well as the nature of the learning process itself must be re-examined in the light of new technology, for the sake of the nation's quality education.

The first step towards improving quality would be to free the teacher from much of his daily routine in order to give him time to serve as diagnostician and organiser or manager of functionally varied learning experiences. The second step would be to provide teachers with a large number of teaching techniques and specific curricular material. A third positive step would be the development of teaching material of a highly individualised nature in each subject. Each of these steps could be realised with the widespread use of electronic teaching aids that could take over much of the routine involvement in teaching and also provide better course materials. Classroom teacher then could give more individual attention to their students.

Lot of educators do believe that if technology is properly supported and wisely used, could help meet most of the pressing educational needs and many teaching problems can be solved partly or wholly by the proper use of the rich experiences that can be gained through certain media. In this technological age, therefore, today's teacher should take the full advantage of the existing technological resources for quality education.

Education and Technology

Any definition of Educational Technology must be subject to the concept held by the definer, and this involves consideration of at least two distinct concepts—the physical science or media concept, and the behavioural science concept. Here various definitions of Educational Technology are being given.

(i) The Educational Technology can be defined as the purposeful utilisation, in combination or separately of objectives, techniques, devices, events and relationships to increase the effectiveness of educational process. Educational Technology is fundamentally aimed at improving the efficiency of educational systems by increasing the rate, depth, precision and value of the learning which takes place.

(ii) Educational Technology concerns the systematic use of modern methods of technologies in teaching and learning. It involves teachers in a variety of roles, some of which are traditional and some still emerging. In this definition special consideration is given to the adaptive role of the teacher.

(iii) Educational Technology is a systematic way of designing, carrying out and evaluating the total process of learning and teaching in terms of specific objectives based on research in human learning, a combination of human and non-human resources to bring about more effective instruction.

Outside the limits of speech, man is dependent upon the tools of his age for his ability to educate or to learn from others. Twenty-first century man has acquired more tools of communication, more power to educate in last fifty years than he ever possessed in the hundreds of thousands of years of pre-recorded history. With the increasing rate of scientific advance and discovery the need has arisen for clarification of new methods of communication and their application. This is the core situatio1n with which educational technology has to deal. The greater the pace of change in the world, the more urgent it becomes for us to develop efficiency in the way our young people learn. This is true because education is a bridge between present and future, it is a bridge between what we are and what we may become—as individual, as a nation, as a world. But the test of the value of a new technique for education is not whether learning occurs. Learning is always occurring but we are to test whether the new technique improves the learning rate and depth of understanding as compared with the existing approach.

Educational Technology is still largely a classroom supplement. Teachers now have access to film projectors, slide projectors, tape-recorders. Video Cassette Recorders (VCRs), Video Cassette Players (VCPs) and computers etc. Teaching machines may ultimately prove more effective in a specific learning situation than text and printed material, since they offer greater control over the contingencies involving in learning.

The teacher normally supplements his verbal output with such materials as textbooks, blackboards, maps, posters, slides, overhead projectors, etc. Essentially these devices are limited to the presentation of immobile two-dimensional/orres.

In United States a Commission on Instructional Technology was established long back to determine whether the belief in technology's value for education is justified and whether it is justified to recommend actions to provide for the most effective possible application of technology to American Education. The Commission took 'Learning' as starting point instead of technology. The heart of education is the student learning and the value of any technology used in education must, therefore, be measured by its capacity to improve learning.

Technology will assist and support educational functions. Thus increasing the productivity of the teaching force and freeing them of the multitude of clerical record keeping chores and the elementary task of simply presenting information for students consumption. This can restore the personal touch to the educational process.

But there are many problems in adopting educational technology.

1. Well intentioned resistance to the introduction of technology—some people think that it will dehumanise a very human process.
2. Getting educational research applied—innovaters and leaders have problems in transitioning from research to application. Many successful researches are not carried out towards its application.
3. Scarcity of trained personnel to install/maintain and supply new methods and equipment.

Few basic principles will affect the successful application of educational technology. The key to success is training and particularly in-service training. The real mass attack on training must take place at school and college level. In-service training needs to be developed on at least at two levels.

(a) At the elementary levels to ensure the elimination of fear and ignorance of the hardware and to show the productive potential in a curriculum situation.

(b) At the advanced level especially in its application to curriculum development.

If educational hardware is going to be used effectively during teaching situations the colleges and schools must be supported by an adequate technical assistance service. Every teacher should take this training in the first few years of his teaching career. Because of the size of turnover of staff in educational institutions, it is essential that in-service training in the handling of technical equipment be continuous until all have learned its use.

Next stage in training could be more advanced, concerned with the techniques of production. One can use this technique in the lecture room situation to take 'Off Air' programmes to enable large groups of students to see a detailed scientific demonstration clearly, or to use it in certain areas of the curriculum.

Computer's Role

In order to use educational technology we should be familiar with the existing hard and softwares.

Hardwares (Technology in Education): Hardwares include all sorts of teaching machines. Some common ones are listed below:

Devices of Moive

(a) 16 mm film projector

(b) 8 mm/super 8 mm film projector (not being used now)

(c) 35 mm slide projector

(d) Opaque projector (Episcope)

(e) Overhead projector (OHP)

(f) Micro-projector

Tape-Recorders

(a) Spool tape-recorders (not much in use now in educational institutions)

(b) Cassette tape-recorder

Television's Power

(a) Closed circuit TV/VCR, VCP

(b) TV telecast

Softwares (Technology of Education): They include the hand-written or printed materials for effective teaching.

(a) Programmed instructional materials

(b) Self-learning modules

(c) Films, slides, OHP transparencies

(d) Audio-video tapes

(e) Multimedia packages

(f) Computer Discs (CDs)

Now let us discuss these Hardwares and Softwares of Educational Technology very briefly.

16 mm Film Projectors : A 16 mm teaching film though less flexible than verbal statement or description, is often far more effective. There is much to be learned which is incapable of demonstration. This can be done by controlling the speed of visual presentation, e.g , the flapping of a bird's wing, the unfolding of a petal, the clogging of an artery and the control of spacecraft etc., 16 mm films are available in India in every field of education. In Delhi there are some good resources for such films, like CIET of National Council of Educational Research and Training (NCERT), British Council and United States Information Service (USIS). Educational Institutions can ask for their catalogues and the films can be borrowed. Similar resources can be explored in each state or city. In addition to this some colleges, lASEs and University Departments have their own film libraries. These films are also available in the market for educational institutions to buy.

16 mm film projectors are now very common and most of the educational institutions have these projectors. These projectors

make it possible to use 16 mm films (software of 16 mm film projectors) which go along with the lesson. These films can be used as introduction, enrichment or follow-up of the lesson. These films are now being videotaped.

8 mm/Super 8 mm Projectors : 8 mm and super 8 mm educational films in different fields are also available in the market. They are lot less expensive than 16 mm films. They can also be produced very easily if the school or college is provided with 8 mm/super. 8 mm movie camera. These films shown with 8 mm/ super 8 mm projector are an asset to classroom teaching. The teachers can give their own commentary or it can be audio taped before hand to be replayed whenever these films are used. But now these projectors are not being used in educational institutions.

35 mm Slide Projectors : 35 mm slides and film strips (software of 35 mm slide projectors) because of their characteristic similarities lead to joint treatment. Both are similar materials, both use the same basic principle of projection. Both can be adopted for sound accompaniment. But 35 mm film strips are not being used now. 35 mm slides on different subjects are easily available in the market, which are not very expensive. Such slides could also be made as desired if college or school has its own 35 mm camera. These cameras are getting common these days in India. 35 mm slides projectors project 35 mm slides. These projectors are available almost in every educational institution. Thus they could be used in coordination with classroom teaching. The teaching value of magnified projection has a dramatic impact and there is a further advantage that the class can examine the pictures etc., on the screen as long as desirable.

Overhead Projector : Overhead projector though very often being used in schools and colleges in western world, is not very common in India even now when we are entering twenty-first century. But now it is being manufactured by several firms in our country. Here the transparencies (software of overhead projector) black and white and coloured-photocopied or hand-made can be projected overhead. Thus the teacher can stand in front rather than at the rear of the classroom. These transparencies use transparent plastic material on which instructor writes or draws in the course of the lesson and this appears on the screen and a large class can see clearly what would be visible to only a small group if the chalkboards were used instead.

Micro-Projector : Microscopic slides can be projected by micro-projector and the entire class can see it at the same time. These projectors are either attachments for a microscopic or separate projectors with built-in micro-lenses. They are used much as slide projector but adjustment is more complex and the image is usually not so bright that is why the micro-projectors require complete dark rooms. Micro-projectors are also available for projecting microfilms.

The Equipments : Two types of recordings are in general use, those engraved on a disc and those magnetised on tape.

(i) The discs vary in the speed with which they rotate on the machines, because of these variations speed as well as size, the 'play back' machines the 'record-player' must be suited to the requirement of the records and vice versa. This is not being used now in educational institutions.

(ii) The second type of recording made on magnetic tape, involves a totally different sort of play back equipment. The magnetic play back or the 'tape records' can also be used for making recordings. These magnetic tapes could be in a spool or in the form of a cassette (software of cassette tape recorder); both of these involve different machines, the spool tape recorder and cassette tape-recorder respectively. But spool tape-recorders are not being used now in educational institutions.

Most of the colleges and schools have their own cassette tape-recorders or players. They can be used very effectively in classroom teaching by imaginative teachers. For example, instead of giving the same lecture to several classes a day or repeating the same lecture every year, a teacher would be able to devote days or even weeks to the preparation of one outstanding presentation to be audio taped and repeated, and up-dated as often as needed.

TV Telecast : Educational Television programme is another technique for effective teaching. The Educational TV project started in 1961 for Delhi schools. Since then it showed tremendous improvement. Due to the coordination with classroom teaching, this programme proved to be very useful for the students. Teachers knew before-hand what lessons at what date and time will be received on TV and what portions of the syllabus they were to cover in the classroom. Now such TV programmes are not being telecast.

Closed Circuit TV : Due to rapid technical advances, specially in the field of video tape recording the emphasis of closed TV (CCTV) has altered over the past several years and has become a powerful media. For this a TV camera, a Video Tape-Recorder and a TV Receiver are needed. The use of CCTV, rather than films etc., is justified by its facility to be immediate and the fact that it is easier to manage. Close-ups of demonstrations of scientific experiments can be shown very clearly to a big class and to several classes at the same time. Some of the good demonstrations or techniques can be video-taped and shown whenever desired.

But due to its high cost and lack of knowledge for its utility it is not very common in our schools, colleges and universities. Instead TV Educational Video Tapes-Video-Cassettes (software of VCRs and VCPs) are used in our schools with VCRs and VCPs. If will be nice if such equipment is used by us quite frequently.

Some Uses of Computers : Classroom uses of the computers generally fall into one of three categories. Computers are being used as a direct means of instruction in many developed countries. This use of the computer is often referred to as computer assisted instructions (CAI). Another widespread use of the computers in educational institutions is for calculating and analysing data. A third use of the computer is a device for computer simulated experiments. Other uses of computers in education are scoring of papers, filling up the grade sheets or mark sheets, time table preparation (scheduling), guidance, counselling and curriculum development. Now CDs and Internet are also in use.

Computer is a powerful and evolving tool for managing and sharing knowledge. Today clever software can turn a computer into a television, a canvas, or make it replay images and music, snap photographs, synthesise human speech, organise databases and libraries, and present a combination of animated drawings.

Computers and communications are progressively becoming cheaper and faster.

Computers: Distance Medical and Surgical Facilities : Convergence of computers, communication, speech, text and images also presents an extraordinary opportunity in multimedia services and applications. These developments will change the way we live, learn, work, transact our business and communicate. For example, these techniques could allow doctors to examine patients in another continent and even monitor surgical operations at very far off places.

Computers: Future Attentive Assistants : Scientists are also working on image and pattern recognition techniques that can make computers ubiquitous. Speech recognition would replace the computer keyboard for most of the uses. There are attempts to develop computer systems for recognising faces, expressions and gestures. Such developments would enable us to create smart rooms which could see that people are in a meeting and shield them from interruptions. Such smart rooms would be networked and furnished with cameras and microphones. Thus these rooms could relay information from the room to other interested parties on the network. The computers could also assess what people in the room are saying or doing. Computers could compare the incoming information with models they have stored in memory, and arrive at decisions by tracking people's movement, identifying them and recognising their expressions. Therefore, in future computers will thus be playing the role of attentive assistants.

Present: The Internet is a large and global network of computers. Anybody can be a part of this network and share information with its users. The Internet provides access to essentially unlimited sources of information. Internet allows dialogue and exchange of ideas through Electronic Mail (E-Mail). Communication can be carried out at all hours and across large distances.

Future: Friendly ways of helping users to find what they want are already becoming available. In the course of time procedures for information quality control will also develop. The Internet will have all the essential features of a massive library system. It will of course take time before Internet possesses a large store of knowledge to rival the best of our libraries. The Internet and its successor technologies will have a profound effect on society.

What India is to Do? We in India should develop a national information infrastructure, where using phone lines, cables, high speed data networks will allow open access for all to the electronic superhighway of information. All our universities and national laboratories should be connected to this information superhighway, so that researchers cannot only have access to important research journals and other library material but can also collaborate across large distances. The status of libraries in our universities is very unsatisfactory. Unless we do something about it, the research in universities will suffer greatly in quality. Low cost computers and internet connectively could provide a satisfactory solution to this problem. Today many of our higher educational and research institutions have working internet facilities, but many of them are operating at low bandwidth. In the area of software India has a lot of potential. We should now aim at high quality software development for automation, networking, design activities and telecommunications. As of now most of the internet software is imported. There is scope for us to design software for specific applications on the Internet appropriate to Indian needs. We should make every effort to see that India is not marginalized in this rapid race of information technology.

Can Computers Recognise the Owner? Have you ever wondered about the fact that while you can recognise your computer, your computer cannot recognise you? How would a computer go about recognising its owner? It would recognise you by:

The Way You Speak: Most PCs today are equipped with a microphone. It would not be too hard to write programmes that can detect and identify voices to a limited extent.

The Way You Look: This is very difficult and involves having a video camera connected to the PC. The image from the camera would then be analysed to identify the person in front of the PC. This is an active area of research.

The Way You Type: Just as handwriting is unique, so is the way in which you press the key on a keyboard. A statistical analysis of patterns of key depressions (for how long, how hard and in what order you press keys while typing) can provide good clues to who the user might be.

The Way You Move the Mouse: Hand-eye coordination is fairly unique in human beings. By analysing the way in which you move your mouse, a PC might be able to figure out who you are.

These are some of the ways in which a PC of the future might recognise its owner.

Programmed Learning Units : Programmed learning was first associated with teaching machines, and there appears to have been two schools of thought. One was represented by the Harvard Psychologist, Skinner who transferred his theories based on the clinical observation of animal behaviour to the field of learning in the classroom. His programmes were divided into different segments each called a frame. The learner reads the frame and because of its form prompted into making a reply, usually written one and is encouraged to go to the next frame and so on through a series of positive reinforcement. The careful shaping of these stimuli and responses was aimed at securing a carefully prescribed behaviour pattern at the end of the programme. The individual could go at his own pace and learning was secure and certain. The second view, seen at one time to be divergent and the learner should be offered alternative answers. This approach was associated with Crowder. The Skinner programmes were called "linear" and the Crowderian ones "branching."

A programmer, nowadays seeks to arrange an environment within which learning activities appropriate to the programme's objectives are provided. No such guidance is given with a text book.

Adjunct Programming another development can be the link between programmed instruction and a good textbook. It combines some of the progressive features of Programmed Instruction (PI) with the comprehensiveness of textbook. The goal of adjunct programming is to enable the student to learn as efficiently as possible from a good textbook.

What is generally considered an advantage of programmed

instruction is the systematic, controlled, and sequential fashion in which content is presented to the learner. In programmed instruction provision can be made for differentiated instruction to accommodate individual differences.

Programmed Learning Units are self-learning programmes. Students tearn on their own with these programmes. Teacher is free to guide those students who really need his guidance.

Self-Learning Modules : Modularization of Instruction is another form of individualisation of instruction and self-learning; Modularization of Instruction is done by selecting, re-arranging or organising material and activities and breaking them into smaller sub-units in order to promote better understanding. The instructions are given in such a way that students know what specific objectives they are supposed to reach. Each sub-unit may have optional activities, from which students choose accordingly, all enabling them to reach the same objectives. Through such instruction the students can direct themselves through learning activities, with minimum assistance from the teacher; *i.e.* they can work at a particular rate that suits them.

Siddiqi developed a Self-learning Module "Man and Environment" and used it in her research study entitled "Development of Self-learning Material for Senior Secondary Biology and Analysis of Its Effectiveness". She found that students who used this module achieved statistically higher than those who did not use the module, and taught by the teacher in a conventional way.

Use of Self-learning Material : You can use programmed learning units and self-learning modules for effective science teaching.

Diverse Objective Oriented Aids

Teaching ideas mainly through one medium, namely, the printed word, is no longer wise either pedagogically or technologically. Taking into account individual differences in the way students learn, it will be wise to use a variety of learning aids assembling them in an integrated form known a multimedia package consisting of (for example) programmed instruction booklets, self-learning modules/books, slides, tapes (audio/video), films, transparencies, experiments, CDs etc. The students who do not learn best through reading a text have, therefore, the chance of learning more or better by working with films, slides, tapes and CDs so forth. For the sake of differences in individuals, knowledge should be presented in different forms.

Such packages though so useful, effective, interesting and instructive are not being used in our country. It will be wise to develop some of such packages at least for try-out.

Example : *A* slide-tape programme is a Multimedia Package. On any topic you can make 35 mm coloured slides (35 mm slides on various topics are also available in the market) by your 35 mm camera. Load your camera with 35 mm coloured slide film. Take pictures. Give the film for developing. You will get a set of 35 mm coloured slides.

Write the commentary for each slide. Audiotape the commentary. Now your Slide-Tape Programme is ready. You can use it again and again in your classroom.

The goals and expectations of science education change, and with them the curriculum. As the curriculum evolves so must the optimum-role of the science teacher. Today's science teacher is faced with numerous problems of how to teach what is given in his hands. Many science educators believe that the traditional teaching methods which are geared towards inculcating students mostly with factual knowledge, should be revised. Educational technology is here for our rescue. It is important that it should be used wisely as some of the earlier attempts to use teaching machines effectively failed because they were employed as alternatives to the presence of a teacher rather than as extension of his capabilities. It is upto us how best we can use the existing tools in science education. There are several tools as mentioned above which can be used in classroom for effective learning. But these materials are not being used in our educational institutions as effectively as could possibly be. Some of them are not available in the institutions due to their high cost or unfamiliarity of their utility. Some of us are against the use of technological tools with a plea that India's economy cannot afford the use of these expensive machines. But even those machines which are already available in the schools and colleges are also not being used fully. Science education is likely to expand substantially even explosively, over the next few decades and that can be achieved through the application of educational technology. It will be wise if the school and college science teachers should gather to learn the effective use of various technological tools and take with them the ideas which they think are wise and feasible for their classroom teaching.

The Expectations

A report commissioned by the US National Science Foundation speculates that by the end of twentieth century electronic information technology will have transformed western home, business, manufacturer, school, family and political life. The report suggests that one-way and two-way home information systems, called Teletext and Videotex, will penetrate deeply into daily life, with an effect on society as profound as those of the automobile and commercial television earlier in this century. This proved true. Now the, same is gomg to happen in developing countries like India in twenty-first century.

The study focused on the emerging Videotex industry, formed by the combination of two older technologies, communication and computing. It was estimated that 40 per cent of households in the US will have two-way Videotex by the end of the twentieth century, and this estimation came out true; Videotex system would enable individuals to create their own newspapers, design their own consumer guides. Furthermore this system will bring an increased flow of information and services into the home and at the same time, carry on stream of information out of the home about the preferences and behaviour of its occupants. All this hopefully is going to happen in the developing countries like India in twenty-first century.

INSAT-IA was up in space on September 4,1982 with capabilities for telecommunications, metereology and country-wide TV telecasts, but it was declared dead on September 6, 1982. Though it was possible to take this failure rather philosophically as a forerunner of future success, yet it was a serious setback to all our communicational developments. Then INSAT-IB was successfully launched by India on August 30,1983, though INSAT-IC launched on July 12,1988 could not be a success. Afterwards both INSAT-ID launched on June 12, 1990 and INSAT-2A launched on July 10, 1992 were a success. (For more satellites launched by India, see the Table 6.1) We enjoy many benefits of satellite technology. An all-India transmission of TV programmes has been possible through INSAT. The satellites bring to us live programmes in any part of the world. Satellite communication, weather monitoring, remote sensing, and collection of information about planets and outer space are some other applications of satellite technology.

It would be nice if we could produce enough software material for maximum utilisation of INSAT. The developing countries like India will have to use TV for reaching out the masses in the dark ghosts of illiteracy/ignorance, disease, poverty and exploitation with a view to providing fundamental education. This is a tremendous task for all educators in general and educational technologists in particular.

It seems that the new media are still quite expensive and their penetration if relatively limited, but future developments hold a promise of considerably cost-reduction and competitive productionization. The cost of computer memory in the developed world for a bit of information was 100 cents in 1954, 1 cent in 1964, 0.5 cent ø 1974 and 0.004 cent in the year 1984. This cost will further decrease in the years to come. In India, the cost of a transistorised radio set has shown consistent reduction inspite of inconsistent price-rise. We do hope that the story would be repeated also a case of TV and Videotex. It is estimated that by 2000, more than six million households would own Videotex in the western world. The developing countries like India would have to chalk out their own plans and priorities in the field of educational technology. In order to do so, we would have to think globally and act locally.

In India, in several States and Union Territories, Educational Technology cells have been started functioning with 100 per cent financial support (for the first 5 years) from the Ministry of Education, under guidance of Central Institute of Educational Technology (CIET) of NCERT in New Delhi. The remaining States and Union Territories will also open similar cells gradually. Hopefully these cells will assist our teachers in effective science teaching using educational technology.

Table. Launching of Indian Satellites

S.No.	*Name of the Satellite*	*Date of Launching*	*Result*
1.	Aryabhata	19 March 1975	Success
2.	Bhaskara-1	7 June 1979	Success
3.	Rohini	10 August 1979	Failure
4.	Rohini	18 July 1980	Success
5.	APPLE	19 June 1981	Success
6.	Bhaskara-2	20 November 1981	Success
7.	Rohini	31 May 1981	Failure
8.	INSAT-1A	4 September 1982	Failure
9.	Rohini	17 April 1983	Success
10.	INSAT-1B	30 August 1983	Success
11.	SROSS-1	24 March 1987	Failure
12.	IRS-1A	19 March 1988	Success
13.	INSAT-1C	12 July 1988	Failure
14.	SROSS-2	13 July 1988	Failure
15.	INSAT-1D	12 June 1990	Success
16.	IRS-1B	29 August 1991	Success
17.	SROSS-3	19 May 1992	Success
18.	INSAT-2A	10 July 1992	Success

NCERT organised the first ever interactive satellite based interactive teacher training programme to train primary school teachers on various topics of primary education using INSAT transponder with one-way video and two-way audio technology.

In the first phase the programme was launched in Karnataka on January 7-13, 1996 (7 days) covering about 850 teachers and 80 facilitators and course directors assembled in 20 different district centres (learning ends).

In the second phase, the programme was organised in Madhya Pradesh on August 2-8, 1996 (7 days) covering about 1400 teachers and 170 facilitators and course directors assembled in 45 district centres (learning ends).

The 7 days programmes each for Karnataka and MP had 14 Sessions, each of which were on various topics such as MLL, use of OB materials, multigrade teaching strategies, teaching of Maths, EVS (Science and Social Studies) and Language etc. Each of the sessions was about 3½ hours (2 hours of live interaction and 1½ hours of individual and group activities). Each session comprised of presentation, demonstration and discussion. Participating teachers interacted with panelists through telephone and fax, followed by group activities.

During the 7 days programme of Karnataka about 600 telephone calls and 240 fax sheets were received, and in case of MP about 700 telephone calls and 200 fax sheets were received, altogether about 7000 questions were asked through telephone and fax.

This experiment was highly appreciated by educationists, distance education experts, education administrators and teachers. Such programmes hopefully will be common in India in the years to come.

Another achievement of this Experiment is the successful networking of various national, state and district level agencies in the implementation of the project.

What is served to India, is what is cooking in Delhi. What you will get in education is now in included in Ninth Five Year Plan.

Educational Technology in the Ninth Plan is going to take a significant and massive turn. The focus in primary education during the Ninth Plan will have to be on quality because without enhanced, retention and performance of students, universalisation of education will remain elusive. The National Action Plan for continuing education of primary teachers envisages a series of change in the Ninth Plan. The main approach is to develop a training module using multi-channel learning which includes self-learning, action learning, face to face interactive learning and learning through interactive television. The entire multi-channel learning is a capsule model instructional design which is the core of educational technology. Self study materials, which are the basis of self-learning, are semi-structured learning modules. Action learning is conceptualised to be action experience and studies within the schools. Face-to-face interactive learning is proposed to build interactive and problem solving skills among the teachers to interact with the guidance of an expert tutor. The interactive television will bring in an opportunity for primary teachers to interact directly with the experts at the regional, state, and national level

The proposal is to set network in selected national, regional, state and district level institutes through satellite communication. The proposal also includes the setting up of block level resource centres with educational technology facilities for face to face interaction. With block and district level training centres, primary teachers would have access to more than 5500 centres in the country.

The proposed training network will have the capacity of training a few million people every year in the country. In view of both extended capacity of the training system and the need for training the supervisors and teacher educators who play critical role in teachers' performance will also be provided specially designed training modules once every 2 years.

This is for the primary teachers. It is likely that the training network will be extended for upper primary and secondary teachers as well. The universities are not far behind. IGNOU has proposed a network called OPENET interconnecting its study centres, state open universities and other distance education institutes and centres. The proposal is to use VSAT for delivery of courses.

From programmed learning, one way television and radio broadcast and educational technology equipments as teaching aids, India seems to be ready to graduate to satellite communication and computer communication. The new educational technology is likely to sweep the country very fast rather we, the teachers should get ready to receive and respond to this massive change which is bemg conceptualised.

Rationale. With the advancement of science and technology many new developments have taken place in the field of education.

The conventional ideas about teaching are proving obsolete and inadequate. With the changing times the expectations from teachers have also increased. A teacher is not only a trainer or instructor in basic skills but he is also an organiser of worthwhile experiences for children. To meet these challenges, a teacher has no option but to adopt new technological aid. With the help of mass media, quality education can be provided to children and adults even in remote and inaccessible areas. The services of competent teachers and subject experts can be made available at any place, without their presence in actual classroom situation. Teacher is now expected to be part of an educational system where in machines, materials and media are important constituents of instructional process. The teacher has, therefore, to understand his roles in the new educational system, and it is for this reason that the present course has been included in the ETE curriculum.

Aims and Objectives

On completion of the course, the teacher trainee will be able to :

— explain the concept and scope of educational technology and use of teaching-learning process develop skills to use and maintain hardwares.

— develop skills of preparing softwares and making their effective use.

— develop skills of effective use of blackboard, school TV programmes, educational radio broadcasts, educational video programmes develop skills to make use of waste material or low cost material available locally for developing teaching aids.

— develop skills for evaluating effectiveness of various technological aids, media and strategies.

3

Revolution in Education

Teaching is an essential part of education. Its special function is to impart knowledge, develop understanding and skills. It generally excludes inculcation of values like truth. It is usually associated with the in parting of knowledge of 3 R's-Reading, Writing and Arithmetic-representing various school subjects. Education, on the other hand, has a wider connotation. It implies 7 R's-Reading, Writing, Arithmetic, (All three denoting school subjects), Rights, Responsibilities, Relationships and Recreation (Requirements and ideals of a modern democratic state). In teaching we limit our outlook omitting those more important means of education which are involved in the school as a systematically organised social community, including its tone or general moral environment, its government and discipline, and that potent influence-the personality of the teacher. James Welton observes, "We treat teaching by itself, because it is an aspect of school life which can be singled out in thought, though it cannot be separated in reality, from the whole of which it forms a part and because it covers a fairly consistent body of doctrine. It is true that the value and success of all school teaching depends on those wider and deeper elements of school life-tone, discipline, etc. which are omitting. But it is true that whilst the latter may be excellent the former may be of poor quality.

Experience and Inherent Nature

Albert Einstein (A Swiss Physicist 1879-1950): The supreme art of teaching is to awaken joy in creative expression and knowledge.

American Educational Research Association Commission in 'Handbook of Research on Teaching' (1962): Teaching is a form of interpersonal influence aimed at changing the behaviour potential of another person.

Amidon and Hunter (1967): Teaching is an interactive process, primarily involving classroom, which takes place between teacher and pupils and occurs during certain definable activities.

Anatole France (French novelist 1844-1924): The whole art of teaching is only the art of awakening the natural curiosity of young minds for the purpose of satisfying it afterwards.

B.O. Smith (1963): Teaching is a system of actions involving an agent, an end in view, and a situation including two sets of factors those over which the agent has no control (class size, size of classroom, physical characteristics of pupils etc.) and those that he can modify (ways of asking questions almost instructions and way of structuring information or ideas gleaned.)

Burton (1963): Teaching is the stimulation, guidance, direction and encouragement of learning.

Clark (1970): Teaching refers to activities that are designed and performed to produce change in student (pupil) behaviour.

Floyed Well (1958): Children are notoriously 'curious about everything except the things people want them to know. It then remains for us to refrain from forcing any kind of knowledge upon them and they will be curious about everything.

Calieleo (Italian astronomer 1564-1652): You cannot teach a man anything, you can only help him to find it himself.

H.E. Morrison (1934): Teaching is an intimate contact between a more mature personality and less mature one which is designed to further the education of the latter.

Israel Sheffler (1966): Teaching may be characterised as an activity aimed at the achievement of learning and practised in such a manner as to respect the student's intellectual integrity and capacity.

John Dewey (1859-1952): One might as well say he has sold when no one has bought, as to say he has taught when no one has learned.

John Bmbacher (1939): Teaching is an arrangement and manipulation of a situation in which there are gaps and obstructions which an individual will seek to overcome and from which he will learn in the course of doing so.

John Chapman (1960): The gift of teaching is a peculiar talent, and it implies a need and craving in the teacher himself.

Joyce and Well (1972): Teaching is a process by which teacher and students create a shared environment including set of values and beliefs (agreement about what is improvement) which in turn colour their view of reality.

J. Wilton: To know where the pupils are and where they should try to be are the first two essentials of good teaching.

Michael Oakeshort (1966): Teaching is two-fold activity of communicating information and communicating judgement.

N.L. Gage (1962): Teaching is a form of interpersonal influence aimed at changing the behaviour potential of another person.

Ned. A. Flanders (1970): Teaching is an interaction, process. Interaction means participation of both teacher and students and both are benefited by this. The interaction takes place for achieving desired objectives.

Paul Goodman (1980): A good teacher feels his way, looking for response.

Thomas P. Green (1971): Teaching is the task of a teacher which is performed for the development of a child.

W.R. Ryburnt (1946): Teaching includes the training of emotions of the child. It is one of the means of giving right feeling to the children.

William Lyon (1970): In my mind teaching is not merely a life work, a profession, an occupation, a struggle, it is a passion. I love to teach, as a painter loves to paint, as a musician loves to play, as a singer loves to sing, as a strongman rejoices to run a race.

Yoakm and Simpson: Teaching is a means whereby society

trains the young in a selected environment as quickly as possible to adjust themselves to the world in which they live.

In the type of teaching as mentioned by Morrison, teaching is reduced to what the teacher does. There is interaction but the flow of instruction is from the teacher. In this type of teaching, the learners may become passive listeners

Brubacher's definition of teaching assigns more place to the learner. This approach tends to be child or learner-centered.

B.O. Smith seems to be more pragmatic in his approach to teaching. He accepts certain limitations of the learner in the teaching learning process.

Smith's definition contains the following three elements:

(a) Teaching is a system of action.

(b) Teaching is a goal-directed action.

(c) Teaching takes place in a situation comprising the controlable and uncontrolable set of factors.

A review of the definitions given above reveals that to play his role competently in teaching, a teacher is expected to understand the significance of the following:

Who is to Teach : The teacher is to teach and he must .. understand himself thoroughly-his strengths and weaknesses and strive to present a reasonably good model before his students.

Whom to Teach : The child is to be taught. Therefore, a teacher should understand him thoroughly-his abilities, aptitudes, attitudes, manners and temperaments and accordingly cater to the individual differences of students.

Why to Teach : The teacher should always keep in view that the aim of education is to develop harmonious personalities, who are culturally refined, emotionally stable, ethically sound, mentally alert, morally upright, physically strong, socially efficient and spiritually enlightened. He should not forget even for a moment that the traditional 3 R's have been replaced by 7 R's, that is, reading, writing, arithmetic (representing various disciplines), rights, responsibilities, relationships and recreation.

Where to Teach : The teacher ought not to visualise the school to be merely a place of imparting information but a place where men of tomorrow are trained to take their place as enlightened citizens in the society and contribute to national development.

What to Teach : The teacher must have mastery over the subject he teaches.

How to Teach : The teacher must use new teaming-learning technology to make his teaching. Effective and inspirational.

When to Teach : Appropriate steps need to be taken by the teacher to develop motivation of the student in the entire work.

Instruction is primarily concerned with the development of knowledge and understanding in the pupil about a thing, system or process. Imparting of knowledge and understanding merely represents one of the several objectives which we want to achieve through teaching. Teaching is concerned with all the domains of pupil's behaviour, i. e., cognitive, conative and affective. Instruction is a part of teaching.

The distinction between teaching and instruction may be seen from another angle. The face to face interaction of the teacher and taught found in teaching is not so much essential in the process of instruction . In instruction, a teacher may be replaced by the programmed material, computer, teaching machine, radio and television etc. A teacher cannot be replaced by these aids. Of course, in teaching a teacher makes use of them. Thus, instruction is one of the several modes of teaching.

Teaching is Giving Information : There are many things that the students cannot find out for themselves. There are many things that they can never know unless they are told. There are many things the use of which they do not know. These things they have to be told. So one essential part of teaching is communicating knowledge. Knowledge must be given in a systematised manner. Teaching should be-made interesting. It must, however, be stressed that knowledge aspect should not be unduly emphasized.

Teaching is Causing to Learn : It is wrong to think, that knowledge can be passed on from one person to another like money. Knowledge will be received only when the students are prepared to receive it. Real teaching consists in persuading the child, by one method or the other to learn for himself. The teacher is an instrument in helping a child to learn how to do things for himself.

Teaching is a Matter of Helping the Child to Respond to his Environment in an Effective Manner : F.N. Freeman observes, "It is not what is presented to the child which educates him, but rather the reaction that he makes to what is presented. Certain children may fail entirely to respond to a lesson, or may respond in a wrong manner. If a child's response to his geography is to memorize the words, without any understanding of the facts they represent, the lesson is ' educative for him (he has not been taught), although it may be educative for the child next to him who reacts properly."

Teaching is Helping a Child to Adjust himself to his Environment : A child is reacting in some way or the other to his physical and social environment, from his very birth. His reactions are both fruitful and harmful. Teaching should help the child to make successful adjustment. This may be done in two ways. Sometimes we modify the environment and at other times strengthen the child. Teaching should make the child socially efficient, that is, a worthy member of society, making his contribution to the common good. Yoakam and Simpson: write, "Teaching is a means whereby society trains the young in a selected environment as quickly as possible to adjust themselves to the world in which they live. In primitive societies this adjustment means conformity with things as they are. In more advanced civilizations, such as ours, effort is made not only to adjust to things as they are" but also to make an advance in the improvement of conditions of life by training the young in modes of thinking and acting which will help to improve the conditions of living that surround them."

Teaching is Stimulation and Encouragement : Teaching should fire the enthusiasm of the child. It is to encourage the child in the development of his natural desires to work, and to be active.

Teaching is Guidance : Teaching is to guide the pupils to learn the right things in the right manner and at the right time. Teaching is to guide the students to do things in such a way that time, material and energy are not wasted.

Teaching is Training the Emotions of the Child : Ryburn observes, "It is also the encouraging and training of the emotional life. This is an aspect of teaching which is very commonly neglected', at least in practice. But our teaching will be only one-sided and distorted unless we take into account the 'necessity for helping the child to develop a stable emotional life." Teaching is to develop the emotional life of the child by providing an atmosphere of love, affection and freedom. Teaching is to provide such activities as will sublimate their instinctive urges to action.

Teaching is Both a Conscious and an Unconscious Process : Teaching is both a conscious and an unconsciously process and the most effective part of it is generally the part of which we are unconscious. The personal relationships between the teacher and the taught have a great bearing on the growth of the child.

Teaching is a Means of Preparation : Though preparation for future is not the only aspect of teaching, yet it is an important aspect: Teaching is to help the immature child to develop physically, intellectually, emotionally and spiritually to participate effectively in the life of the community.

Teaching is Formal as well as Informal : Formal teaching is deliberately planned, systematically organised and is always purposive. Teachers are just formal agents of teaching. School is not the only agency of teaching. Informal teaching is carried on by the parents, brothers and sisters at home, playmates, student community outside the classroom, etc. The few hours of the school are insufficient for the full development of the child. Formal and informal teaching must coperate, if good results are to be achieved. School should 'supplement' not 'supplant', the training imparted by the home and *vice-versa.*

Teaching as a Skilled Occupation : Every successful teacher is expected to know the general methods of teaching and instruction in creating suitable learning situations. He is also expected to be familiar with the general objectives of education.

Teaching is an Art : Art implies the intelligent action of a human being through which it is possible to modify an ordinary course of events. Teaching is an art which can be improved through research.

Teaching is a Form of Social Service : The teaching profession is regarded to be a sort of social.servjce and the teachers as servants of society in whose hands has been entrusted the task of shaping and developing the behaviour and conduct of the young children for maintaining and improving the social patterns.

Teaching as a Relationship : Teaching is a, relationship which is established between three focal points in education, the teacher, the child and the subject. Teaching is the process by which the teacher brings the child and the subject together. The teacher and the taught are active, the former in teaching and the latter in learning.

Teaching as a Skilled Occupation : Every successful teacher is expected to know the general methods of teaching and instruction in creating suitable learning situations. He is also expected to be familiar with the general objectives of education.

Teaching is Both an Art and Science : Silverman (1966) has expressed the nature of teaching in these words, "To be sure teaching-like the practice of medicine-is very much an art which is to say, it calls for exercise of talent and creativity. But like medicine, it is also a science, for it involves a repertoire of techniques, procedures and skills that can be systematically studied, described and improved. A good teacher, like a good doctor, is one who adds creativity and inspiration to the basic repertoire."

Teacher's Role

1. Creating learning situations.
2. Motivating the child to learn.
3. Arranging for conditions which assist in the growth of the child's mind and body.
4. Utilizing the initiative and play urges of the children to facilitate learning.
5. Turning the children into creative beings.
6. Inspiring children with the nobility of thoughts, feelings and action.
7. Giving information and explaining it.
8. Diagnosing learning problems.
9. Making curricular material.
10. Evaluating, recording and reporting.

Sri Aurobindo describes the marks of good teaching in these words, "The first principle is that nothing can be taught. The teacher is not an instructor or task master, he is a helper and guide. His business is to suggest and not to impose. He does not actually train the pupils's mind, he only shows him to perfect his instruments of knowledge and helps and encourages him in the process. He does not impart knowledge to him, he shows him how to acquire knowledge for himself. He does not call forth the knowledge that is within, he only shows him where it lies and it can be habituated to rise to surface. The distinction that reserves this principle for the teaching of adolescent and adult minds and denies its application to the child, is a conservative and unintelligent doctrine. Child or man, girl or boy, there is only one sound principle of good teaching. Difference of age only serves to diminish or increase the amount of help and guidance necessary, it does not change its nature."

John Dewey (1859-1952) states, "The more a teacher is aware of the past experiences of students, of their hopes, desires, chief interests, the better will he understand the forces at work that need to be directed and utilized for the formation of reflective habits." Further he writes, "The teacher is a guide and director, he steers the boat but the energy that propels it must come from those who are learning."

Albert Einstein (1879-1955) has observed, "It is the supreme art of the teacher to awaken joy in creative expression and knowledge.

Montaigne, a French philosopher (1533-1592) advises, "A tutor should not be continually thundering instruction into the ears of his pupil, as if he were pouring it through a funnel, but, after having, put the lid, like a young horse, on a trot before him, to observe his paces, and see what he is able to perform, should according to the extent of his capacity, induce him to taste, to distinguish, and to find out things for himself, sometimes opening the way, at other times leaving it for him to open."

Joseph Payne (English educator, 1808-1876) writes, "The teachers part in the process of instruction is that of guide, director or superintendent of the operation by which the pupil teachers himself."

Swami Vivekananda (1863-1902) describes the role of the teacher in teaching as, "The true teacher is he who can immediately come down to the level of the student." Following are the marks of good teaching :

Good Teaching Recognises Individual Differences : Good teaching treats each child as unique. Good teaching recognises that catering to individual differences brings strength. It must be remembered that standardized procedures do not fit every pupil.

Good Teaching is Causing to Learn : Good teaching enables the child to learn for himself. It is not stuffing the mind of the child with information. Good teaching is what we can make the child do for himself.

Good Teaching Provides Opportunities for Activity : The child is inherently active. Passiveness on the part of the child implies that he is not in good physical and mental health. A good teacher keeps the students active. He is aware of the fact that to keep the students disciplined, he must fill the time with work and he does so accordingly.

Good Teaching Involves Skill in Guiding : A good teacher motivates his teaching. He stimulates " through his personality and his activities the personalities and activities of the pupils." He creates such situations as lead to desired types of learners.

Good Teaching is Kindly and Sympathetic : Good teaching must create an environment of acceptance, sympathy and understanding.

Good Teaching Decreases the Distance i.e. to either Teacher and the Taught : Teachers should come out of their ivory tower and come as close with the students as possible.

Good Teaching is not Tied to Any Method : Methods, techniques and devices should be adopted to local situations and considered as servants and not masters.

Good Teaching is Cooperative : Good teaching is an active and living process. A good teacher seeks the cooperation of the learners.

Good Teaching is Kindly and Sympathetic : A good teacher always creates. A cordial atmosphere in the classroom. He always ensures his pupils's emotional stability and security. He is loving, kind, affectionate and sympathetic to his pupils. He bears in mind this fact "love the child and he will love you, hate him and he will hate you." He avoids scolding and sarcasm.

Good Teaching Involves Careful Planning : Good teaching keeps in view that everything cannot be taught to children at every time. A good teacher carefully studies the mental make-up of the pupil he teaches, studies the individual differences of pupils and then prepares his subject-matter. An unplanned lesson often results in a failure and involves a waste of time, energy and money also.

Good Teaching is Democratic : A good teacher always respects the individuality of his pupils. He keeps democratic ideals, contents, methods and objectives in view.

Good Teaching Provides Desirable and Selective Information: The good teacher does not try to teach all the available information that he gathers form books and experience. On the other hand he makes a judicious selection and teaches all that is useful to live a good life as responsible member of the society.

Good Teaching Helps the Child to Adjust Himself to His Environment : Man has been struggling against natural forces since ages. He is expected either to adjust himself to these natural forces or to adjust the forces to himself. A good teacher helps the child in both directions.

Good Teaching is Progressive : A good teacher aims at improving his modes and techniques steadily. He also helps the child to make suitable progress in life.

Good Teaching Leads to Emotional Stability : There are very powerful inherited urges which always cry for expansion. A good teacher knows that unguided expression leads to wilderness, and therefore, helps in providing his pupils suitable opportunities which assist in training and sublimating their urges and emotions.

Good Teaching is Both Diagnostic and Remedial : A good teacher makes use of the various measuring instruments which have been provided by psychology and discovers the intelligence, aptitudes and interests of children and accordingly plans his work.

Skills

Challenge of Education-A Policy Perspective (1985) : A publication of the Ministry of Education, and a forerunner of The National Policy on Education-NPE 1986, has something worth quoting, on quality of education. It states, "It is difficult to define quality, particularly with reference to educational processes. However, it could be stated that a quality conscious system would produce people who have the attributes of functional and social relevance, mental ability and physical dexterity, efficacy and readability and above all, the confidence and the capability to communicate effectively and exercise initiative, innovative and experiment with new situations. To these personal attributes one could add the dimensions of a value system conducive to harmony, integration and the welfare of the weak and disadvantaged."

Quality teaching also known as effective teaching is the chief instrument of quality education. It is essentially concerned with translating the objectives of education into action and practice. It is concerned with how best to bring about pupil learning by various activities. Quality teaching may be defined as the teacher's ability to stimulate students intellectually and move them emotionally to instill in them love for learning and develop suitable skills and attitudes.

Quality teaching is based on the premise 'All teachers should teach well and all students should learn well'.

An understanding of the following facts would go a long way in quality teaching:

1. Effective teaching is a comprehensive concept. Several variables are involved in teaching.
2. All types of variables play their part in teacher-learning situation.
3. 'What' and 'how' of effective teaching should be carefully comprehended.
4. There are several models of teaching and each should be considered in the overall context of teaching.
5. All models are complimentary to each other.
6. A teacher should adopt an electric approach in the selection of a model.
7. Developing a personal model of teaching in consonance with the requirements of quality teaching should become the cherished goal of every teacher.
8. Skill in creating intellectual excitement has two components: The clarity of an instructor's communications and their positive emotional impact on students.
9. Quality teaching results from a teacher's skill attracting

both intellectual excitement and positive rapport with students.

10. The development of good rapport is based on three qualities in the teachers interaction with students: the teacher cares for student progress, the teacher has consideration for students as learners and the teacher respects students as individuals.
11. The three elements involved in teaching competence while contribute to teacher's authority and prestige are: Mastery over the subject, interest in the subject and effective learning situations and experiences.
12. Quality teaching presupposes an understanding mind; a feeling heart and a lofty personality.
13. In quality teaching the environment is of mutual cooperation and of purposefulness. A play-way spirit is the chief characteristic of the work.

Potent Role

A *'A'* is for alertness on the part of the teacher to the multifarious needs of the learners. Alertness is very helpful in taking appropriate decisions and timely corrective measures.

'A' is also for adaptability in handling several situations.

B 'B' is for businesslike attitude. It is to be ensured that every learner in the class, remains busy in realizing the goals set.

'B' is for balanced behaviour.

C 'C' stands for cooperative teaching-learning. The learners must be made active partners.

'C' is for clarity of purpose. The teacher and the learners must be clear about the goals for the achievement of which they are working.

'C' is for clarity of the subject-matter taught. A teacher must make all possible efforts to make his lesson clear. Difficulties of the learners must be appreciated and clarified.

D 'D' stands for democratic classroom environment.

'D' is for discovery. Children should be guided to find out new facts, ideas and principles. It helps children in becoming independent and resourceful learners.

'D' stands for democratic discipline.

E 'E' stands for expectancies. Each learner should be expected to learn. No learner should be considered without any potential.

'E' stands for enthusiasm. The teacher himself must demonstrate enthusiasm for his work.

'E' stands for appropriate etiquettes.

F 'F' is for feedback. Feedback helps the teacher and the learners to take timely corrective measures for the completion of the task.

'F' stands for faith of the teacher in himself.

G 'G' is for goal-setting. Appropriate goals should be set for the learners. They should also be made clear about the suitability of goals. Efforts may be made to associate the learners with the setting of goals.

H 'H' is for hard work on the part of the students as well as teachers.

'H'is for humour. Humour on the part of the teacher releases fatigue and tension.

'H' stands for human touch.

I 'I' stands for involvement of all the learners in classroom activities and experiences.

'I' stands for impartial attitude.

'I' stands for inspirational teaching-learning.

J 'J' stands for just attitude.

'J' stands for judicious rewards and punishments.

K 'K' stands for knowing children's abilities, aptitudes and interests.

'K' stands for the knowledge of the sub-matter.

L 'L' stands for linking present, past and future knowledge.

'L' stands for leadership qualities.

M 'M' stands for motivation.

'M' stands for management of the class.

N 'N' stands for needs of the learners and their satisfaction.

O 'O' stands for open-mindedness.

'O' stands for out of class activities.

'O' stands for objectivity in approach.

P 'P' stands for praise. Verbal and non-verbal praise of children can motivate them to hardwork.

'P' stands for personal contact with every learner.

Q 'Q' is for quiz. From time to time, quiz competitions may be arranged in the class.

'Q' stands for quality teaching.

'Q' stands for question-answers.

R 'R' stands for review of the lesson.

'R' stands for relationships.

'R' stands for resourcefulness.

S 'S' stands for success experience. Success motivates the learner to achieve more.

'S' stands for scientific temper.

'S' stands for self-analysis and self-control

T 'T' stands for technology of teaching.

'T' stands for tutoring which involves removing difficulties, individually or in small groups.

U 'U' stands for undivided attention to teaching.

'U' stands for unbiased attitude to the treatment of controversial issues.

V 'V' stands for visual aids.

'V' stands for variety of experiences.

'V' stands for voice-modulated.

'V' stands for variation in the presentation.

W 'W' stands for welcoming attitude.

'W' stands for warmth towards students.

X 'X' stands for X-ray of the teaching process. It implies finding out of the difficulties and potentials of the students.

Y 'Y' stands for yardstick i.e. same standard basis of making a judgement on the performance of the students.

'Y' stands for you, implying that you (student) are the most important element in the teaching-learning process.

'Y' stands for zenith or excellence.

Either J. Swenson in the Teacher's Letter (1952) states that each of the following seven wonders brings a new challenge to the classroom teacher:

First Wonder : How much children are ready know before they come to school. They bring with them rich resources of knowledge, skill and understandings-mostly self-learned.

First Challenge : How much do I know of these rich resources? How far do I go in searching them out? How do I use what I find?

Second Wonder : Children's eagerness to learn. It is natural for children to inquire, to discover. It is unnatural for them to be passive, disinterested.

Second Challenge : How do I use this eagerness to learn? In what direction should it be channelled? Am I feeding it or killing it?

Third Wonder : The never-ending process of learning. Every hour of the day, no matter where he is with whomever or whatever he works, the child learns.

Third Challenge : Is he learning what is best for him, now and later? Am I setting the stage for constructive learnings?

Fourth Wonder : The infinite variety of abilities, personalities, needs, and interests of pupils. He who says, "I know children" has not taken time to study the marvels of their growth.

Fourth Challenge : Do I know as much as I should about each child's abilities, personalities, needs, interests? How can I learn more? Do I accept differences or rebel against them?

Fifth Wonder : The concomity of learning. Simultaneously, children learn subject matters, traits of personality, habits of working, attitudes and appreciations-many of them permanently.

Fifth Challenge : Do I push so hard toward a single goal that I push the children away from another of equal importance? Do I leave these "marginal learnings" to chance?

Sixth Wonder : The faith, respect, loyalty and tolerance to children. When a teacher treats them well : sometimes even when he does not : they will respond with respect and understanding.

Sixth Challenge : Do I have an equal faith in them and in their motives? Am I as loyal to them and their welfare? Do I treat them with respect and understanding?

Seventh Wonder : The ability of children to teach. Each child learns form the other, and even the teacher can learn much from children. .

Seventh Challenge : Do I use my opportunities to learn from children? Do I listen, literally and figuratively, to the lessons they can teach?

Various Theories

Several attempts have been made to analyse activities involved in teaching with a view to understand it scientifically, design teaching materials and methods for realising the specific objectives efficiently, and to evaluate and modify it in the light of the feedback.

Plenlders, Ned. S. (1959) of the University of Minnesota was the first educator to categories all the sets of verbal behaviours (teaching activities) of a teacher in the classroom while interacting with students. He classified these activities into three categories: 1. Teacher Talk. 2. Pupil Talk and 3. Silence/confusion.

1. Teacher talk was further categorised as under:
   (1) Indirect influence which includes (a) Accepts feelings, (b) Praises or encourages, (c) Accepts or uses pupil ideas, (d) Asks questions.
   (2) Direct influence which includes (a) Lecturing, (b) Giving directions, (c) Criticising or justifying.
2. Pupil talk which induced (a) Pupil talk response, (b) Pupil talk initiation.
3. Silence or confusion.

Komesnr, N.P. (1966) tried to analyse teaching into various specific activities like introducing, demonstrating, contrasting, explaining, proving, justifying, explaining, defining, appraising, amplifying, rating, interpreting, questioning, elaborating, identifying, conjecturing, confirming etc.

Gagel NL. (1968) attempted .to analyse teaching in terms of technical skills. According to him, "Teaching skills are specific instructional techniques and procedures that a teacher may use in the class room. They represent an analysis of the teaching process into relatively discrete components that can be used in different combinations in the continuous flow of the teacher's performance."

Clarles, S.CT. (1970) analysed teaching in terms of some specific activities that are designed and performed to produce change in student's behaviour. Those activities may be of cognitive, affective or conative nature and belonged to different levels.

Brown, B.B. (1968) analyses teaching by considering it as a manysided activity which includes several activities like questioning, giving information and listening etc.

Passi, B.K.. (1976) states that teaching constitutes a number of verbal and non-verbal teaching acts like questioning, accepting pupil response, rewarding, smiling, nodding to pupil response, movements, gestures, etc. These acts, particularly in combination, facilitate the achievement of objectives in terms of pupil growth.

Dhingra, N.K. and Singh Ajit (1982) present the analysis of teaching as, "Teaching can be analysed in terms of teacher behaviour at least at three levels viz, component teaching skills, competent teaching behaviours and atomistics teaching behaviours."

Teaching Technology : Concept and Meaning

Teaching technology involves the mechanism of instructional process in the classroom situations, levels of teaching, theories of teaching, principal teaching operations and establishing relations between theories and teaching operations.

Teaching technology as a concept can be classified into four well-defined components. These components are: (i) Manpower, (ii) Methods, (iii) Materials, and (iv) Media.

As a method, it implies making use of a few devices such as programmed learning, team teaching, micro-teaching, personalized system of instruction, etc.

As materials, it comprises instructional materials, comprising programmed text-books, manuals, guides, text and other written/ print materials, which expose to the learner the contents of these sources of materials.

4

Salient Features

Management of Education Technology or E.T. is a complex task. It involves planning, organisation, staffing, training, materials, management and much more. Selection, procurement, preparation, planning and utilisation of all the wide-ranging media make the process very much complicated, and the procedures call for extreme care and caution, skills and strategies for maximising learning experiences. All this implies not only effective management but also proper management of E.T. Hence, the discussion has been made on the planning, organisation, co-ordination, monitoring and application of E.T. by developing suitable infrastructure for acquisition, maintenance, utilisation, networking and support system for ensuring effectiveness and efficiency.

The Motives

After going through this unit, you will be able to-

- know various aspects and implications of management.
- plan and execute the E.T. application in various formats, types and methods.
- organise E.T. in different types of schools.
- co-ordinate various aspects of E.T.

- develop infrastructure for procuring media and man-power recruitment and posting.
- maintain media of different types properly.
- provide networking and support system for effective utilisation of E.T.

Technology Management

Management of E.T. involves different activities and processes aiming at effective and efficient functioning and application of various media. The E.T. application and operations seek to achieve higher levels of satisfaction and quality in education. Efficiency of E.T. requires a high degree of perspective planning and execution of technology, improvement of teaching-learning skills and greater motivation of the learners. Modern management is goal-oriented and result-based. It envisages a constant and continuous process of change to generate new ideas, insights, methods and techniques to cater to the needs of different clientele groups. The educational manager can prove effective if he knows the fundamentals of educational management and technology and takes decisions appropriately in time to meet the goals.

Management is controlled by certain general principles like planning, organising, co-ordinating, monitoring and evaluation. It deals with multifarious resources, human, physical, ideational or academic which have to be handled properly to realise the instructional objectives. It is a systems approach in which all elements are interlinked and interdependent. If one link is weakened or broken, the entire, process can be damaged or adversely affected. It is, therefore, desirable that there should be harmonious co-ordination and efficient organisation. Since E.T. includes a wide range of media and materials, its management requires a series of activities relating to planning, organisation, co-ordination, monitoring and evaluation for maximising the learning experiences. These are as follows:

E.T. for Schools: Planning is the prerequisite exercise for any effective activity. It implies a basic function "do how" that is how the aims and objectives need be realised. Before launching upon a particular job or enterprise or implementing any project, the manager is required to take decisions about the methods and strategies for effectively and efficiently achieving the objectives. This implies that for E.T. planning the school management has to have the basic data, facts and figures, background information and audience as well as the school profile at hand and take decisions on the basis of such fundamentals.

Modern planning needs to be democratic, scientific and decentralised. There must be adequate participation of all concerned-teachers, students, media experts and E.T. specialists or E.T. trained personnel, in the planning process. The persons not only at the helm of affairs, but also at the grassroots level must be consulted for planning effectively. In view of the objectives, expenses involved and size of the E.T. project, the plans/projects may be long-term or short term or medium-term. This kind of democratic planning becomes more productive and creative, promoting high morale, motivation and commitment of teachers as well as students.

E.T. in other Institutions: E.T. has to be provided to all types of schools, rural, urban, tribal, non-tribal, primary, high or higher secondary schools. The resources available in these institutions vary in range, quantity and quality. The roll strengths of students and teachers also range very widely. Similarly, E.T. also comprises all kinds of media and materials, ranging in vast complexity and control, expenses and distribution. Hence, after planning, the next important phase of organisation of execution comes into play. Both human and material resources are to be well organised for achieving the instructional objectives set for various media and materials.

Effective organisation ensures maximum utilisation of resources. Otherwise, there would be wastage of resources and duplication of work. Interpersonal relations need to be improved for making an organisation efficient to apply E.T. according to needs, abilities and interests of students. Therefore, one E.T. application must be strengthened and supported with other kind of media and materials. Formal and informal contacts and linkages must be established for mutual cooperation.

There must be decentralisation and delegation of powers and greater autonomy can ensure better functioning. Vertical structure of relations must be flattened and horizontal linkages and relation should be expanded. Adequate consultancy and advisory services should be provided for improving the tone and morale of personnel and efficiency of the systems.

Manning E.T.: For organising E.T. effectively, it is essential that suitable human resources are deployed in time and adequately. The personnel should be recruited in time and they must be equipped with required knowledge and skills. There should not be any mismatch of persons with the specific skills required of them. The right man should be posted at the right place. He should know how to operate the media or utilise the materials. Nowadays the work is becoming more complex, more skill-based and more knowledge/expertise-based. Management should, therefore, be quite active and responsive to matching human resources with particular/specific job and work place.

The first step in matching jobs and individuals is to make job specifications or descriptions available to the management. A job description sets for the objectives, duties, relationships and results expected of a person on the job. An operator of the projector, overhead or film, for example, should have adequate training and experience in handling the machines effectively. In order to match job and individuals, job descriptions or job-chart should be more explicit and specific. That is, for example, in case of a projector operator, it may be specifically mentioned that he can be able to do minor repair in case the machine goes out of order.

The second step in matching jobs and individuals is translating the duties or spelling out 'individual specifications'. In considering an individual for a particular job, his qualification, past experience, accomplishments and conduct in the past or in earlier positions must be taken into consideration. In case of a fresher, his behaviour and conduct in the viva voce or practical test have to be appraised with more care and objectivity.

After a person is recruited and posted, it is felt necessary to guide and supervise his/her performance and ascertain his/her strengths and weaknesses. It is to be assessed whether in order to make him/her more capable, any specific on the job or in-service training is essential or desirable. He/she has to keep his/her knowledge, skills etc., abreast with the latest trends and innovations. Therefore, very often in-service education/training is to be provided continuously and systematically. Introduction of new machines or media makes it imperative on the part of the manager to provide suitable training to the incumbent. The inservice education/training may be of various types as follows:

(a) Refresher training courses for giving advanced knowledge and skills.

(b) Orientation on training for wider exposition and better acquaintance with latest developments.

(c) Staff discussions/faculty meetings.

(d) Participating in professional meetings, conferences, seminars, workshops, etc.

(e) Making various distance education courses and career development programmes available.

(f) Encouraging staff members to take up researches, experiments, extension work and publication activities.

Since machines/media as well as materials of multifarious nature and types are to be utilised, adequate co-ordination is necessary to avoid wastage and duplication of work. In any kind of organisation, in spite of all resources available, without proper co-ordination, the entire process gets plugged because of a little negligence or through-oversight. All facilities and services should be properly unified and harmonised for promoting effectiveness in operation or execution. The plans and programmes should be made operative only through proper co-ordination of various resources, both human and physical.

To ensure adequate co-ordination, communication has to be vertical as well as horizontal and any gaps or lapses in this communication process can spell disaster or wastage of resources. The responsibilities assigned to different individuals are to be co-ordinated through written or verbal communications without hindrances and bottlenecks. Inter human relations should be properly maintained and monitored, so that their activities and assignments can be properly streamlined, co-ordinated and accomplished. Proper understanding and cooperation should be ensured and sharing of information, joint discussion, staff participation and rapport should be promoted among different functionaries and personnel for effective functioning and implementation of E.T. programmes.

The Assessment

Last, but not the least is the importance of monitoring and evaluation which are essential for effectiveness of management. Since there are various agencies and sectors involved in the process, it is imperative that timely and proper monitoring are really necessary. There are mainly two kinds of evaluation from time perspective. One is short-term and another is long-term. But evaluation should be continuous. It may also be formal or non-formal. It may also be formative or summative or both; evaluation can be done internally and externally. In order to bring about improvement in the system, it is necessary to study the strengths and weaknesses, deficiencies and difficulties in the implementation so that suitable steps can be taken to highlight the strengths and success, take remedial measures for avoiding weaknesses and deficiencies encountered and experienced in different factors and segments of management. Short-term evaluation is necessary for periodic check-up and getting feedback on the progress made. If the project is a major one implemented over a long time and involves a good number of persons and agencies, it is felt desirable to undertake long-term evaluation.

Formative and summative evaluation is conducted for ascertaining the needs and for assessing the effectiveness of the programmes. For example, before producing ETV programmes, the needs and conditions, background experience and knowledge are to ascertained. It may be in the form of audience profile or survey. This is called formative evaluation which is required for planning. On the other hand, after producing and telecasting the programme, summative evaluation is taken up for measuring the effectiveness or success of the programme or a series of programmes. On the basis of the evaluation results, planning can be made either to continue the programme if found suitable or discontinue the same, if it is found a failure. But the findings must be useful for bringing about improvement or desirable changes in the process for ensuring more effectiveness. Similarly, in order to ensure impartiality and objectivity, evaluation should be done by an external agency. But in order to check up any lacunae or progress in organising a programme, it is desirable to conduct evaluation internally. The persons working in the same organisation can evaluate the programmes being implemented or which were implemented.

The Hindrances

In the management of E.T. a number of problems are experienced at various levels and in different sectors. These problems may be related to infrastructure i. e., facilities, human resources, procurement of media, financing and maintenance of media, networking and support services. These are discussed below:

Infrastructure is the physical and human resources which are basic requisites for managing a particular institution or a project. For smooth functioning of an organisation both human and material resources are necessary. But in this context, we are going to discuss infrastructure as regards material or physical resources which are required for transaction of curricular and co-curricular activities from planning to evaluation. Hence, the infrastructure includes buildings, equipment, media, furniture, laboratory, library, studio, auditorium and so on. For planning and developing the necessary infrastructure, the following factors are taken into consideration.

(i) Determination of material resources.

(ii) Specifications of the facilities according to requirements.

(iii) Quality determination.

(iv) Quantification of facilities.

(v) Development of indicators for per capita requirement.

Determination of Material Resources : Many kinds of physical facilities are required for organising the programmes in an educational institution. Besides buildings, other resources like media, equipment, studio, auditorium, etc., are to be provided for various activities. With a view to making the teaching-learning process effective, all these material facilities are to be determined appropriately and in time, so that the programmes will not be affected adversely.

Specification of the Facilities : The material facilities should be determined as per prescribed standards and specifications. The specification of facilities implies the description of materials in the context of their quality, utility and standards. Unless specifications of these facilities are made clear and specific, there is a possibility of wastage and under utilisation. Hence exact specifications can ensure proper utilisation or resources.

Quality Determination : Nowadays materials and media are available in a wide variety of makes and brands. Some of them are of high quality whereas others are of poor standard. It is, therefore, felt desirable to determine the nature of the materials in order to optimise their use. Unless the quality of the products or materials is specified and standardised, there will be difficulties not only in procurement but also in using and maintaining the same. Poor quality materials, for example, leads to poor functioning and maintenance, which again calls for frequent replacement affecting the output very badly.

Quantification of Facilities : Management of material resources includes the quantification of facilities on the basis of per capita requirements. The quantum of materials of different types has to be assessed and full deployment and utilisation of resources are to be made at the right time. Time and space management in terms per capita and per hour need to be calculated for quantifying the facility requirement.

Development of Indicators per capita Requirement : With a view to ensuring efficient management of material resources alongwith quantification of per capita need, it is necessary to develop material requirement indicators. This should be done as the amount of material facility is required to produce a given amount of output. It can be possible if combinations of material facilities are shown in an input matrix and various combinations are found out to see whether they have influenced the outcomes.

After the basic infrastructure is developed, specifications are determined and requirement of various types of media and materials are estimated. Steps need be taken for procurement of media which are of multifarious grades and quality, uses and expenses. In every organisation there are fixed and formal procedures and principles for procurement of media and materials. These are to be followed scrupulously as far as possible and procurement should be made in time in adequate amount and quality.

Now it is essential to see that these media and materials are properly used in implementing different programmes. In this context, the following two considerations need be made for ensuring adequate utilisation of the facilities.

(i) Planning the Utilisation Process

(ii) Optimum Utilisation of Material Resources

Planning the Utilisation Process : For streamlining the procurement and utilisation of material resources, it is felt essential to know what type of material facilities are available and how they are being utilised in the teaching-learning process and various co-curricular activities. Sometimes we procure materials that are not used adequately and on the other hand, we cannot procure the materials which are sufficiently required. Thus, on the one hand there is inadequacy and on the other hand, there is wastage of resources. Hence a checklist can be prepared to show the time of their procurement and use, by whom used and on what occasions. This will help not only in knowing the extent of utilisation of various materials, but also for providing these facilities adequately.

Optimum Utilisation of Material Resources : It is the duty of the management to see that material resources are used to the maximum. We find that in most of the educational institutions, media and materials are not adequately used. It has to be ascertained which media and materials are over-utilised, under-utilised or properly utilised. Planning has to be made for optimum utilisation of physical resources.

Since media and materials are expensive and useful, we cannot afford to neglect their proper upkeep and maintenance. Unless they are kept in right condition, in right places and in right amount, difficulties are experienced in production and utilisation of curricular programmes. Suitable steps need be taken for saving them from wastage and under-utilisation.

Saving physical facilities from wastage is an important aspect of infrastructural management. It has two aspects (i) the media and materials need be protected from damages like wrong uses, wrong storage etc. (ii) they should be saved for future repeated uses. Students coming in batches or one generation after another must be given adequate facilities for their learning and skill development. Particularly valuable machineries and media need be used and preserved carefully.

Again there are two dimensions of proper maintenance (i) it lengthens the life of the media and materials and (ii) it keeps them in readiness or in good condition for repeated uses. As the prices are increasing by leaps and bounds, maintenance has assumed a greater significance. But it poses a serious challenge to both personnel working in an organisation and the clientele for whom media are to be used.

The personnel in charge of the material resources are actually the custodians who should be knowledgeable and vigilant. The media can have better longevity through proper maintenance and meticulous attention. Different caring and curing mechanisms like lubrication, watering, warming, cooling, repairing and renewing from time to time are to be adopted scrupulously.

The first step towards better maintenance is to train the persons concerned. Due to explosion of knowledge and technology many media are getting obsolete and complicated, unless the persons who are custodians of media and materials are trained and oriented properly in time. They must have:

(a) a thorough knowledge about various media and materials for cleaning and caring them.

(b) an adequate skill in using various tools and materials, and

(c) a positive and scientific attitude towards the study of various custodian services at different phases.

In order to effect efficiency and economy of time and energy, it is essential that the custodians should have adequate knowledge, skills and attitude. The media and materials are sometimes unused, underused or over-used and at times misused also. All this cuts down their longevity. All the media and materials procured must be mentioned in stock register or in the directory with specification, gradation and utilisation possibilities. The media should be used with proper recording about the date, time and purpose. Maintenance and storage procedures should be mentioned in a register.

It is also felt necessary to maintain a condition profile of each item of media/materials which can give a status account of all important ones in terms of quantity as well as quality. On the basis of the data given here, decisions will be taken for repair, replacement, maintenance or even write-off of the unusable and damaged media. Besides, a detailed checklist of various items of facilities can be maintained for the purpose.

Man behind the machine is more important than anything else in the management. Persons need to be deployed for managing, operating and maintaining all relevant activities. Persons with requisite qualification and experience have to be recruited according to the job requirements. Today work is becoming more knowledge and skill-based and the management has to be active and responsive to emerging needs of media and matching human resources with various work places and jobs. Manpower planning and management has therefore assumed a great significance nowadays.

The first step in this direction is to make job specifications and descriptions available which mention the objectives, duties, relationships and results expected of a person on the job. Job description should be more explicit and concrete in terms of work and outcomes. It should also spell out, for instance, how decent relationships intended, what innovative and renovative measures are to be taken or what management technique need be followed for getting better results.

Another major step in manpower planning is to translate the allotted duties into activities. Individual specifications are to be chalked out and a job chart should be given to every incumbent about the work expected to be done by him to achieve specific objectives or reach targets. An 'individual specifications chart' may tell about the training and education, past experience and achievement, personality traits and characteristics which are important points for considering his work and performance.

Manpower management should take into account the following:

(i) The knowledge, understanding, values, attitudes and skills required for proper performance.

(ii) Manpower requirements should be estimated well ahead of recruitment.

(iii) Development needs should be assessed periodically and steps for appointment of additional hands should be taken accordingly.

(iv) Persons on jobs need to be motivated to maintain adequate levels of performance.

(v) Appropriate rewards and incentives should be provided through career advancement programmes and promotion.

Further, the following steps need to be taken for developing manpower.

(i) Refresher courses giving advanced knowledge and skills should be organised from time to time.

(ii) Orientation courses should be wider organised for better and further exposition to wider facilities.

(iii) Staff/faculty discussions and deliberation should be organised regularly.

(iv) Persons have to be deputed to professional meetings. seminars, workshops and conferences.

(v) Various distance education courses can be availed of, for career development.

(vi) Staff members can be encouraged to conduct research studies, extension and publications;

(vii) Personnel may be given certain amount of freedom and flexibility for taking initiative.

(viii) Periodic review may be made for ascertaining the rate of progress and problems, if any.

(ix) Continuous interaction, feedback and monitoring are essential for better performance.

(x) Strengths of the employees can be capitalised whereas weaknesses can be considered for sorting out the problems or overcoming the hurdle.

(xi) An objective system of awards and punishments should be developed in manpower management.

With a view to promote effectiveness in our educational system, it is desirable that proper networking of agencies and facilities should be developed. Nowadays a large number of agencies and organisations have been set up to perform the same kind of jobs at different levels. Unless suitable steps are taken for establishing linkages for co-ordination, co-operation and collaboration, there will be duplication of work, wastage of resources and loss of time and energy. In spite of all our developments, we are still facing constraints and crunches at the financial level, particularly for academic and educational programmes. Therefore, it is imperative that adequate networking of institutions and services should be developed at different stages for ensuring economy and efficiency.

Media and materials are gradually multiplied and getting sophisticated. Every new brand and generations are bringing with them new changes and improvements. Unless a proper support service system is developed it will be difficult to maintain the media of all types. Wear and tear of the machines is a must due to their uses and utilisation. Sometimes expensive media are damaged due to mishandling and wrong storage practices. They have to be repaired or cured and cared for their smooth functioning. Otherwise the programmes depending on the same media will be seriously affected or cannot be implemented properly. Hence suitable men and machineries for operation, repair, care and curing of the media must be deployed in time and adequately.

To conclude the above discussion, it may be mentioned that this unit has focused on the need and importance of management, its types and implications for bringing about efficiency and effectiveness in the E.T. system.

We have tried to discuss the planning and organisation of E.T., recruitment and training of personnel co-ordination, monitoring and evaluation which are essential parts of management.

Under the problems that are faced by the management are developing infrastructure, procurement of media and their proper maintenance, manpower planning and management for optimisation of performance and outcomes.

In order to ensure economy, efficiency and efficacy in the media management, development of suitable networking and support system involving co-operation, co-ordination and collaboration among various agencies and institutions is very necessary.

The Approach

The use of Educational Technology has been emphasised in both the National Policy of Education, 1986 and revised NPE, 1992, to improve both the quality and quantity of education for the first time in the history of Indian Education. No earlier document of national significance had pointed out the importance of educational technology so clearly and so strongly as it has been done by the NPE, 1986. Spelling out its deployment, the NPE, 1986 (p. 22) has observed, "Educational Technology will be employed in the spread of useful information, the training and retraining of teachers, to improve the quality, sharpen awareness of art and culture, inculcate abiding values etc., both in the formal and non-formal sections."

According to Eric Asbhy (1967), mankind is now in the midst of the Fourth Revolution in Education-the Age of Electronic Media which comprises radio, television, audio/video recorder, computer, and so on. The NPE '86 has therefore added (p. 22): "In the villages without electricity batteries or solar packs will be utilised to run the programme." It has also suggested that in order to avoid structural dualism, modern educational technology must reach out to the most distant areas and the most deprived sections of beneficiaries simultaneously with the areas of comparative affluence and availability.

The Programme of Action (POA), 1986 (p. 180) has rightly pointed out that several efforts have been made in the past to use technological aids for improving the quality of education. Audio visual units and film libraries were set up at the Centre and in States for promoting the use of educational films and projection aids. Educational Technology Centres and Cells were established at the national and state levels respectively for facilitating the use of various media, particularly radio and television. Although School Broadcast programme has been in vogue for more than four decades, it has not yet been accepted whole-heartedly and in massive scale throughout the country. Educational Television Programme, in spite of its glamour and potentiality, has not yet been popular in the educational institutions.

In many States and Union territories, State Institutes of Educational Technology (SIETs) and at the national level the Central Institute of Educational Technology have been producing, utilising, monitoring and following up the television and radio programmes for improving the quantity and quality of education. Under the project "INSAT for EDUCATION" launched in 1982, the SIETs have been generating educational software for children. The Audio Visual Research Centres (AVRCs) and Educational Media Research Centres (EMRCs) have been producing Educational TV Programmes for college/university students. Some Technical Teacher Training Institutions (TTTIs) have also been developing facilities for production of TV as well as other media programmes.

Video Technology has made a headway in the field of education. The Electronic Trade and Technology Development Corporation (ET & TDC) has formulated a TELETEACH Project to prepare software on videotape. A good number of secondary schools have been selected by the Ministry of Education for equipping them with VCRs and viewing equipment to work as viewing centres.

Computer Education has been popular in the country at various stages of education. The Computer Literacy and Studies in Schools (CLASS) Project has been implemented in hundreds of Schools and with availability of microcomputers there, the students have been familiarised with the application and potentiality of computer as learning medium. Computer education courses are now available in many universities besides Ph. D., M. Tech., and B. Tech Programmes conducted by the IITs and other technological institutions. Diploma level courses are being offered by a few dozens of polytechnics.

Although educational broadcasting has the inherent advantages of greater reach, management, convenience and cost effectiveness, the non-broadcast/non-project media and materials are more oriented to individual learning and more appropriate to the indigenous clientele and developing economy. These media would also help in enriching the learning process. Large scale use of audio and video programmes in broadcast and non-broadcast modes would generate enormous demand for qualified manpower to work in educational media set-ups. It would be necessary to develop maintenance structure and train "technician entrepreneurs" for taking up such responsibilities. As enunciated in the POA (1986) "Education requires media support which is related to the curriculum as well as enrichment. Curriculum-based education also requires materials which the teacher can draw upon in the course of this teaching. This could be provided in the form of charts, slides, transparencies, etc. Video technology offers considerable potential for improving the quality of education especially at higher levels."

Similarly computer technology is likely to influence education enormously and can play an important role in enhancing the efficiency of the teaching-learning process, making children more creative and providing them with an individualised learning environment. Computer literacy would be crucial in preparing children to cope with microcomputer explosion which has the same potential for social change as the Industrial Revolution. It is essential to integrate the same progressively with the school curriculum.

Diverse Views

The modern world is confronting two general problems which are not only affecting the pattern of human life, but also inflicting their full impact on education. These two problems are called "information explosion" and the "population explosion." They are like two horns of dilemma in education-more things to learn and more people to be taught.

The term "information explosion" really means an explosion of knowledge. We all know, new frontiers of knowledge are opening day by day and the horizon of human knowledge and understanding is expanding very fast. In most of the subjects, moreover, knowledge is cumulative, so that every now and then, there is more to be learnt. Especially in arts subjects, new facts and figures take their place along with the old. In sciences although new knowledge or information often supersedes the old, the students and scientists have to learn both. Besides, closer relations among countries of the world resulting from wide international communications make information explosion more acute and complicated.

The second problem is "Population Explosion" which is immensely affecting traditional pattern of education. The problem of population explosion is more serious in the developing countries than the developed ones. For example, in India population has been increasing in geometrical progression. India now has more than 1000 million people.

Michael J. Apter (1968 p. 10) has rightly observed, "The increase in population has of course tended to occur fastest in the developing countries. For this reason the problem it poses for education is the greatest in these countries. Conversely, the information explosion has the greatest immediate effect on the technologically advanced countries. Fortunately, no countrv has experienced the full effects of both at the same time. Nevertheless, there is a fair degree of overlap between the effects of the two." The developing countries like India, however, are facing serious difficulties both from population as well as information explosion. Because they have to provide education for a larger population year by year and cover more and more technical and scientific ground for making up the deficiency. Since most of the countries are confronted more or less with the problem of more persons to be taught and more information to be learnt, this general problem is called "Education Explosion."

The problem of "Education Explosion" has both positive and negative aspects. On the positive side the problem has unprecedented record to its credit. The bright features are—

1. Most countries of the world have spent more on education during the last fifty five years than we have in recorded history.
2. More enrolment of pupils than any time in the past has been made during the last three decades. It has more than doubled in most countries since 1950.
3. The educational systems of the world have produced 90% of all the writers, artists, scientists and technologists who have even lived during this time.
4. The products of our educational systems are so creative that they are making the quantum of knowledge double in scientific and technological fields.
5. The youths educated by the modern educational system during the last five decades have published more books and magazines both regards the number of copies as well as that of titles.

Seth Spaulding (1970 p. 9) Director of UNESCO's Department of School and H. E. has thus aptly remarked, "The record is, then impressive. We are, in essence, providing more education than ever before in history and the products of our systems are apparently more creative than all our forefathers put together."

The other side of the coin is however as follows:

1. Although in most of the countries educational expenditure has been enormous, it is estimated that as many as one third of the children of school-going age have not yet seen the inside of a school. If at all they enter the schools, less

than one third of them are able to complete lower elementary education. As many as 50% of the pupils' are only repeaters. The wastage and stagnation in many educational systems thus make cost of schooling spectacular and increase the number of illiterates and semiliterates.

2. In spite of the phenomenal quantitative expansion of education the world has still an army of illiterate adults.
3. Almost all governments of the world now recognise education more as an investiment rather than as a social expenditure. Accordingly the so-called "investment" has been expanded enormously. But many countries are still finding it difficult to reach the quantitative targets like physical facilities and material resources suggested by various international conferences on education.
4. Grave doubts are expressed as to the relevance and effectiveness of education in the modern society not only in India, but also in most of the developed and developing countries of the world. Education cannot serve its purpose unless it is relevant to contemporary and future problems of the community and of the world. For example, education should deal with the pollution problems, population problems, agricultural problems, technological problems and war and peace. If succeeding generations are not able to tackle these problems successfully, education will be deemed to be a failure.
5. Although education has promoted the growth and development of science and technology, education itself has not yet been able to utilise their traits for being more effective and relevant. Seth Spaulding has rightly said, "The way we manage and administer our educational enterprises would probably bankrupt any other kind of business. Although education has shared in the creation of technological age, education itself has not learnt how to use the fruits of technology to improve the efficiency and the quality of its own institutions. In attempts to 'catch up' quantitatively education has usually attempted to multiply what has gone in a pre-technology system of schooling."

In essence, Mr. Spaulding (1970 p. 10) has said that we have provided more and more money to more and more of that we may be doing poorly. We hope that we could do it better. Educationists of international distinction have suggested that it will be possible only by developing suitable curriculum and applying educational technologies to make the curriculum more effective and the school more efficient.

Global Recognition

Educational technology, in its global sense, includes the entire process of the setting of goals, the continuous reforms of curriculum, the tryout of new methods and materials, the evaluation of the system as an integrated whole and resetting of goals on the basis of the findings of evaluation and innovations. But it is often identified as pointed out by Spaulding, with various devices and processes which make possible the recording, storage, manipulation, retrieval, transmission and display of data, information and printed and photographed materials with an efficiency and speed unheard of, even 20 years ago. If these capabilities are considered as part of a broad curriculum for research and development design, they have tremendous potential in education.

Potent Factors

Technological materials and methods useful in the teaching-learning process range from chalkboards to television sets. Technology of education involves books and blackboards, paper and pencils, models and maps, charts and globes, tapes and slides, radios and televisions, projectors and computers. It comprises both "hardware" and "software" and both audio and visual materials. It also includes decisions about the educational objectives to be achieved and decisions about the size of the learning group, the learning sequence, teaching methods and selection of media.

In its wider perspective, therefore, educational technology deals with the systematic application of the resources of scientific knowledge to the process that each individual has to pass through in order to acquire and use knowledge. "Educational Technology" writes Geoffrey Hubbard (1974), Director of the National Council for Educational Technology, England "is the complement of curriculum reform concerned with the Method where curriculum reform is concerned with the content... Given an acceptance of the concept of educational technology as the process of improving learning method, we are faced with the problems of encouraging innovation in an educational system whose greatest strength is in decentralisation and autonomy. Certainly nothing will be achieved by elaborating authoritarian solutions. What is needed is more discussion of the contribution the different elements of the system can make to the problems facing education. Widespread dissemination of experience (both successful and unsuccessful) of innovations and supporting services, including training, consultancy and information activities are necessary to assist the teacher in the selection and introduction of the new methods appropriate to his own particular situation."

According to GOM Leith "Educational Technology is the application of scientific knowledge about learning and the conditions of learning to improve the effectiveness and efficiency of teaching and training. In the absence of scientifically established principles, educational technology implements techniques of empirical testing to improve learning situations." Hence educational technology seeks to apply scientific knowledge about learning and the conditions of learning for improving its effectiveness.

Sphere of Operation

We find that a large number of new methods and media constitute educational technology. But there is no proper co-ordination and articulation in their use. That is why, no satisfactory results are achieved by such a wide range of materials due to lack of a systematic planning and organisation. Henri Dieuzeide (1970), Director of UNESCO's Division of Methods, Materials and Techniques has aptly remarked, "The new techniques do in fact offer a vast range of possibilities, but their field of application often seems to be a wasteland scattered with spare parts which no one knows how to put together to form an efficient system. Here it is useful to discuss the difference between technology in education and technology of education. We have to move from one to the other, i. e. from the former to the latter. Technology in education is concerned with equipment, preparation of adhoc messages and integration with traditional teacher-centered activities. But as discussed earlier, technology of education deals with the active use of mass media and computer science for the individual pupils learning process under the teacher's supervision. Hence the latter one i. e. educational technology is more scientific, more psychological and more pedagogical than the former one i.e. technology in education."

With the advance of science and technology there are new learning aids which have revolutionized the learning process, in particular and education as a whole. In modern society with its emphasis on mass education and successful citizenship training, the requirement is for efficient learning. Education has now become an assembly-line like mass production factories. A nation can prosper if its education can be made effective. Education can be made efficient, if it uses modern technology. Technology in education will be useful, if it is properly planned and organised on psychological and pedagogical principles. Henri Dieuzeide has rightly observed, "The transition from technology in education to the technology of education involves a thorough appraisal of the existing educational system, of its objectives and of the means used to attain them, before any decision is reached to employ these new techniques for specific teaching purposes. The teacher-turned technologist can then gradually assume the functions of an 'educational engineer' whose job is to increase the output of the entire scholastic machine."

Although educational technology can be interpreted in a rather narrow sense as the use of sophisticated hardware in teaching or in a broad sense as the use of any new educational technique, in fact the concept means more than the sum total of all the media and methods, materials and techniques used for better teaching and learning. It involves or should involve greater psychological and pedagogical preparedness, a scientific attitude and a coordinated approach to the educational process as a whole. It should reflect one's professional interest and zeal for making experiments and innovations for development and success of education.

Educational Technology implies the use of all educational resources—men and materials, methods and techniques, means and media in an integrated and systematic manner for optimizing learning. According to the modern educationists, learning not teaching is the crucial task of the entire educational process and emphasis of teachers is regarded as a system which facilitates learning and makes learning effective as well as efficient. Efficient in the sense that the learning with the use of Educational Technology becomes easy and interesting, durable and comprehensive. Efficient in the sense that it is economical and financially viable. In fact, effective communication of educational messages in an economic way is the main objective of educational technology.

Organs of Computer

Educational Technology is not a new-comer, although the concept as such is comparatively new in the field of education. The educational process was teacher-centered, the method of rote-learning was important, a few textbooks were the main resource and chalkboard was the only aid. Subsequently, a number of audiovisual materials were introduced and used in the teaching-learning process. It was usually thought that teaching machines, film-projectors, slide-projectors, language laboratories, tape-recorders, cassettes, radio, television, video-tape recorders, computers, and so on, are educational technology. In brief, all the audio-visual equipments are regarded as the Educational Technology. But this is only one aspect of educational technology and is called hardware component. Another aspect is new-methods of teaching, tested principles and practices, innovation, e.g., programmed learning, micro-teaching, team-teaching etc., are called software component of educational technology. Both software and hardware constitute the concept of educational technology and both of them go hand in hand to maximise the effects of teaching-learning process. Thus, increased efficiency of the process is the keynote of the Educational Technology.

Elements of Influence

(i) increasing influence of science and scientific knowledge and skills of education.

(ii) appearance of a number of audio-visual aids which needed to be put together in order to avoid confusion and wastage of resources i. e. multimedia approach to education.

(iii) development of programmed learning approach.
(iv) explosion of numbers and knowledge, facts and figures.
(v) teaching revolution and recent development in pedagogy.
(vi) emergence of a systems theory.
(vii) expansion of educational broadcasting and computers.

Significant Impact

(i) Curriculum and development.
(ii) Revolutionary change in teaching and learning methodology and practices.
(iii) Shift in emphasis from teaching to learning.
(iv) Media application in education and the development of media taxonomy.
(v) Quantitative and qualitative expansion of education.
(vi) Emphasis on non-formal education and special education systems.
(vii) New assessment criteria and procedures.
(viii) Emphasis and research, continued evaluation and recycling process in education.
(ix) New role and position of teachers and an increasing emphasis on in-service training of teachers.
(x) Appearance of resource libraries and teacher's centers.
(xi) Changes in structural patterns of educational organisations to facilitate interaction between programme producers, course designers and users.
(xii) Application of economic considerations and cost-effective criterion in education.
(xiii) Use of ET in the field of lifelong and continuing education.

The Facts : The use of E. T. encompasses all types of education formal, non-formal and informal education, primary, secondary and higher education, adult and continuing education. ET has been applied largely in the field of distance/open learning system. Thus, educational technology is very comprehensive and all pervasive, covering all stages of education. Its scope is very broad, flexible, open and ever-widening. It is an emerging field that includes all modern methods, media and materials that are being invented every now and then, and being utilised for improving the quality and quantity of education.

This chapter is intended to enable its readers to know the background and context of ET application, its meaning and implication, nature and scope of educational technology.

The NPE, 1986 and its revised version in 1992 have laid great stress on the application of ET in all aspects and stages of education. The Programme of Action, 1986 and 1992 have given the strategies and set goals for achievement during the 7th, 8th and 9th Five Year Plans.

The modern world has faced two dilemmas (i) Explosion of Population and (ii) Explosion of Knowledge. Both have posed challenges to the mankind and these can successfully be tackled with the help of modern methods, media and materials that constitute educational technology. There has been unprecedented expansion of education in all dimensions, but the quality has to be promoted with the help of educational technology.

ET can make education and learning effective and interesting. Previously, the audio-visual aids and approaches were used in education, but these were used in an unplanned and unsystematic manner. It was called Technology in Education. But now technology of education or educational technology is being used and applied in the field of education in a systems approach and well-planned manner. This ensures cost effectiveness and efficiency in education.

Educational Technology has now influenced all stages of education starting from pre-primary and university education, from formal to non-formal education and from distance to continuing education. The various media like radio, TV, computer etc., have influenced the education system and have enabled educational planners and educationists to provide enormous facilities and alternatives for educational expansion at all levels. Quality of education can be greatly improved to benefit the pupils by using Educational Technology.

5

Changed Scenario

Programmed learning is one of the important invocations of the 20th century in the teaching-learning process. It is a self-instructional technique for providing individualized instruction or learning experience to the learner. In programmed learning, the subject matter or learning experience is logically sequenced into small segments. The learning experience is self-corrective.

The English writers prefer to use the term programmed learning and the American authors prefer the use of programmed instruction.

It is held by some educators that 'Gita' is the first example of programmed learning. They hold that the text of the 'Gita' has several ingredients of programming: initial behaviour, small steps, active participation of the learner, terminal behaviour, immediate feed-back and self-evaluation by the learner.

Several educators regard Socrates as the earliest programmer. Socrates used to guide his followers to gain knowledge by conducting them conversationally along a path from fact to fact and insight to insight.

Programmed learning emerged in the beginning of the 20th century from the efforts of American psychologists. E. L. Thorndike

(1874-1949) was the first psychologist whose findings bear direct relevance to programming. Other important psychologists who have made significant contribution in the field are Sidney L. Pressy, Robert M. Gagne, Robert Mager and B. F. Skinner.

Programmed learning is related with the 'Law of Effect' as explained by Thorndike. Sidney L. Pressey, a psychologist of Ohio State University, is credited for developing in the middle 1920's practical machines which could teach as well as test. The teaching machines as developed by Pressey present a series of questions to a student and inform him immediately whether his response is right or wrong.

In 1943, Skinner and his two other colleagues started programming by teaching a pigeon to roll a small bowling ball by operant conditioning. By 1954, Skinner and James G. Holland devised the auto-instructional methods which have served the present generation as the basis for present work in programmed instruction. In Skinnerian programmed instruction, whether mechanised or otherwise, the learner is initially asked a question which he can easily answer correctly without any previous study of the particular lesson. The learner is taught by the sequence of questions. He is asked more and more as the lesson proceeds in very small steps.

In 1955, Norman A. Crowder developed what he calls "automatic tutoring by intrinsic programming" as against "extrinsic programming" developed by Skinner.

Robert Mager (1958) gave a new concept known as "Learner Controlled Instruction" which is a kind of Socratic dialogue in reverse, in which the learner led the instructor. The instructor remained silent until the learner himself stimulated the instructor with questions that suggested the needed illustrations, demonstrations, practice or some other help.

Stoluron, at Illionis, aimed at developing a process which should provide for greater individualization by measuring needs and developing programmes that require a computer to assist instruction.

In 1962, T. F. Gilbert gave formalized expression of his technology of education called Mathetics. Pennington and Slack expressed in 1962 further detailed methods of preparing lessons from mathetic principles.

Programmed learning is a process of arranging material to be learned in a series of small steps designed to lead a learner through self-instruction from what he knows to the unknown of new and more complex knowledge and principles. A programme takes the place of a tutor and leads the learner through a set of frames of specified behaviour designed and sequenced to make it more probable that he will behave in a given derived way.

In programmed learning, it is said that the most efficient, pleasant and permanent learning takes place when the student proceeds through a course by a large number of small, easy-to-take steps. Wilbur L. Schramm (1962) lists the essential elements of programmed instruction as: (*a*) an ordered sequence of stimulus items, (*b*) to each of which a student responds in some specific way, (*c*) his responses being reinforced by immediate knowledge of results, (*d*) so that he moves by small steps, (*e*) therefore, making few errors and practicing mostly correct responses, (*f*) from what he knows by a process of successively closer approximation, toward what he is supposed to learn from the programme.

Following definitions provide a comprehensive view of programmed instruction.

Dale, Edgar (1962) : Programmed learning is a systematic, step by step, self-instructional programme aimed to ensure the learning of stated behaviour.

Das, R. C (1993) : Programmed instruction is a method of individualised instruction where each individual learns by himself at his own rate. Programmed learning consists of elements of new knowledge called 'steps' which are arranged in a sequence in such a way that a student can easily learn by himself.

Espich, James E. and William B (1965) : Programmed instruction is a planned sequences of experiences, leading to proficiency in terms of stimulus response relationship.

Gulati and Gulati (1990) : Programmed learning as popularly understood is a method of giving individual instruction in which the student is active and proceeds at his own pace and is provided with immediate knowledge of results. The teacher is not physically present. The programmer, while developing programmed material has to follow the laws of behaviour and validate his strategy in terms of student learning.

Jacobs and Others (1966) : Self-instructional programmes are educational materials from which the students learn. These programmes can be used with many types of students and subject-matter either by themselves, hence the name "self-instruction" or its combination with instructional strategies.

Kampfer (1970) : Programmed learning is a device which presents an exercise or a problem to a student, inducing him to respond; and revealing to him whether or not his response is correct.

Leith, G. O. M (1966) : Programme is a sequence of small steps of instructional material (called frames), most of which require a response to be made by completing a blank space in a sentence. To ensure that expected responses are given, a system of cueing is applied, and each response is verified by the provision of immediate knowledge of results. Such a sequence is intended to be worked at the learner's own pace as individual self-instruction.

Luonsdaine Arthur, A (1964) : An instructional programme is a vehicle which generates an essentially reproducible sequence of instructional events and accepts responsibility for efficiently accomplishing a specified change from a given range of initial competencies or behavioural tendencies to a specified or terminal range of competencies or behavioural tendencies.

Marke, Susan (1969) : Programmed learning is a method of designing a reproducible sequence of instructional events to produce a measurable and consistent effect on the behaviours of each and every acceptable student.

Navi, N. S. (1984) : Programmed instruction is a technique of converting the live instructional process into self-learning or auto-instructional readable material in the form of micro-sequence (the segments of subject-matter) which the learners are required to read, make some right or wrong response, correct wrong responses or confirm right responses and attain the complete mastery of the concept explained in the micro-sequences.

May, K. O. (1965) **:** Educational programming is the scheduling and control of student behaviour in the learning process.

Smith and Moore (1962) **:** Programmed instruction is the process of arranging the material to be learned into a series of sequential steps. Usually it moves the student from a familiar background into a complex and new set of concepts, principles and understandings.

Stolurow (1966) **:** Programmed learning can be described as a process in which a teacher presents (*i.e.*, communicates), a subject matter to a learner so that he responds to it (i.e. communicates to the teacher) the next item of information to be presented.

From the above mentioned definitions of programmed learning, following characteristics may be derived:

1. It is a method of individualized instruction.
2. In this technique, instructional material is logically sequenced and broken into suitable small steps or segments of the subject matter called 'frames'.
3. For sequencing a particular unit of the instructional material, the programmer has to pay due consideration to the initial or entering behaviour of the learner.
4. In actual operation, the beginning is made by presenting a 'frame'. The learner is required to read or listen and then respond actively.
5. Programmed instruction system has an adequate provision for feed-back.
6. The interaction between the learner and the learning material or programme is very important.
7. Programmed learning provides self-pacing to the learner.
8. Programmed learning provides for continuous evaluation.

Different Aids of Teaching

There are three basic types of programmed instructional material—The teaching machines, the programmed textbook and scrambled textbook.

The Teaching Machine **:** A teaching machine is intended to function as a private tutor. It is simply a mechanical devise or piece of apparatus designed to present to the student a sequential programme of learning activities comprising instructional items which requires the student to make an overt response and which provides the student with immediate knowledge of the accuracy of his response. It represents the practical application of laboratory technique of education.

Programmed Textbook : Each page of the programmed textbook consists of usually four or five panels. The student begins with the top panel on page one, responds to it, turns to page two to get his answers confirmed on the top panel, goes to the top panel on page three, responds to it, confirms the answer by turning the page, and so on.

The Scrambled Textbook : In a scrambled textbook, branching or intrinsic technique is used.

Principle of Small Steps : It is shown by experiments that even the dullest students can learn as effectively as the brightest students if the subject matter is presented to them in suitable small steps. When we divide the task to be learnt into very small steps, and ask the students to learn only one step at a time, then probably all the students will be able to learn one small step at a time and sequentially learn all the steps. It is a difficult task to climb a mountain but once steps are built even a child can climb the mountain very easily. This is known as the 'Principle of small steps'.

Principle of Active Responding : The second psychological principle is that the students learn better and faster when they are actively participating in the teaching-learning process. In our classroom teaching the teachers to ask a few questions and the students respond. But is not possible for the teachers to ask all the students to respond at each small step. A teaching machine text or a programmed text contains a large number of questions—one question at each small step and the students respond actively. The principle of active responding is used for the programmes. The teaching machines and programmes have proved to be superior because they provide opportunity to every learner to respond at every small step.

Principle of Reinforcement : Every response even approximately correct must be reinforced immediately. Delayed reinforcement fails to work. This is possible only when a teacher has to teach only one student at a time. The most ideal situation is when the teacher can cater to the needs of his students individually. But in classroom teaching this is hardly possible. No teacher, however efficient and sincere he may be, can reinforce each correct response of each of his students as soon as it is made in a classroom situation where he has to teach abut 40/50 students. The teaching machines and the programmes do the job more efficiently.

Principle of Self-Pacing : The programmed instruction is based on the basic assumption that learning takes place effectively if the learner is allowed to learn at his own pace. Therefore, a good programme of the material always takes care of the principle of self-pacing. A learner moves from one frame to another according to his own speed of learning.

Principle of Student-Evaluation or Student Testing : Continuous evaluation of the student and the learning process leads to better teaching-learning. In the programmed instruction, the learner has to leave the record of his responses because he is required to write a response for each frame on response sheet. This detailed record helps in revising the programme.

Important stages in the Development of the Programmed Instruction

Preparation. This is the first stage in the development of the programme. It includes:

(*i*) Selection of the topic.

(*ii*) Writing assumptions about learners.

(*iii*) Defining objective in behavioural terms.

(*iv*) Writing the entry behaviour (present status) of the learner.

(*v*) Developing specific outline of the content.

(*vi*) Preparing a criterion test.

Writing of the Programme : The programme is written under these heads (*i*) Writing draft frames in a sequence i.e. from simple to complex. (*ii*) Editing the draft frames by a team of experts usually comprising a subject-matter expert, a skilled writer and the programmer.

Try Out Revision. It includes (*i*) Trying out the programme on a few individual learners and finding out their reactions and making necessary changes in the light of reactions, (*ii*) Trying out the programme on a group of learners and making necessary changes on the basis of their reactions; and (*iii*) Trying out the programme in the field.

Evaluation. This implies finding the success or the failure after implementing a programme.

Illustation and Teaching

Introduction : This a programme meant for you for the study of salient features of the Constitution of India.

In this programme you will find paragraphs which are called frames. Study each frame carefully and write down what is required. Answers are given at the end. After stating your answers, check them. If your answer is wrong or you do not understand anything, you can again go back to the frame. It is not a test but instead it is a self-study programme.

Frame 1 : The Constituent Assembly of India was set up under the provisions of the Cabinet Mission Plan to frame the Constitution of India which was formally adopted on 26th Nov. 1949 and came into force on 26th January 1950. It took nearly three years to complete the work.

(*i*) What was the work assigned to Constituent Assembly?

(*ii*) Under whose provision was it formed?

(*iii*) When did our Constitution come into force?

(*iv*) When was it adopted?

(*v*) How much time did Constituent Assembly take to complete its work?

Frame 2 : The Preamble of the Constitution has a great significance but is not a part of the Constitution. The Constitution was framed by the people of India through their representations. It stresses the fact that the reign of the land lies with the people of India.

(*a*) Is the Preamble a part of the Constitution?

(*b*) By whom was the Constitution framed?

(*c*) In whose hands does the reign of law of India lie?

Frame 3 : The Preamble of our Constitution is as under:

We the people of India having solemnly resolved to constitute India into a Sovereign Socialist Secular Democratic Republic and to secure to all its citizens:

Justice, social, economic and political;

Liberty of thought, expression, belief, faith and worship

Equality of status and of opportunity; and to promote them all;

Fraternity assuring the dignity of the individual and the unity and integrity of the Nation.

In our Constituent Assembly this twenty-sixth day of November, 1949, do hereby adopt, enact and give to ourselves this Constitution.

Note : Three new terms—Socialist, Secular and Integrity were added to the original text of the Preamble when it was amended in 1976 with the 42nd Amendment.

The Preamble stresses the democratic basis of the Constitution by stating that the People of India gave to themselves this Constitution. It also states objectives like justice, liberty, equality and fraternity.

(i) Who has given the Constitution of India?

(ii) What kind of justice has been ensured by the Preamble?

(iii) What type of Republic is to be constituted?

(iv) What kind of equality has been given to its citizen?

(v) How many types of liberty can a citizen enjoy?

Frame 4 : Another important feature of the Preamble is that the people themselves adopted and enacted the Constitution. Thus, the representatives of the people frame the laws of the country and they have the power to change or amend the Constitution.

(*a*) Who frames the laws of the country?

(*b*) What has the power to amend the Constitution?

Frame 5 : The Constitution of India has many unique features which distinguish it from Constitutions of other countries. The framers of the Constitution freely borrowed ideas but took care to adapt these to the needs of the country.

The Constitution makes India a Sovereign, Socialist Secular, Democratic Republic. The word Sovereign means that India is completely free from external control. No outside power has the right to interfere either in her internal administration or direct her in the conduct of her foreign policy.

This was emphasised to ensure that India was no longer 'dependent' on the British Empire as she had been before Indian Independence Act 1947 or 'dominion' as she had been from 15th August, 1947 to 26th January 1950.

(*a*) What kind of status did India enjoy during 15th August 1947 to 26th January 1950?

(*b*) Was India sovereign between 15th August 1947 to 26th January 1950?

(*c*) What is the meaning of the word 'sovereign'?

(*d*) Does the Constitution of India have unique features?

(*e*) Did the framers of the Constitution borrow ideas?

Answers

1. (i) To frame the Constitution of India.
   (ii) Provision of the Cabinet Mission Plan.
   (iii) 26th January 1950.
   (iv) 26th November 1949.
   (v) Nearly 3 years.
2. (*a*) No.
   (*b*) People of India through their representatives.
   (*c*) People of India.
3. (i) People of India.
   (ii) Social, economic and political.
   (iii) Sovereign Socialist Secular Democratic.
   (iv) Equality of status.
   (v) Five.

4. (*a*) Representatives of the people.
   (*b*) Representatives of the people.
5. (*a*) Dominion.
   (*b*) No.
   (*c*) India is completely free from external control.
   (*d*) Yes.
   (*e*) Yes.

Pattern of Assessment

Merits of Programmed Instruction : 1. A well-programmed instruction is a great thrust in the direction of individualised instruction, as it is tailored to the needs of the individual learner in the class. 2. It permits individual learner to progress at his own speed. An intelligent learner needs no longer to be bored or allowed to lose interest on account of his slow progress of other learners of the class. He can make progress as he is capable of. 3. Since a programme requires continuous response from the learner, it overcomes the inertia and passivity on the part of the learner. 4. The teacher can give explanation in the classroom if the error is common or he may arrange individual conferences on specific points. 5. Learning material in a programmed instruction is presented in such a way that learning becomes an interesting game and the learner is motivated to meet the challenges set by his own capabilities. 6. Programmes are developed by experts. They are empirically tested and modified till they are standarised. A number of learners can use a single good programme and thus evade textbooks. 7. In programmed instruction the learner is immediately reinforced to correct his response and this reinforcement sustains the motivation of the learner. 8. The self-instructional technique presents material in which its complexity is simplified through the analysis of the subject-matter into small and more easily assimilated segments of information. 9. The introduction of programmed instruction is of great significance for developing countries which are set on the path of educating millions of learners and are short of teachers. 10. Good teachers are freed from the boredom of routine classroom teaching and they are in a position to devote more time to more creative activities. 11. The programmed instruction has been used more successfully in teaching the discernment of the logic of various disciplines and inspiring students to creative thinking and judgement. 12. Certain motor skills and intellectual abilities normally taught by frequent drills and rote memorisation can be very efficiently taught by self-instructional devices. 13. Self-instructional materials have been found to be very useful in the West in revolutionisng the social setting of the classroom. Problems of discipline have been solved and a new hope for eliminating emotional and social problems has been generated. 14. Programmed instruction enables the teacher to diagnose the problems of the individual learner. 15. The introduction of programmed instruction is very helpful in certain situations where human instructors are not easily available in the required number, for instance small schools in the isolated or hill areas.

Programmed materials have been severely criticised as a threat to replacing the teacher.

It is also argued that there is too much emphasis in learning facts and very little emphasis on the mastery of principles and concepts.

Some critics of programmed instruction maintain that the user of a programme does not now where he is headed to.

They also point out that the learners are not aware of the organisation and programmed instruction is unrelated to other aspects of instruction.

It is also argued that the programmed instruction material is very costly and only rich nations can afford it.

It is also stated that the development and use of programmed instructional material require expert knowledge and training. An average teacher finds it very difficult to make use of this device.

As a result of experimental studies and research, following types of programmed instruction have emerged.

1. Linear or Extrinsic Programming
2. Branching or Intrinsic Programming
3. Mathetics Programming

4. Rules System of Programming
5. Computer Assisted Instruction (CAS)
6. Learner Controlled Instruction. (LCS)

The first three styles—linear, branching and mathetics are the basic formats. The rules system represents the deductive and inductive approach to teaching. The other two types, Computer Assisted Instruction (CAI) and Learner Controlled Instruction (LCI) are not the basic format of Programming. They are, infact, the ways and means of providing instruction. Here we have taken up only the basic type of programming.

Concept of Linear Programming : B. F. Skinner is the originator of linear programming. It is also called a single tract programme. According to Skinner, a creature, a bird or a human being can be led to a desired behaviour by means of a carefully constructed programme consisting of small steps leading logically through the subject-matter from topic to topic, provided each step is reinforced by some kind of favourable experience or reward. The increments in information which the learner is expected to absorb are small. The favourable experience or response increases the probability of the same response to occur again in the future. The process of rewarding the correct response to a stimulus increases the general tendency to give a response.

The sequence of frames and path of learning in programmed learning is systematic and linear. That is why, this type of programming is referred to as linear programming. Hence all the learners have to proceed through the same frames and in the same order.

In a linear programme, learner's responses are controlled externally by the programmer sitting at a distant place. Hence linear programming is also termed as extrinsic programming. In branching programming, learner's response is controlled by the learner himself internally. It is, therefore, also called intrinsic programming.

Merits : 1. Immediate knowledge of results acts as a great motivator and releases anxiety and tension. 2. The smallness of the frames brings the sub-goals within the reach of the learner and thereby facilitates secondary reinforcement. 3. Repetition strengthens the responses and ensures learning. 4. Easy nature of the programme provides 'success experience' to the learner.

Limitations : 1. In linear programming, the learning process becomes quite dull on account of the following reasons (*a*) Subject matter is broken into very small pieces, (*b*) Responding is quite mechanical and restrictive, and (*c*) The learning process is quite slow. 2. The use of linear programming is limited to some subjects and topics. 3. Linear programming cramps the imagination of the learner and initiative for creative, integrative and judgement learning. 4. Linear programming encourages guessing. 5. Linear programming does not develop the discriminating power of the students.

Concept of Intrinsic Programming : Branching or intrinsic programming was developed by Norman A. Crowder (1954) an American technician. According to Crowder, branching or intrinsic programme is one which adopts to the needs of the learners without the medium of any extrinsic device such as a computer. It is not controlled extrinsically by the programmer.

Norman A. Crowder was a technician who was working in the United States Air Force. He was faced with the problem of efficiency of vocational training. His programme is based on intuition. His approach at the most is practical. This type of programme employs multiple choice response patterns. The learner is required to select one right answer out of several responses presented to him.

Merits : 1. Big size of a frame as well as the branching minimises unnecessary repetitions and responding, thus reducing the amount of learning time and fatigue. 2. The pitfalls and consequences of erroneous logic are usually explained in the remedial frames so that the learner not only gets the correct responses but also understands why some other response is not correct. 3. Instead of simple response it provides alternatives in the form of multiple choice. 4. Through its broad frames, branching programme provides for more freedom to respond and scope of choosing one's path of learning according to one's need. Thus, it helps in maintaining the interest and initiative of the teacher. 5. Branching programme is helpful in the development of the power of discrimination of the learner. 6. Branching programme helps in the development of creativity and problem-solving ability. 7. Branching is most useful in the areas beyond facts, definitions and basic skills. 8. The frames being of a large size contain a good deal of information and this may enable the programmer to enrich the style and expand his ideas.

Limitations : 1. The multiple choice questions provided in this programming may lead to guess work on the part of the learner and he may not understand the subject matter of the frame. 2. The setting of appropriate multiple choice questions suiting to the entire material of the frames proves a difficult task. 3. No branching method can provide infinite branching to take care of all possible needs of every individual student. 4. The cost of branching programme is very high when compared with traditional teaching approaches. 5. The branching programme is not suitable for small children as they are unable to express symbolisation. 6. The programme needs revision after every five years. 7. It is difficult to cover the entire subject matter of the curriculum in the stipulated time. 8. The diagnostic questions framed by the programmer may or may not suit the needs of the individual learner. 9. The programme cannot shape the behaviour of the learner.

Teaching Instruction and Programmed Instruction. According to Edger Dale, "Teaching' is a broad, vague, ill-defined term and instruction' is a purposeful, orderly, controlled sequencing of experience to reach a specified goal. 'Programmed instruction' is a sub-head under instruction and represents a more rigorous attempt to develop a mastery, over specified goals to secure 'insured' learning."

Programme learning cannot replace the teacher. Any innovation in the school programmes and practices must remain in the hands of the teachers. The radio and T.V. did not displace the teacher. Similar is the case with programmed instruction. It is upto the enlightened teachers to take up the challenging task of preparing programmes. We have got a wide market. The programmes can be sold all over the country. A student who is convinced that he can learn better, achieve more with the help of this programme, will definitely prefer instead of buying this programme to buying a text book. By taking up this challenging task we will not only help the cause of education, help our fellow teachers by setting them free from the routine task of information, giving help to the students to achieve more, but we will be helping ourselves also.

It may also be remembered that these gadgets can be used mainly in the cognitive field and possibly in the psycho-motor field to develop certain abilities and skills of the students as an individual. A teacher is something more than all these gadgets put together. He has to bring about socialization of the individual; he has to promote socially desirable attitudes and interests and mould the personality of the students. The effective domain is almost reserved for his care. At present the teacher is not able to devote his energy and time to this important task as most of his time and energy is consumed by his routine job as an information giver. We always talk of education for three 'H's'—the head, the hand and the heart. But it has almost remained a mere slogan. Programmed learning, teaching machines and other gadgets will set teacher free from routine work. These are labour-saving devices for the teacher so that he may function more effectively in a field of his own choice.

Technique involved in programmed instruction can be used in teaching different subjects. Teaching of mathematics, science, social studies and elements of Indian languages can be done effectively with the help of this new technique. The teacher has to formulate objectives of teaching a particular subject, undertake content analysis of the subject matter in the light of objectives, frame a chain of questions which will lead the pupils in the direction of the objective and present the questions to his pupils who are expected to try their hand at answering the questions independently. The teacher will have to play the role of a friend, guide and philosopher in the class when the pupils are engaged in solving the riddle and at the same time acquiring knowledge or skill. The question of class discipline may not arise as the pupils will be found busy doing the task assigned to them by the teacher. The teacher will have to do remedial or corrective teaching as the weakness of his pupils will be located in the very act of learning. The pupil will also undergo a process of self-evaluation as he completes his work.

Role of the teacher in the changed context of Programmed Learning may be stated as follows :

1. Teacher as an advisor in helping students in the selection of programme learning material.
2. Teacher as a discussion leader for focussing the attention of the learners on important points.
3. Teacher as a guide to clarify doubts and elaborate on various points asked by the learner.
4. Teacher as an evaluator of the learning outcomes.
5. Teacher as a consultant to the various agencies engaged in production of programmed material.

The programmed learning approach can be adopted in normal classroom teaching in the following ways:

1. A teacher can make use of the principles of programmed learning such as active responding, minimal errors and confirmation while teaching various subjects in the conventional manner.
2. A teacher can define behavioural objectives in advance of teaching.
3. A teacher can validate the instructional systems of a class in terms of the performance of learners immediately after teaching is over.
4. A teacher can regulate questions and answers. The answer of a learner can be immediately reinforced by informing or telling whether it is correct or incorrect.
5. A teacher can plan the entire instructional programme of a classroom and can treat the terminal behaviour, the pre-requisite skills and content analysis in advance.

Komoski (1960) an expert has observed "Two thousand years ago the world's first public administrator, a gentleman by the name Quintilian wrote what might be called a handbook for teachers." In it he has one bit of advice which will serve as an excellent starting point for a discussion of programmed learning and its potential uses. His advice is: "Do not neglect the individual student. He should be questioned and praised."

Programme and Instruction

Programmed instruction is still in its infancy in India. Programmed instruction as an optional or elective paper has been included at the B. Ed./M.Ed. level in a few universities in India. It also forms a part of the paper of Educational Technology/ Educational Innovation. However, as regards its classroom use, it may be observed that it is almost nil. As far back in 1966, the Kothari Commission suggested to develop programmed material in different subjects to test the suitability of the technique in Indian conditions. An Association of Programmed Instruction has been formed to coordinate the research being done at different centres in the country. The association also disseminates the information on new studies through its journal issued from time to time. The National Council of Educational Research and Technology has also done some work in the field. In spite of all these efforts, it may be stated that the application of programmed instruction has not yet made an appreciable impact on our classroom teaching. Our methods of teaching still remain traditional, by and large.

6

Audio Visual Aids

Production of Audio

Production forms an important part of the process of audio development. Planning production, distribution, utilisation and evaluation are five significant steps of educational broadcasting on play-back of cassettes/tapes. These steps are interrelated, and efficiency in all these stages results in good and suitable educational radio/audio programmes. Deficiency at any one or two stages spoils the entire radio/audio programmes. Although no stage is less important, production is found to be very significant and its success largely determines the effectiveness of these programmes.

In this unit we intend to discuss the software development's various features of production, importance of audience profile, script writing, tryout of the script as well as the radio/audio programmes in order to make these material effective and interesting.

After going through the unit, you will be able to

- know the need and importance of software for radio/audio
- realise the importance of production of these programmes

- acquaint yourself with various features of production
- identify the need of audience profile for good production
- feel the significance of script writing
- know the need for editing the radio/audio programmes

The Working : Among the stages of planning, production, distribution, utilisation and evaluation, production is most important step of audio/radio broadcasting. The curricular needs and objectives should be identified and planning has to be made for production of suitable audio/video programmes. Audience profile is found useful at this stage to know the needs and interests of the clientele group. After planning, suitable script is prepared by subject experts on a particular topic and then production takes place either in the studio or outside. Various steps are taken by the producer to see that the programme is recorded properly. Sound being the main strength of the radio/audio programme, the "clarity and the quality of what is heard is fundamental to the understanding of the listener" (John C. H. Ball 1974).

Hardware and software are like two wings of audio-production. All kinds of machines and equipment are essential, but the material therein on the academic input of the programme is called software. Both of them should go hand in hand to make the programme meaningful and effective. Hardware has its origin in physical and engineering sciences and software owes its origin to the social and behavioural sciences. Software is developed according to the principles of these science and is used for modification of behaviour known as learning.

Software development is closely related to psychology and pedagogy. It is very much associated with the principles of programme learning and is characterised by task analysis, identifying objectives, selecting suitable strategies, reinforcement etc. The software approach is often referred to behaviour technology aiming at modification of behaviour or enriching learning experiences. Achievement of educational objectives is possible only through adequate use of software inputs and organisations. Procurement of hardware is one-short activity but software production is a time taking process which has to be continuous and academic by nature. Software had to be need-based, need-specific and relevant. Teachers and students can easily produce software and also programmes according to the curricular needs and provisions. Agarwal (1981) has rightly observed, "One of the major lessons of SITE is that the planning for software rather hardware requires more time. Hence the planning for software aspects must start many years prior to the planning of hardware aspects." Therefore, preplanning should be made for software development much before hardware planning and production. A systems approach to software planning and production is desirable and the entire teaching learning process should be viewed holistically with reference to the curricular needs and interests as well as abilities of the clientele group. Optimum achievement of the instructional objectives has to be emphasised for software development.

Software production for audio programmes requires a combination of content knowledge, production techniques and communication strategy to reach the target audience. It is rightly said that as merely copying a picture from a book into a large sheet of paper does not make a good illustration, similarly just recording a chapter or story of a book does not give an audio programme. Some basic questions should be answered for understanding the production needs. Some of these questions are-

(i) Software for whom?

(ii) With what needs?

(iii) With what objectives?

(iv) With what background experience and knowledge?

(v) With what means and medium?

(vi) By which agencies?

(vii) With what infrastructure?

(viii) With what advance preparation?

(ix) What targets are set in terms of time and money?

Answers to these questions are very relevant for properly planning and producing the audio programmes. Sometimes while answering these questions we see that change in one does not suit the needs of audio production. The stereotyped ways or outdated rules and regulation do not promote creativity and productivity.

The objectives of software production may be one or more of the following.

(i) To inform

(ii) To entertain

(iii) To impart skills

(iv) To instruct

(v) To solve problems

(vi) To generate thinking and curiosity

(vii) To stimulate imagination and creativity

(viii) To change aptitude and interests

(ix) To modify behaviour

Some of these objectives can be easily realised, but some are not so easy to be achieved. Some objectives are quite challenging and some are very stimulating. The production process is long drawn-out and adequate insight into the process is developed for ensuring effectiveness of the audio programme.

Diverse Kinds

Before producing any programme, its medium of production, its nature, its strength and weaknesses have to be properly understood by the personnel concerned including scriptwriter and producer. Otherwise due justice cannot be done to its potentialities, nor its deficiencies can be made up and limitations can be overcome, so that programmes can be meaningful and interesting. The strengths and weaknesses of radio and audio programmes have been discussed before. In spite of its potentialities, it suffers from a few limitations and steps are taken for effective audio production. The following points need be taken into account for production of suitable audio programmes. These are (i) Instructional Objectives, (ii) Audience Profile, (iii) Content, (vi) Format, (v) Sound/music Effects.

Instructional Objectives : In the curriculum, there are various provisions which are dealt with in the textbooks presented in radio and television or audio/video programmes. Some topics are identified for radio programmes in view of their presentation facilities in the same medium. There are some specific objectives and teaching points which are dealt within the audio programme and attempts are made to realise those objectives. To the extent these objectives are realised, the programme is proved to be a success proportionately.

Audience Profile : Before production of an audio programme it is essential that the producer and scriptwriter should have a clear concept about the background knowledge, experience, attitude, interests etc. "Know your audience" is the basic motto of the electronic media production. Radio/audio programme can be planned and developed successfully with adequate knowledge about the audience. Broadcasting on audio programming without this prerequisite is a dull diction or a dry exercise. The psycho-socio-economic and political background of audience for whom the audio programmes are mainly meant, should be given prior attention, so that the programmes can be produced effectively.

As mentioned in the para (i) above, curricular content/ provision should constitute the backbone of the programme. The audio programme should be based on the subject matter or main highlights. It may be merely a syllabus-based or an enrichment programme.

Format : The styles of presentation called format of the audio programmes should be varied. Some of these are stories, talks, discussion, interviews, demonstrations, dramatisation and so on. Some topics are very good for dramatisation, but not for discussion or demonstration. Some are quite effective in interviews, but not suitable for other styles. The scriptwriter should have the necessary skills and competence in developing such formats. Any interesting audio programme should be produced in a suitable format.

Sound/Music Effects : Since sound is the most important strength of the audio programmes, it is essential to make use of various sound effects and musical effects at appropriate places.

Script is the backbone of the audio programme and the basic material for the audio programme. It is not the final product, but the basis for the audio programme. It is aptly said that if you have a good script, half of the battle is won in making a good audio/ radio programme.

A script is prepared to communicate a theme or an idea to

listeners through radio or audio programme. The link between the scriptwriter and listeners is established through the producer who translates the script into sound. Necessary instructions should be given by the scriptwriter to use relevant and meaningful sound effects and musical sounds at appropriate places. For example, if the scriptwriter wants a boy to participate in a dialogue for a specific reason, this should be indicated in the script. If the scene on the deck of a ship is given in the script, sound of sea waves, singing of sea-gulls, etc., should be suggested.

Every radio programme is introduced by a compere or an announcer. If the scriptwriter is to tell specifically to the listeners, it can be mentioned by him in the beginning very clearly. It should be indicated in the script, whether it should form a part of the script or just an announcement. But such an introduction should be brief and catchy. After making an interesting beginning, occasional attention-catchers must be used for making the programme interesting.

Similarly, the end of the script should be natural and not abrupt. But climax should not be the end. Care should be taken for a smooth, but heart touching end. In the educational audio programmes, it is desirable to make some repetitions for reinforcement and recapitulation. Such repetition should not be made haphazardly, but in a planned manner repeating only the important highlights.

Some activities can be suggested for the listeners who should not be just passive participants. Appropriate support materials may also be suggested by the scriptwriter for ensuring efficiency.

It is not desirable to show off the knowledge or use any technical jargons and very bombastic words. Simple language and style are to be preferred. Demoralisation or sermonising is to be encouraged.

Too many teaching points should not be in a script and too many facts and figures are to be discouraged.

Scripts for Audio Programming : Script being the basic framework of educational audio programme, utmost care should be taken to make it suitable for reflecting the above concepts and principles. In this context, the guidelines developed by the British

Council Media Departments, London are found to be quite relevant as well as comprehensive. These are given as follows:

1. The script is the most important of an audio programme. Unless it is excellent, every other aspect of production is useless.
2. To be successful it must be written in the right language for the listener.
3. The right language is the language the listener can understand. So it must take into account the listener's background, education and interest. The writer must therefore think carefully about the structure he is going to use and the vocabulary.
4. The words the scriptwriter uses are not read by the listener-they are listened to. So the words must appeal to the Ear, not to the Eye.
5. Writing for the Eye relies on the conventions of writing-punctuation-paragraphs-type sizes-columns-headlines. The reader can go at his own speed. He can go back to check any point of difficulty. He can stop reading, put the writing aside and return to it later.
6. Writing for the Ear is quite different. The listener can not be given too many facts. He cannot be given too many figures. It is essential to sustain his interest—therefore the script must be presented in an interesting way. It must develop logically. The radio writer may have to repeat, expand and reinforce. He must use the form of language which is simple and informal. It is Spoken Language. The listener must be held—otherwise he switches off mentally.
7. How is the listener held? The radio writer must think of the listener as his personal friend....

   He must talk with the listener, not at him.

   He must hear in his mind all the tones of voice that will communicate the script.

   He must visualise the listener.

   He must read the script aloud to himself and ask----

   "What do I sound like?"

   "What do I mean?"

As discussed earlier, the script is the basis of all work in educational media including radio or audio cassettes. It contains ideas and content to be presented in an interesting way on a particular medium-here, radio/audio. The script for radio/audio programme would be different from one for television. Script writing for any medium requires an understanding of the potentials and limitations of the medium, production and distribution processes.

In India, workshops are organised for developing scripts of various kinds with or without any knowledge of the medium, production and distribution technicalities. Even though they might not have heard good examples of audio programmes or audio materials like audio tapes/cassettes, the writers would be exposed to some good programmes/materials and production machines and processes. They, under the guidance of experts develop scripts of their own. They should ask and answer all the questions listed earlier before they start writing scripts.

It is natural that a few drafts would not be upto the standard, because the quality of an educational audio script is not judged merely by the correctness of its information/content. That is essential but more than that the format, use of sound/music effects, etc., are also of great importance. A good script might have undergone three or four revisions and modification before it emerges as the final script. A flow-chart of such exercise is given below:

Audio programme is dependent on an aural medium quality of what is heard and clarity of recording is of paramount importance. Reception on short waves due to variable conditions in the ionosphere, can adversely affect speech clarity. R. L. Hilliard writing about school broadcasting observed, "The conscientious radio broadcaster aims to transmit sound in such a way that the listening public will be able to understand speech clearly and enjoy the reproduction of music—After leaving the transmitter, sound is subject to all sorts of losses and quality degradations before it reaches the listeners' ears. Therefore, it is necessary to keep the technical quality of the sound as high as possible at all times while it is under the control of the station."

John C. H Ball (Ibid) in this context said, "By quality here we mean quality directly in relation to audibility. It is of first importance then the producer of programmes is aware of the reception conditions in the area to which he is broadcasting and he takes them into account." It is therefore, necessary that proper recording of the audio programmes and their broadcasting or playback should be made under favourable and congenial conditions. Hence besides production quality, listening conditions need to be suitable.

Audio programmes should be interesting any way. Otherwise these cannot be heard at all or heard, not received adequately. Ball has aptly said therefore, "The class teacher may consider the programme useful and so switch on the radio, but unless it is also 'interesting' the children will switch off their ears." Besides, content and format of the programmes, the quality in production, broadcasting and playback has to be ensured for increasing effectiveness in the educational institutions and distance education system. In the AIR we have a quite well-deve-loped infrastructure for production of audio cassettes/tapes.

Although Akash Vani is responsible for production of educational radio programmes, it depends on the outside resource persons for preparing scripts. However necessary editing of the script is made by the producer. A case-study of school broadcasts at Delhi revealed that "It is mostly of the nature of substituting some difficult words with simpler ones, and/or curtailing/adding the spoken matter. The accuracy of facts presented in the material is generally accepted, as no other subject matter specialist is consulted in the matter. This practice allows a material passed off for broadcast without providing a safeguard for checking its accuracy at the editing stage". This practice at New Delhi holds good for all the Akash Vani Stations and the instances of errors in educational programmes are also not rare.

Hence writing of scripts free from all errors thematic as well as linguistic is very important for success of the educational broad-casting. It may be regarded as a specialised job. The scriptwriters are usually appointed from among subject experts which does not always happen well. Therefore care should be taken for preparing fool-proof scripts for the purpose. It is better to get them approved by subject experts and then use for production of programmes in presentable form by the producer who is a media man.

It was thought desirable as well as more practicable to train the specialist to write scripts for educational radio. In order to write suitable scripts, besides content knowledge the writer should have knowledge about various formats, audience profile, different techniques for attracting attention and sustaining interests, ability in creative expression, proficiency in language and presentation styles and techniques. During a training course or workshop, the prospective scriptwriters should be exposed to these theoretical as well as practical aspects of the programme. It should be realised that good scriptwriters are not born, but made through sincere efforts, long practice, keen interest and love for the job.

At present a good number of institutions like IGNOU and UGC through their production centres are producing many kinds of educational audio cassettes/tapes. These are being produced by groups of subject experts, and media experts and the audio materials are sold at no profit no loss basis. Besides, some private firms are also engaged in producing audio tapes for various educational courses/classes. They produce these audio tapes on commercial basis and the quality of their production is not always satisfactory.

As discussed earlier, audio tape/cassettes and radio are aural media and these programmes have their own limitations. Some people have aversion to listening only. They dislike to hear only words, words and words. Again what is heard is fleeting and changing from moment to moment. That is why, radio/audio programme is called evanescent and taxing to its audience.

In view of these handicaps, attempts are being made to provide support to the spoken words. Illustrations are used to explain, to create interest, to motivate and to help concentration. That is, vision is supplemented with audio or radio. This is done in many ways-viz., by showing pictures or flash cards or by projecting slides or film-strips even by organising activities. France Berrigan and Anne Gibson (1978) have rightly observed in their paper "Radio and Audio-Vision in the British Open University: Towards Individualisation", "At the simplest level, having a visual support does seem to help concentration. It is easy enough for the mind to wander during a twenty minute radio talk or discussion. To support what is said by an illustration or an activity helps to concretise the subject matter."

Research conducted by Gallagher (1977) has revealed that students prefer radio-vision to radio alone and this justifies more of it in the advanced countries of the world. Radio-vision has become more popular day by day and the latest trend is towards more audio-vision in the field of educational broadcasting.

The Perception

Abroad: The British Open University is a remarkable achievement in educational technology and has been using various kinds of media for providing its students with rich learning experiences. It has developed multi-media packages for various units in all subjects—arts, sciences, technologies and humanities. Particularly, its attempts to support radio-programmes with print materials, posters, coloured post cards, slides and film strips are really quite laudable and enlightening.

Since 1964 the BBC has started with radio-vision programmes systematically. In Sweden, Norway and Denmark, radio-vision series are specifically broadcast along with educational radio programmes in general. Even in Kenya, its Ministry of Education used to broadcast radio vision science programmes in conjunction with the Centre for Educational Development Overseas (CEDO), London. In 1976 the Audio-visual Media Research Group was asked to evaluate several programmes with special emphasis on a radio-vision programme. But it was found that there was a wide range of materials being used for radio-vision programming. At that time there was no record of the number of courses or programmes using radio-vision and no way of measuring the cost of this medium to the OU. It was therefore decided to carry out a study to discover the range, extent and cost of radio-vision in the university. According to the study undertaken by Berrington and others (1987) radio-vision described the simultaneous use of radio and vision which promotes better utilisation.

The extent of radio-vision showed that Mathematics made

most use of the medium. The second most extensive use is in Science. The range of materials used for radio-vision includes diagrams or tables in broadcast notes, charts, maps, samples or specimens, film strips and transparencies. Radio-vision materials in the Arts Faculty consist of coloured or black and white photographs, colour postcards, drawings and plans, etc. It is interesting to know that 62% of all Open University courses in 1977 were making use of radio vision. But 23-33%, i.e., a quarter of all radio programmes made use of the technique in some way or other. Thus the innovation has made a headway in the visual area and has shown a significant development in the educational broadcast.

The experience in use of radio-vision shows that much more effort has been devoted to the provision of elaborate visual support material for radio-vision than to the design of the sound component. Berrington and others have in their study rightly pointed out "Many radio-vision programmes overload students, requiring sustained concentrating as well as expecting a great deal of pre-broadcast preparation to assemble materials. Often programmes seemed to race through the material, allowing in-sufficient time for the detail to be located, or observed" (1977).

Besides, many radio-vision programmes are designed with a predetermined work pace, when broadcast makes no allowance for individual learning styles and varying speeds of comprehension. This is, of course, due to the very inherent limitation of the sound broadcasting. Once the listener fails to locate a reference, he is likely to lose concentration and miss valuable information.

In India: During the Satellite Instructional TV Experiment (SITE) period (1974-75) an in-service training course in Science was organised by the Centre for Educational Technology, NCERT in collaboration with the Educational Technology Cells of Andhra Pradesh, Bihar, Karnataka, Madhya Pradesh, Orissa and Rajasthan for the teachers of the elementary schools. A Multi-Media Package was developed by the CET for this course which included radio-vision programme in its sound broadcast component.

Explaining these radio-vision programmes to the teacher monitors who were to conduct the course, it was mentioned by the CET (1975), "Radio-Vision means a radio-programme accompanied by visuals which may be on flash cards as in this case (shadows) /or as posters as in the case of next programme "Vikas aur Vigyan" or on slides/film strips. A topic like "shadows" needs visuals. In the materials sent to you, have included "Sketches/diagrams as eleven cards numbered serially. You should display these cards one by one, the programme will cue you for such display by announcing look at card no. so and so? Please ensure that the participants are made to sit in such a manner, at such a distance that where these sketches, they could easily see them while listening to the radio-feature. The teacher monitor here has to be alert to change the sketch when next sketch is referred to."

It was found that with the help of these suitable graphics accompanied by commentaries from radio, the principles of shadow in various situations were well-explained to the trainees. Similarly, few posters used in the other radio programme "Development and Science in Villages" helped to clarify certain difficult concepts and made the radio teaching interesting and meaningful.

The question "In the age of TV, has pedagogical Radio a future?" stimulated the Department of Education, South Gujarat University, Surat to take up a research project "Radio-Vision as a Partial Substitute to Educational TV." The experience of SITE programme provided further impetus for the venture. Although TV is considered to be a better medium of communication for the rural masses, the question arises, "Are we in a position to provide TV to all the inhabitations of our country?" Secondly, "Have we been able to exploit fully the potential of Radio as an educational medium? "Loud thinking over these questions further stimulated to examine the "effectiveness of Radio-Vision as a medium of instruction." As reported in the Newsletter of the Indian Association of Programmed Learning (1978), the major aim of the project was to study the efficacy of radio-vision as a medium of instruction in formal and non formal education situations (1978). The findings of this study were quite encouraging.

Sharma (1980), Oberi (1981) and Sharma & Tripathy (1980) have conducted a good number of studies in the use and efficacy of radio-vision programmes. All these experiments have reported that radio-vision programmes produced significantly better results as compared to traditional classroom instruction.

Production of audio/radio programmes is a significant process. It assumes special significance when such programmes are educational. Although hardware and software are two wings of audio production, software is more important, because we can procure the machineries and equipment from the market if funds are available. But software materials need to be developed with the help of persons having adequate knowledge in psychology, pedagogy and content areas. Software is to be need-based and need-specific relating to a particular group of clientele.

Important features of audio production are instructional objectives, audience profile, content, format, sound and music effects. Importance of script writing cannot be overemphasized. A few basic guidelines should be followed in developing suitable scripts for radio/audio programmes.

In the AIR there is quite a well-developed infrastructure for production of audio programmes. Besides script writing which is quite significant a number of precautions need to be taken for sound recording, editing, broadcasting, etc., to ensure better quality and higher reception.

Some innovative measures have been taken for overcoming the deficiencies and limitations of audio programmes. Radio/ Audio-Vision is one of such innovations for providing visual support to aural presentation through the use of slides, illustrations, maps, charts, etc. In India NCERT and South Gujarat University have made some notable experiments in radio/audio-vision while the BBC and some other agencies have done the same abroad.

Broadcasting Role

Educational broadcasting has the potential to accelerate the pace of national development in general and bring about qualitative as well as quantitative improvement of education, in particular. This is more significant in developing countries like India where the socio-economic condition is yet to reach a take-off stage and universalization of elementary education is still to be realized as per the Constitutional Directive. Therefore, there has been an imperative need for furthering national development in all facets of life and for providing increased access to education, both through formal and non-formal systems and reducing the massive wastage and stagnation at all stages of education. Educational broadcasting is required to be a potential instrument of educational advancement and an integral component of educational inputs in traditional as well as distance or other alternative learning systems for different categories of learners.

Existing Conditions

The Asian Programme of Educational Innovation for Development (APEID) technical working group in its draft final report in the context of formulating guidelines for the development of educational broadcasting services has laid down the following for consideration:

- Guidelines should have application to the universalization of education and the special needs of rural communities.
- There is a great variety of administrative patterns and in the stages of development in educational broadcasting among member countries.
- Advice should be practical for implementation, and should have a proper regard for limits of financial and other resources.
- Radio is a cheaper form of broadcasting than television, both in the production and transmission of programmes and in the facilities required for reception. It has the advantage of greater penetration of the general population.
- Notwithstanding the previous statement, television is a powerful educational tool and must be given full consideration by governments and ministry policy-makers when determining priorities for the allocation of resources.

In view of the above considerations, the APEID group was rightly conscious of its limitations and has aptly observed that the guidelines that were laid down by it are not either general principles or specific statements that are not applicable to any one country or educational system. Therefore, it was felt necessary to discuss and spell out these guidelines in further detail of specificity in national seminars or workshops of various Asian countries. In India, such a national workshop was held at New Delhi from 1 to 6 December 1980 under the joint collaboration of the Ministry of Education and Culture as well as the UNESCO's APEID. This workshop in the fitness of things specifically viewed educational broadcasting including both radio and TV programmes:

(a) as a means of motivation by informing and encouraging people to participate in national development;

(b) as a major component of the non-formal education system by providing an alternative approach to the education of out-of-school children, youth and adults;

(c) as a direct instructional medium dispensing with the need for an intermediary;

(d) as an enrichment of the formal system of education where it can fill instruction gaps, up-to-date knowledge and bring in new learning experiences;

(e) as a training component for teachers (instructors) and supervisors; and

(f) as a means of imparting vocational (agricultural and industrial) and professional (medical and engineering) skills.

Education Purpose

The national workshop thus wished that educational broadcasting would be multipurpose and sought to make multi-pronged efforts for educational advancement. It would not only move away from narrow syllabus-based approaches, but also would try to reach the learners directly. It would aim at reduction of load and drudgery in the classroom and make teaching-learning process interesting and effective. Both radio and TV programmes would serve all categories of learners and provide all kinds of learning experiences—knowledge, understanding, appreciation, attitude and skills. The new curriculum with emphasis on SUPW, citizenship training and national integration could be better realized with the help of educational broadcasting.

In planning and production of programmes both the media-radio and television-would emphasize the following national priorities.

(a) Universalization of elementary education, both formal and non-formal;

(b) Non-formal education for adults, linking education to economic and social tasks;

(c) Development of vocational and professional skills;

(d) Training for citizenship;

(e) Popularizing science with a view to developing a scientific outlook;

(f) Promoting national integration, and

(g) Providing information about themes of national importance-population education, energy conservation, preservation of wild life, environmental sanitation, nutrition and health.

With a view to realizing the above national objectives and priorities, it has been decided that educational broadcasting should form an integral part of the total educational system. It means that the responsibility of policy and management of educational broadcasting should be with the educational authority. It has been suggested that advisory bodies and educational technology institutes should be set up at the national and state levels for extending advice from time to time and taking up the management. These advisory and executive bodies should take up responsibility for all kinds of educational media. This responsibility must include formulation of policy, programme planning, production, utilization, evaluation and feedback, training of personnel, providing support materials and publicity. This must also comprise administration and accounting of the organization. Although these institutions should be part of the educational infrastructure, they should have operational freedom.

Educational broadcasting by its very nature must address itself to mass audience. It must also serve the national interests and goals. But it is also necessary that it should take cognizance of local needs, language differences, cultural variety and other similar factors. Therefore, besides national framework within which the priorities, broad areas, themes, objectives, utilization and evaluation procedures of educational broadcasting should be spelt out, similar action should also be taken up at regional, State and even local levels. Planning, production and evaluation should be a collaborative venture involving curriculum developers, subject experts, teachers, scriptwriters, social scientists and producers. Even audience would be involved in planning, production and evaluation for ensuring credo and reality in programmes.

In order to ensure optimum and effective utilization of educational broadcasts, the national workshop suggested that all schools and learning centres should be adequately equipped with listening and viewing facilities. Although the government should take up the main responsibility for this, public funding, participation of the community and national as well as international voluntary agencies may also be explored. Adequate steps should be taken for maintenance and operation of the receivers. Even necessary incentives may be made available to teachers for bringing their own radio sets. Educational broadcasting should also form an integral part of teacher education programme. Besides, in-service training courses should be organized for orienting the teachers and supervisors media; various kinds of support materials should also be provided to teachers and students by the educational authorities. Research and evaluation should form a significant part of the total process of educational broadcasting. Both short-term as well as long-term, formative and summative research studies should be carried out to achieve better results.

Role of Radio : There was a time when education was the privilege of a select section of society. But today, it has become a necessity for all of us. Previously, its main objective was to impart some knowledge and skills required for the white-collared jobs or other few vocations. But now it is necessary for all kinds of jobs that are available in any part of the world. Education is regarded as a potential instrument of social change that is thought desirable at a particular point in time. It is intended to bring about social upliftment, political awareness and promoting economic growth of the masses in general. Governments of different countries have, therefore, taken up the responsibility of universalising school education and widening the access to tertiary and technical education. It has been ensured not only in the Constitution of most of the countries, but also in the International Charters of UNO and UNESCO.

Education is not limited to the classroom teaching only. It is broad-based and multi-dimensional. It is lifelong, universal, free and open. Education is learning and learning is life. Learning, living and working should go together. Education is not only lifelong, but also life-wide. Hence, there is no end to learning and no frontiers of learning. School is not the only institution of learning. It has ceased to monopolise the sources of learning. Schooling is not the only education or education is not the only schooling. The traditional curricula, methods, organization and examination are found irrelevant to the modern age. Therefore, flexibility and multiplicity of media and materials are to be encouraged. Since the children of today are the citizens of tomorrow, they have to be provided with all kinds of facilities and techniques for effective as well as efficient learning.

Teaching by Broadcasting

In this context, radio has been playing an important role for promoting relevant and interesting education. It brings the outside world into classrooms and makes the educational programme very attractive and useful. It not only informs, but also inspires the audience. It inculcates values, develops virtues and encourages imagination. Therefore, radio has been used as a potential medium for helping in realization of educational objectives most efficiently. Being an inexpensive medium, it has reached villages and is now available in the nook and corner of the society. Radio is, at present, not only one of popular mass media, but also a potential instructional tool in the formal, informal and non-formal education.

Although All India Radio (now Akash Vani) introduced programme for children from the Bombay station as early as in 1929 and from Madras station in 1930, the pioneering school broadcast programme started in 1932. The other stations followed suit and have been broadcasting educational programmes quite successfully.

Educational broadcasts are now a little over 70 years old. The educational broadcasts for secondary schools are mostly syllabus-based and the subjects covered in these programmes are English, modern Indian Language, Science, Social Studies, Sanskrit, etc. Secondary school broadcasts aim at helping students and teachers by giving up-to-date content-knowledge, providing new approaches and methods of teaching and filling curricular gaps. A few non-syllabus programmes are, however, broadcast in order to break away from the stereotyped formal education, for doing away with monotony in the curricular topics and also to stimulate awareness and curiosity about the modern world dealing with themes ranging from popular science to current affairs.

Besides secondary school broadcasts, primary school programmes have recently assumed greater importance. This has been done in order to reduce wastage and stagnation at the primary school stage by making the school situation attractive and interesting.

Dullness of the classroom, irrelevance of curriculum and rigidity of school timing are the reasons for the high percentage of drop-outs. Hence along with the various attempts of the Governments at the State and the centre, the AIR has shifted the emphasis of educational broadcasting towards the primary stage. Besides introducing primary school programmes with the existing school broadcasts, priority is being given to the primary school service. The AIR has given preference to tribal and interior areas for expansion of instructional broadcasts. The personnel incharge of these services are being recruited from among those who are familiar with the tribal culture and languages. The programmes are being related to their education, health, hygiene, nutrition etc., with a stress on bringing the audience into the mainstream of national life.

There are also broadcasts for tertiary or university students which are of two kinds. One is a general and enrichment service which mainly constitutes the Youth Programme. These broadcasts are not syllabus-oriented and topics of general interest are discussed therein. The second category is the radio support to correspondence or Distance Education. These broadcasts are related to the course of studies and are planned in consultation with the Correspondence Education authorities of the respective universities.

Since it is not possible to cover all the students under formal educational system, efforts are being made to provide facilities to the drop-outs and those who have not entered into the schools so far, through non-formal educational system. The AIR has not lagged behind to support this system through its educational programmes. As such non-formal education broadcasts were started from 5 stations since 1976 on an experimental basis. These programmes were broadcast to non-formal education centres where rural workers assemble to study in the evening between 7 or 8 p.m. and 9 or 10 p.m.

The National Adult Education Project was implemented on massive scale by the Government of India in order to remove illiteracy from the country since October 2, 1978. The AIR also has committed itself to supporting the project with suitable programmes for publicity motivation and training of instructors/helpers. Since learning directly from the teacher is minimal and there is more emphasis on learning through various mass media, educational broadcasts are expected to play an important role in non-formal system.

Farm Schools of the AIR is another example of non-formal education through the AIR. It was inaugurated in the year 1973 and thousands of farmers have been registering for different courses under this service. A series of lessons on selected agricultural topics are planned and produced according to local needs.

The AIR is now laying more emphasis on the planning and production of science programmes in both the formal and non-formal spheres of educational broadcasts. Special Science Cells have been set up in most of the major stations of the country to improve the quantity and quality of science programmes.

There are also special programmes for teachers and teacher-educators in most of the stations. These are intended to familiarise the teachers with methods of teaching, curricular changes, advanced content, and so on. This service has been more necessitated in recent years on account of large changes in school curriculum and methodology particularly in subjects like science, mathematics, social studies and English. Teachers have to be oriented to these changes and their knowledge in content and methodology needs to be updated. Hence teachers programmes have assumed more importance today than before.

A Pilot Project for teaching of mother-tongue as a first language through radio was started in Jaipur, Rajasthan during July, 1979. The project was organised by the Centre for Educational Technology, NCERT. This project aims at teaching Hindi to children in the first years of their schooling. Evaluation of this innovation showed substantial improvement in the achievement of children.

During the SITE experiment in 1975-76, in-service training in science was organised with the help of a multimedia package consisting of radio programmes as an important component. This package was developed by the Centre for Educational Technology, NCERT and the training programme was implemented by the CET and ET Cells of 6 SITE States. About 43, 000 teachers of primary schools and M. E. schools benefited from the programme and experience was quite interesting. Besides this, a few other innovations are being tried out both in rural and urban schools.

Every radio station with school broadcasting service has a unit with only three persons-a producer, scriptwriter and a production assistant with a general assistant to help. There is a consultative panel for school broadcasts comprising usually eminent heads of schools and experts who monitor the broadcasts and advise the station. As spokesmen of the programme-users they point out the deficiencies as well as useful features and suggest measures for better planning and utilisation of the educational broadcasts.

Planning of programmes is done in consultation with the Education Department. There are advisory bodies for various subjects who help the station in choice of subjects and in drawing the broadcast schedule. This help is provided through the State Institute of Education, State Council of Educational Research and Training, State Institute of Languages and State Institute of Science Education depending on institutions available in a particular State at the time.

With the establishment of Educational Technology Cells in many States since the year 1974 the collaborative efforts between the AIR and the Education Department have been promoted satisfactorily. The E. T. Cells have been taking an active interest in educational broadcasting-provision of radio sets, planning programmes, producing and distributing teachers' notes, training teachers in the use of media and scriptwriting. The State Governments have been actively participating in various training programmes, particularly in the Radio-cum-Correspondence courses by funding and organising workshops and seminars and producing support materials.

Most of the personnel in charge of Akash Vani educational broadcasts are recruited from among experienced trained teachers and educationists who have a favourable aptitude and positive attitude towards the medium. They are also trained in the Akash Vani Staff Training Institute at the centre and subsequently updating is provided there or at the two Regional Centres of the Institute or at specially organised workshops. The training is both in-service or on the job as well as formal. Exchange of ideas and mutual sharing of experiences are facilitated at the periodical seminars, workshops and conferences held at the regional and national levels. With a view to sorting out the problems and devising ways and means for overcoming them, the Director of Public Instruction, Directors of SCERT and Educational Technology Officers are invited to participate in these seminars and workshops. Most of the producers are also deputed for training abroad and get exposures from BBC, NKH, ABC or AIRD (Kualalumpur) which improve their expertise and outlook in the field.

Since quality of educational programmes depends on the quality of scripts, nowadays a number of scriptwriters are being trained at the national as well as state levels. The Centre for Educational Technology, NCERT has been organising training courses for radio scriptwriters from various parts of the country. The E. T. Cells also are organising scriptwriters workshops in collaboration with Akash Vani and CET experts. Akash Vani also occasionally organises training of teachers in properly using radio and writing scripts in special workshops. This is mostly done on requests from the State educational authorities. Although Akash Vani Staff Training Institutes are mainly intended for Akash Vani personnel, they and individual stations organise such workshops for outsiders on special grounds.

With a view to bringing about improvement in the educational broadcasts, it is imperative to evaluate them and get feedback from the audience. This is done through so many techniques. The immediate antenna for sensing the reactions of the listeners is the value of letters received by the station. A format for setting immediate feedback is printed on the Data-Schedule of programmes or any teachers' note supplied to teachers who are requested to furnish data in the same. The filled in proforma are sent back to the station. Some stations send printed proforma in bulk to the radio user schools and get them back every week for processing and reporting These reports provide immediate feedback from the field.

At times, producers also pay visits to school, and listen to the programmes with the students there. The reactions collected from students are of immense use to the producers for their guidance.

In most of the stations there are Audience Research Units which undertake surveys and studies for assessment of individual programmes in various subjects like drama, farm programmes educational broadcasts, and so on. Since these units have a small staffing pattern, they are not able to take up many research studies. Usually they conduct surveys of programmes in a series.

A number of external agencies like State Institute of Education, SCERT, Educational Technology Cells, Centre for Educational Technology and some other organisations also have started undertaking studies in this area. Even some scholars, for their Ph.D., M. A. and M. Ed. degrees, are taking up research studies in educational radio programmes.

The findings of these studies are largely revealing as well as useful. They are found quite necessary for planning, producing and utilising the educational broadcasting. Akash Vani as well as the Education Departments should take adequate note of them.

Since radio is one of the popular mass media, there are pressing demands for other services like drama, music, women, workers programmes, and so on. At the time it is felt that more time chunks should be made available for adult education, workers education, open universities or distance education and teacher education. In order to partly tackle this demand, the Akash Vani authorities are trying to fit these developmental ideas into the already existing special as well as general audience programmes.

Provision of radio listening sets in the schools and centres for non-formal education is not at all adequate. Another problem likely to be faced is that educational broadcasting would lose its initial glamour and might get into rut. But in the changing society it has to be accepted as a universal reality and attempts should rather be made to recreate new attraction and novelty in the medium through various innovations and experiments. For example, radio-vision or audio-vision with the help of slides, filmstrips, graphics etc., can make the radio programme interesting and attractive. Nevertheless, from cost-effectiveness consideration and due to relative convenience in production and utilisation, radio broadcasts can be appreciated and preferred to TV programmes.

The educational planners and administrators are yet to realize the importance of educational technology in general and educational broadcasting in particular. Although resources are available, they are not properly utilised for provision of radio sets and other media in the schools. Whatever media are available they are not suitably used in the teaching-learning process. An initial orientation towards the media is, therefore, felt imperative for heads of institutions and educational supervisors.

Adequate cooperation and coordination among the producers, user teachers, educationists, evaluators and planners are not yet forthcoming in our country. Whatever attempts have been made in this connection are quite enlightening, but they are very occasional and fragmentary. Such collaborative efforts are therefore necessary in all aspects of educational broadcasting-from planning and designing to production and evaluation in a very systematic and inter-disciplinary manner. Systems approach and cost-effectiveness are the two parameters that need consideration for planning optimum learning through radio broadcasts.

T.V. Aid : Inventor of television, John L. Baird, would never have thought that his brain child would exercise such a great influence on the world over. The American author James S. Kinder has aptly remarked, "Television has literally captured the country.

Its expansion has been much more dramatic than of radio or the automobile. It has become an important part of our way of life, so much so that it is difficult to say whether it is a luxury or a necessity." This is the state of affairs not only of America, but also in most of the developed as well as developing countries. Its glamour has caught the attention of all irrespective of economic and political or religious affiliation of the country.

John Baird was able to transmit a visual across a few metres for the first time in 1924. Marconi also succeeded in starting experimental television. The BBC initiated its television service in 1936 with only 300 TV sets. But in 1939 it closed down this service and could not muster its strength till 1946 for starting the same again. It, however, flourished in the developed countries particularly in the Western world during nineteen sixties.

In 1956, the General Conference of UNESCO was held in New Delhi and it was decided therein that a pilot project should be implemented in India to study the use of television as a medium of education and community development. In 1959 an agreement was signed between AIR and UNESCO for starting the project on an experimental basis. This was inaugurated in Delhi by the erstwhile President of India Dr. Rajendra Prasad on the 15th September, 1959. Thus the experimental television service was started with the objectives of "experimentation, training and evaluation" as a part of the UNESCO project. It was experimentation with the new medium, training of the personnel for running it and evaluation of the new medium as a vehicle of communication and education.

Television sets were installed at first only at 21 community centres of adult education and social welfare services. A tele-club was formed at each centre and was expected to promote organised viewing, conduct post-telecast discussions and convey the viewers' reactions and comments as feedback to the All India Radio. A convener was appointed at each club for this purpose and the programmes were telecast for one hour every Tuesday and Friday. TV programmes were educative and informative and of various formats like talks, plays, ballets, interviews, discussions, music and documentary films. Besides, important occasions like

Independence Day, Republic Day, State visits of foreign dignitaries, Holi and Diwali festivals also had their coverage.

This TV service was operated from the Akash Vani Bhavan in New Delhi and the area of coverage was within 12 to 15 miles. About 150 to 200 persons were viewing the programmes at each of the 21 centres. During 1960-61 a series of social education programmes were telecast in collaboration with UNESCO. As many as twenty such programmes were telecast from December, 1960 to May, 1961. The topics covered were, for example, traffic and road sense, community health, good manners and rights and duties of citizens. After the completion of these programmes another series of twenty programmes were telecast. The nature as well as impact of these programmes was evaluated by the National Fundamental Education Centre and Indian Adult Education Association, New Delhi. The findings of the experiment were quite encouraging and significantly beneficial.

Tele-lecture Concept : The first move towards educational television was made by AIR in January-March, 1960 and an experimental programme was telecast for school children of New Delhi every Tuesday from 3 to 4 p.m. in lieu of the evening programmes. Although a number of difficulties were experienced in assembling batches of students at nearby community centres with TV sets, the experiment, on the whole, was inspiring.

A Ford Foundation Project, in fact, laid the foundation stone of educational television service. A four-year agreement was made with the Ford Foundation for launching a regular TV programme for schools in Delhi. According to this Agreement 600 TV sets were installed in secondary schools by 1965. This service was inaugurated on the 23rd October, 1961. Eight E. TV programmes of 20 minutes each were telecast every week for the students of secondary schools. These programmes were also repeated in the afternoon in order to make them available to students of the second shift. The subjects covered by these programmes were Physics, Chemistry, Hindi, English, Geography and current affairs.

The agreement also provided for the supply of technical equipment, deputing AIR personnel abroad for training and making experts on educational TV from America available to the AIR.

Initially, 250 TV sets were installed in secondary schools having AC Electricity supply and it was proposed to cover all the high schools in Delhi. As the number of schools equipped with TV sets increased, benefits of ETV programmes were extended to 36,000 students of science and 96,000 students of English.

After four years of execution, the project was evaluated by Dr. Paul Neurath, a New York City University Professor of Sociology. The overall impact of the ETV programmes was quite satisfactory. G.C. Awasthy on the basis of his personal contacts with schools, reports from the viewing schools, discussions with teachers and AIR personnel has observed that the results of the projects were very encouraging. AIR has also claimed that as a result of TV programmes, academic performance of students viewing ETV programmes had improved, interest in science has increased and standards of teaching had improved.

Regular TV service was inaugurated in Delhi on the 15th August, 1965 and a landmark was made in early 1966 with launching of the Krishi Darshan Programme for farmers. The AIR was organising this project in collaboration with the Institute of Agricultural Research, the Delhi Administration, and the Atomic Energy Commission. The experiences of this project were quite enlightening and interesting.

The famous Satellite Instructional Television Experiment (SITE) was implemented during the year 1975-76. This project however, originated during the year 1965-the year of International Cooperation and initiative was taken by the UNESCO. In a meeting of the UNESCO on Space Communication, an Advisory Panel was set up and an International Committee of Media Experts submitted a report after carefully examining the issue. It was decided to take up a pilot project in India on TV programmes through satellite. It was felt that the project would help India in solving her problems of food scarcity, mass illiteracy and ignorance about developmental strategies.

The SITE was inaugurated by Smt. Indira Gandhi, the Prime Minister of India at Ahmedabad on the Ist August, 1975. The TV programmes could be telecast with the help of a satellite called ATS-F loaned by the National Aeronautics and Space

Administration USA. The TV programmes related to Education, Agriculture, Health, Family Planning, National Integration, and so on. The telecast was for four hours a day out of which one and a half hours in the morning were meant for primary school children and two and a half hours in the evening for adults. The total time was equally divided into three segments for six States of India in view of the capacity of satellite for telecasting on video with two audio channels.

The project was intended to cater to the development needs of the rural community and with this in view, about 2,400 direct reception television sets were deployed in different cultural, linguistic and agricultural regions located in 6 States-Andhra Pradesh, Bihar, Karnataka, Madhya Pradesh, Orissa and Rajasthan. The ETV programmes were produced by the TV Base Production Centre, Doordarshan and Indian Space Research Organisation (ISRO). Besides students programmes, a number of ETV programmes were also telecast for teachers who participated in the in-service training courses in science. A few organisations at the State and national levels like ISRO, NCERT, Ministry of Education, E. T. Cell and universities were engaged in conducting research studies on impact of TV programmes on the rural audience. The findings of these studies were, on the whole quite inspiring and useful.

After the SITE, the Government of India decided to provide TV viewing facility in 40 per cent of the SITE-served villages by setting up terrestrial transmitters in the six SITE States. As the infrastructure and studio facilities already existed in these States, it was easier for the Doordarshan authorities to take up the SITE continuity programme in these areas by setting up low-power terrestrial TV transmitters.

With a view to utilise the INSAT capability for educational development, the Ministry of Education initiated action for preparing plans of operation as early as in July 1979. In view of the experience and involvement of the Space Application Centre, Ahmedabad in different aspects of TV, it was decided to elicit their cooperation in preparing a basic document for consideration and discussion. It was expected that the document would provide, inter alia, an outline of the institutional, human, technical and financial resources available and those that could be developed in the country and were necessary for a national system of utilisation of television for education. In response to the Ministry's request, the SAC prepared a background paper entitled "INSAT." The paper outlined the INSAT capability, the ground segment requirements for TV, the possible hardware for satellite utilisation and an approach for developmental communication.

A meeting was convened by the Ministry of Education on the 30th January, 1980 to discuss the background paper and all connected issues involved in the satellite utilisation for radio and television programmes. The Education Secretary presided over and representatives from SAC, NCERT, A. I. R., Doordarshan, Planning Commission, UGC and Ministry of Education attended the meeting. It was decided that urgent steps should be taken for planning software in connection with INSAT utilisation by all the user Ministries in general and by Education Ministry, in particular.

The Ministry of Information and broadcasting set up a Working Group under the Chairmanship of the Secretary, Information and Broadcasting on the February 2, 1980 in order to draw up a software plan for INSAT utilisation. The Group consisted of members from various affiliated organisations and different user ministries. The Working Group finalised its report in September, 1980 and mainly recommended that the concerned Ministries should develop programme production capability and take upon themselves specific responsibility for producing programmes. The Ministry of Education after due consideration took the decision that educational authorities would be entrusted with programme production and indicated to the Working Group that the major educational objectives of a satellite television would be to promote alternative approaches to education for children, youth and adults. The thrust of the specific programmes would be to emphasize direct teaching, moving away from curriculum-oriented approach and aim at reduction of load in the classroom, and improvement of the quality of programmes through training of manpower.

Another Study Group set up by the Ministry of Education under the Chairmanship of Shri S. Sathyam, Jt. Secretary, Education also developed a policy for the use of TV, identified approaches, priorities, target audiences and themes for programmes, considered in detail the implications arising out of the decision that the educational authority shall be responsible for the production of educational television programmes in terms of an infrastructure and manpower requirements, identified key areas for training and developed training courses in detail and suggested lines for further action.

In April, 1980, the Government of India was invited by the UNESCO Regional Office for Education in Asia and Oceania, Bangkok to participate in their Asian Programme of Educational Innovation for Development (APEID) in the field of educational technology. As the participating countries were required to organise national workshops, the Ministry of Education, Government of India, in collaboration with UNESCO convened National Workshop on Educational Broadcasting from December 1 to 6, 1980 at New Delhi. The basic reference document for the National Workshop was the Draft Guidelines on Educational Broadcasting which was developed at a Technical Working Group Meeting on Educational Broadcasting organised by the UNESCO during 1979 in Malaysia. The NCERT, AIR and Doordarshan authorities extended necessary cooperation in organising the National workshop.

The National Workshop was attended by 41 participants representing various media and educational interests from all over the country and consisting of media practitioners, media experts, planners, administrators, teachers, trainers, educationists, researchers and social scientists. The workshop assumed special significance on account of the nation's renewed emphasis on educational broadcasting on the eve of putting INSAT in the orbit. The main highlights of the workshop were as follows:

1. Recognition of Educational Broadcasting. New priority role to move away from syllabus-oriented approaches into non-formal systems and lesser dependence on intermediaries.
2. Stressing team mode of production, making the planning and production of educational broadcasts a collaborative effort of the producers, educators and social scientists.
3. Calling for an integration of educational broadcasting within the total educational system and for the purpose

recommending autonomy to the Centre for Educational Technology at the national level and creating autonomous State Institutes of Educational Technology at the State level which will be necessary professional and technical structures for Educational Broadcasting.

4. Laying more emphasis on research and evaluation as an essential component of Educational Broadcasting at all stages of planning production and utilisation.
5. Evolving a national framework spelling out the priorities, broad areas, themes and objectives of the programmes.
6. Entrusting the responsibility of planning, production and use of educational broadcasting to the educational authority.
7. Urging immediate action on all fronts to prepare for the utilisation of the television facilities under INSAT.

The Report of the National Workshop has rightly mentioned that the participants representing a cross-section of varied professional background and interests were able "to take collective look at the problem of educational broadcasting, share the individual and group experiences and to pool their expertise in the creation of new approaches towards making broadcasting a meaningful educational tool, the free spirit of which came out across the barriers of syllabi age-groups, and traditional restrictive educational philosophies. It is to be hoped that the liberal thinking that permeated the workshop will be instrumental in shaping Educational Broadcasting and pave the way for exciting educational horizon behind and beyond INSAT."

7

Teaching Aids

The Basics

Audio-Visual aids, audio-visual material, audio-visual media, communication technology, educational or instructional media and learning resources—all these terms, broadly speaking, mean the same thing. Earlier the term used was audio-visual aids in education. With the advancement in the means of communication and that of technology, educators coined new terms, More specifically media refers to films, filmstrips, recordings, etc. The use of newer terms Educational Technology or Instructional Technology is primarily due to the dynamic expansion of programmed learning, computer assisted instruction and education T.V. This revolution in the field of audio-visual education is the outcome of the development in electronics, notably those involving the radio, tape recorder and computer.

Brief History of the Use of Audio-visual Aids : A Dutch humanist, theologian and writer Desiderious Erasmus (1466-1536) discouraged memorization as a technique of learning and advocated that children should learn through the aid of pictures or other visuals. John Amos Comenius (1592-1670) prepared a book known as *Orbis Sensulium Pictus.* (The world of Sense Objects) which contained about 150 pictures on aspects of everyday life. The book is considered to be the first illustrated textbook for childhood education. This book gained wide publicity and was used in childhood education centres all over the world. Jean Jacques Rousseau (1712-1778) and other educators stressed the need of pictures and other play materials. Rousseau condemned the use of words by teachers and he stressed 'things'. He pleaded that the teaching process must be directed to the learner's natural curiosity. Pestalozzi (1756-1827) put Rousseau's theory into action in his 'object method'. He based instruction on sense perception.

The Approach

Burton : Audio-visual aids are those sensory objects or images which initiate or stimulate and reinforce learning.

Carter V. Good : audio-visual aids are those aids which help in completing the triangular process of learning i.e., motivation, classification and stimulation.

Edgar Dale : Audio-visual are those devices by the use of which communication of ideas between persons and groups in various teaching and training situations is helped. These are also termed as multi-sensory materials.

Good's Dictionary of Education : Audio-visual aids are anything by means of which learning process may be encouraged or carried on through the sense of hearing or sense of sight.

Kinder, S. James : Audio-visual aids are any device which can be used to make the learning experience more concrete, more realistic and more dynamic.

Mckown and Roberts: Audio-visual aids are supplementary devices by which the teacher, through the utilization of more than one sensory channels is able to clarify, establish and correlate concepts, interpretations and appreciations.

Factors of Significance

Audio-visual aids or devices or technological media or learning devices are added devices that help the teacher to clarify, establish, co-relate and co-ordinate accurate concepts, interpreta-tions and appreciations and enable him to make learning more concrete, effective, interesting, inspirational, meaningful and vivid. They help in completing the triangular process of learning viz., motivation-clarification-stimulation. The aim of teaching with technological media is 'clearing the channel between the learner and the things that are worth learning'. The basic assumption underlying Audio-visual Aids is that learning—clear understanding—stems from sense experience. The teacher must 'show' as well as 'tell'. Audio-visual aids provide significant gains in informational learning, retention and recall, thinking and reasoning, activity, interest, imagination, better assimilation and personal growth and development. The aids are the stimuli for learning 'why', 'how', 'when' and 'where'. The 'hard to understand principles' are usually made clear by the intelligent use of skilfully designed instructional aids.

According to Gandhiji, "True education of the intellect can only come through a proper exercise and training of bodily organs—hands, feet, eyes, ears and nose."

Commenting on the use of audio-visual aids, the Kothari Commssion 1964-66 observed that it should indeed bring about an 'educational revolution' in the country. It further stated that the supply of teaching aids to every school was essential for the improvement of the quality of teaching.

The National Policy of Education, 1986 and as modified in 1992 has laid a great stress on the use of teaching aids, especially improvised aids, to make teaching-learning more effective and realistic.

In the words of Edgar Dale, "Because audio-visual materials supply concrete basis for conceptual thinking, they give rise to meaningful concepts enriched by meaningful association, hence they offer the best antidote for the disease of verbalism."

Some of the important values of the proper use of audio-visual aids are given below:

Antidote to the Disease of Verbal Instruction : They help to reduce verbalism. They help in giving clear concepts and thus help to bring accuracy in learning. As observed by Raymound Wyman (1957) "We (teacher) tell students, and we provide them with written material so much of the time. Words are wonderful.

They are easily produced, reproduced, stored and transported. But the overuse or excessive use of words can result in serious problem, chiefly, the problem of verbalism (using or adopting words or phrases without considering what they mean) and forgetting."

Best Motivation : They are the best motivators. The students work with more interest and zeal. They are more attentive.

Clear Images : Clear images are formed when we see, hear, touch, taste and smell as our experiences are direct, concrete and more or less permanent. Learning through the senses becomes the most natural and consequently the easiest.

Vicarious Experience : It is beyond doubt that the first-hand experience is the best type of educative experience. But it is neither practicable nor desirable to provide such experience to pupils. Substituted experiences may be provided under such conditions. There are many inaccessible objects and phenomena. For example, it is not possible for the pupils living in India to see the Eskimoe. Similary, it is not possible for an average man to climb the Mount Everst. There are innumerable such things to which it is not possible to have direct access. So, in all such cases, these aids help us.

Variety : 'Mere chalk and talk' do not help. Audio-visual aids give variety and provide different tools in the hands of the teacher.

Freedom : When audio-visual aids are employed, there is great scope for children to move about, talk, laugh and comment upon. Under such an atmosphere the students work because they want to work and not because the teacher wants them to work.

Opportunities to Handle and Manipulate : Many visual aids offer opportunities to students to handle and manipulate things.

Retentivity : Audio-visual aids contribute to increased retentivity as they stimulate response of the whole organism to the situation in which learning takes place.

Based on Maxims of Teaching : The use of audio-visual aids enables the teacher to follow the maxims of teaching like 'concrete to abstract', 'known to unknown' and 'learning by doing.'

Helpful in Attracting Attention : Attention is the true factor in any process of teaching and learning. Audio-visual aids help the teacher in providing proper environment for capturing as well as sustaining the attention and interest of the students in the classroom work.

Helpful in Fixing up New Learning : 'What is gained in terms of learning, needs to be fixed up in the minds of students. Audiovisual aids help in achieving this objective by providing several activities, experiences and stimuli to the learners'.

Saving of Energy and Time : A good deal of energy and time of both the teachers and students can be saved on account of the use of audio-visual aids as most of the concepts and phenomena may be easily clarified, understood and assimilated through their use.

Realism : The use of audio-visual aids provides a touch of reality to the learning situation. By seeing a film show exhibiting the life of the people of the Tundra region, students learn it more effectively in about 2 hours than by spending weeks by reading.

Vividness : Audio-visual aids give vividness to the learning situation. A film on Buddha provides a vivid picture of his life and teachings.

Meeting Individual Differences : There are wide individual differences among learners. Some are ear-oriented, some can be helped through visual demonstrations, while others learn better by doing. The use of a variety of audio-visual aids helps in meeting the needs of different types of students.

Encouragement to Healthy Classroom Interaction : Audio-visual aids, through their wide variety of stimuli, provision of active participation of the students, and vicarious experiences encourage healthy classroom interaction for the effective realization of teaching-learning objectives.

Spread of Education on a Mass Scale : Audio-visaul. aids like radio and television help in providing opportunities for education to people living in remote areas. They also help in promoting adult education.

Promotion of Scientific Temper : In place of listening to facts, students observe demonstrations and phenomena and thus cultivate scientific temper.

Development of Higher Faculties : Verbalism promotes memorisation. Use of audio-visual aids stirs the imagination, thinking process and reasoning power of the students, and calls for creativity, and inventiveness and other higher mental activities on the parts of students and thus helps the development of higher faculties among the students.

Reinforcement to Learners : Audio-visual aids prove effective reinforcers by increasing the probability of re-occurance of the response associated with them and thus render valuable help in the teaching-learning process.

Positive Transfer of Learning and Training : Use of audio-visual aids helps in the learning of other concepts, principles and solving the real problems of life by making possible the appropriate positive transfer of learning and training received in the classroom.

Positive Environment for Creative Discipline : A balanced, rational and scientific use of audio-visual aids develops motivation, attracts the attention and interests of the students and provides a variety of creative outlets for the utilisation of their tremendous energy and thus keeps them busy in the classroom work. In this way, the overall classroom environment becomes conducive to creative discipline.

The Use

In addition to reading, vicarious experience can be gained from still pictures, films, filmstrips, resource persons, simulations, mockups, television, and the like. The more concrete and realistic the vicarious experience, the more nearly it approaches the learning effectiveness of the first level. Of course, unless the learner realizes that he is dealing with a substitute, his learning may not be comparable to that of real-life learning.

Interest in the role of the senses in learning was already there in educational circles when instructional media began their ascendancy. It has long been recognized that the various senses condition the reception of messages in the communications act. Research done by Cobun (1968) indicated that:

1 per cent of what is learned is from the sense of TASTE.

1.5 per cent of what is learned is from the sense of TOUCH.

3.5 per cent of what is learned is from the sense of SMELL.

11 per cent of what is learned is from the sense of HEARING.

83 per cent of what is learned is from the sense of SIGHT.

Retention of what is learned is likewise related to sense experience.

Observation and research by Cobun tended to show, holding time as nearly constant as possible, that people generally remember:

10 per cent of what they READ.

20 per cent of what they HEAR.

30 Per cent of what they SEE.

50 per cent of what they HEAR AND SEE.

70 per cent of what they SAY.

90 per cent of what they SAY as they do a thing.

Popular Sayings

I hear, I forget.

I see, I remember.

I do, I understand.

Characteristics

1. They should be meaningful and purposeful.
2. They should be accurate in every respect.
3. They should be simple.
4. They should be cheap.
5. As far as possible, they should be improvised.
6. They should be large enough to be properly seen by the students for whom they are meant.
7. They should be up-to date.
8. They should be easily portable.
9. They should be according to the mental level of the students.
10. They should motivate the learners.

Rules and Regulation

Principle of Selection : Teaching aids prove effective only when they suit the teaching objectives and unique characteristics of the special group of learners. Following points may be kept in view in this regard :

(i) They should suit the age-level, grade-level and other characteristics of the learners.

(ii) They should have specific educational value besides being interesting and motivating.

(iii) They should be the true representatives of the real things.

(iv) They should help in the realization of desired learning objectives.

Principle of Preparation : This principle requires that following points should be attended to:

(a) As far as possible, locally available material should be used in the preparation of an aid.

(b) The teachers should receive some training in the preparation of aids.

(c) The teachers themselves should prepare some of the aids.

(d) Students may be associated in the preparation of aids.

Preparation of Physical Control : This principle related to the arrangement of keeping aids safely and also to facilitate their lending to the teachers for use.

Principle of Proper Presentation : This principle implies the following pioits :

(i) Teachers should carefully visualise the use of teaching aids before their actual presentation.

(ii) They should fully acquaint themselves with the use and manipulation of the aids to be shown in the classroom.

(iii) Adequate care should be taken to handle an aid in such a way as no damage is done to it.

(iv) The aid should be displayed properly so that all the students are able to see it, observe it and derive maximum benefit out of it.

(v) As far as possible, distraction of all kinds to be eliminated so that full attention may be paid to the aid.

Principle of Response : This principle demands that the teachers guide the students to respond actively to the audio-visual stimuli so that they derive the maximum benefit in learning.

Principle of Evaluation : This principle stipulates that there should be continuous evaluation of both the audio-visual material and accompanying techniques in the light of the realisation of the desired objectives.

More Problems : While all these aids are becoming more and more popular day by day, there are still some problems to be faced and solved. These are :

Apathy of the Teachers : Teachers in general are yet to be convinced that teaching with words alone is very tedious, wasteful and ineffective.

Indifference of Students : The judicious use of aids arouses interest but when used without a definite purpose they lose their significance and importance.

Ineffectiveness of the Aids : Due to the absence of proper planning and the lethargy of the teacher and without proper preparation, correct presentation, application and discussion and the essential follow-up work, the aids do not prove their full usefulness. A film like a good lesson has various steps—Preparation, Presentation, Application and Discussion.

Financial Hurdles : The Central and State Governments have set up Boards of Audio-Visual Education and have chalked out interesting programmes for the popularization of teaching aids but the lack of finances is not enabling them to do their best.

Absence of Electricity : Most of the Projectors, Radio and TV cannot work without the electric current which is not available in a large number of schools.

Lack of Facilities for Training : Training colleges or specialised agencies should make special provision to train teachers and workers in the use of these aids.

Co-ordination between Centre and States : Good film libraries, museums of audio-visual provision to train teachers and workers in the use of these aids.

Language Difficulty : Most educational films are in English. We should have these in Hindi and other important Indian languages.

Not Catering to Local Needs : Little attention is paid in the production of audio-visual aids to the local sociological, psychological and pedagogical factors.

Improper Selection of Films : Films are not selected according to the classroom needs.

Today, the problem is not whether visual aids should have a place in education. Their place has been recognised long ago. The problem, now, is that of extending the benefits of these aids to all teachers and all children. The future can be bright if there is proper planning on the part of the Government and co-ordination between producers, teachers and students. Useful and effective aids can be produced after getting the reaction of the audience and doing research work in the field. A great deal is being done already but a lot more still remains to be done.

Big media include computer, VCR and TV. Little media include radio, films strips, graphic, audio cassettes and various visuals.

(i) Models

(ii) Mock-ups

(iii) Specimens.

Three dimensional aids are the replicas or substitutes of real objects. All the learning experiences which can be utilised for classroom teaching are shown by Edgar Dale in a pictorial device—'pinnacle form'—which he called the 'cone of experience'. If we go up the pinnacle from its base, we find that every aid has been arranged in the order of increasing abstractness or decreasing directness. In a simple language, it may be stated that the 'cone' classifies the audiovisual aids according to their effectiveness in communication—aid at the base of the cone as 'most effective'—relative effect gradually decreases.

At the pinnacle of the 'Cone', the direct, purposeful experiences are represented. At the pinnacle of the 'Cone', the verbal symbols are represented. The experiences included in the cone are as indicated below:

Direct, Purposeful Experience : The experiences gained through the senses are direct and purposeful. It has been amply observed, "An ounce of experience is better than a tonne of theory, simply because it is only as an experience that any theory has vital and verifiable significance." This, direct experience is gained through the aids mentioned at the base of the cone.

Contrived Experience : When the real thing cannot be perceived directly, its simplification becomes necessary. Contrived experience is like a working model which is an editing of reality and differs from the original either in size or in complexity. The real object may be too small or too big, may be confused or concealed. In such a situation imitation is preferred for better and easier understanding.

Dramatic Participation : In dramatics, certain real events are presented through the play, the pageant (kind of community drama, usually based on local history), pantomine (actors do not speak, make movements), tablean (pictureline scene in which the characteristics stand still, silently), and the puppets.

Diverse Sorts

Actual Objects : Actual objects and specimens are indispensable in science and other subjects. They are very vivid and impressive. They make a direct appeal to the senses of children. It is not possible for a child to have a clear picture of a river, a factory or a mountain unless he has seen these. The teaching of history and geography can never be effective without visitsing places of importance, valleys, lakes, old forts, monuments, etc. The students get a correct idea of various minerals when they are shown these objects. In framing the multiplication table, counting of beads and sticks prove to be very useful at the earlier stages.

Blackboard : Blackboard and a piece of chalk prove very helpful in illustrating concepts and ideas to the students. These can be used for drawing diagrams and sketches, etc. Blackboard is a simple and unique device which, in spite of new devices and techniques in teaching, is irreplacable as well as indispensable. It is the oldest and the best friend of a teacher. It is the mirror through which students visualise all about the teacher's mind regarding the lesson in hand, his way of explaining, illustrating and teaching as a whole. It is the cheapest teaching device and continues to be the *'sine quo non'* of our educational system. It is the most universally used aid. Writing on clay and sand was the ancient form of blackboard writing. It helps 'crystallizing' the main points, 'summarising' and 'reviewing'.

Varied Ways

1. The teacher can illustrate the main points of the lesson on the blackboard.
2. Abstract statements can be clarified in the exposition stage and a summary containing the salient features can be given at the recapitulatory stage.
3. Questions and problems can be listed on the blackboard.
4. Pupils' interest in classwork can be stimulated by blackboard writings and drawings.
5. A teacher can use the blackboard for graphs, graphics, sketches, maps and statistics, etc.
6. A blackboard provides a lot of scope for creative and decorative work.
7. The teacher can erase writings and drawings and start afresh.
8. It helps the teacher to focus the attention of his students on the lesson. It takes heed of varying capacities and rates of grasp of the students.
9. A teacher can review the whole lesson for the benefit of the class with the help of the blackboard.

Fixed Blackboard : Fixed in the wall facing the class and normally made of wood or concrete cement.

Blackboard on Easel : A portable and adjustable blackboard put on a wooden easel can be taken out of the classroom while taking classes in the open.

Roller Blackboard : Made of thick canvas wrapped on a roller mostly used for teaching higher classes.

Graphic Board : It has graphic lines and is used for teaching mathematics, science and statistics.

Magna Board : A board which enables teachers to make three-dimensional demonstrations with objects on a vertical surface. Small magnets are used to hold suitable objects fixed wherever they are put on this vertical surface.

Following points may be kept in view while using the blackboard :

1. Blackboard should be kept clean so-that writing on it could be easily read by the students from all parts of the room.
2. Writing on the blackboard should be legible.
3. Letters and drawings should be large enough to be seen from all parts of the room.
4. Writing should be started from the top left corner.
5. Writing should be in straight rows.
6. Extreme lower corner of the blackboard should not be made use of as writing on it cannot be seen easily.
7. Material on the blackboard should not be covered by standing.
8. Only salient points of the subject-matter should be written on the blackboard.
9. Diagrammatic visual presentation involving many processes should be prepared before the beginning of the lesson.
10. It should be ensured that blackboard is well lighted by natural or artificial means.
11. Everything needed for the blackboard should be got together before the class begins *i,e.,* collection of chalk, rulers, T. Square, Compass, Projector, etc.
12. While writing on the blackboard, the teacher should ensure that the class is attentive.
13. Duster and not hand or handkerchief should be used in cleaning the blackboard.
14. Occasionally students may be asked to write or draw diagram on the blackboard.

15. Teachers should develop the ability to draw freely on the blackboard. The map or chart or diagram that grows before the very eyes of the students is much more useful and valuable than a well finished map, chart or diagram.
16. It should be ensured that the blackboard is periodically serviced.

A chart is a combination of pictorial, graphic, numerical or vertical material which presents a clear visual summary. The most commonly used types of charts include outline charts, tabular charts, flow charts and organisation charts. Other types of charts are technical diagrams and process diagrams. Flip charts and flow charts are also being used. Ready made charts are available for use in teaching in almost all areas in all subjects. But charts prepared by a teacher himself incorporating his own ideas and lines of approach of the specific topic are more useful. Charts serve the following purposes:

1. For showing relationship by means of facts, figures and statistics.
2. For presenting materials symbolically.
3. For summarising information.
4. For showing continuity in process.
5. For presenting abstract ideas in visual form.
6. For showing development of structure.
7. For creating problems and stimulating thinking.
8. For encouraging utilisation of other media of communication.
9. For motivating the students.

The following is a list of basic types of charts in terms of arrangements and the kinds of ideas which they may express :

1. The narrative chart, an extended left-to-right arrange-ment of facts and ideas for expressing:
   (a) The events in a process such as shoe making, oil cracking, or the like,
   (b) The events in the development of a significant issue to its point of resolution or to present status (sometimes

a time limit). Example: the events leading to the separation of the Bangladesh from Pakistan, the events leading to the establishment of the idea that an individual should be free and that he should have a voice in his own government and the events leading to increased regulation of business by government,

(c) Technological improvement over a period of years such as improvement in transportation, communication, manufacturing etc.

2. The tabulation chart, a left-to-right, top-to-bottom arrangement of facts and ideas for expression:

   (a) Numerical data for making comparisons,

   (b) Lists products, mountains, rivers, or the like in selected areas.

3. The cause and effect chart, usually a limited left-to-right arrangement of facts and ideas for expressing:

   (a) Relationship between standard of living and such factors as economic system, availability of natural resources, level of technological advancement,

   (b) Relationship between `a culture and neighbouring cultures,

   (c) Relationship between rights and responsibi-lities,

   (d) Relationship between a complex of conditions and change or conflict,

   (e) Relationship-between the elected and the electors,

   (f) Relationship between community workers and the community which supports them.

4. The chain charts, a circular or semi-ircular arrangement of facts and ideas for expressing:

   (a) Transitions, such as the transition from raw materials to useful products,

   (b) Cycles, such as the water cycle.

5. The evolution chart, a left-to right arrangement of facts and ideas for expressing:

(a) Changes in specific item from beginning to date, perhaps with projections into the future. Example: origin of the automobile and its subsequent development, early basic homes and changes in basic homes to date,

(b) Change in standard in food consumption, length of work, weak purchasing power of a rupee, or the like.

Diagrams : Diagrams are very helpful in supplementing vertical illustrations in teaching. Difficult operations may be explained with the help of diagrams. The parts of a flower or leaf can be suitably explained by means of sketches drawn by the teacher in front of the class on the black-board: Simple diagrams can be used to explain different phenomena in geography and science. The diagrams of battle plans and forts can be drawn on the blackboard. The area and volume, etc., in mathematics can be illustrated through diagrams. A teacher is expected to possess the skill of drawing diagrams easily, neatly, rapidly and readily on the blackboard.

Epidiascope : The epidiascope is an instrument which can project images or printed matter or small opaque objects on a screen, or it can project images of a 4" X 4" slide. With the help of any epidiascope, any chart, diagram, map, photograph and picture can be projected on the screen without tearing it off from the book. No slide is needed for this purpose. An epidiascope serves two purposes. It works as epidiascope when it is used to project an opaque object. It works as epidiascope when it is used to project slides (by operating a lever). It works on the principle of horizontal straight line projection with a lamp, plane mirror and projection lens. A strong light from the lamp falls on the opaque object. A plane mirror placed at an angle of 45° over the project, reflects the light so that it passes through the projection lens forming a magnified image on the screen.

Film Strip : A film strip is 35 mm wide and has a series of 12 to 48 picture frames arranged in a sequence so that they develop a theme. A film strip can be prepared by taking a series of photographs using a 35 mm camera and then by taking a positive print of the negative film on another 35 mm film.

Globe : Knowledge of map is unreal without the knowledge of globe-the true map. It is the true representative of earth's physical personality. A globe gives a true idea of the total environment at a glance in a classroom situation. It is through globe that a child can understand the concepts of time, space, wind's planetary relations and proportion. Hence, every school shall have globes. Four types of globes may be kept in every school. (1) Political globes, (2) Phy-sical globes, (3) Washable projection globes, (4) Celestial globes.

Graphs : Graphs are flat pictures which employ dots, lines or pictures to visualise numerical and statistical data to show relationships or statistics.

Line Graph : In a line graph, data is represented with the help of simple lines horizontally or vertically drawn. For increasing the interest and readability of concepts, pictorial illustrations and cartoons are occasionally used on the line graph.

Bar Graph : A bar graph consists of bars arranged, horizontally or vertically from a 'zero' base. The colour, length and size of the bars represent different values.

Circle Graph : Data may be presented in a circle graph.

Magic Lantern : Magic lantern is the earliest invention in the history of audio-visual aids used for projecting pictures from a transparency (slide) on a wall or screen. When the figure or illustration is very small and it is required to be shown to the entire class, a transparent slide of the small figure is prepared. Then, this slide is placed into the slide carrier part of the magic lantern. This magic lantern device projects it on the screen by enlarging its dimension and making the vision more clear and sharp.

Significance of Map Study : In several subjects, especially social studies, the learning of many geographical, historical and economic concepts remains unreal, inadequate and incomplete without map media. A resourceful teacher by motivating the pupils will turn the fear of map into the genuine love for them. This, however, presupposes the invariable uses of maps at every possible opportunity by the teacher in the classroom, and the possession of individual atlases by the pupils. Every student should also know certain elementary aspects of map preparation such as copying, enlarging and reducing, symbolizing, colouring, and preparation of key. Most of the students develop an aversion to maps because they do not know skills relating to map preparation.

Meaning of Map : A map is an accurate representation of plain surface in the form of a diagram drawn to scale, the details of boundaries of continents, countries, of etc. Geographical details like location of mountains, rivers, altitude of a place, contours of the earth surface and important' locations can also be represented accurately with reference to a convenient scale with suitable colour scheme.

1. Understanding and interpreting the key of index.
2. Understanding the lines-boundary lines, lines of communication, lines indicating the rivers, contours, meridians and parallels.
3. Understanding the colours, tints, shadows, symbols in a map or globe.
4. The top of every map is not north, but the direction of northern pole is north.
5. Distinction between the various types of maps such as relief, political, distribution maps, etc.
6. Understanding of the position of earth in the universe. Many students suffer from a notion that the earth leans in June towards the Sun northwards and in December southwards and thus the seasons are formed. Earth never dances that way. The student shall understand that the inclination of earth is constant and the learning effect changes due to its rotation around the sun.

Relief Maps (regional and the world) : This requires the knowledge of colours, contours, symbols and the other connected ethics of map making.

Historical Maps : Maps in history reveal the changing times and the growth and decline of various kingdoms. Knowledge of lines of boundaries and other symbols is necessary.

Distribution Maps : Generally, the student shall associate with the following types of distribution maps: (1) Vegetation maps, (2) Population maps, (3) Economic maps, (4) Statistical maps,

(5) Dot maps, (6) Pictorial maps, (7) Language, race and other human division maps, etc.

Geographical Maps : Contour maps, weather maps, seismological maps, archaeological maps, rainfall maps, geological maps, etc.

Microfilm : The microfilm and microfiche are used widely for storage and retrieval of information. Microfilms contain photographed reading material on 35 mm film, each frame being the reduced photograph of a printed page. Thus, printed matter of a book can be stored in *a* small loop of 35 mm film. When the microfilm is passed through *a* microfilm reader, an enlarged image approximately of the size of the printed page is formed on a ground glass (rear-view) screen and the observer can read the matter. By moving the film through the microfilm reader, images of different pages can be obtained and read.

Models : Models are substitutes for real things. A model is a three-dimensional representation of a real thing. Models are concrete objects to explain clearly the structure or functions of real things. A model is a replica of the original. Models enable students to have a correct concept of the object. Being three dimensional, models evoke great interest and simplify matters. Models enable us to reduce or enlarge objects to an observable size. It may not be possible or even practicable to make students see the whole of a large industrial unit or even a large machine unit, but a model will give the correct perspective. Preparation of models could, form a topic for project work. It is essential to create interest in creative activity in students. Models are working as well as static. A working model will secure immediate attention and serve as motivation to learn. Model can be prepared with several kinds of materials like cardboard, plastic, plaster of paris, wood, clay, and thermocol etc. (See also under three Dimensional Aids)

The Secondary Education Commission, on the role of school museums observed, "Museums playa great part in the education of school children as they bring home to them much more vividly than any prosaic lectures, the discoveries of the past and the various developments that have taken place in many fields of science and technology." Again the Commission observes, "We believe it is necessary from the educational point of view to establish such museums in important centres at least wherein both ancient and modern collections will be exhibited and in some cases even demonstrations given of the actual process of development of various scientific discoveries. Nothing can impress students in the formative age so much as the actual visualising of these experiments in a graphic manner,"

Museums are made up of materials used in classroom teaching which, in many cases, are collected, classified and exhibited by students, with or without the help of a teacher. The museum activities may be an extracurricular function of the class or the school or they may be incorporated into a scientific-experimental method of teaching. The objectives of this type of museum are:

(a) to form within the school or the classroom an embryonic community dedicated to the usual occupations reflected in the school life of adults;

(b) to permit visual instruction and experimentation with actual museum specimens;

(c) to stimulate enthusiasm for study and research among both teachers and students;

(d) to stimulate interest, co-operation and participation in the cultural activities and scientific research conducted by the larger museums;

(e) to instruct students in proper scientific methods of laboratory, research and museum conservation and exhibition techniques;

(f) to form, in the absence of larger museums in the community, a nucleus from which the classroom museum can grow beyond the limits of the school to serve ultimately the community and the region as a whole.

Exhibit Programmes, Interpretation, Visual Communication: What then are some of the ways in which museums as cultural and educational centres of the community can communicate successfully with their transitory visitors of heterogeneous composition? Based on various audience-testing experiments the following media can be used to heighten the effectiveness of visual communication.

Dramatic Labels : Usually they are far too short in the museums or far too long. They actually frighten away rather than entice the average museum visitor. Experiments suggest that large letters placed at the focal point of the case or exhibit area will successfully headline the exhibit and catch the visitor's attention. Like a newspaper headline, the main label tends to direct the eye to smaller, less conspicuous letters that outline the most important points of the exhibit.

Dramatic Lighting : Light is a means of visual communication as well as an attention getter. Coloured lights that change, fade or highlight an exhibit can be used with great dramatic effect. Light can also be used to tell a story and to convey a sense of passing time. Light is particularly important in art museums.

Dramatic Utilization : Again experiments suggest that museum visitors should be given a chance to touch exhibits as well as to see them. Of course, much depends on the nature and expendability of the object involved but certain types of material-objects of wood, stone and metal and special "touch me" samples of animal skins and fabrics-can be used with great success to satisfy the visitor's urge to which while permitting a minimum of danger.

Dramatic Sound Effects : Sound, like light, can be used to heighten the dramatic effect of visual communication. For example, an Amazon rain forest exhibition can be made vastly more effective by adding the sound of tropical rain, the croaking of frogs, the chattering of monkeys, and the beat of drums. An exhibit of mediaeval art can be made more meaningful if it is accompanied by music of the same period:

Effective Use of Space : Special concepts are also important in planning visitor traffic patterns within the exhibit areas.

Pictures are very much liked by children and especially of lower classes, pictures provide an environment of 'reality'. A lesson in history can be made interesting and stimulating by showing the pictures of kings and queens, costumes and dresses, forts and weapons, monuments and tombs, etc. Similarly in a geography lesson, we can show the pictures of animals, deserts, lakes, mountains and rivers, etc., and also the various aspects of lives of people of other lands with great effect.

Following points need to be kept in view while showing pictures to the students:

1. Child's point of view should be the main criterion in the selection of pictures.
2. Pictures should be relevant to the topic.
3. As far as possible, pictures may be coloured.
4. Pictures should be accurate and of a suitable size.
5. It is desirable if the teacher himself prepares the pictures and takes help from the students.
6. Pictures should be shown in such a way that all students in the class can easily watch.
7. Too many pictures should not be displayed in one lesson.
8. After showing the picture, it should be removed from the view of the students.
9. Sufficient time should be given to see the picture.
10. Students who are good at drawing should be encouraged to draw pictures.

Gadgets of Modern Nature

The combination of a microscope and a slide projector is an instrument called micro-projector. The microscope is used to see very minute parts of objects by magnifying the same hundreds of times. The minute part usually of a plant or an animal is put on a glass slide and a magnified image formed by a combination of leuses in a microscope which can be seen by an individual through the naked eye. The micro-projector attachment consists of a projection lens; a plane mirror fixed at 45 degrees to the vertical plane and a vertical ground glass screen. It is very useful in teaching science.

Over head projector is a device that can project a chart, a diagram, a map, a table or for that matter, anything written on transparent plates, upon a screen or the white wall before students in a class. This makes teaching illuminative, illustrative and impressive. It also saves a great deal of the teacher's time used in drawing or writing. These transparencies can also be preserved by the teacher for future display while taking up the same topic.

It is very simple to prepare such transparencies. All that a teacher has to do is to draw or write, as the case may be, upon transparent plates with any dark ink with a fibre tipped pen. Any material meant for display before the class while teaching can also be typed on such transparencies using a good carbon paper. In case transparencies are to be washed out for use, washable water colour can also be used for writing on the transparencies.

With a slide projector, photographic slides can be projected on the screen or the wall before the class. Photographs of relevant matter meant for teaching in the class can be developed on celluloid slides and displayed with the help of such a projector. The teacher's lesson can also be recorded on an audio cassette and played with a tape recorder suitably synchronising with the slides by manipulating a remote control switch. Such an arrangement is called a tape-slide sequence. In case there are several slides to be shown in quick succession, the tape-slide sequence can bring as interesting an effect on the viewers as do the movie films. An ordinary slide projector has a frame containing two slits into which slides are put for focusing. They are manually and continuously replaced by other slides one after another. An improved type of a slide projector consists of a circular disc with more slits where even a hundred or more slides can be inserted in a sequential order which can be projected on the screen with the help of a remote control switch to be suitably manipulated by the teacher as he delivers the lesson.

Puppetry is one of the old and popular arts in India. The use of puppets has been very popular in China, Egypt, Greece and Japan. Puppets can serve as an effective aid to learning. They can be made to illustrate lessons in civics, geography, history and hygiene. Puppets throw a lot of light in an interesting way on the life of historical personages if they are accompanied by effective narration. There should be plenty of dancing and music in the display of puppetry. While presenting puppet programmes, the age and tastes of the pupils should be duly considered. A short puppet play is always preferable to a long play. Puppets are of three types:

(i) Hand puppets which fit in the hand like a glove and are operated from below by fingers,

(ii) Rod puppets which are operated from below the stage by a combination of rods and springs,

(iii) Marionettes or string puppets which are figures with moving limbs. These are operated from the above by means of strings.

Reprographic is a branch of technology dealing with methods of duplication or reproduction. Duplication involves making a number of identical copies of the original. Reproduction enables preparation of one or more identical copies of the original, same size or of different size in monochrome or colour. Equipment and processes, included are: duplicators, reflex printing and photography.

Record players are a means of audio playback. They are older types of hardware using records of discs for the needed playback. Four sizes of records 7", 10", 12" and 16" are in common use. There are also high speed record player with standard stylus. The record players now in use are equipped with speed changer mechanisms permitting the playing of the slower long-playing 45, 33⅓ and 16⅔ r.p.m. records played by microgrove stylus. The use of recorded pieces in education has great value in language learning, appreciation of poetry and literature and presentation of brief dramatised episodes from history, from development of musical knowledge and discrimination. Long-playing records with 20 minutes of recorded information per side provide several diverse selections inscribed on each side and are very suitable for classroom instructional purposes. The needed selection for a particular learning situation can be easily identified by the specific microgrove ring it occupies on the record. 'Talking books' for the blind also consists of recordings of essential literature for the visually handicapped. The older, manually wound spring powered gramophone's place now has been taken up by electrically powered multi-speed record players and changers with built-in amplifying unit or linked to separate amplifying units and speakers. Likewise, the older mechanical recording has given place to electrical imprinting involving greater clarity and fidelity.

A tape-recorder in its own can be very effective for classroom instruction. Pre-recorded tapes consisting of lessons by eminent teachers on any subject can be played in the class. Such instructions become impressive not only because of the novelty but also because of their being well-thought out and planned. The tape-recorder has proved to be a boon in teaching foreign languages like English. Pre-recorded tapes on English lessons can be played in the classroom to teach not only the contents of the lesson but also proper accent, pronunciation and intonation which an average English teacher very much lacks.

Pre-recorded video tapes can be played through TV in the classroom. Video films on educational topics shown through TV in the classroom have the same effect on the students as the ordinary cinematic educational films do. Video films have the added advantage over ordinary films in that the arrangement is compact and requires little space and time for manipulation. It is the most convenient of all audio-visual teaching-learning materials.

The potential advantage of video cassette lies in the fact that control of the equipment and the learning process is placed in the hands of the learner through control over the mechanics of the machine, i.e. stopping, starting, timing, reviewing and previewing and consequently the capacity to order the sequence of events, controls the rate of learning, and facilitates practice sequences.

The potential exists for providing the basis for learning a wide range of motor, intellectual and cognitive and interpersonal skills, as well as affective aspects. These are important aspects which printed materials cannot deal with adequately.

This facility could be particularly useful where distance education programmes are involved with updating skills and techniques of workers in the field. For example, new horticulture techniques can be transmitted to field workers to improve farming techniques. Mid-career retraining can also be catered for.

In some countries as a way of regionalizing a centrally produced programme, video cassette programmes are being built round the study centre concept, a location where several video machines are available to which students bring their study notes. The students run the programmes as individuals. Sometimes study centres provide for group sessions during which video cassettes are played. Unless some supplementary teaching is provided, this technique can become another version of broadcast technology.

In other countries some institutions assume that students can gain access to such equipment and make programmes which will be used on an individual basis as either supplementary learning material or integral to the teaching programme.

The problems associated with video cassettes are of two kinds: (i) cost; and (ii) production of programmes.

(i) Equipment costs cannot always be kept down by using lower quality equipment. Cheaper equipment formats do not enable technical material such as animal or plant tissue to be represented adequately or tapes to be reproduced in quantity without loss of fidelity.

(ii) Video production for educational purposes calls for new techniques different from the entertainment modes. Producers, directors, scriptwriters need to be knowledgeable about teaching and learning. Many of the old techniques of film and television will no longer be of use. For example, the very basic concept that programmes must have a beginning, a middle, and an end will no longer apply as a cassette could just as easily consist of a series of short video events which sets a problem, teaches a technique, or brings together a range of visual material to make concepts or principles clear.

Up-to-date Avenues : Three dimensional aids serve as good substitutes for the real objects. There is no doubt that an encounter with real objects serves as an unmatchable source of learning. But on account of several reasons it may not be possible to bring the real objects in the classroom. The real objects may be too large to move or store in the classroom. It may be too small to be seen for a group of students. It can be too complicated in real form to be understood. Its movements may be too slow to be studied completely. It can be too expensive to be purchased by an educational institution. Being handicapped in such situations, a teacher has to search for some good substitute for the real objects.

Models diagrams, mock-ups and specimens are the important three dimensional aids.

Models are the replicas or copies of the real objects. Models are usually of three types: solid, cross-sectional and working.

Models are concrete objects, some considerably larger than the real object. Sectional models explain clearly the structure or functions of the original. In some cases working models of the original are used where the specific function of the original is duplicated and could be explained easily.

Following are the important functions of models:

1. Models simplify reality.
2. Models concretise abstract concepts.
3. Models enable us to reduce or enlarge objects to an observable size.
4. A model provides the correct concept of an industrial unit or a bridge or a dam like, the Bhakra Dam etc.
5. A working model explains the various processes of objects and machines.
6. Preparation of models could form a topic for project work. This is very helpful to create interest in creative activity in pupils.

Cardboard, plastic, plaster of paris, wood thermocol' and metal, etc., can be used in the preparation of a model.

A mock-up refers to a specialised model or working replica of the object being depicted. In a mock-up, a certain element of the original reality is emphasised or highlighted to make it more meaningful for the purpose of instruction. While a model is a recognizable limitation of an object (though larger or smaller than the original one), a mock-up may or may not be similar in appearance. Mock-ups of aeroplanes, automobile engines, bridges, ships and tunnels, etc., may be demonstrated for explaining their structure and actual working. Mock-ups are often used in technical institutions for training purposes.

A diorama is a three dimensional scene in depth incorporating a group of modelled objects and figures in a natural setting. The diorama scene is set up on a small stage with a group of modelled objects kept on the foreground which is blended into a painted realistic background. Dioramas are very effective in the teaching of biological and social sciences.

Devices and Tools

Use of Slides : Slides are transparent pictures projected by shining light through them. The commonly used sizes of slides are 2″ x 2″ and 3¼ Slides are used on a variety of materials-glass coated or etched or clear or sensitized. These are used as very effective teaching aids.

Advantages in the projected pictures and photographs for effective teaching and learning are numerous. Slides-

- create interest and curiosity among students.
- explain the concepts very well.
- can be viewed by the entire class.
- can be shown in a semi-darkened room.
- can be used according to convenience.
- can be utilised according to the slow or quick learning needs.
- can be used according to our desired pace.

Slides are mainly of two kinds (i) handmade and (ii) photographic. Slides in series or linked together in a sequence make a film-strip or film slide or strip film. Film strip is a roll of 35 mm positive film which has sprocket holes in both sides and contains a sequence of pictures like slides.

Preparing Slides: Slides are prepared easily and with inexpensive materials. That is why, in developed countries even the primary school students prepare slides not only as a learning aid, but also as a means of self-expression. Plain, coloured or etched glass, binding tape, cellophane, coloured pencils, and coloured inks are the materials needed for producing slides. With a little artistic skill, practice and ingenuity, slides can be prepared and mounted.

Photographic slides are printed on sensitized glass on a large scale by commercial firms. The teachers and students who have never developed or printed photographs/pictures, cannot prepare photographic slides so easily. These slides are made on glass plates coated with an emulsion similar to that used for making film negatives. The plates are developed, fixed, washed and dried as are other photographic plates. After the plates are fully dried, these should be projected in a lantern or small light for examination. Then these should be mounted for making them durable.

Slides can be printed from negatives by either contact, reduction or enlargement. Since contact printing is very easy, it can very well be printed by a camera. Any negative that makes a good print can make a good lantern slide. The photographic slide is merely a positive print from a negative. Thus a dark room and ancillary photographic facilities should be made available for developing, exposing and printing the slides.

Nowadays, handmade slides are prepared by drawing/writing on the transparent films. Then the film is cut into pieces and mounted on a cardboard or plastic mount available in the market. Photographic slides can be prepared using positive films. Preplanning is necessary before preparation of slides. After selecting a topic for teaching through slides, we have to write a script. Then the filming is done to develop slides in a series of items/aspects of the topic.

The latest method of preparing slides is by using computer graphics on the colour screen and shooting the same directly from the screen. The computer provides a lot of flexibility in planning and preparing slides.

Utility of Transparencies : Overhead Projector (OHP) is an important electronic teaching aid. This machine projects an image from a transparency which is transparent. The graphic picture and message of transparencies are reflected on a screen. The teacher while teaching can use transparencies and show the graphics and message. Besides, readymade transparencies, very often the teacher can write certain important points and draw figures or pictures on glass or cellophane sheets with the help of a specific type of pen which can write various colours. The glass and cellophane can be wiped out and cleared with a cloth. Sometimes cellophane is available not in sheets, but in rolls.

As discussed earlier, transparencies are readymade or are written or drawn on by the teacher in the classroom then and there in course of teaching. Commonly available cellophanes used for transparencies are in sheets. Cellophanes are also available in rolls.

The advantages of transparencies/OHP are as follows:

(i) They serve as an attractive chalkboard/blackboard.

(ii) While using transparencies, the teacher can face the class without any difficulty.

(iii) The classroom need not be darkened for projecting transparencies.

(iv) The teacher can write or draw extemporaneously on a 10" x 10" surface of transparencies.

(v) Small objects can be shown on the machine simply by placing them on the projection stage.

(vi) The graphics and writings on transparencies can be shown to students very clearly and colourfully.

Producing Transparencies

Single Transparency: It can be prepared by writing on the cellophane sheets with the help of an OHP pen. Even graphs, figures, and diagrams can be easily shown in different colours. Generally black, blue, red and green colours are used as they are more visible on projector screen. Coloured transparency can also be used in the classroom to give variety and attraction.

Xeroxing from any printed material can be made on transparencies and magnified or reduced according to requirement. Tracing can be done on transparency from the original material.

Roll Transparency: Besides single transparency, we can use roll of trar.sparency on which writings and pictures can be made in a sequence and can be projected on OHP in classroom while the teacher would be explaining/narrating/demonstrating.

The roll transparency can be moved backward forward as required.

Whenever it is felt that something is to be added or shown alongwith the previous writing/graphics, we can make overlays by placing the addition on the OHP stage. Thus with ingenuity and dexterity, we can bring about effectiveness in the use of transparencies.

Cartoon's Utility

A cartoon is a novel way of using pictures or symbols or bold exaggerations for presenting a message or a point of view concerning a personality, news, situations or events. At present, even in schools/colleges, cartoons are profitably used as a useful teaching aid for interpreting or highlighting some social, political, economic, literary and scientific data. Cartoon is more attention drawing and in a small space, gives a lot of imagination, particularly on the current happenings. Very often cartoon is blended with humour and satire.

Cartoons are of different types and are prepared/used with imagination and creativity. These are used more and more in newspapers and magazines for focusing attention of the public on certain social, political, economic and other problems and issues. Hence the types of cartoons can be innumerable.

Educational uses of cartoons are many due to their universal appeal irrespective of age, sex and cultural differences. The main advantages of cartoons are as follows:

(i) These are very good attention-capturing devices and motivate the students.

(ii) These can reveal the truth or reality about the people, events and incidents in an interesting way.

(iii) These are useful in modifying behaviour and developing positive attitude, interests and character of learners.

(iv) These are capable of creating humour and interest among the viewers and explaining various concepts.

(v) These are helpful for providing opportunity for self-expression and creativity among children.

Making Cartoons: Cartoons as useful teaching aids can provide information and knowledge about various subjects and current issues in an interesting way. Before preparing cartoons, it is essential to locate suitable topics and pictures from newspapers, magazines, etc. But the teacher himself should prepare cartoons according to the class room needs. Students need be involved in the process of preparation in order to maximise learning experiences.

The material for cartoons should be selected by the teacher who should keep the following points in view:

(i) It should be suitable to the age, class and experience, level of students.

(ii) The writing and graphics used in the cartoon should be meaningful and intelligible to them.

(iii) Cartoons should be of adequate size, so that the details can be made visible to the entire class.

(iv) The symbols used in the cartoon should be clear and understandable.

(v) Cartoons need to be both amusing and instructive.

(vi) Students must be actively involved in the process of preparing cartoons.

(vii) Cartoons should be prepared according to the educational objectives and background of students.

Teaching aids are now available in a wide variety and novelty ranging from traditional graphics to electronic materials and media. With a view to making the teaching-learning process more interesting and effective, it is necessary to select suitable teaching aids suitable to the instructional objectives and students' needs as well as their background. It is, however, desirable that besides commercially prepared readymade materials, students and teachers should join hands in preparing suitable aids according to their interests, expertise and resources available. If learners participate in preparing the teaching aids, their involvement results in enhancing their knowledge and skills. It also makes understanding enjoyable and effective.

For those men and women who take to the vocation of teaching, it has no promise of wealth and fame, but they to whom it is dear for its own sake are among the nobility of mankind. As Henry Von Dyke has said about teachers and teaching "Ah! there you have the worst paid and the best rewarded of vocations. Do not enter it unless you love it. I sing the praise of the unknown teacher, king of himself and leader of the mankind." This, we may say, is the philosophical meaning of teaching, but is very relevant and meaningful also.

Of course, we cannot measure the significance of teaching by mercenary standards, but in terms of emotional and psychological satisfaction. Teaching is not a mechanical process of transmitting knowledge and information from the teacher to the students. It is not a monologue but a dialogue. In the dialogue one may be vocal and another not so vocal, but can give vent to his feeling in the form of queries through facial expressions and some sounds of exclamation or irritation.

Teaching is regarded as an art. Like a piece of music or painting, it touches the heart, brightens the mind and gives pleasure to everybody. It has to inspire and motivate the learner to go ahead on the road of exploration and discovery, to open new vistas and to reach new horizons. But traditionally teaching is equated with telling. The old concept of teaching as giving of information has been discarded by the modern psychologists. Now the educationists feel that teaching is to motivate the student to learn and acquire the desired knowledge, skills and also desirable ways of living in the society. The main objective of teaching is to enable the pupil to respond to his environment effectively.

Teaching, to be precise, is a process of communication for achieving certain objectives. These objectives, of course, should be desirable and specific to various groups of learners. Kulkarni (1986) has therefore defined teaching as " the process wherein conditions are deliberately created (environment organised) to enable a specified learner (or a group of learners) to behave in a specified manner to perform or to experience certain desired objectives." Teaching thus aims at helping learners to learn or change their behaviour in a relatively permanent manner and involves arrangement of situations for facilitating learning.

The important general maxims of teaching are: it should proceed from the known to unknown, from analysis to synthesis, from simple to complex, from whole to part, from concrete to abstract, from particular to the general, from empirical to rational, from psychological to logical, and so on. Good teaching recognises individual differences among students; it should be interesting and need based. It should be challenging as well as sympathetic to the learner. It ought to promote productivity and self-study. Teachers should take the social and psychological background of pupils into account. Good teaching should be dynamic and well-planned. Teachers in order to make their teaching effective need to acquaint themselves with curriculum, school routine, standard of the class and if possible, brief bio-data of students. Successful teachers should project themselves as sympathetic and sincere, warm and friendly persons to their pupils.

Concept of Learning and Teaching : In Layman's language, living is learning. As we grow, we learn, we are apt to learn than any other living beings. We adjust with our environment better than any other being. We influence our environment and the environment also influences our living styles. The interaction between the living being and environment results in the change of behaviour and such change is learning.

That is why, learning is called the modification of behaviour. It implies change in knowledge, understanding, skills, interests, habits, attitudes, and so on. Learning thus consists of all changes in thinking, feeling and doing in course of life. The human child the most helpless of all creatures and his helplessness is again longer than that of any other living being.

It is said that such helplessness of the human child gives a greater scope for learning. The world is full of problems. The human being faces problems in his everyday life. But he tries to solve them with his own knowledge, insight, reasoning, skills and techniques of adjustment. Human life is thus a continuous process of learning a series of experiences gained through living.

Skinner has therefore defined learning as " process of progressive behaviour adaptations. Crow & Crow has considered learning as "the acquisition of habits, knowledge and attitude." According to Munn learning is "more or less permanent incremental modification of behaviour which results from activity, special training of observations." Mc Connel has precisely defined learning as "the modification of behaviour through experience."

Kulkarni (1986) has summed up all these elements of learning in his definition. According to him learning means "relatively permanent change in behaviour which occurs as a result of experience or practice. On the whole, learning can be defined as the process of effecting changes in behaviour that brings about improvement in our relations with environment. Learning is rightly called the pivotal issue in education. The main aim of education is to effect desired changes in the behaviour of students. Learning is thus a natural outcome of the individual as attempts to meet his basic and normal needs.

The learner cannot afford to be passive in the process. He has to interact with his environment. Learning is a complex process by which an organism faces new problems, acquires new knowledge, develops new mode of behaviour which tends to persist and create a general behaviour pattern of organism in more or less degree. This brings about changes in behaviour-in doing, expressing one's thoughts, feelings and attitudes called learning.

As regards its main characteristics, learning is growth through experience; it is an adjustment to the environment; it is a synthesis of old and new expressions; it is purposeful and intelligent; it is both individual and social; it effects conduct of the learner. There is a difference in adult learning and child learning. For instance the adult learns through concentration of mind on essential and useful rejecting the useless. Children on the other hand, learn through all senses in a natural and active way. The vastness of adults experience may help or hinder their learning, whereas children's learning is immensely promoted due to their strong spirit of curiosity, inquisitiveness and free and frank mind towards the outside world. Therefore children should not be forced to learn in adult ways and methods with narrow utilitarian objectives

Prior to the last century teaching was considered as a rigid, formal and stereotyped process of transmitting knowledge and figures. Education was taken as a bipolar process with teachers at the giving end and students at the receiving end. Teachers were deemed to be the only source of knowledge, may be through manuscripts or printed materials. Schools were the knowledge shops and teachers are the information managers or vendors. Methods of teaching were logical, sequential and routine devoid of proper attention to the psychological needs and conditions of learners-their interests, curiosity, freedom and flexibility. Emphasis was laid on rigid discipline, blind memorization and hard reinforcement. Verbalism was enforced and no audio-visual aids or materials were utilised in the field of education.

The learner was always kept at the receiving end and was considered as an empty vessel to be filled with knowledge and information, facts and figures. At the advent of the 20th century, a child is considered a tender plant whose growth is facilitated by the teacher as a gardener. The child is taught according to his abilities, attitude, interest and aptitude. He is helped to learn and to grow. Cultivate the growing child or give him intellectual exercises or train him in the horizontal sense of directing or guiding his growth. Children are motivated to search and experiment, to gather facts and information, They learn by doing and learn how to learn both individually and in groups. Various media and materials are used for making learning more interesting and effective.

Recently, learning has assumed more importance than teaching. It has been rightly observed by the International Commission on the Development of Education. (1972, p. 150) that there has been a change in the learning process which is tending to displace the teaching process. New theories of learning highlight the principle of contiguity and the importance of needs and motivation, of choice of content of the hierarchic nature of learning the inter-relationship between educational content and environment, etc. Multimedia systems have to now acquire more significance, and educational technology has been popularly used for effectiveness.

Now stress is on the mathetic principles. Of learning rather than on the traditional pedagogic principles of teaching. Mathetics, the science of the pupil's behaviour, has recently gained more importance than pedagogy, the science of the teacher's behaviour. The term "Mathetics" is derived from the Greek root signifying the learner and the process of learning is given high priority. The mathetic principle is now used for designing various programmes for individual learning by pupils. And pedagogy has been replaced by mathetics and teaching by learning.

Teacher education aims at the improvement of the quality and efficiency of teaching. This objective is not properly realised in our country due to so many factors. Absence of adequate feedback devices in our teacher education system is felt to be the greatest shortcoming in the way of modifying as well as improving teacher behaviour. A number of techniques have been developed and introduced during the last decade for providing feedback and modification of teacher behaviour. Simulated Social Skill Training (SSST) is one of these techniques and like a few others it has been tried out as an innovation in teacher education for providing suitable feedback and modifying teaching skills.

The pioneering effort in the development of this technique is attributed to the State University Research Foundations, Columbia, USA where originally a taxonomy of teacher behaviour was developed. The SSST techniques include four dimensions-sources, direction, function and sign. In fact, this technique is utilised for training in role-perception and role-playing.

The fundamental assumption underlying this technique is that there are certain patterns of teaching behaviour which are essential for effective teaching. It is also assumed that these patterns can be identified and described in certain behavioural outcomes. Like any other skill they can be practised, and used in teaching appropriately and effectively. A particular pattern of teacher behaviour can be called a social skill for the training purpose and can be identified and practised intrusively for its acquisition. This will facilitate modification of behaviour for professional growth.

Simulated Social Skill Training has been the basis of role-playing, socio-drama and psycho-drama. The general objective is to place a person in a situation which provides spontaneous interaction to enable him to practise a certain pattern of behaviour. The person who gets the training is called the actor, the individuals providing the spontaneous environment are called foils and one or two supervisors recording behaviour for professional or maintaining notes for later evaluation are known as supervisors.

The objectives of simulation exercise are as follows:

(i) Modifying student behaviour,

(ii) Motivating learners,

(iii) Bringing about changes in attitudes,

(iv) Understanding one's role properly,

(v) Realising other's role and responsibilities,

(vi) Helping students to assume emerging roles,

(vii) Discussing crucial social problems and generating awareness.

Simulation exercises promote free expressions and participation in situations that are very close to reality without involving them in the actual circumstances. The participants are encouraged to understand real problems and freely think and decide themselves for improving their conditions-social, psychological, educational, and so on.

The following procedure is usually followed for SSST exercise:

1. Each trainee in the group may be designated as a lecturer and all have to be prepared for changing their roles. That is, everybody must have a chance to play the role of an actor, a foil and an observer.
2. Each skill may be discussed and practical topics be suggested for suiting the skills. One topic may be selected for the first exercise and additional topics for other exercises. Each trainee should select a topic convenient to him for playing the role of an actor.
3. A schedule may be drawn up as to who will start teaching, who will introduce the actor and who will stop the interaction and when they should be stopped.
4. Prior decision may be taken on the procedure of evaluation, on the kind of data for recording and how best the data and views can be presented to actor.
5. The first practice session may be conducted and the actor be provided with feedback on his performance. If necessary, the procedure may be changed for the second session for improving the training procedure.
6. The procedure may be modified and topic be changed so that each actor takes it as a challenge and interest is sustained. Thus, the task should neither be too easy nor too difficult.

SSST exercise, in order to be successful, requires the following abilities of the trainees:

1. The ability to ask open or closed questions and to know when each is appropriate in classroom teaching.
2. The ability to ask a question which lifts the current level of abstraction or a question which lowers it and the ability to ask a series of questions which gradually lifts or lowers the level of abstractions.
3. The ability to ask questions in which the concept and logical connectives have previously been expressed by pupils.
4. The ability to summarise what pupils have said and then end by asking a question which moves the discussion into the next step in logical sequence of problem-solving.
5. The ability, both to demonstrate and to explain the rates of logic in classroom discourse, including helping to maintain consistency in the meaning of words, and helping to distinguish matters of fact, opinion and value.

Devices' Role

Role-playing refers to special kinds of memorised, often impromptu, dramatisation put on by a group of students. This may be planned and practised or may be spontaneous outgrowth of the study of some important problem in class. Socio-drama and psycho-drama are also taken as role-playing. They are used to probe into deeply rooted prejudices and behaviour patterns which are difficult to change. Socio-drama relates to social problems whereas psycho-drama is used as a device to provide scope for change of behaviour and reception of suggestions for doing better.

In short, role-playing aims at the following:

(a) Illustrating interpersonal problems;
(b) Adopting simulation techniques to solve problems;
(c) Developing insight into personal attitudes, values and behaviours;
(d) Understanding adequate awareness about social and psychological issues;
(e) Understanding feelings and opinions of others;

(f) Developing interpersonal communication skills; and

(g) Enabling even the shy and introverts to express their views.

Role-playing comes naturally to children. Without rehearsals or coaching they assume various roles through which they project themselves into adult experiences. It is an excellent medium for conveying new information or practising a skill. It can integrate with other learning techniques and materials.

On the whole, the important steps in organising the role-playing are as follows:

1. Identifying a suitable problem situation;
2. Selecting the pupils for playing the roles;
3. Assigning roles to the students;
4. Orienting the students to the techniques-identifying with characters, understanding the issues, playing the characters, etc.;
5. Allowing time for preparation;
6. Playing the roles as actual characters;
7. Encouraging peers to express their views on the role-playing;
8. Giving remarks and summing up by the teacher.

The most effective role-playing situations are those which grow out of problems concerned with people, their actions and their beliefs. Role-playing skills and the disposition of students/ trainees to participate in such an activity are improved by good playing and organisation. The role-playing techniques prove successful with older children and adults as well as with young children.

Through these they get rid of shyness and develop social poise, ease and smartness. In order to bring about adequate solutions to social problems and psychological problems, sociologists and psychologists respectively adopt role-playing techniques like socio-drama and psycho-drama. Teachers also find them as effective devices for teaching attitudes and interests to children most naturally and interestingly.

The advantages of role-playing may be summed up as follows:

(i) Generating awareness and sensitising the students to learning problems;

(ii) Minimising shyness and inhibitions through role-playing;

(iii) Gaining insight into behaviour patterns;

(iv) Helping students in adjustments;

(v) Giving scope for free expression of feelings.

Role-playing does not prove successful on account of the following:

(a) Shy and introvert students do not play the roles properly and spontaneously;

(b) They cannot articulate well and give vent to their feelings and views;

(c) The technique is found to be a time-consuming and wasteful exercise if roles are not played realistically.

Teachers can cleverly find out solutions to current problems and gain insight into the real feelings and opinions of the students who are likely to play their future roles in the present simulated situations.

The Training Group is briefly called T Group and is used as an exercise in human/social relations. Participants in this Training Group get the opportunity not only to share their perceptions of each others behaviour, but also to get an insight into their own behaviour. This helps in bringing about an awareness which provides suitable feedback for modification of behaviour.

The Working : Training Group consists of eight to twelve trainees and one or two experienced trainers. No agenda is fixed nor any leader is appointed for conducting a meeting/discussion which is extended over 2 or 3 hours. This may be held once or twice a week.

Discussion will be initiated on a topic by a trainer. Some trainees may express dissatisfaction with the set up and some may find fault with the trainers. Thus in the initial meetings conflict and frustration increase to a great extent.

The trainees are however, encouraged to give bent to their feelings. In subsequent meetings they become sober, honest, frank and introspective. The trainer will give necessary guidance through suggestions and clarifications. He will help the group to come to effective interaction.

The Training Group Technique enables the experienced teacher to improve his behaviour and the pupil teacher to improve his skills and abilities as a good teacher. The training group gives opportunities to live through enquiry in order to improve one's own behaviour and to get perception of the group behaviour. This technique has the justification for creating efficient means of continued self-assessment and adequate readiness in teacher education. It provides a context of a human relations programme to make the teacher more receptive and more sensitive to the problem of social interaction. Through proper feedback devices developed through this training, the effectiveness of teaching programmes and the behaviour or a teacher are improved.

8

Teaching Devices

Developments in teaching and learning materials reflect wider societal and technological advances. The latter half of the twentieth century has witnessed a massive expansion in technological advancements that began cautiously with radio and television and which, via language laboratories and calculators, have now developed into the World Wide Web and the information superhighway. These technological wonders have been adopted by teachers in classrooms and lecture halls with the aim of enhancing the learning experience. Technological teaching and learning aids have assumed greater significance in recent years as one of the major developments that have dominated higher education teaching in the 1990s. We explore the perceptions of computer-assisted learning materials (CAL) from two perspectives: the students who attend the courses; and the tutors who design and teach the courses.

Diverse Techniques

The teaching and learning materials evaluated form part of a suite of computer-aided learning materials known as GeotechniCAL. These have been developed as materials to support the teaching of geotechnical subjects within the syllabus of undergraduate degrees in Civil Engineering, and were funded through the UK Higher Education Funding Councils under the auspices of the Teaching and Learning Technology Programme (TLTP).

The GeotechniCAL project comprises five strands, the primary developers are the Universities of Durham, Glasgow, Portsmouth, South Bank and West of England. Details of each of the strands in the GeotechniCAL project can be found on the World Wide Web at http://CL24.uwe.ac.uk/geocal. Other universities (twenty-two in all) have been involved in small amounts of authoring and in the provision of feedback and formal evaluation of the materials.

This article considers the evaluations of two of these strands carried out at Durham University. The first study relates to evaluation of the ConFound package developed at Durham University. Students at Durham University were involved in the formative evaluation of this package. The second study relates to the Site Investigation package developed by South Bank and Portsmouth Universities. Again this was evaluated by Durham students but at a later stage in the development, near the end of the project.

It is important that the evaluation process is not viewed as a one-off exercise at the end of the project but as a continuing process and an integrative element of development, with this in mind, two evaluations were undertaken. Formative evaluations of the Geotechnical materials were carried out at an interim stage to provide feedback to the developers. Summative evaluations were carried out at the end of the project to identify whether the product was seen to be of direct use to users. Both students and tutors participated in the formative and summative evaluations.

Technique of Measurement

Students are increasingly familiar with mechanisms for course monitoring, evaluations are a means of providing feedback to institutions, course providers and external auditing bodies, and hence students are generally amenable to participating in evaluation processes.

Rather than using whole classes of students as evaluators it can sometimes be more useful to select a small representative group who can provide more detailed feedback. This is particularly true at the stage of formative evaluation when specific feedback to the developers is needed to help them to improve their product. The establishment of a core group of evaluators is particularly important if there are several pieces of software to be compared and evaluated. This core group can also identify whether changes that have been made as a result of previous feedback have been beneficial.

Although it is not always easy to arrange, it was felt important that the student evaluations should be carried out by an independent evaluation coordinator who was unknown to the students. This is one way in which the evaluation of the materials can be separated from other elements such as the course(s), the tutor(s), the assessment of the student's personal knowledge of the subject and of their general progress. That is not to suggest that these are equally important elements of learning that need to be monitored and evaluated, but they are different and to combine them with the evaluation of the CAL materials may cause confusion. The independent evaluation had the additional advantage of allowing students to make critical observations about the learning materials, and to offer insights that they may have felt impeded in offering to known tutors. In this case study, the first author was able to fulfil the role of independent evaluation coordinator.

For the interim evaluations of the ConFound package at Durham University a core group of eight student evaluators was established. Of the eight students, there were three females and five males. They represented two sub-groups, one group that described themselves as comparatively experienced software users and the other that described themselves as less experienced. Neither group, however, were novices in the use of computers.

The students were identified by numbers (not names) to ensure anonymity. It was considered important to protect identities and to maintain the goodwill of the group so that they could be called upon again, at a later stage, to evaluate this and other pieces of software during the course of the GeotechniCAL project. Not identifying the students by name also stressed that the evaluation exercise was in no way connected with any assessment of their personal knowledge of the subject or of their general progress.

The GeotechniCAL initiative was outlined to the student

evaluators. Their role and the reasons that lay behind the various aspects of the evaluation were explained and discussed. This provided the group, and individuals within the group, with the opportunity to ask questions for clarification of particular points and helped to forge group identity.

A pre-test of the subject knowledge that the software aims to teach was carried out, using a multiple choice questions test. The Durham test comprised nine multiple choice questions. After completing the test the students were then given a further copy of the test, to complete while using the software. This helped the students and the teachers to assess the subject knowledge content of the software under evaluation.

Computer's Utility

The students were given the opportunity to use the software. The learning objective set was to obtain the knowledge required to resist the test. This gave a focus to their use of the software. The students were allowed to spend as long as they wanted using the software, However, to avoid demotivation, the test was designed so that it was feasible to obtain the necessary information in a session lasting approximately one hour. In fact, students chose to spend between 60 and 90 minutes with the software.

Technique of Assessment

The students were asked to complete the standard evaluation form developed for use within the GeotechniCAL project.

The evaluation questionnaire was designed to elicit both quantitative and qualitative information. It is based on an earlier questionnaire produced by Dr. Les Davison, coordinator of the GeotechniCAL project. The form used at Durham invites responses on a four point scale to 30 statements grouped under the headings:

- Background (information about the learner);
- Documentation (the documentation supporting the software);
- Content (the level of detail of the subject knowledge of the topic);
- Usability;

- Presentation (of the material);
- General (other general aspects).

The reverse side of the form provides opportunities for qualitative responses under the headings: I particularly liked; I did not like; My suggestions for improvement; and Any other comments.

A semi-structured interview format was used R group interviews. They typically lasted between 21 and 30 minutes. The interviews were recorded using an audio-tape recorder. The following headings were used to guide the discussion:

- For how long did you use the software ?
- Would you like a teacher/technician present when you use this software ?
- Do you think other members of your course would use this software?
- What did you particularly like about the software?
- Can you make suggestions for improvement?
- Are there features you would like to have included?
- How easy was it to use this software? What precise difficulties did you have?
- Could you understand all of the questions in the questionnaires?
- How helpful was the supporting documentation?
- What other documentation would you have liked?
- Would you prefer to use software, read a book/do library work or attend a lecture?

These questions were not asked in any particular order. It was considered important to provide some feedback to the evaluation group, as quickly as possible. Feedback helps to sustain interest and motivation and ensure continued involvement in the project. At the time of the follow-up interview the students were provided with a set of the correct answers alongside which they could compare their own responses on the subject knowledge multiple choice test. They were also sent a copy of the evaluation report.

The process of summative evaluation followed a different

pattern. After each session using the GeotechniCAL software the student evaluators were interviewed in a group. These follow-up interviews provide a very valuable enhancement to the information gathered from the questionnaires. In discussion some students felt able to provide more specific examples of the points they made in the written feedback. Others took the opportunity to make comments and suggestions that they did not wish to commit to paper. There was also the intellectual stimulation of ideas that a group discussion precipitates. The ideas generated in this way would have been lost if students had been confined to responding to questionnaires and written responses individually.

This section describes an evaluation of the Site Investigation module within the GeotechniCAL suite. The module was evaluated at Durham University with a combined group of final year MEng students following civil engineering options and MSc students following courses in Engineering Geology and Geo-Environmental Engineering. The group consisted of 5 females and 40 males.

Site Investigation is a topic which is taught jointly to the MEng and MSc courses at Durham University.

This would normally have been delivered as a 19 hour lecture course. On this occasion, a three hour supervised CAL session was arranged in place of three hours of lectures. Prior to the session the students had received only one lecture as a basic introduction to the topic. No introduction to the CAL materials was given in the lecture. Instructions to the students at the start of the CAL session were kept to a minimum; they were only instructed which icon to click on. They were then told to work through the tutorial materials until they felt sufficiently confident to attempt the game element of the package. No paper-based documentation was provided, but a lecturer and a demonstrator were on hand throughout the session to respond to student queries. The students were asked to complete the standard evaluation form developed for use within the GeotechniCAL project. Forty-two of the 45 students returned evaluation forms at the end of the CAL session.

Details of the outcomes of the evaluation have been reported by Thompson and Toll. The majority of the students were very positive about the package, preferred it to alternative forms of learning and indicated a clear willingness to spend more time using it. They did identify the need for more guidance and reported that they found the quantity of information difficult to assimilate. However they liked the pictures and video clips; the interactive nature of the software; the humour the 'ease of use and the simulation of a 'real life' situation.

The results of the evaluation were fed back to the student group in a subsequent lecture. Since the evaluation had been so positive, and the majority of students had identified a willingness to spend more time with the package, the option was put to the students that a further three hour CAL session could be arranged in place of three lecture hours. The students were asked to vote for another CAL session with a show of hands. Perhaps surprisingly in view of the comments made in the evaluations, not one student voted in favour of this option. When asked to vote against, 37 of the 45 students raised their hands. Therefore, although they liked the software, found it more interesting than lectures and wanted to spend more time using it, the students clearly did not want it to replace lectures. From the comments on the evaluation forms it was clear they would be prepared to use the software in their own time, or in parallel with the lectures. They felt that conventional lectures provided them with a better means to achieve their main aim of acquiring a set of structured notes for revision purposes.

It has already been noted that twenty-two universities were involved in the GeotechniCAL project, although only five were the primary developers. Tutors from universities other than the developers were involved in the evaluations. In many ways these can be seen as untypical examples of tutors who teach in engineering departments because their involvement in the project indicated a commitment to the use and development of CAL materials. However, they represented an expert view and bad not been closely involved in the development. This group comprised old and new universities, with students from diverse backgrounds on a range of undergraduate and postgraduate courses, including BSc/BEng, MEng and MSc courses.

At the formative evaluation stages of the ConFound package, two tutors were sent copies of the software and a tutor questio-nnaire. They were asked to complete the questionnaire and/or to provide comments on the software in free format based on their own perceptions of the software. Their comments generally covered half to one A4 page.

At the summative stage, the tutors were asked to provide more detailed feedback on the software after having used it with a group of students. They were asked to comment on their own perceptions and also how successful they felt the software had been when used with students. They were again sent the tutor questionnaire to complete, but were also asked to provide an additional detailed report. The tutor evaluators used the headings on the questionnaire (Documentation, Content, Usability, Presentation, Potential uses) as sub-headings in their reports. These were typically 6 pages in length.

Defined Tools

The Concept of Tools : Fixing devices in teaching are those devices that help in fixing the knowledge and understanding in the mind of the child, i.e. that help in making durable impressions and strengthening the hold of the child over the subject-matter. It is our common experience that children often do not take first impression and if they do, they usually lose it shortly. It must be borne in mind by the teachers that the minds of the students are not like stone, to be engraved. On the other hand, their minds are like wax to be moulded and then hardened. Fixing devices in teaching first mould and then harden the minds of the students-first create impressions and then make these impressions durable through practice or repetition. The law of practice and repetition is the basis of fixing devices. It is undoubtedly true that a reasonable amount of practice makes one perfect. Fixing devices will not allow the first impressions to disappear. They will improve the grasp of the students over the subject-matter taught to them.

Following are the chief fixing devices:

1. Drill
2. Review
3. Questioning
4. Describing Outstanding Problems

Drill implies practice with understanding and with a clear idea of objectives involved in drill. Drill, if not done in a balanced way, can be abused and misused. It should not be regarded as a mere repetition of an act to attain proficiency or perfection in a performance, irrespective of the needs and interests of the students. Drill is not a mere mechanical repetition of a lesson or a part of a lesson. Drill is helpful in reading, spelling and pronunciation in languages, learning tables in arithmetic, developing skill in handwriting and remembering dates and facts in social studies and principles and rules in natural sciences.

Effective drill is not only helpful in developing knowledge and skills, but also it is a means of developing and maintaining good-habits when they are once established. Intelligent drill is always effective and purposeful and unintelligent drill is purposeless and wasteful besides being boring and monotonous. As Yoakam and Simpson have observed, "Drill is a serious work-activity which has for its purpose the perfection of a skill or the strengthening of association to make them more permanent." This purpose could be achieved only with intelligent drill.

1. The students should be well acquainted with the objective of the drill.
2. The students should understand the material which they are to repeat.
3. The material to be memorised or drilled should belong to the 'whole' of which it is a part.
4. Drill should be well-organised. Drill exercises should be short and distributed over a period of time.
5. The student who is put on drill exercises should be oriented to the process of practising or drill from the very beginning.
6. Drill exercises should be graded. To start with, we can put the student on easy exercises and gradually on difficult ones.
7. The material to be drilled, or memorised, should be meaningful.
8. Drill work should be constantly supervised by the teacher so that good responses are secured from the very beginning.
9. Student's attention should be centred on definite improvement.

10. Drill should be treated as an individual affair and it is a wrong practice to ask the entire class to undertake all types of drill work, unless absolutely necessary.
11. Drill should be varied and it may take different forms so as to avoid monotony.

Practical Application

Meaning and Significance : Review is a 'retrospective view' of what has been learned or experienced. According to the literal meaning it means to 'view again'. In the words of Bossing, "The term review connotes not a mere repetition of facts to fix them more firmly in mind, but rather a new view of these facts in a different setting that-results in new understandings, changed attitudes, or different behaviour patterns." According to Rusk, "Review means getting a new view or renewal of an old view to assure a better view or grasp of relationships studied."

Dr. Yoakam and Simpson think, "the review involves a recall for purposes of renewing the learning already passed and of, carrying it on to mastery, his the reorganisation and integration of experiences," H.N. Rivilin regards review as, "deepening the students insight into the problem.....increasing his appreciation of its ramifications." Review must recall essential facts and appraisals of segments of experience in a final summary that actually involves a new view and a new understanding and provides a basis for changed behaviour.

A good review involves a new way of handling the instructional raptorial and instructional process and as such is very helpful in stimulating children's interest. Reviews can be very dull affairs they are conducted as drill by merely repeating materials over and in exactly the same way each time. A variety of forms of review should be used to make a review interesting. Review may be conducted by preparing charts, graphs, tables and introducing games and quiz etc.

Purposes of Review : Following are the purposes of review:

1. Fixing in mind activities or materials learned.
2. Organising the materials and experiences into larger units for understanding.

3. Enabling the students to gain perspective.
4. Providing for desirable expansion and supplementation of materials and experience.
5. Providing an apperceptive basis for future study.
6. Diagnosing student weakness in preparation and understanding.
7. Diagnosing teacher weakness.
8. Creating new interest in old materials.

Forms of Reviews : Some of the important forms of review are as under:

(a) The daily lesson review.
(b) Topical review.
(c) Review by answering questions and making questions or co-operative review.
(d) Review by making a chart, graph, model, a statistical table, map, diagram, picture, etc.
(e) Review by application.

Daily Lesson Review : At the beginning of the period, the teachers would do well to devote a few minutes to review what has been already covered previously. The previous lesson may be summarised, 'Recapitulatory' type of questions, may be asked.

Topical Review : This implies the review of the topic already covered. Take for instance the Gupta period. After covering all the rulers of the dynasty, a few lessons may be devoted to the review of the whole dynasty.

Co-operative Review : Questions and answers both by the teacher and students can serve the purpose of review when the topic is finished.

Review by Making Charts, Models, etc : The teacher may use black-board for this purpose and draw diagrams or tables etc., to give the salient points of the lesson in an interesting manner. Students can also be asked to do all those activities in the class.

Review by Application : Practical application is also used in the conduct of reviews. The students may be asked to apply the knowledge gained to new situations.

Review Activities

(a) Noting the chapter and paragraph headings in books.

(b) Studying the summaries of sections, chapters and parts of books.

(c) Underlying facts in paragraphs.

(d) Making marginal notes in the book.

(e) Reading a few of the selected references.

(f) Making a bibliography.

(g) Paraphrasing poetry.

(h) Making out sets of test questions.'

(i) Making a collection of articles, objects, etc.

(j) Writing out observations.

(k) Reciting.

(l) Making a chart.

(m) Making a graph.

(n) Making a statistical table.

(o) Making an outline map.

The Comparison

Area	*Drill*	*Review*
1. Aim	Development of skill	Longer retention and greater thorughness
2. Method	Exact repetition of the material	Presentation of the material in different forms.
3. Nature of recall	Recall of every detail	Recall of only salient points
4. Appeal	Mechanical association and therefore memorisation	Logical association and therefore involvement of thinking
5. Spirit	Dullness	Interesting, hence sustenance of interest.

The Guidelines

1. More essential points should be emphasised in review and minor details disregarded.
2. Usually that subject-matter should be reviewed in which the students are weak.
3. Exercise in the text-book may be used for review.
4. There should be reviews at short and long intervals.
5. Review to be effective should organise previous knowledge.

The Assessment

Significance of Questioning : It is well said about the importance of questioning:

"I keep six honest serving men,

They taught me all I know,

There names are what and why and when,

And how and where and who."

Significance of Questioning : The art of questioning is the most potent weapon in the educational armoury of the teacher. "Good questions", writes F. Theodore Struck, "by their very nature, are educative, and they have a very prominent place in all kinds of learning." Questioning plays an indispensable part in 'learning', 'teaching', and 'testing'. If used in the right way, at the proper time, questions lead to new realms of understanding; they serve as means of organizing knowledge, or correlating the results of educative experiences; of tying together units of learning; and of integrating personality. One who questions faultlessly teaches effectively, is not without meaning. Salmon holds that a bad questioner is a bad teacher; he may be a good lecturer. In the words of Ryburn, "It is not exaggeration to say that the success of a teacher in any particular lesson, and in teaching in general, depends upon his ability to question well." According to Raymont, "The acquisition of a good style of questioning may be laid down definitely as one of the essential ambitions of a young teacher."

Purpose of Questions

1. To test the previous knowledge of the students.

2. To enable them to recall something.
3. To enable them to recognise something.
4. To enable them to think over something.
5. To enable them to reason about something.
6. To elicit something from students.
7. To stimulate interest and effort on the part of students.
8. To keep the children mentally alert.
9. To promote initiative and originality.
10. To stimulate the curiosity of the students.
11. To ascertain whether they are following the lesson or not.
12. To link new knowledge with old.
13. To revise the lesson and thus fix the facts in the minds of the students.
14. To secure the cooperation of the students.
15. To diagnose the weak points of students.
16. To formulate general rules.
17. To synthesise.

These questions are generally asked at the beginning of the lesson. These serve the following objectives:

(i) Test the previous knowledge of the students.
(ii) Link the new knowledge with the already learnt knowledge.
(iii) Motivate the child and arouse his curiosity.

These questions enable the teacher to test the readiness of the students' mind and their entering behaviour. Questioning at this stage enables the teacher to follow the maximum 'From known to the unknown'.

Questions should be relevant to the topic. The number of questions should be very small, say three or four.

Skills in Developing Questions : These questions are said to be the backbone of the lesson. They are used:

(i) to develop a particular line of thought;
(ii) to lead pupils to discover facts for themselves;

(iii) to formulate new generalizations in an inductive way;

(iv) to focus attention on important points;

(v) to develop knowledge step by step;

(vi) to enable the students to use their powers of observation, of comparison and concentration;

(vii) to break the narrative in order to ensure that the class is following; and

(viii) to make the inattentive students attentive ones.

A great skill is required on the part of the teacher to ask developing questions. The teacher has to lead the students to think and discover facts for themselves. While narrating a story, the teacher should not ask questions.

Recapitulatory Questions : Such questions are generally put at the end of a lesson or at the end of each section of the lesson. Such questions serve two purposes:

1. To enable the teacher to know if the children have picked up the ideas he wanted them to learn.
2. To serve the purpose of revision and to give a good opportunity of practice.

Skills in Evaluating or Testing Questions : These questions relate to periodic internal as well as external evaluation. Types of Questions

Comparison or Contrast : Example: What is the difference between wealth and capital?

Decision for or Against : Example: Do you consider it correct to call Chandragupta Maurya as the first Emperor in India?

Application in New Situations : Example: Suggest measures to remove illiteracy in your village or town.

Classification : Example: Are the following free goods or economic goods-air, sun-shine, machinery, gold, food?

Relationship between Cause and Effect : Example: What is the relation between population and economic prosperity?

Example or Illustration Example : Describe cases when prices rise with the decrease in the supply of some commodities.

Statement of Aim : Example : Why is the author interested in the study of problem children?

Criticism : Example: Do you think Ashok was justified in following the policy of 'Non-violence'? Elucidate.

Inference : Example : From the data given, which place do you consider to be more hotter?

Discussion : Example : Discuss the most important proposals for bringing down the prices.

Definition : Example : Define elasticity of demand.

Recall : Example: What do you consider the three most important inventions of the last century?

Summary : Example: What were the causes of the downfall of Mughal Empire?

Observation : Example: Observe this experiment.

Formation of New Questions : Example: What questions did occur to your mind after listening to the exploits of Samudra Gupta?

Three Levels of Classroom Questions : Questions are broadly divided into three levels as under :

1. Lower order questions.
2. Middle order questions.
3. Higher order questions.

Recall

1. When was Jawaharlal Nehru born? (Recall of fact)
2. What is the definition of force? (Recall of definition)
3. What are the laws of gravitation? (Recall of laws)

Recognition

1. What words in this sentence are adjectives? (Seeking recognition of certain words as adjectives)
2. What is this? (Showing a barometer in the class) (Seeking recognition of an object)

Translation

1. What does this model represent? (Seeking the translation of an idea contained in a model into the verbal form)

2. How can we represent 'happiness' of the child in a picture? (Seeking the translation of an idea into a pictorial form)
3. Define 'state' in your own words. (Seeking a change in the mode of expression of a definition)

Comparison

1. Compare the city life and the village life. (Seeking comparison to search for similarities and dissimilarities)
2. Compare the similarities between the powers of the Prime Minister and Chief Minister? (Seeking the compa-rison through pointing out similarities).

Explaining Relationshtips **:** How is price rise related to demand and supply?

Application **:** Considering natural resources and climatic conditions of this place, which industry can come up here?

Analysis **:** Does the evidence support the generalisation that farmers in India are in debt?

Syntheses **:** What sort of life do you expect without printed material?

Skills in Questioning **:** The teacher should bear in mind the following in this connection.

1. The question should be asked first and then the student asked to answer it. The main advantage in asking the question first is to set the whole class thinking to find out the answer. On the other hand, if a particular student is asked to stand or sit, as the case may be, and then the question is put to him, other students may not show much interest.
2. Questions should be evenly distributed. No child should be neglected. At the same time questions should not be given in a regular order round the class. Generally there is a tendency to put either too many questions or too less to the students sitting at the back or in the front. Such a tendency should be avoided.
3. Plenty of time should be allowed for pupils to think out the answer. However, the time allowed will depend upon the nature of the question.

4. The inability of a child to answer a question should be accepted. The teacher should avoid to waste a lot of time in trying to get an answer out of a child who cannot answer.
5. A volley of questions asked in a rapid-fire manner is upsetting.

Characteristics of Good Questioning

1. The language of the question should be simple.
2. Questions should not be ambiguous, lengthy and vague. They should be clear, brief and to the point.
3. They should be suited to the ability of the children to whom the questions are put.
4. Questions should be relevant to the topic.
5. Questions should be graded. They should neither be too easy nor too difficult. If the problem is too easy, the child will not take any interest in it. If it is too difficult, he will get discouraged.
6. Question once asked should not be repeated unless the teacher is sure the class has not followed it.
7. The teacher should try to vary the form of his questions.
8. Two questions should not be asked in one.
9. Questions should be interesting as far as possible.
10. Questions should be framed in such a way that these do not encourage guess work. The teacher should not generally admit answers like 'yes', 'no', or other single words.
11. Questions should be of developing nature. Every question should grow out of the response of the previous one. Questions should be in a sequence so that lesson may develop properly.
12. Suggestive questions such as "Was Sardar Patel an iron man?" should be avoided as they fail to encourage mental activity.
13. Leading questions such as "Do you know that Subhas chandra Bose was the founder of the Indian National Army?" should not, be asked.

14. Echo questions such as "Mahatma Buddha was born at Lumbini. Where was Mahatma Buddha born?" should not be asked.
15. Phrases like "Can anyone answer this question?" should be avoided.
16. Questions should be addressed to the entire class.
17. Questions should be asked in a pleasing manner.
18. Questions should be put in such a way that every student thinks that he will be asked to answer whether he is good or weak.
19. Adequate time should be allowed to answer.

The teacher's attitude to pupils' questions.

1. The students should be encouraged to ask questions.
2. Relevancy in questions should be insisted upon.
3. The teacher must insist on courtesy. Several pupils should not be allowed to ask questions at the same time. Everyone should be asked to listen to a question.
4. Pupils' questions may be made the starting point for a small project.
5. The teacher should be frank enough to admit his inability to answer a question when he does not know the answer. However, in due course, he should be able to answer that question. For the sake of prestige in the eyes of the students, he should not give a wrong answer.

Judicious Blending of Talking and Questioning : Questioning is not a one-way traffic. There is an ample scope for the teacher as well as the students to put questions. The teaching-learning process is effective only when the teacher as well as the pupils are active and co-operative. The aim of the teaching-learning process is to enable the child learn in such a way that it enables him to adjust himself to the environment. As both the teachers and the pupils are attempting to realize the same goal, it is evident that they must be active and not passive.

Skill in Answering : The same care and skill in dealing with pupils' answers, as in questioning them should be shown. After all, what for do we ask questions? Not for the sake of question!

The aim is to motivate children, to create interest, to test what the child knows and what he does not know, to encourage and stimulate thinking and fact-finding and to clear ambiguities and doubts. The quality and the nature of the answer reveal whether the purposes of questioning are fulfilled or not. Rather it may be put that questioning is a means to teach something that is revealed through the answers. Questions and answers may be compared with the blades of scissors. Both are indispensable in the teaching-learning process as both the blades are required to cut a piece of cloth.

Answers reveal the deficiency of the students as well as the teachers. They are the touchstone to test the effectiveness of the teaching-learning process. If the answers are not satisfactory, it clearly indicates that either there is something wrong with the teaching process or with the learning process. Either the teacher has not taught in the proper manner or the students have not understood the subject-matter. Therefore, answers provide an important tool to make necessary changes in the teaching-learning process.

Classification of Answers : A close analysis of the various types of answers shows that these can be put under the "following six categories:

(i) Right and correct answers.
(ii) Correct but incomplete.
(iii) Partially correct and partially wrong.
(iv) Wrong but intelligent.
(v) Ridiculously wrong.
(vi) Mischievous.

How to Deal with Answers : No hard and fast rule can be laid down for dealing with various categories of answers. Ward and Rascore write in this connection, "There are no rules. It is unwise to pass over all wrong answers as it is unwise to deal with all. Some are genuine misconceptions, which the teacher must clear up at that time or later on, others are imperfect and incomplete answers, genuine also, which must be rounded off, others are haphazard or stupid and should be treated with contempt or else with such brief but emphatic words of disapproval as the teacher may have a command." The following are the different ways of dealing with answers.

Appreciation : The teacher should in general appreciate the answers of the students as appreciation will encourage the students to think further. Even if the answers are wrong but teacher feels that the child is making genuine attempts, due appreciation should be given.

Analysis of Wrong Answers : When the answers given by most of the students are wrong, the teacher should try to analyse their causes. The causes may be as under:

(i) Defective or difficult language used by the teacher.

(ii) Defective explanation of the subject-matter taught.

(iii) Inattentiveness on the part of the students.

(iv) Lapses of memory.

(v) Toughness and complexity of the subject-matter.

In such cases, the teacher should accept the responsibility and should not feel shy of teaching the subject-matter again.

Encouragement of Children : When the answers are partly right and partly wrong, the students should be encouraged to analyse themselves the nature of their mistake. The teacher may ask further questions to analyse the nature of the mistake. When all the factors which are responsible for wrong answer, or answers are not clear to all the students, they may be asked to build up the real answers once again. It is unwise on the part of the teacher to be impatient and to make the necessary completion or correction himself.

Treatment of Wrong Answers : When a particular student gives a wrong answer, the teacher should not pass on till he gets the right answer without explaining why the first answer is wrong. The child must be made to understand why his answer is wrong. He is not likely to gain anything from the right answer if his doubts remain unexplained.

Answers Carrying Some Version, other than Expected by the Teacher : The teacher should accept and appreciate correct and complete answer although it may differ from the answers as expected by the teacher. There are a few intelligent students in every class who believe in novelty and do a lot of extra-reading. The difference in approach should be explained by the teacher.

The Form of the Answers according to the Nature of the Lesson: Whether the answer should be in bits or incomplete sentences depends upon the nature of the lesson. Complete sentences may not be insisted upon in arithmetic, science and in some cases in history or geography. But in a language lesson where the aim is to develop the power of expression, the teacher should insist upon complete sentences. No general rule can be laid down. It is up to the teacher to decide the form of the answer. But it must be stressed that whatever be the form, answers should be in a clear, simple and concise language.

Answers based on Right Understanding : The teacher must make sure that the answers as given by the students are really based on genuine mental activity. Parrot fashion words, though they may have sense, are not based on any thought or understanding on the part of the child. The teacher must go deeper and ensure that the child really knows what he says.

Answers Given in Unison : Answers given in unison should be discouraged. Such answers lack educational value and, therefore, should be disallowed. Assertive students should not be allowed to usurp the right of others who are slower or are perhaps making a mistake. Students should not be allowed to interrupt others while they are answering questions.

Observance of Courtesy : The teacher should see that the ordinary courtesy is observed in answering questions. The students should stand or sit and address in the proper way.

Encouragement to Shy and Submissive Students : There are always some students who feel shy and become nervous when questions are put to them. Though they know the answers quite all-right, yet they remain mum. The teacher should, in all such cases, give more encouragement and appreciation.

Repetition of Good Answers : Good answers of the students should be referred to the class, got repeated, preferably by another pupil. The teacher should avoid to repeat a correct answer himself, unless he wants it to be specially stressed.

Discouragement to Irrelevant Answers : The students should be made to realize the cause of the irrelevant answer. The teacher should analyse thoroughly whether the irrelevant answer is due to some mischief on the part of the student.

Development of the Summary of the Lesson with the help of the Answers : The answers given by the students at the recapitulatory stage may be used to develop a summary of the lesson. All the answers io brief may be written on the blackboard and the students encouraged to develop an integrated summary with the help of these answers.

Conclusion **:** Correct, clear and thoughtful answers result from clear and thought-provoking questions. The better means of evoking responses from the students are sympathy, patience and encouragement rather than impatience, harshness or snubbing them. Right and correct answers imply that the teacher is using right and correct methods of teaching and the students are learning in an appropriate manner. It may, therefore, be concluded that the pupil's answers to the questions are equally important if not more than the questions of the teacher in teaching-learning process.

Questions properly planned, carefully worded, evenly distributed, scientifically and psychologically asked, honestly answered and intelligently followed up are very profitable and in fact indispensable in the effective teaching-learning process. Colvin gave recognition to questioning in these words, "The efficiency of instruction is measured in a large degree by the nature of the questions that are asked and the care with which they are framed. No teacher of elementary or secondary school subjects can succeed in his instruction if he has not a fair mastery of the art of questioning."

Skill of Probing Questions **:** The term probing implies going deep in the matter in hand. It is defined as the art of response management comprising a set of behaviours or techniques for going deep into student's responses with a view to elicit the desired responses. N.K. Jangira and his associates (1980) named the skill of probing questions as the skill of response management on account of its emphasis on the ways and means of response management.

The skill of probing questions comprises the following component behaviours or techniques:

1. Prompting
2. Seeking further information

3. Refocusing
4. Redirection
5. Increasing critical awareness

Prompting : In the teaching-learning situation, prompting refers to the cues or hints provided by the teacher through well defined questions to the students for arriving at the desired response from the undesired situations like no response, incorrect, partially correct or incomplete, sentences. It may be noted that here the teacher himself does not provide the answer to the questions asked in the classroom by him or any student but tries to manage the situation by giving cues.

The selection of specific prompt (cues or hints or restructuring or phrasing of the question) in a particular situation depends upon factors like previous experience of the students, ability of the students to manipulate the relevant facts, concepts or principles, logical consistency of the response and the level of maturity, etc., of the students.

Seeking Further Information : For seeking further information from the students, questions like 'give some examples" make it more clear' by giving some evidence, are often asked.

Refocusing : In refocusing, the teacher asks the responding student either to relate his response with something already studied by him or to consider implications of his response in a more complex and novel situation.

Redirection : This technique is generally used in a 'no response' or 'incomplete response' situation and requires putting or redirecting the same question to several students for eliciting the desired response.

Increasing Critical Awareness : This technique is applied in a correct response situation to increase critical awareness in the students. Questions like, How would you justify it? Why do you assume so? How does it happen? are helpful in asking the responding student to justify his response for the purpose of increasing critical awareness in him.

9

Feasible Activities

In an introductory class of audio-visual education from B.Ed. students it was asked some of their earliest school experiences. Following were some of their answers:

(i) "The earliest school experience was when I made things out of plasticine."

(ii) "When in class 3rd we made a model of iglu out of sugar cubes."

(iii) "When I went to see a zoo in my 2nd grade."

(iv) "When we did gardening in a small comer of the school."

(v) "When I played the role of little red riding hood in kindergarten."

(vi) "The puppet show I saw in the school."

Dozens of similar experiences were reported by these (college) students. All these are varied experiences but we see one similarity, they could remember the experiences where they are involved in doing something, when they were active, when more senses were involved. These are some of the experiences where effort was not made to memorise them, on the other hand we do not always remember the facts or concepts that we try hard to memorise. From this we can generalise that learning becomes comparatively permanent when concreteness is there in the experiences. The various experiences help in developing concepts.

The process of building concepts operates naturally from the time a child begins to draw certain conclusions from his experiences and applies these conclusions to new situations. It continues thereafter as he makes new generalisations from new experiences and experiences in which new and old experiences are combined. The overall activity of building concepts, therefore is a realistic definition of Education. Now we can say that two elements are involved in building concepts: (1) Certain amount of concrete experiences, and (2) Combining and recombining these concrete experiences in many ways. When we apply this to classroom teaching, audio-visual aids play a very important role in concept formation and therefore in permanent learning.

Important Facets

If we see teaching of science in schools of our country by and large we wili find teachers lecturing or even reading out from the books and explaining few things on the blackboard. Some teachers use some demonstrations, charts and models but not very frequently and many a times students memorise things without understanding. Audio-visual aids if properly used help in teaching learning process in many ways (as given below) and can ensure quick and effective learning.

(i) The timely use of proper aids compels attention, develops interest and motivates students.

(ii) They break the monotony of teacher's talk, reduce verbalism, save time (of long verbal explanations) and give a better idea of the real things.

(iii) Audio-visual aids can make learning experiences far more concrete; therefore clarification of concepts, better understanding and long lasting learning are possible.

(iv) Great many teaching problems can be solved partly or wholly by the proper use of rich experiences (through audio-visual aids); therefore they offer great opportunities for improved learning.

The Kinds : Variety of audio-visual aids can be used in science teaching. They can be classified in various ways.

(a) One way of grouping them is as follows:

Visual Aids : charts, photographs, diagrams, static and working models, etc.

Auditory Aids : radio, recordings on tapes, and cassettes.

Audio-visual Aids : films, T.V. etc.

(b) Another way of classifying can be:

Graphic Aids : diagrams, photographs, charts, play cards.

Three-Dimensional Aids : models, specimens, real objects, apparatus, dioramas etc.

Projected Aids : slides, films, etc.

Aids Through Activity : excursions, projects setting and maintenance of aquarium, vivarium, botanical garden etc.

Verbal sysmbols
↓
Visual symbols
↓
Radio Recordings
↓
Still pictures
↓
Motion pictures
↓
Exhibits
↓
Field trips
↓
Demonstrations
↓
Dramatic participation
↓
Contrived experiences
↓
Real Direct experiences

Fig. Edger Dale Cone of Experiences

Some of these aids are more concrete in nature and some of them are comparatively more abstract. Edger Dale has arranged the various audio-visual aids in pictorial form which he called "Cone of Experiences".

This is a kind of visual aid to visualise and explain the interrelationship of various types of audio-visual material as well as their position in learning process.

At the top of the Cone are verbal symbols which are most abstract and at the base are the direct purposeful experiences which are most concrete form of experiences. This is only a pictorial form where all sorts of aids and experiences are arranged in a Cone. The various bands of the cone representing various experiences and aids, should not be considered as rigid divisions or watertight compartments. They overlap and blend with each other. For example you can be a viewer of an exhibit or a person who made it, you can observe a demonstration or can demonstrate it yourself. It is also not being suggested that the various aids and materials are arranged in the form of their effectiveness but they are arranged from most abstract to most concrete. As a teacher we should also know that abstract ideas, concepts, or generalisations are not possible without rich meaningful concrete experiences. A science teacher has to pick and choose the aids according to the maturity levels of the students and the topic to be studied. We will discuss the strengths and limitations of each in teaching sciences.

Fabulous Experience

The base of the Cone of experiences represents "direct purposeful experiences." Here the word 'purposeful' is very important. Every direct experience may not be very meaningful, therefore, it may not be purposeful. We have to see the direct experience in terms to learning outcome. In cases where the real things are too small or too big to comprehend, direct experiences are not very effective and therefore are not purposeful. For example, "structure of atom," "working of a factory." "water supply in a city" etc., can be understood better by some indirect experiences like models, maps or charts, etc.

In teaching science many direct experiences can be given to

the students for effective comprehension. Some examples are: observing real flowers, leaves, plants, insects; dissecting animals; taking a walk through woods; going to the seashore and observing marine animals; doing salt analysis in the lab; setting and maintaining an aquarium, etc. In such cases learning is by direct participation.

The science teacher has to decide what direct experiences will be purposeful for his classes and then try to give them as many experiences as possible because direct and concrete experiences soon become associated with abstractions and help in developing more difficult concepts.

What are Contrived Experiences? Next in the hierarchy towards abstraction are contrived experiences. Examples of contrived experiences are static models, working models, specimens, dioramas, etc. Contrived experiences may differ from the original in size (big things are made smaller and smaller things are made bigger) and complexity. It usually is a simplified and edited version of the real thing, where the unnecessary details can be removed to make the learning clear. For example a petroleum refinery is difficult to comprehend in a real situation but its model will be more meaningful. In the same way models of places where it is difficult or impossible to reach and see can give a clear idea, like models of globe, volcano, parts and systems of the body, bottom of the ocean, view of a forest, polar region, etc. Sometimes we imitate the whole natural habitat in the form of dioramas and keep in museums. Cut-away or half cut models are extremely useful in teaching internal structure of eye, ear, stem, root and automobile, etc.

There are some examples where nobody has seen the real thing, the models are made on the basis of indirect evidences like model of atom, DNA structure. Here the whole concept is developed on the basis of these imaginary models.

While teaching through the models, teacher should give the idea of the real thing, regarding their size and complexity. All models are not correct reproduction of their originals, they are only simplified versions.

Objects and Specimens : Objects and specimens are very common in science laboratories. These are also examples of contrived experiences. We collect rocks from various places. Different kinds of plants and animals are collected; pressing, preserving and sniffing are done for storing and study purposes. The objects and specimens are taken from the real settings. They are samples of real things minus real settings. The specimens are collected and stored so that they are readily available for study purposes. Another most important advantage of objects and specimens which is not otherwise possible in direct experience is that they can be arranged into groups and classes.

This has been placed on the 3rd band of Cone of experiences. Dramatisation means substitute for real experience of reconstruction of the original reality. There are many things we cannot possibly experience at first hand. There is a great value of dramatisation in education. Students can participate in a dramatisation or watch some kind of dramatisation. Both are valuable experiences but participation is much more meaningful and closer to reality than only watching.

The question is "What is the scope of dramatisation in science teaching?" Dramatic acts are quite popular in languages and social sciences. In sciences also the scope is not limited.

The films made on the work of various scientists are only possible because of dramatisation. Such films are quite effective as such experiences are otherwise not possible.

Students of primary and middle classes participate in scientific dramatised act in schools, such activities are also brought to science fairs etc. Some very abstract and uninteresting ideas are taken for dramatisations, for example, different students act as various components of solar system with proper costumes, dialogues, songs, music and dance, and the abstract concepts become clear and leave a long lasting impact on participants and viewers; students act as various petroleum products and explain how they are formed and utilised like coal, petrol, vaseline, synthetic rubber and plastic etc. Functions of vitamins and other components of food can also be taught through dramatisation.

It is also possible to use dramatisation in classroom teaching where costumes are not necessarily required but different students can remember their parts and act out in the classroom.

Interdependence of various components of an ecosystem and balance of nature can also be explained interestingly through dramatisation. An imaginative science teacher can think of many such topics which can be taught more effectively through such activities. Thus dramatisation can become an effective teaching aid in teaching science.

Way of Displaying

Demonstrations are quite familiar activities in science classrooms. Their merits and demerits have been discussed at length in the Cone of experiences they have been placed on the fourth band from the base because it is essentially a process of observing. It differs from the first three bands, which are essentially doing. Demonstrations are used to show how something is done or not done. When demonstration is followed by doing on the part of students, it becomes very much meaningful.

Demonstrations are used to clarify ideas, and help to develop skills, processes and attitudes. They are not limited only to demonstrations through apparatus only. They can be used to clarify abstract ideas on the chalkboard, through slides or motion picture also.

Demonstrations can be improved to a great extent if certain points are kept in mind while planning and doing a demonstration.

- Plan all steps of demonstration in advance.
- Rehearse the demonstration before going to the classroom.
- Keep the demonstration simple as far as possible.
- Keep the students involved.
- Make it sure that all the students can see it.
- Outline various points on the board.
- Keep summarising various steps.

Activities Outside

A field trip or excursion is a planned visit to a point outside the regular classroom. It may be in the school, out in the community or it could be a long trip to far away places. Usually in field trips to places like visits to a factory, observatory, agricultural institute, poultry farms, museums etc., we often see other people doing things. As spectators we are not involved but we directly watch it and get a first hand knowledge. Therefore field trip is an excellent bridge between the work of the classroom and the work of the outside world. The chief difference between a field trip and other educational experiences is that the student get their experiences in the field and not in the classroom. Because of its nature to be mostly observation it is kept on the 5th band of the Cone of experiences as less concrete than other experiences discussed before. But if the field trips are planned and arranged in such a way that they go beyond observation, for example of a sea-beach, on a pond where they can also touch, feel and collect things, it becomes a *direct experience* for them. Such a variation in the field trip indicates again how the bands of the Cone interlap and blend into one another.

Importance of the Field Trips : Excursions or Field Trips are of great educational value especially in science subjects. The classroom is a limited place, bounded normally by four walls and meagrely equipped for the task or providing students with worthwhile experiences. The environment outside the classroom has no bounds; it has almost every conceivable situation that a teacher might wish to utilise. In school corridor students may study writing system for supply of electricity to different rooms and laboratories, may determine the power (in watts). On school grounds there may be various types of plants, birds, insects, different kinds of soil, sunshine and shadows, building materials, bicycles, scooters and cars. And just beyond the school boundaries lie the unlimited resources of community.

Contributions of Field Trip

(i) Field experiences are first hand experiences. They arise from direct learning situations. Sometimes they play the same role or even better in the learning of science as do experiments and demonstrations.

(ii) Field experiences tend to be much more meaningful and permit easier transfer of learning to solutions of real life problems.

(iii) Fieldwork if properly organised awakens many interests that classroom work cannot arouse. Fieldwork is the study of actual objects which stimulate more curiosity than to ideas. Out of almost any situation encountered in the field can develop into some challenging problems.

(iv) Fieldwork permits first-hand study of many things that cannot be brought into the classroom because of size and other inconvenience, *e.g.*, it is only outside the class that the students can be acquainted with the flora and fauna of the area.

(v) Fieldwork permits a class to engage in activities that are too noisy or too violent to be used in the classroom, *e.g.*, a model airplane, gasoline engine if demonstrated in the classroom would disturb the other neighbouring classes too.

(vi) Outdoors, students are able to work with large size materials, *e.g.*, an iron piece pipe makes a more impressive lever than a routine stick and erosion is better demonstrated from a garden hose than with a tiny trickle from a yet drawn in a glass tube.

Some Special Experiences of Field Trips : Fieldwork brings students in contact with many objects. The observation and manipulation of objects in the environment are bound to arise questions. Attempts to answer questions give rise to new problems.

Field trips can be used for review and drill. Ideas learnt in classroom can be better fixed in mind in actual situations, *e.g.*, by visiting factories the ideas of running a plant and the products manufactured can be better fixed in students' minds, or visiting a zoological park or a botanical garden, more abstract ideas about animal and plant life can be more clarified to students.

Difficulties Experienced in Arranging Field Trips. Lack of availability of good inventories regarding field experiences, school policies, and transportation problems create hurdles in arranging field trips. Therefore the teacher will have to take a key role if he wants to arrange the trip.

1. Survey of the place of excursion should be taken before going to the field trip, so that the teacher knows before-

hand what their students are to see there; or what relevant literature should be studied if places are far away.

2. Objectives of the field trips should be very carefully identified to make a field rip a success. If this is done teacher knows what he is going to teach and the students know what they are going to learn there.
3. Permission from the authorities and parents of students should be taken well in advance.
4. Appropriate activities compatible to the identified objectives should be listed and given as well as discussed with the students beforehand.
5. If there is a need for transport and place to stay they should be arranged in advance.

Preparation of Students

1. It is essential to brief students after arriving at the area. This should be as minimum as possible. A long lecture may deprive the students of an opportunity to explore the place.
2. Students should be divided into small groups appointing a group leader for each group. Group leaders may help in running fieldwork smoothly and quickly.
3. You as a teacher should be aware of the fact that there are slow as well as rapid learners. Activities and responsibilities should be so divided among the students as to be equally shared by both type of students without any feeling that they are slow learners or rapid learners.
4. Students should be made aware that there may be some difficulties like: (a) noise while visiting any working plant in a factory, (b) listening to the guide due to distance while standing around him, or (c) technical language used in explaining particular process; and they should try to solve such difficulties themselves as far as possible.
5. Students may be advised to take notes and draw diagrams, whenever they think it is necessary.

Teacher's Role. The teacher's role is very important for a successful field trip. Some of them are listed below:

1. Watches students closely and gives specific help as and when needed.
2. Recognises student's achievement.
3. Avoids frequent interruption in student's work but occasionally if it is justified.
4. Does not lecture while in field ?
5. Avoids loud voiced comments.
6. Acts as a guide, resource person or consultant.
7. Does the relevant follow-up activities of the trip ?

Follow-up Activities : Follow-up activities are very important in any kind of field trip, it may be a short trip just outside the classroom or a long excursion to various far away places.

Follow-up activities vary accordmg to the nature of excursion. If the field trip is taken just outside the classroom in the school lawns to find the population densities of various species of plants, the follow-up activity will include the pooling up of data collected by each student or each group of students and discussion on the result. If the field trip is an observational trip to places like factories, mills, observatories or hospitals, discussion about what they have learned is important. Field trip can also be taken to study the fauna and flora and collection of specimens from seashore, hill stations or any other places. If such field trip is taken by the students follow-up activities will include pressing of plants, preservation of animals, drying of insects, classification and displaying of material.

If proper care has not been taken just after or during the trip (in case of long trips) the materials collected cannot be utilised properly and goes to waste. Sometimes the students and teachers are quite enthusiastic while planning and taking the field trip, but forget about the material after the big excitement or do not do the follow-up activities properly, therefore, the field trip is not as effective as it should be.

In short we can say that follow-up activities should be planned according to the objectives of the field trip. Science teachers should plan their objectives for the field trip well and do the follow-up accordingly for better understanding.

The Displays

Kinds of Exhibits. There is a big variety of exhibits. Sometimes they are three-dimensional working models, sometimes a series of photographs or photographs mixed with charts, models and real objects. But exhibits are essentially something one sees as a spectator. Usually one is not involved in handling any thing or working with the material. Science teachers take their students to show the science fairs where different kinds of exhibits can be seen. They are also of great educational value. Sometimes they may also influence the attitudes.

When students are involved in making exhibits, it becomes a direct experience for them. Investigatory science projects done by students can be displayed as exhibits. Exhibits can also be used by the science teachers to teach subject matter.

Museum : Museums are places where items and exhibits of knowledge are assembled, protected and studied. In big cities there are public museums of various kinds like art museums, history museums, science museums, and natural history museums etc. Here we are concerned with science and natural history museums. In our country there are not very many science and natural history museums. But if they are available in your cities, advantage should be taken from them.

Mostly Science and Natural History Museums (Science museum in Bangalore, Natural History Museum in Darjeeling and New Delhi) have two functions:

(i) presentation and display of the materials, and

(ii) to work with classroom teachers on specific curriculum unit. If this facility is given by the public museums, science teachers should take full advantage of such arrangements.

The other kind of museums are college and school museums for various subjects. Biology museums are quite common museums established in some form or the other in many schools and colleges. Museum should not be considered as a collection of various items and objects. It is more than that, it must be viewed with an idea, a process, and an objective. Therefore science museums should not emphasise only on the product of science but due importance should also be given to science processes.

There is a big scope of displaying of specimens and objects collected by students. Models and projects made by students could also be displayed there. In fact development of museum can be taken as one of the science club activities.

Movies' Power : Next on the cone towards little more abstraction comes the TV and motion pictures because we are only the viewers of these audio-visual aids. First we will discuss the motion pictures.

16-mm Educational Films : It is not possible to learn everything by doing or first-hand viewing. We have to get some of our experiences indirectly, 16-mm films play a very important role in giving this indirect experience. Motion pictures present an abstracted version of the real events omitting unnecessary and unimportant details, they can, sometimes dramatised events so effectively filmed that we feel as though we are present at the reality itself. No other medium has brought so much information and scientific knowledge to the classrooms as the educational sound motion pictures.

There are various kinds of motion pictures. Here we are concerned with the *educulional films.* Educational films include *documentary* and *instructional films.* Though some documentary films can be used in classroom teaching but they are especially planned for classroom teaching purposes. On the other hand *instructional films* are specially planned to achieve certain educational objectives and are made in specific subject areas tor teaching purposes. These films can be background films or direct teaching films. They help to promote to achieve a skill, an attitude or to convey certain facts, information, phenomenon or theory. As a science teacher we will be mainly concerned with the instructional films in our areas.

Though we are only spectators before a motion picture but the learning outcomes are quite effective because of certain specific values of motion pictures.

For 16-mm films, 16-mm movie projectors are needed. Now video cassettes of 16-mm films are available, which can be seen on TV. with V.C.P. or V.C.R.

The Strength

(a) Motion pictures motivate the students and compel attention.

(b) Movement can very effectively be shown by motion pictures which is not possible in any other aid except direct experience.

(c) It is an edited version of reality, the editing involves manipulation of time, space and by eliminating distractions; it gives relationships of things, ideas and events that might well be overlooked in real life. For example, food web, food chain, etc., can be seen as continuous processes which is not possible in reality.

(d) Time can be controlled in a motion picture with the help of slow motion photography, "movements in animals, insects, flight of birds" can be understood very easily. With the help of time-lapse photography it is possible to see the blooming of flowers, germination of seeds, growths of plants, etc.

(e) Motion pictures can enlarge or reduce the actual size of the objects for better compensation. By means of microscopic lens attachments microscopic organisms like algae, fungi, protozoas, and blood circulation in capillaries etc. can easily be seen and understood by students.

(f) By X-ray cine photography techniques movements of internal organs of animals—action of arms, legs, movement of the heel, swallowing of food, heart-beating/living movements, etc., can be shown.

(g) Motion pictures can bring past and distant present into the classroom.

(h) With the help of animation techniques motion pictures can show processes which cannot be seen by human eye even with the help of microscope or telescope. For example, behaviour of molecules in solids, liquids and gases, phenomenon of nuclear fission and fusion, etc.

(i) Motion pictures can reproduce the record of events like lunar and solar eclipses, etc. which are not always possible to see. Complicated techniques can be filmed and reproduced when required.

(j) Motion pictures promote understanding of abstract relationship, offer a satisfying aesthetic experience, influence and even change in attitudes.

With so many values, motion pictures not only expedite the rate of learning but they also increase the scope of teaching. This is an important consideration in the field of science where mass of learning and the learning processes are expanding so rapidly that it is to keep hand up with them. Motion pictures enable the teacher to clarify the difficult concepts in less time than with any other technique.

In order to get the most effective use of films or video tapes, the following necessary information and skills should be acquired:

(i) Where to obtain appropriate films or video tapes?

(ii) How to use such films and video tapes in your teaching?

(iii) How to operate the 16-mm film projector, V.C.R, V.C.R.?

School, college and university teachers have to spend some time to find films or video cassettes which they can integrate into their courses. It is possible to find suitable films or video cassettes on various science subjects. Securing catalogues will be important for this purpose.

For an effective use of films or video cassettes, preparation and follow-up are two very important steps to be taken by a teacher. Teacher should select the film or video cassette which goes along with the topic. The film or video cassette should be previewed and important points to be covered in the lesson should be outlined.

It will be advisable to frame few short answer questions. These questions can be given to the students before showing the film or video. During the follow-up activity unanswered questions and other important points should be discussed. Such activities help in coordinating the film or video with the topic. In the absence of such coordination sometimes the film or video becomes a wastage of time and effort.

The next point is to learn to operate the 16-mm projector and V.C.P./V.C.R. which is not very difficult to learn. Ordinarily only a few hours instruction followed by a brief practice results in satisfactory operation. Simple threading and operating instructions are given somewhere on the projector, which should be followed carefully. The possibilities of error should not discourage the teacher but it should be taken as challenge. The thrill of this educational device will compensate for minor disappointments.

Caution to be Observed in Using Films or Videos : Motion pictures may not necessarily be effective for teaching everything. As a teacher you have to be cautious about certain things.

- You have to think about the *effectiveness* of the film or video. If other experiences like direct or contrived are more meaningful, film or video should not be used.
- Sometimes the film or video gives a wrong idea about the *time notion* and *size notion.* It should be clarified to the students by comparing it with a known object or by giving a familiar example.
- If inexpensive devices are available with the *same effectiveness* as motion pictures, then less expensive devices should be used.
- Teacher should see that the film or video is adequate for the comprehension of his/her students.

Role of T.V.

School T.V. Programmes : Television has all the potentialities of motion picture with a little more concreteness because of the "on the spot coverage" and the nature of the TV programmes, as most of them are specially produced for a particular audience. This is more so for educational TV programmes. In many countries educational TV programmes include series of science programmes.

Educational TV in India : Experimental TV Service was inaugurated on September 15th, 1959. This programme was planned for educational and cultural values of community and designed for community viewing. In the meantime Ford Foundation in India was approached to assist in the development of educational TV. Ford Foundation team of TV experts visited India in February 1960. In 1961 Television was started in India as an educational TV project. The project was launched in close collaboration with the Delhi Directorate of Education and with the financial assistance of the Ford Foundation in 1961.

The educational TV programmes were integrated with the school syllabus based on the principle of direct teaching. Direct teaching implied that the TV programmes were directly related with the school syllabus. They were proposed to help in classroom teaching by bringing into classroom additional resources through the medium of TV. The students were benefited from talented teachers, best and expensive equipment and other audio-visual aids which were not usually available in schools. In the project the teachers were also fully involved from the planning to evaluation. This arrangement of instructional TV was working well in Delhi schools because there was a set prescribed syllabus. In some other advanced countries there is not any set syllabus for all but they have different syllabi choosen by teachers and students. Their educational TV programmes are not strictly integrated with the syllabi.

In Delhi the educational programmes started in General Science, Social Studies, Physics and Chemistry. Later Biology Maths and Geography were also included.

For proper functioning of educational TV and better coordination between Doordarshan and Schools a Television Branch was set up in 1967 in Delhi Directorate of Education. The TV branch used to divide the syllabus term-wise and week-wise, and select lessons for TV teaching. To ensure close relationship between TV and classroom teaching, a package of a uniform time-table, set examination days and working hours, and a uniform weekly syllabus in the form of a TV booklet was to be distributed to all viewing schools in the beginning of the school session. Such TV booklets used to be prepared for each subject taught on TV. But now we do not have such school TV programmes in Delhi or elsewhere in the country.

This kind of educational TV programme if started again can solve several problems of science teaching in our schools.

The Merits

1. It solves the problem of unequipped laboratories to certain extent. Students are able to see effective demonstrations

and expensive apparatus which is otherwise not possible for them to see.

2. TV teachers prepare and rehearse a lesson, spend enough time to collect relevant material and up-to-date information.
3. It has all advantages of films plus being a live presentation seems more natural. Only relevant portions of films are shown, along with teacher's explanation and other visual material.

The Demerits

1. It is a one way process and students are passive viewers.
2. There is no opportunity for an active participation of the learner during TV lesson.

Better Utilisation of Educational TV : The disadvantages can be removed if some preparation is done and precautions are taken by the classroom teacher.

For effective use of any mass media three things are important: proper reception, proper seating arrangement, carefully planned preparation and follow-up.

Good reception is one of the basic important things for effective viewing. The television branch in Delhi had the respon-sibility of installing and maintenance of TV sets. The coordination had to be done by the teachers and administration of the school. Classroom teacher was also be familiar with proper handling and minor adjustments of a TV set.

Next important thing is the proper seating arrangements. If a big crowd is sitting on the floor (without any discipline) in an auditorium or classroom, not sure of proper viewing, this kind of arrangement will be a waste of time. The classroom teacher was to see that there was proper seating arrangement.

TV presentation is only one part of the learning procedure. Preparation for the TV lesson or the pre-telecast activities and the follow-up or post-telecast activities by the classroom teacher are equally important without which the TV lesson may not be very much meaningful.

Pre-telecast activities included the preparation by the subject teacher. Preparation varied with class to class and also depended on the topic, the classroom teacher could see the topic of the TV lesson in advance from the TV booklet. During pre-telecast activities his job was to make the students ready to receive the TV instructions. He could ask motivational questions. If some background knowledge was needed it was to be given at this time. The time-table was arranged in such a way that there were about 10 minutes before and after the actual telecast, usually the presentation was of 20 minutes duration, and class periods varied from 35-40 minutes.

After the TV presentation follow-up activities included clarification of points of doubts raised by students. Recapitulation questions could also be asked to see how much they have grasped. With little encouragement by the classroom teacher many activities could be followed by students as continuation of the TV presentation for better understanding.

The TV branch of Delhi also tried to evaluate the lessons. They used to send a printed pad of evaluation check sheets to each school for the constant feedback of TV lessons. If various people connected with educational TV production do their jobs consciously the E.T.V. programmes can be quite effective. You as a science teacher has to play an important role. During your practice teaching you can observe some science lessons on video tapes, evaluate them according to the evaluation check sheet developed by you and give suggestions for further improvement.

Role of Radio : Next stage on the cone of experiences after motion pictures is the number of those devices which can be called as one-dimensional aids. We will take the scope of each in teaching science one by one.

Photography

Kinds of Still Pictures. Various kinds of still pictures can be used in teaching science. They include photographs, illustrations and slides. These visual materials are of great importance in teaching learning situations.

Photographs and illustrations can be used without projection, slides can be projected on the screen with slide projectors. Therefore pictures can be divided into two kinds: (i) unprojected, and (ii) projected.

Unprojected Pictures : Photographs, illustrations and clippings of photographs from magazines and newspapers can be collected for teaching purposes. Pictures give a correct impression of the object or situation and motivate and enrich teaching. It is good to have relevant pictures on the walls of science rooms—pictures of great scientists and some of their apparatus, etc. Pictures can also be used in teaching for motivation, introduction, presentation or recapitulation as the need may be.

Pictures and illustrations with some theme can be displayed on a bulletin board.

Bulletin Board : It is a place for posting "bulletins", as the name suggests. Bulletin boards can be used in many different ways and as an effective "teaching device". Bulletin boards inside and outside the science rooms and laboratories can be used for putting visual materials (pictures, illustrations) with relevant heading and some labelling for supplementing the teaching. It should be of scientific interest and importance. With proper teacher guidance and motivation bulletin boards can provide opportunity of developing creativity, responsibility and interest among the students. Other than displaying the photographs and illustrations, bulletin boards can also be used for displaying reports of science projects done by students, science news and cuttings from science magazines, collected and presented by them.

Projected Pictures : Projection of visuals have certain advantages. For example, projection magnifies the material, therefore, a bigger group can easily see it. It is somehow motivating, therefore, compels attention.

Different kinds of projectors aroused in classrooms for projecting still pictures. They all are very easy to use, with little planning on the part of the teacher, teaching can be quite effective.

Opaque Projector of Episcope : The opaque projector projects and simultaneously enlarges material directly from original books, magazines, etc. All kinds of written, printed or pictorial matter in any sequence can be projected for teaching purpose. It can also project opaque thin objects like leaves, shells, sample of fabrics, butterflies, moths, etc.

Designs for posters, maps, pictures for displaying on bulletin boards etc., can be projected in the desired enlarged forms and then traced. The opaque projector though has many unexplored possibilities but is not being used much because of its bulk, weight and requirement of a very dark room.

Slide Projector : Such projectors usually project 35 mm slides. It is essentially a simple machine, easy to operate, inexpensive and light weight. It has most of the points of practical importance. Slides can be shown individually in any desired order.

Slides' Utility

(i) Slides are of great value in visual teaching situation, when motion is of little or no importance, for example, in teaching structural details.

(ii) Great variety of visual material such as pictures, charts, graphs, diagrams, maps, tables, anything that can be photographed can be put on a slide.

(iii) Slides are available in black and white and coloured forms on many science subjects covering a wide range of topics and levels.

(iv) Slides are comparatively inexpensive.

(v) Slides require only a slight darkening of the room.

(vi) In some little more expensive projectors the slides can be moved automatically either from a master control or from a synchronising device on a sound track. This arrangement of slide-tape programme is an effective device as the well prepared commentary makes it more meaningful.

The use of this visual aid will be more meaningful if following points are considered while using them:

(i) The science teacher has to explore if suitable slides are available on the particular topics.

(ii) Second step is the careful preview. The preview helps in deciding on how to use the material to the best advantage. Is it stimulating enough for introduction on the whole lesson could be developed with it or only suited for summarising the lesson.

(iii) Teacher has to think about the purpose also. If showing of motion is necessary for understanding, then slide is not the best medium.

(iv) If teaching involves a series of step by step development, one leading to the next logical sequence the slides are well suited.

Showing slides is only one part of the process. Good discussion and further activities could be developed from it.

The Micro Projector : One of the more specialised types of projection equipment is the micro projector. As its name indicates it shows enlarged images of stained sections of microscopic slides or other biological material mounted on microscopic slides so that the bigger group can see it. The advantages of micro projector are that:

(i) It presents an enlarged picture of the object on the slide for common view.

(ii) It assures the teacher that his students are seeing precisely what he wants them to see.

Some manufacturers make low power projection attachments for slide projectors. Some are simple extensions of a microscope using a more powerful illumination system with a small view screen. This can be easily shown in small groups. But the full scale micro-projectors are quite expensive.

Projectors of any kind are a boon to classroom teachers. These technological tools, if coordinated wisely make the classroom teaching quite effective, because of the novelty of presentation, students become motivated and interested.

Language and Voice Modulation : These are primarily auditory aids. If the speaker on radio or recordings uses simple everyday language with meaningful associations with familiar examples the listening can become quite concrete. On the other hand if the language is difficult without any associations, it could be an abstract thing for listeners. Being only an auditory aid language and voice modulation etc, play a very important role in the effectiveness of these programmes

Values of Radio : Immediately we are able to get the news of important events from all over the world, which is not possible from any other media except vedio or TV. Many events are of great importance for science classes, some of which are mentioned below :

(i) Radio brings reality to the classroom The spectator who describes the events with his tone and description can brings sense of participation amongst listeners.

(ii) Radio programmes if well rehearsed and well presented in the form of stories bring the personal feeling of the actor, different sound effects and voices make them more realistic and meaningful.

(iii) It brings variety to the classroom and helps in teaching

(iv) Though in a well prepared programme enough expenses may be involved but radio being a mass media technology, on the whole it is inexpensive.

The Limitations

(i) It is still a one way communication

(ii) Availability and maintenance of radio set may be a problem.

(iii) Radio broadcast timings always do not coincide with the class timings. Provision of radio broadcasts in the school time table is made only in a very few schools.

Educational Radio Programmes in Our Country : Educational broadcasts for schools in the AIR were regular features from the last few decades. These programmes included science lessons for students and teachers at various levels. Teachers' programmes were on content as well as on methodology. Before the board examinations revision lessons on various science subjects were quite popular. These were used to be given by experienced science teachers and educators

The school broadcast was a separate unit of AIR in New Delhi. The unit tried to coordinate between various agencies to improve the effectiveness of the broadcasts. Meetings were held where people were invited from Directorate of Education Delhi, Municipal Corporation Delhi, New Delhi Municipal Council and Delhi University to plan future programmes and give suggestions for their improvement.

Radio broadcast schedule in the form of a chart was prmted and sent to the schools in the beginning of the year. Teachers could utilise the relevant broadcast in their classes. Radios and transistors were or could be easily available in the schools. If the teachers are conscious of the radio programmes students can be benefited Pre- and post-broadcast activities improved the effectiveness of the programmes as discussed in TV programmes.

Recordings : All the values of radio can be applied to recordings also. But the disadvantages can be eliminated like timing, administration and one way communication problems. Recordings from many sources can be utilised in the classrooms, like spool-tape records and cassette records.

Advantages of Recordings

(i) Recordings can become two way communication as it can be stopped, discussed and replayed wherever it is necessary, it can be controlled by us.

(ii) Recordings on cassette or spool-tape-recorder can be made in the school also. A commentary can be written and recorded on the available slides in your subject in the school for effective use and re-use.

(iii) Good radio programmes can be recorded and replayed in class whenever needed.

(iv) Scientific talks by eminent personalities can be taped and reproduced in the class.

Kinds of Visual Symbols : They include the abstract representation of real pictures. Various kinds of visual symbols used in communication are drawings, sketches, diagrams, graphs, cartoons, flat maps, etc. They all can be projected on screen, and can also be shown on the blackboard or on the overhead projector.

Diagrams and charts etc., are part of everyday work for most of the science teachers. Almost all the science teachers use blackboard to show in the structure and happenings of various things in their subjects.

Commercially made charts are available in various subjects. Charts and other graphic aids are also made by various Governmental agencies. Central Institute of Educational Technology (CIET) of NCERT New Delhi develops various kinds of graphic aids for school purposes. Charts are also made in schools by teachers and students and can be utilised in teaching science quite effectively.

Chalkboard : Blackboard now is usually called a chalkboard because of variations in colours. It is one of the very important but quite neglected aid of the classrooms. If it is properly used can become a valuable aid in teaching science.

It should not be taken for granted that you already know the use of chalk board, but the techniques should be learned and practised especially as a trainee teacher.

Importance of Chalkboard

(i) This aid is used with all other aids for better clarification, for example, the main points of a demonstration planning and summarising of a field trip, questions for a motion picture and so on can be written on the board.

(ii) It gives a concrete form to abstract and vague statements and ideas.

(iii) It helps in developing the skill of drawing a particular diagram..

(iv) It is less time consuming and comparatively cheaper.

(v) It can be used for some students activities like quizes, competitions and discussions, etc.

(vi) Some chalkboards can be used for permanent outlines of maps, graphs, tables and other special materials where some filling up can serve the purpose.

(vii) If properly used chalkboard becomes an attractive point and holds students attention.

Effective Use of Chalkboard

(i) Clean the board properly before using it.

(ii) Try to write neat and bold so that it is legible.

(iii) Do not write too much on the board. Start writing from top left hand. Give headings and sub-headings in the written summary.

(iv) If diagrams are used for referring or introduction, they can be made beforehand. If you want the students to draw the diagrams then it should be drawn in front of them and they should be asked to draw side by side. In the same way a complicated process should not be drawn beforehand, but it should be developed before them for clarification and better understanding.

(v) If necessary, some tools can be used to draw on the board.

(vi) Coloured chalks should be used for making complex diagrams.

Overhead Projector : Any thing which is written or drawn on a chalkboard can also be projected by an overhead projector with some additional advantages.

An overhead projector projects material overhead or over shoulder the teacher using it on to a screen behind and above him. They generally have 25 cm x 25 cm writing area which is big enough for writing. What is required to be shown on the screen is written on a glass plate covered with sheet or roll of transparent plastic. Variety of fabrics tipped pens or china marking pencils are used for writing and drawing. Wet cloth can be used for erasing and re-using the sheets.

Advantages of Overhead Projector

(i) It is very simple and convenient to use the machine.

(ii) "Ibis projector unlike any other projectors is operated from the front of the room and the teacher faces class as he or she writes or points on already made transparencies.

(iii) Plastic roll attachment is quite useful. Diagrams, points of the lesson, assignments, tests and similar material can be effectively presented gradually with a minimum of time and effort.

(iv) An important feature of overhead projector is the provision of "overlays" or 'build ups," which have successive layers of transparencies in black and white coloured or both showing cumulative stages of development, sequences and sectional views, which is quite effective in many scientific processes and phenomenon.

The Limitations

(i) Though it is not very heavy but a voluminous projector.

(ii) It is quite expensive and needs some planning.

This is the most abstract and one of the most important forms of experience we get and give to our students. Our job as a teacher is to make sure that the various terms, ideas, words, principles and other abstractions used should be meaningful for students. The ideas and concepts which can be translated into verbal symbols come by getting other concrete experiences. Rich experiences gained by students help them to understand the verbal symbols meaningfully and therefore they can read and understand the textbooks also. Ability to speak or read the word does not mean that one also understands the object, process or phenomenon.

If from the very beginning science is taught by reading books or abstraction only, students usually acquire the habit of memorising and accepting verbal formulation given by others. This is no way of teaching science.

Various kind of experiences discussed on the core of experience from direct purposeful experience to visual symbols, all help in the development of verbal symbols meaningfully. Then reading is not only the process of reproduction of verbal symbols but also involves a thinking process, which includes meaning of words.

Textbooks and other reference books provide the most to the students, because all teaching is not possible by any one particular aid or experience. But the textbooks should be written in understandable vocabulary of that level. Sometimes in primary classes the language of science textbooks is much more difficult than the language in the language textbooks of that particular class. Another important aspect is also the style of writing and format. In writing and specially in teaching if references and examples are given from their environment and known things learning will be more meaningful.

Practical Use

A variety of teaching aids has been discussed in this chapter with some details. It is difficult to select few aids and to say that they are more important than others, or mis should be used more often than others etc. The value of an aid does not depend wholly on its quality itself but it also greatly depends upon the way it is used and the particular time it is used.

The qualities of various aids have also been discussed. No matter how perfect the aid may be, if it is irrelevant to the occasion of its use then it is of little value and an ordinary aid with not too many qualities becomes indispensable if it is used relevantly at the right time. For example, there is film which shows the animals under the sea or life in a desert in relation to their ecology. Neither the materials nor this relationship could be shown in a class by any other media or field trip as effectively as the film could. But always it should not be used as a substitute for other materials of the classroom.

Devices of Teaching

Teaching aids arouse the interest of learners and help the teachers explain the concepts easily. They make learning easy, effective and interesting. There are audiovisual aids such as blackboard, maps, charts, globes, pictures, etc., which are traditional in nature. Nowadays electronic media have come in a big way and are apt to influence not only communication and education, but also the manner and behaviour, lifestyle, attitudes, and interests of the clientele. These media and materials provide direct as well as vicarious or improvised learning experiences to the students at all levels of education. These include traditional aids as well as electronic media evolved from time to time in large variety and great novelty.

Learning becomes effective when students are actively involved in the process. To the extent his different senses are related, his learning becomes successful to that extent. For using various senses in the teaching-learning process, different materials are utilised in the classrooms. The learning experiences are thus made quite relevant, meaningful and effective. That is why, these aids are called 'multi-sensory materials', or 'instructional aids' or 'instructional materials.' These materials mainly being of two kinds, audio and visual, they are known as 'audio-visual aids' or A-V materials. As these aids are to be used as an integral part of the entire learning situation and are not just ancillary or supplementary, many educators are not happy with the term 'aids.' Therefore, the term 'material' is safely used and sometimes the term, 'technique' is also used to mean how these materials can be used.

Important Objectives

After going through the module, you will be able to

- know the role and importance of audio-visual teaching aids
- classify teaching aids on the basis of their characteristics
- acquaint yourself with the various uses and applications of these aids
- enlist a number of guidelines for preparation of some selected teaching aids viz-charts, models, slides, transparencies and cartoons.

Varied Sorts : The teaching aids or the audio-visual materials may be divided into three categories: (i) visual (ii) audio and (iii) both audio-visual. The materials which appeal only to the sight are of the first category. Examples of these materials are slides, film strips, transparencies, silent motion pictures and projections with the opaque, the techistoscope and the over-head projector. Other materials traditionally used in the schools are textbook, illustrations, photographs, prints, graphs, charts, maps, globes etc., which may be taken as visual aids. The chalkboard, felt board and bulletin board are also visual materials appealing only to the sense of 'sight.' Displays and exhibits like specimens, mock-ups, electric maps, diagrams and some dramatisations like pageants, pantomimes, puppetry and dancing are regarded as successful visual materials.

Secondly, radio, gramophone, tape recorders and different magnetic recordings provide audio materials which are appealing to the sense of hearing only. Thirdly, television programmes, tape slide programmes video tape recordings and films are materials which appeal to both eyes and ears and are very effective audio-visual materials. Dramatic plays, role-playing, socio-drama, verse choirs, etc., are a few types of dramatisation that can be used with satisfying results.

These three types of materials either audio or visual or both audio-visual cannot be exclusively categorised. There is no distinct compartmentalisation and the list of such materials is not exhaustive. Imaginative and resourceful teachers can invent, explore and discover various sources collecting and developing these materials.

Tools of Projection : Audio-visual aids are also divided into (i) Projected, (ii) Non-projected and (iii) Activity aids. When aids are projected on screens or even against white-washed walls to give an enlarged image of the material, they are called projected aids. Projected aids include slides, film-strips, films, and transparencies which bring about better results and are more effective. The darkened room reduces distractions and the bright image on the screen secures the attention of learners. By the use of different colours, the aids become more attractive and impressive.

Non-projected aids are generally still materials including maps, charts, globes, models, display boards, bulletin boards, etc. These aids are not so costly, and no sophisticated aids are required for their use. Therefore non-projected aids can be easily used with good results.

Lastly, the activity aids include field trips, excursions, exhibitions, museums, demonstrations and dramatisation. Organisation of various activities in and out of the campus make the programmes effective as well as interesting. Planning, execution and evaluation of those activities ensure better effects and help in improving these aids to bring about quality in education.

Aids can be classified not in categories, but in a continuum. For example, while using textbook or an audio tape, the learner can use and learn from them at his or her own pace, he/she may go back and read the paragraph or listen to a portion of the programme according to his need and convenience. Hence these aids are learner-controlled. On the other hand, a TV/radio programme when listened to by a learner, the message is transmitted at a stretch without his intervention, even though it may not be according to his pace or interests. Thus mass media like radio or TV cannot be controlled by the learner who may of course switch it off if he is not interested in it. Therefore various aids can be arranged in a continuum ranging from no control to high control by the learner.

Teaching aids can be classified on the basis of the size of the group of learners or an individual learner for whom they are meant and utilised. Take an example of a programmed lesson on a Computer-Assisted Instructional (CAI) programme which is prepared for individualised learning. It takes into account the difficulties usually encountered by an individual learner who is learning on his or her own without any help from others. Non-projected aids like maps, charts, models are used for a small group of learners. A class consisting of about 50 students can take advantage of these aids.

Use of Charts : Projected aids, however, like films, film-strips, slides, can be shown to about 80-100 students sitting at a place. Mass media like radio, T. V., newspapers can reach thousands of audiences at a time.

Chart is either or both graphic and pictorial representation designed for the orderly and logical visualisation of relationship between facts or information and ideas. It uses only graphics or pictures or both graphics and pictures to represent a large mass of data or to show their progression. It may be related to an individual or an institution, an object or incident, an idea or ideas which are represented for easy reference. For example, nowadays, a large number of dowry deaths are published in the newspapers. One can compile and classify all information relating to dowry deaths over a period of a month or a year, datewise or monthwise and a particular variable, say time gaps after the marriages were held, is taken for a chart. Thereby it can show deaths taking place within a week, a month, a quarter, a half-year, a year or two, three, four, five, six, seven years. The chart can easily represent the progression of the incident.

Charts are useful at various stages of teaching and in different classes. Their importance lies in the very nature of representation and communication. The desired information, facts and numerical data relating to a particular subject or incident are visually represented in a beautiful and pictorial form. They prove more effective in the task of systematic presentation of facts, ideas and relationship than other graphics-pictures, graphs, diagrams and photographs.

For instance, the inner structure of a coal mine, the functioning of various subsystems and their interrelationships can be better represented in a chart than in a picture or a photograph. Similarly, a polling booth and its functioning can be better shown in a graph than in other traditional media or material.

The different uses of charts are given below:

- To present data and information in a summarised form.
- To show the relationships through comparison and classifications.
- To give the visual representation of the abstract ideas and facts.
- To enable learners to get clarification and meanings at a glance.
- To facilitate discussion and narration on a particular issue or problem.
- To create interest, draw pupils attention and provide motivation in a topic or issue.
- To generate awareness about the gravity and seriousness of the issue or problem.

There are, on the whole, six types of charts. These are development, pictorial, tabular, genealogical, flow and skills. The developmental or progress chart is very commonly used. The pictorial chart is used to present facts through interesting illustrations. The tabular chart is widely used to bring out a mass of related data in a compact form. The genealogical chart is extensively used in history and biographical books to show dynasties and generations. The flow chart is used to show a process or sequence in various subjects like political science, industry or government. It is also called organisation chart for showing relationships and interrelationships in an organisation. The skill or experience chart is an orderly presentation of skills and experience items prepared by teachers for showing language skills, planning skills, etc., for evaluating pupils' activities.

Time Chart: Time chart is used for showing the sequence of time of various events or for depicting chronologically all the happenings relevant to the development of a process, certain organisation or any problem.

Issues Chart: This chart is used for highlighting the contrasting views of individuals and organisations on a burning issue or problem.

Flow Chart: This chart is meant for representing an organisation or an industry or a hierarchy of structure administrative or supervisory. Various geometrical designs like triangles, quadrangles, circles and arrow marks are given to indicate the development of an organisation or a system.

Table Chart: This chart represents data in tabular form. The basic importance of this kind of chart is to indicate a mass of data precisely and represents time-relationship, contrasts as well as comparisons among various events and ideas.

Pictorial Chart: This type of chart is very attractive with illustrations, diagrams, sketches etc., which represent various ideas and objects.

Charts are comparatively cheaper and easier for construction than many audio-visual aids. Generally these are prepared by teachers and students. Nowadays, commercial firms have come up for producing various types of charts on mass scale at cheaper rates. But specific purpose charts are produced more by teachers than these commercial firms. Involving students also in the process of constructing the charts provides effective learning experiences. In order to make charts efficient teaching aids and informative as well as interesting material, adequate planning and preparation are necessary. In spite of variety in the nature of charts, there are common features viz., caption or title, the message or content. The message may be verbal, graphical or pictorial or a combination of both. Generally, the caption is mentioned in bold letters either at the top or bottom.

Charts are a very simple type of A. V. aids and their preparation is quite easy. Generally, charts are prepared on card paper or on mounting board. The following steps and aspects are followed in the preparation of charts:

Verbal Message: Suitable words should be selected. These words should be plain, precise and meaningful. Too many words in a chart make it clumsy and sometimes distracting. The size of the words should be quite visible and also readable by all students in a class. Important points need be highlighted in a chart. Sometimes different colours are used for differentiating one concept or idea from another. The difference in colouring also helps in catching attention and marking the differences.

Graphic Message: Very often a verbal message is supplemented or reinforced by graphics such as graphs, diagrams, maps, pictures, figures, photographs and so on. The size of the graphics should be appropriate to that of the chart. Colours are used effectively in drawing graphics on charts or may be enlarged with the help of an epidiascope or overhead projector. Sometimes pictures, maps, graphs etc., from a newspaper or magazine or books can be pasted or superimposed on a chart. Necessary planning is made prior to preparing a chart.

Models' Utility

A model means an imitation, a replica or a copy of a thing, act or process. It is a three-dimensional aid with desired flexibility, size, complexity, safety and cost for effectively achieving instructional objectives. Models are the actual representation of the real objects. The original size or shape of the actual things is changed, i. e., enlarged or reduced to suit the learning group. That is why, models are more advantageous and more convenient than actual objects or process. For example, a fly is so small in size in actual condition that it cannot be used as an aid in the classroom, but an enlarged model of a fly can easily show its structure and various organs very well. Similarly, a process or a phenomenon actually in operation cannot be explained to students, but models of the same can be effective aids in explaining the details of their functioning. Models are also most suitable from safety point of view. For instance, you cannot take your young students inside mines to show the actual functioning of the mining system. But it can be explained very well through models.

To explain the details of actual objects in a clear and leisurely manner which is not possible in case of real objects:

- To show the minute parts of a system or a process through a model which cannot be done when it is actually in operation.
- To use models economically and effectively in the class-rooms.
- To use models more successfully than two dimensional aids like pictures and illustrations.
- To show the internal functioning of a system or objects which are not visible from outside with the help of cross-sectional or dissectable models.
- To use models with safety and convenience. To utilise models with adequate flexibility and freedom.

There are mainly three types of models:

(i) Solid models, which are used generally for recognising external features viz relief maps

(ii) Cross-section models which show internal structure like heart, brain, etc., and

(iii) Working models which demonstrate functions or processes viz a machine, gear box, etc.

Each type of model has distinctive advantages and uses. Solid models are commonly used and easily prepared. Cross-section models are cutaway models that enable viewers to look into the inner design and structure of a system, say a gas engine or a coal mine. Working models are designed to show students how an organ or a process works. Sometimes, contrasting colours are used for showing different parts and how various parts are fitted to work or move together. These are very fascinating and provide exciting learning experiences to students. Engineering and medical students are familiar with such models.

Models can be prepared or procured from the market. Normally the solid models can be prepared by students and teachers.

Previously, relief maps and models of various fruits, etc., were prepared by them, But the other two kinds of models are difficult to be constructed. It is a valuable learning experience for pupils to participate in the preparation of models. Some teachers are very good in preparing models and are well-trained to do the job. They can take initiative and motivate students to collect the materials and participate in the construction of models.

Materials like cardboard, plaster of paris, wax, paper, thermacool, etc., are used for preparing models. At the school stage, (in the past) students brought soft soil and teachers prepared models of various kinds, of course, mainly of solid models. Even wooden models were prepared for showing the functioning of an object or system. Even in teaching Mathematics and Science, many things can be prepared to make abstract ideas concrete and real objects. In Engineering, Medicine and military training, a good number of models are prepared for making the concepts clear and meaningful.

Since models are three-dimensional, they are capable of representing the real objects in a better way than the two-dimensional graphic aids. It is also better to get them prepared in the schools, with active cooperation of students. A teacher, therefore, should acquaint himself with the steps and essentials of their preparation, which are discussed below:

(i) At first the objectives and scope of preparing the models should be decided in relation to lesson.

(ii) Decision about the materials to be used for preparing the model need to be taken carefully. The material may be clay, plaster, papermache, paper or cardboard.

(iii) Real object of the model to be prepared should ideally be kept in view or in its absence in mind. That is, at least a picture or photograph should be kept handy before preparation.

(iv) A rough sketch or a rough model can be prepared at first before finally preparing the model.

Since there are various types of materials ranging from cheap clay to costly plasters, we have to decide the material according to our financial provisions. Skills in preparing the model differ according to the quality of the material. These are briefly discussed as follows:

Clay Models : Clay available in the beds of lakes, ponds and rivers is found suitable for modelling. That clay should be without or little sand. No hard material like seeds, stones, etc., should be there. At first dry clay is powdered and is added with water allowing three/four hours for softening, so that it can be squeezed in any manner we like. Then such soft clay can be immediately used for model making or be kept in fine-lined box or in an earthen pan, so that as and when we need, it can be used for preparing a model.

Small models can be prepared with clay in the light of the object or graphic. In case of making big models, hay, wire, bamboo sticks or such other things can be used for giving strength to the model. Anyway, clay coating is to be given in the end and be dried or baked to add more stability. The baked clay models can be coloured according to our choice.

Papermache Models : Papermache is made of any fibrous paper, i. e., brown paper, news paper, etc., by cutting into pieces and soaking them in water for some hours (can be heated also for getting quick results). Superflous water can be poured off and the soaked material be powdered for getting consistency and softness. A little glue and starch may be added to the pulp for making the mache more adhesive-like and unbreakable. And then models are prepared out of such mache by pressing it into a plaster of clay mould. Sometimes oil or any greasy substance is added to moulds for getting better results. Then models may be dried thoroughly and colour be applied according to our design. Occasionally, without moulds also models can be prepared out of mache making a structure with the help of bamboo sticks, wires etc., and then papermache coating is given to it.

Plaster of Paris : Plaster of Paris can be used like clay and papermache for preparing models. Moulds can be used or prepared by hand with plaster of paris which is readymade for model-making with all softness and malleability. Wires and bamboo sticks were used for making structures or for freehand structuring or using moulds and plaster of paris is applied according to our requirements.

Cardboard and Thick-paper Models : For preparing models, cardboard, thick paper, chart paper etc., are used with profit. Artists and artisans prepare designs of plants, animals, birds, human figures with necessary colours, costumes and other make ups. Bridges, tunnels, dams and other kinds of scientific and geographical designs can be prepared with these materials with required dexterity and skills. Various geometrical models can easily be prepared to explain the principles and formulae.

10

Micro-Teaching

Micro-teaching is one of the most important development in the field of teaching practice. It is originated in Standard University in 1963. The workers in the centre for Research and development in teaching have evolved and approach to practical teacher-training. It is more analytical method and completely new approach to provide the feedback. It is considered as a mechanism of feedback device for the modification of teacher trainees.

The Growth

A doctoral candidate Leith Acheson got information through a newspaper article about portable video-tape-recorder invented by German scientist in 1961. He was working with Robert Bush and Dvight Allen who had received a grant to study those experiences which might be relevant a grant to study those experiences which might be relevant for teaching in terms of an innovative teacher-education programme. Acheson saw the possibility of using the video-tape to provide immediate feedback to the teacher trainees in term of what occurred in the demonstration lesson. Acheson and other Standard graduate students started to explore several different uses of the partible video-tapes-recorder and its potentiality in modifying the behaviour of pupil-teachers towards desired objectives.

The Concept

Micro-teaching is like a simulated social skill teaching to provide the feedback to teacher-trainee for the modification of teacher-behaviour. It is training concept that can be applied at various pre-service and in-service stages in the professional development of teacher. Micro-teaching provides teachers with a provide setting or instruction in which the normal complexities of classroom are reduced in which the teacher gets feedback on his performance.

Basically, micro-teaching is a scaled down teaching encounter in which a teacher teaches in, small unit to a group of 5 to 10 students for a small period of 5 to 10 minutes and one teaching skill is practice during teaching. Micro-teaching is a new training design for pupil-teacher which provides an opportunity to practice one teaching skill at a time and with information about their performances immediately after completion of their lesson.

Micro-teaching is a clinical teaching programme which is organized to explore the trainee to an organized curriculum of miniature teaching encounterl moving from the less complex to the more complex.

The basic principles of micro-teaching are simple. A pupil-teacher teaches a short lesson of about five minutes duration to small group of pupils. At the end of the lesson, the pupils are left and student-teacher discuss the lesson with their supervisor. After a short interval, the pupil-teacher reteaches the lesson with a different group of pupils making use of the feedback from the supervision and attempts to improve this pervious lesson.

Allen (1966) defines micro-teaching as a 'Scaled down teaching encounter in class size and period.'

Clift and Other (1976) have recently defined "Micro-teaching is as a teachers' training procedure which reduces the teaching situation to simpler mid more controlled encounter achieved by limiting the practice-teaching to a specific skill and reducing teaching time and class size."

Mc Aleese and Unwin (1970) suggest that the term micro-teaching is most often applied to the use of closed circuit television

(CCIN) to give immediate feedback of a trainee teachers performance in, a simplified environment, but suggest that micro-teaching is the best viewed as a form of simulated teaching usually incorporating reduced complexity and some feedback placed along a simulation specture ranging from the purely abstract textbook of teaching practice through the actual classroom teaching."

Micro-teaching is defined as "a teacher-education technique which allows teacher to apply well defined teaching skill to a carefully prepared lesson in a planned series of five to ten minutes counters with a small group of real classroom' students, often with an opportunity to observe the performance on video-tape."

Importance

The above definitions indicate the following features of micro-teaching:

1. It is a real teaching but focuses on developing teaching skills and competencies.
2. It is a scaled down teaching.
   (a) To reduce the class size 5 to 10 pupils.
   (b) To reduce the duration of period 5 to 10 minutes.
   (c) To reduce the size of the topic.
   (d) To reduce the teaching skill. A single skill is practised.
3. It is a highly individualized training device.
4. It provides the feedback for trainees performance.
5. It is training device to prepare effective teachers.

The Hypothesis

Micro-teaching is an idea, at the core of which lie five essential proposition :

1. Micro-teaching is a real teaching, but its focus is on the development of certain teaching skills and not the development of pupils-abilities.
2. Micro-teaching lesson reduces the complexities of normal classroom by scaled down class size, content and time.
3. Micro-teaching focus on training for the development of

specific teaching skills. One skill is practised during course of teaching and brings it upto the mastery level.

4. Micro-teaching permits for the increased control of practice by providing the feedback to the pupil-teachers. A high degree of control can be imposed on the training programme.
5. Micro-teaching greatly expands the normal knowledge of results or feedback to teaching. It is highly indivi-dualized training programme.

The Working : Clift and Others (1976) have given three phases of micro-teaching procedure:

Knowledge Acquisition Phase: It involves two major activities:

(a) To observe demonstration skills, and
(b) To analyse and discuss demonstration.

Skill Acquisition Phase : Three activities are performed under this phase in the following sequences:

(a) To Prepare micro-lesson,
(b) To practice-teaching skills, and
(c) To evaluate the performances.

The evaluation activity provides the basis to re-plan the lesson for reteaching the same topic to practice the same skill.

Transfer Phases : After acquiring skills in the second phases, the trainees are given an opportunity to use the skills 'in normal classroom teaching situation.

The micro-teaching procedure involves the following steps:

1. A particular skill is defined to trainees in terms of teaching behaviour to provide the knowledge the and awareness of teaching skills.
2. These specific skills are demonstrated by an expert or shown through video-taped or film to the teacher- trainees.
3. The student-teacher plans a short lesson in which he can practice a particular skill.
4. The pupil-teachers the lesson to a small group of pupils-

which is observed by supervisor or peers or video-tape or audio-tape.

5. The teaching is followed by discussion to provide the feedback to the trainees. The video-tapes or audio-tape may be displayed to observe his own teaching activities by the trainees. The Awareness of own teaching performance provides the reforcement to the pupil-'teacher.
6. In the light of the discussion and suggestions, the student-teacher replans his lesson in order to practice the same skill effectively.
7. The revised lesson is retaught to different group of same class for the same duration to practice the same skill.
8. The re-teaching is followed by discussion, demostration suggestions and encouraging the teaching performance. In this way, the feedback is provided again to the trainee.
9. The 'teach-reteach' cycle is continued till desired level of skill is achieved. It is the mastery of teaching skill.

The Use : The following are the main advantages of micro-teaching:

1. It is scale down teaching hence it is called micro-teaching.
2. It is real classroom teaching which is used for developing teaching skills.
3. It is highly individualized training device. The cycles of reteaching and re-planning are determined by pupil-teacher or teacher-trainee.
4. One skill is developed in one time by reducing the complexity of teaching process.
5. Under this device attempts are made to develop the mastery of teaching skills.
6. There is a provision for integrating skills after developing mastery of teaching skills.
7. It is an effective feedback device for developing teaching skills.
8. An observation technique is used for teaching cycles. The trainee can observe and analyse his own teaching.

9. Under this device, demonstration can be done by an expert to improve his teaching skill.
10. The close circuit television (CCTV) is used to provide immediate feedback to the trainee.

The Drawbacks

It has the following limitations.

(1) Teaching is very complex situation but it employs very simple teaching situations. It may not work in actual class.

(2) It requires teaching laboratory or small classes for re-teaching which are not available in our schools.

(3) It is very time consuming device for developing teaching skill. A large number trainee can not be given such opportunities of re-teaching and re-planning.

(4) It employs more controlled situation with a limited practice-teaching to specific teaching skill.

(5) It deviates from normal classroom teaching for which trainee are prepared. He may not face real situation.

Micro-teaching can be used effectively by employing the, following suggestions:

1. Micro-teaching is to best viewed in the form of simulated teaching in corporating reduced complexity of teaching.
2. In our schools, micro teaching can only be used in simulated conditions. The student-teachers have to play the role of teacher as well as students.
3. Micro-teaching can be used in the actual classroom teaching by reducing the size of topic, duration of time and one skills can be practised. The size of the class should remain the sane it should not be reduced.
4. Under this device attempts are made to move from the less complex teaching to the more complex teaching.
5. More than one teaching skills are to be practiced in organizing teaching simulated conditions.
6. The best way that micro-teaching should be in corporated by simulated social skill training. It is highly feasible.

Teaching, an Art

Micro-teaching is used for developing certain teaching skills. A teaching skill is defined as a set of teacher behaviours which are especially effective in bringing about desired changes in pupil-teachers. There are various teaching skills which can be developed among pupil-teachers. Allen and Ryans (1969) have suggested the following fourteen teaching skills:

1. Stimulus variation
2. Set induction
3. Closure
4. Silence ad non-verbal cause
5. Reinforcement
6. Asking questions
7. Probing questions
8. Divergent questions
9. Attending behaviour
10. Illustrating
11. Lecturing
12. Higher order questions,
13. Planned repetition, and
14. Communication completeness

B. K. Passi (1976) has described the following thirteen skills in his book 'Becoming Better teacher' : 'A Micro-teaching Approach':

1. Writing instructional objectives,
2. Introduction of a lesson,
3. Fluency and questioning,
4. Probing questioning,
5. Explaining,
6. Illustrating with examples,
7. Stimulus variation,
8. Silences and non-verbal cause,
9. Reinforcement to student's-participation,
10. Increasing pupil-participation,

11. Using Black Board,
12. Achieving closure, and
13. Recognising attending behaviour.

The meaning of importance teaching skills have been discussed here:

Stimulus Variation : This skill involves deliberate changing of various attention producing behaviour by the teacher in order to keep pupils attentive at high level.

Set Induction : It refers to the development of cognitive rapport between pupils and teacher to obtain immediate involvement in the lesson.

Closure: This skill is complementary to set induction. It is more than a quick summary of the portions taught and the pupils are able to related new knowledge with the previous one.

Silence and Non-Verbal Cause : The use of silence and non-verbal cause is powerful device in order to encourage pupil-participation in classroom teaching.

Skill of Reinforcement : It involves teacher encouraging pupils response using verbal praise, accepting their responses or non-verbal causes like a smile.

Fluency in Questioning: This is a skill in asking questions. By fluency means the use of as many question as possible in a given period of teaching.

Probing Questions : Probing requires that teacher asks questions that need pupils to go beyond superficial first answers of question.

Recognition and Attention Behaviour: The successful teacher is more sensitive to note the interest of boredom of pupils through visual causes.

Skill of Explaining : An explanation is a set of interrelated statements made by teacher in order to increase the under standing in the pupils about ideas and concepts.

Skill of Increasing Pupil-Participation : This skill involves the four components creating set questioning, encouraging pupil activities and pausing in such a way that pupil participation is maximised.

Skill of Writing Objectives : It involves the following activities identifying objectives, analysing the task and writing objectives in behavioural terms with regard to adequate learning.

Skill of Using Blackboard : This skill requires legibility, neatness appropriateness continuity simplicity of blackboard work. It is very essential skill for a successful teacher. The effectiveness of presentation depends upon the proper use of blackboard.

Skill for Class Management : This skill involves a number of activities that a teacher performs for creating and maintaining conducive environment for learning in the classroom.

Skill of Using Audio-Visual Aids: It implies the effective use of appropriate teaching aids to make teaching interesting and desired objectives can be achieved. The effective use of audiovisual aids makes the pupil active and attentive in classroom.

Skill for Giving Assignment: This skill consists of the pupils to organize and assimilate the learnt material.

Skill of Pacing Lesson : The pacing of a lesson means variation in the teaching speed. This skill involves adjustive devices for satisfying the needs of thc pupils or student-variation.

The Use of Higher Order Questions : This skill involves the questions which can be answered by memory or sensory description. The question consist of rules, principles and generalization.

Divergent Questions : It requires the respondent to organize elements into new pattern, predict, and infer from the situation. This skill involves higher order of thinking creativity.

Lecturing : require's the effective presentation of content by using appropriate techniques and devices of teaching aids. This is, known as communication competency.

Planned Repetition : It is a powerful skill in focusing and highlighting important points of teaching.

Competencies of Communication : It is a skill which is developed by sensitivity training for a clear communication of ideas and concepts in teaching. The teachers are more -responsive to possible miscommunication.

Teaching Skills and their Components

Skill	*Components*
Writing instructional objectives	Clarity, relevance to the content, adequacy with reference to the domains and level of objectives, attainability in terms of pupil outcomes.
Organising the content	Logical organisation according to content and psychological organisation as per need of the pupil.
Creating set for introducing the lesson	Greeting, accepting creating, securing attention and giving instructions, establishing rapport, ensuring facilities like chalk, duster, aids, apparatus etc.
Introducing the lesson	Linking with past experiences, link between introduction with main parts, use of appro-priate devices/techniques like questioning, examples, exhibits arousal.
Structuring class room questions	Structuring questions at different levels which are grammatically correct, precise and relevant to content.
Question delivery and distribution	Questions delivered with appropriate speed, with proper intonation and pitch, allowing pause for thinking, and questions well distributed covering even non-volunteers.
Response management	Management of pupil responses using techniques like prompting, eliciting further information, refocusing and asking critical awareness questions, accepting-rejecting, redirection.
Explaining	Clarity, continuity, relevance to the content using beginning and concluding statements, covering essential points.
Illustrating with examples	Simple, interesting and relevant to the point being explained.
Using teaching aids	Relevant to content, appropriate to the pupil's level, proper display and appropriate use.
Stimulus Variation	Body movements, gestures, change in into-nation and pitch, change in interaction pattern and pausing.
Reinforcement	Use of praise words and statements, accepting and using pupil ideas, repeating and rephras-ing pupil ideas. Use of pleasant and approving gestures and expressions, writing pupil answers on blackboard.
Pacing of the lesson.	Adjusting the speed of the lesson to the level of the pupils and difficulty level of the content.

Contd...

Skill	***Components***
Prompting pupil participation	Providing opportunity to pupils to increase participation through asking questions, creating climate of participation, use of silence and nonverbal cues, calling upon pupils' physical participation.
Use of Black board	Legible, neat, adequate with reference to the content covered.
Achieving closure of the lesson	Summarization, establishing link between the present learning with earlier as well as future learning, creating a sense of achievement in pupils.
Giving assignments	Relevant to the content covered and level of pupils.
Evaluating the pupil's progress	Relevant to the instructional objectives. Use appropriate questions and observations.
Diagnozing pupil learning difficulties and tasking remedial measures	Identifying learning difficulties along with causes, remedial measures suited to the type of the learning difficulties and the level of pupils.
Management of the class	Attention behaviour reinforced and directions given to, eliminate non-attending behaviour, clarity of directions, appropriate handling of pupils disruptive behaviour.

After completing the preparation along the lines indicated above implementation of the programme of micro-teaching in an institution require the following steps.

The Orientation : Orientation of the faculty was envisaged under step above. Now it is the turn of the student-teacher. They need to be given an overview of the concept and procedure of micro-teaching, analysis of teaching into skills to be practised and the skill learning strategy. This may be done in an atmosphere of free and fair discussion.

Skill Presentation : The teaching skill selected for practice by the student-teachers may be presented. The presentation or the modelling exercise includes discussion about its rationale and role in teaching, its meaning, and definition of the allied terms, component teaching behaviours comprising the skill, sample illustrations of the component behaviours, sample micro-lesson, plans and observation tools. Materials on selected skills has been provided in the second section of this handbook. Material is available in Passi (1976) and "Special Package on Core Teaching Skills" being prepared in the NCERT.

This step is also a part of the modelling. After discussion of the teaching skill, the teacher-educator gives a demonstration lesson on the use of the teaching skill. This lesson is observed and the teacher-educator is provided feedback on the lesson based on systematic observation and recording as pointed out in Unit IV.

Preparation of Micro-lesson Plan : The student-teacher selects a concept for the preparation of micro-lesson plan. The concept has to be such that it is reasonably amenable to the practice of the skill. The component behaviours of the skill may be made conspicuous in the micro-lesson through labelling in brackets. Samples are available in section two of the handbook. The lesson, is confined to six minutes of teaching.

Creating Micro-teaching Setting : Seating arrangements for the pupils for practising the skill, the college supervisor and the peer supervisor may be made. Blackboard, chalk, duster and other materials required for the micro-teacher may be arranged.

Practice of the Skill : The students teacher the lesson for six minutes. The lesson is observed using observation schedule.

Providing Feedback : On the basis of the observations, the student-teacher is provided feedback on his teaching performance. The feedback is provided in terms of his use of the component behaviours comprising the skill under practice.

Replan-Reteach-Refeedback : The students teacher replans his lesson in the light of the feedback received. The lesson is retaught and refeedback is provided as in (f) and (g) above.

Repeat the Cycle to Master : The student-teacher repeats the Micro-teaching cycle till he attains mastery over the skill under practice. The mastery level will depend upon the efficiency with which he can use it and the time available for practice.

Integration of Skills : The skills are mastered as outlined under steps: (a) to (i) above. The training in the integration of teaching skills may be provided as indicated in Unit IV of the handbook.

Judging the Devices

The teaching skills being developed through micro-teaching lessons are to be evaluated or observed by the peers of supervisor. The rating schedule in used as criterion measure. The most popular evaluative instrument for assessing the effectiveness of micro-teaching is the Stanford Teacher Competence Appraisal Guide (STCAG).

The problem of evaluation of micro-teaching effectiveness is much more difficult. The more important question is whether micro-teaching experiences lead to improve the teaching skills in a normal classroom teaching.

Allen and Ryan (1969) have given ail evaluation sheet for assessing the skill of reinforcement. It consists of four dimensions of the reinforcement skills.

1. The correct responses of the students are praised or rewarded by saying 'fine', 'good' 'excellent' etc.
2. The teacher use non-verbal cues (smile) to encourage students.
3. The teacher gives credit to students answering a question partly correct.
4. The teacher refers to possitive aspects of a student's previous responses.

These dimensions are recorded, by the teacher has used to category number of times. The categories are assessed on scales ranging from three to seven points. The STCAG consists of a number of scales rating the broad aspects of a teacher's performances.

The following are the main uses of micro-teaching:

1. It is an effective-feedback device for the modification of teacher-behaviour.
2. The knowledge of practice and teaching skill can be given by the use of micro-teaching.
3. It is useful for developing teaching efficiency in pre- service and in-service teacher-education programmes.
4. The specific teaching skills are developed by the micro-

teaching experiences e.g. reinforcement skill probing questions, etc.

5. It is a training device for improving teaching practice and to prepare effective teachers or better teachers.
6. The mechanism of feedback device can be combined with other devices such as stimulated social skill training and interaction analysis device which provide continuous reinforcement to the trainee-performances.
7. The training of teacher becomes individualized. Each trainee makes progress in developing teaching skills at his own rating depending upon his ability.
8. It permits increased control and regulates teaching practice.
9. Micro-teaching can be done either in teal classroom conditions or insimulated conditions.
10. It is an economical device and use of videotape enables the trainee to analyse his own teaching performance.
11. It lessons the complexities of the normal classroom teaching by scaled down teaching.
12. It focuses attention on teaching behaviour to modify and improve in a desired direction.

While teaching, a teacher encounters a variety of pupil behaviours. Obviously, he would like the pupils' desirable behaviours and criterion responses to be retained and undesirable behaviours to be eliminated. For reinforcing pupils desirable behaviours and criterion responses, he uses positive verbal and non-verbal reinforcers. These reinforcers not only strengthen the pupils' desirable behaviours, but also develop confidence in them. Besides, they enhance their positive self-concept. Absence of a positive, reinforcer for pupils, desirable behaviours may erode their confidence and lead to poor self image. Positive reinforcement encourages pupils to participate actively in classroom transactions. It stimulates them to achieve more thereby, creating a sense of achievement.

Skillful management of reinforcers helps a teacher to promote pupils' learning. The skill of reinforcement refers to the effective use of reinforcers. It can, therefore, be defined as "the effective use of reinforcers to modify pupils' behaviour in the desired direction."

Skill Components : In order to learn the effective use of the skill of reinforcement, it is desirable to specify its component behaviours which are presented in this section.

Positive verbal reinforcers can be further divided into two broad categories. The first category includes the use of praise words, such as 'good', 'excellent'. "fantastic", "splendid', 'right', 'yes!, correct', 'continue', 'go ahead , etc. The second category of positive verbal reinforcers refers to a teacher's verbal behaviour other than the use of praise words. The statements accepting pupil's feelings, repeating and rephrasing pupil responses, summarising pupil ideas, etc., fall in this category of positive verbal reinforcers.

The Assessment

The Meaning : When a question is put in the classroom, there are a number of possible pupil response situations such as no response, wrong response, partially correct response, incomplete response or correct response. The skill of probing questioning is going deep into pupil responses through step by step by step questioning with a view to eliciting the. criterion response. Let consider various, response situations one by one.

No Response Situation : No response situation refers to the failure on the part of the pupil to frame and express verbally a response to the question that he is required to answer. The opportunity to respond is the essential condition to identify and-response situation. Special reference to opportunity for responding has been mentioned because it is observed that teachers tend to think a no response occurrence even without providing opportunity to the pupils to give response. They put questions to the class, pause for a few second and taking the silence in the class as an indication of no response, start explaining, repeating or restructuring the question. This is an unhealthy practice mid should be avoided. Only after a designated pupil fails to answer, we may infer a no response situation.

Definition of Skill : Many a time, it happens that a teacher explains in the classroom a scientific principle or a mathematical rule or an abstract idea and observes that his pupils are not comprehending it. In such a situation, the teacher attempts to explain the concept or generalisation more and more but he fails in his attempt. The concept or generalisation requires more than mere explanation for the pupils to understand. This presents a challenge to the teacher. An unskilled teacher may deal with this challenging situation by rebuking the pupils for be inattentive in the classroom and asking them just to memorise the concept or rule. But a skilful teacher handles this situations in a different way. He illustrates the scientific principle, generalisation. This makes them easier to understand for the pupils. Obviously, examples are one of the most effective tools in the hands of the teacher to make to concept or generalisation simple and easier for pupils to understand. Thus, examples can be defined as the observation or situations of occurrence of a concept or generalisation and the skill of illustrating with examples can be defined as the selection and presentation of the example, relevant to the concept or generalisation to be taught to the pupils so as to make it easier for them to understand it. The examples, of courses, may be drawn from the pupils experiences.

Components of the Skill : The next logical question is as to whether all examples make the concept or generalisation easier to understand ? If not, what type of examples are helpful and appropriate in realising this objective? Experiences with the use of examples for illustrating concepts and generalisations have shown that effective examples have definite characteristics. A teacher should known these characteristics and keep them in mind while formulating examples for illustrating a particular concept or generalisation. The component behaviours, based on these characteristics are presented in this section.

Meaning of the Skill : Learning in the classroom depends to a large extent, on the attention of the pupils on the learning, task. It is therefore., essential for the teacher to secure and sustain pupil attention for making his teaching effective. Continued used of the same stimulus or activity for longer period induces inattention. The inattention is caused in two ways. Firstly, continued focus of the pupils on the same stimulus for a long time restricts his postural mobility. As a result, they feel fatigued. Secondly, the continued use of the same stimulus for longer duration introduces the element of monotony which brings in dullness. The problem of inattention is further aggravated because of the short span of pupil attention. Their attention tends to shift from one stimulus to another frequently. They find it difficult to attend to one stimulus for more than a few minutes. The problem of inattention is a challenge to the teacher. Unless he is in a position to secure and sustain pupil attention, optimum learning cannot take place. It is, therefore essential for the teacher to secure and sustain pupil attention to what he is discussing in the classroom. How to accomplish this task during classroom teaching is a problem that confronts every teacher ?

The Strength

Meaning and Definition of the Skill : A pupil is required to learn a number of concepts, phenomena, generalisations, procedures, functions and reasons for certain occurrences. He is to learn about their attributes, constituent elements, relationship and applications. A teacher organises, a number of learning experiences in the classroom towards this end. He uses a number of interrelated statements related to the concepts, phenomena, generalisations and functions with a view to developing in pupils an understanding about them. The set of interrelated statement used for this purpose is termed as explanation and the process is termed as explaining. The term explaining can, therefore, be defined as the use of interrelated statements about a concept phenomenon, generalisation with a view to providing its understanding to someone else.

An explanation to be understood by pupils the explainer has to keep in mind the previous knowledge of the pupils. The previous knowledge refers to the knowledge already possessed by pupils. Since previous knowledge of the pupils of different grades, cultural background and geographical regions is always different an explanation about a concept which is appropriate for one group of pupils may not be appropriate for another group. The quality of an explanation. However, depends on the degree of understanding it generates in the explainess.

Man has wants and these can be satisfied by the used of goods. For instance, when an individual is hungry, the satisfies his hunger by taking food. He is said to have consumed the food. Similarly (explaining link), a smoker when uses a cigarette and gets satisfaction, he is said to have consumed a cigarette. Thus (explaining link), the direct use of goods and services for the satisfaction of human wants is known as consumption.

Whenever we consume eatables they lose their utility. Food water, rice, fruit and vegetables get destroyed when these are consumed. Therefore (explaining link) some confuse consumption as the destruction of utilities. But (explaining link) this is not so. Sometimes (explaining link) utility of certain commodities are destroyed of their own. For instance (explaining link) when any fruit decays, it loses its utility. A house may catch fire and get destroyed. The decayed fruit and the burnt houses have lost their utilities. But (explaining link) these cannot be said to have been consumed. Because (explaining link) an act of consumption implies satisfaction of human wants. The decayed fruit and the burnt house have not satisfied human want while losing their utilities.

Besides (explaining link) goods, services are also consumed. When a person travels in a bus and pays for the ticket, he consumes the transport services. A teacher's services are consumed by the pupils when they learn from him in the school. In the same way (explaining link) a doctor's, a lawyer's and a tax consultants services are consumed by the need consumers who pay fees for their services.

Consumption, therefore, (explaining link) stands for the satisfaction of human wants. A commodity which loses its utility without satisfying a human want cannot be said to have been consumed. Besides goods services, are also consumed (concluding statement).

Production of Video

Both hardware and software are needed for video production as incase of any other media and these two components call for more or less amount of time and money according to the nature and quantity of these requisites. But software is given more importance than hardware due to the fact that the former is developed by the experts with adequate knowledge in pedagogy, psychology and content subject. Knowledge in learning strategies, reinforcement techniques, reading readiness, attention and interests and content is felt essential for developing suitable video programmes for the clientele groups. The software approach is often referred to behaviour technology aiming at modification of behaviour and enriching learning achievement. Maximisation of learning experiences can be possible through the adequate use of software inputs in man-machine systems.

Procurement of hardware, even production and transmission services are more or less one-shot activities, but software development is a continuous process and purely academic in nature. Software must be relevant to the curricular needs specific to the courses/clientele. Teachers and students can interact and develop the material according to their capabilities and requirements. The entire process must be taken as integrated and interrelated. The objectives should be precisely identified and software has to be developed by educationists and academics. These useful material can be utilised in video production.

Software production for educational TV or video cassettes requires a combination of knowledge of subject matter, media production techniques and communication strategy to reach the target audience. Just recording a chapter of the book cannot make a good video tape. The video/TV productions are only tools for communication and some basic questions need answering and understanding before production. Some of these questions are:

(i) Who is the target group?

(ii) What is their socio-cultural background?

(iii) What are their needs?

(iv) What are their experiences?

(v) Material to be produced by what means/medium

(vi) By which agencies/personnel?

(vii) What advance preparation is needed?

(viii) With what infrastructure?

(ix) What targets are feasible in terms of time and money to produce the material?

The production personnel, especially the scriptwriter should answer these and other allied questions and understand the production techniques before developing the software for the video programmes. The infrastructure for administration and production should be quite adequate and oriented to produce good quality video programmes without much hindrances and handicaps.

The Motives

The objectives of such communication may be one or more of the following:

(i) To impart relevant knowledge
(ii) To inform
(iii) To entertain
(iv) To teach skills
(v) To present concepts
(vi) To generate curiosity and interest
(vii) To stimulate creative and imaginative ideas
(viii) To develop problem-solving ability
(ix) To bring about change
(x) To modify behaviour and attitudes

These objectives are to be realised through the scripts. Some objectives are very easy for realisation. These objectives are also not hierarchical. Media communication to be effective needs insight and understanding of the target audience and their needs according to which scripts and materials for video programmes are developed for realising the specific objectives.

The Working : Scripts are the basis of all production activities. These soft-ware materials need to be translated into action i.e. video programmes. Sometime scripts for educational video programmes are developed through workshops where writers of various abilities with experience and insight, discuss the programme briefs, objectives, audience profile and prepare drafts in a rough proforma. These drafts prepared under the guidance of experts are presented and discussed in the workshops. Again the scripts are revised, redrafted and utilised for video programmes. These scripts undergo several revisions before good quality materials are ready for video production.

Video Script

The process of writing a script for ETV and video pro-grammes is essentially the same as designing any learning activity. But writing video scripts means using your "ideas and imagination in a different way." i.e., giving visual treatment to your ideas. The first thing, therefore, to understand and learn about video script writing is that it is not a process of writing words or sentences and thinking of pictures to accompany them. On the other hand, it is an imaginative and creative process and is essentially and basically an art of imaginative programme creation, using the available resources. It is because of this reason that it is said that television programmes are evolved from the combined or pooled talents of the producer, the scriptwriter and occasionally others directly involved, such as designer, graphic artists, etc. Satisfying success can be achieved in this exercises more conveniently and confidently, if we look upon the process of evolving an ETV video script as a cyclic process, as shown in the diagram below.

E.T.V. Programmes

Before going into the details of each of the steps involved in the process of evolving an ETV script, it is, however, essential to point out the two important facts that all scriptwriters must always keep in mind.

1. Television is a one-way medium
2. Television is a mass-medium

Both these factors exert considerable limitations on the designing of ETV programmes. One has to bear in mind that there should be no gap in the content and the script should, as far as possible, be self-sufficient in communicating the desired messages. This limitation makes script writing a difficult job which demands special care and attention, better imagination and visualisation, mastery of the subject and mature experience in identifying the requirement of the viewers. So the script should evolve step by step and different steps be presented vividly and linked so smoothly and naturally, one after the other, that the average viewer understands and follows the total content without any difficulty.

Secondly, because television is a mass medium, an ETV

programme will be viewed by a large number of students, including the talented, the average and the below average. It may be very difficult to cater to the needs of all the three categories simultaneously throughout a programme. Therefore, the programme has to be planned and prepared in such a way that all the three categories benefit to the optimal extent, providing involvement and satisfaction to each one of them. This can be achieved by devoting the major part of the programme to the average students and also offering some satisfying material for the talented as well as the below average ones, so that the interest of all the three categories is sustained and the programme attracts and serves viewers from all sections of audience.

Introducing the entertainment element in a television programme is useful, but a balance is to be maintained by the scriptwriter between entertainment and education. In case of younger age group audience, entertainment programmes are desirable but this element must be exploited cautiously and carefully so that children are not carried away by the entertainment part so much that the actual message is not at all received by them. Thus, a successful scriptwriter always keeps in mind the psychology, interests and needs of his target audience. He has also to remember that visuals are the main carriers of the message and sound effects and words have a role to play but only in support of visuals, Television script writing is thus the other name of thinking in terms of visuals to convey the intended message, combined, of course, with sound effects, music and words to make it a continuous programme in order to achieve the desired objectives.

Different writers follow different methods and techniques for writing scripts and it varies from writer to writer. However, for purposes of explanation and convenience of beginners, the process of script writing may be described under the following main steps:

Defining Objectives and Selecting Content Outlines : Once the topic for writing a script has been assigned, the scriptwriter should be informed about the target audience, their age-level and specific objectives and the programme.

This is to be followed by deciding the content to be presented in order to achieve the established objectives. Specifying objectives and visualising content in detail is an essential discipline in the production process. At this stage, the detailed visual ideas on which the programme will be based are evolved. "How can we convey that concept visually?" "How can we grasp the attention of the viewers?" This stage demands creativity and imagination. The success of the programme will heavily depend on the care taken at this stage.

Research and Selection of Materials : Research is important to all programmes. Finding information from books, periodicals, reports, atlases, encyclopaedias, dictionaries and from experts in the field, checking details, locating pictures, selecting film locations, etc., are the part of research. Once the materials have been collected after research, the relevant materials which match the content and lead to the achievement of the desired objectives, can be finally selected for making the programme.

Selection of Resources to Present the Content : The scriptwriter has to be very imaginative in his selection of resources to match the content and the objectives. It is the most important step in the process. Success of the programme depends on the imaginative use of visual resources, keeping in mind the time and money available for the programme. This process of selecting resources implies the conversion of the programme content into suitable and appropriate visual terms, i.e. how the content can be presented visually. It needs imagination, research and experience to accomplish this job successfully and to achieve the desired quality of the programme.

Organisation of Resources into a Programme Structure : This is the process of giving the programme a shape and a form-visual treatment. It includes deciding how the programme will vary according to the needs, interest and how the parts of the programme will be linked together and knit into a natural sequence, so that the programme may have varying interest levels and appear to be evolving from one sequence to another. In this process, each sequence would have to be linked with the previous one in respect of content, visuals, sound effects and other demonstration materials. But at the same time, care may be taken to see that there is a good coherence in the whole programme, something to bind everything into one natural and effective unit. At this stage, it is helpful to draw a time-line of the programme, showing how much time is to be spent on each element of the programme keeping in view the way the selected resources are to be used.

Developing a Story-board/Draft Script and the Final Script : All the visual themes alongwith necessary links thought out and planned by the scriptwriter need to be communicated to the producers for understanding the shots and logical sequencing of the programme. This could easily be communicated if the scriptwriter presents his ideas in the form of a story-board. For developing the story-board, the scriptwriter may divide the white sheet of paper into two vertical columns. Pictures in sequence may be described within different rectangles (ratio 3: 4) drawn on the left hand side of the paper. The supporting words, sound effects and music may be indicated in the right half of the paper.

From the story-board and final script, the producer writes the camera script which contains the technical information necessary for the production of the programmes.

To sum up, the following guidelines should be borne in mind by the scriptwriter while writing a script for an ETV programme.

(1) First of all, the scriptwriter must realise and accept the factual position that scripts are not written but they are evolved.

(2) He should always keep in mind the target audience and their needs.

(3) The script must be simple, direct and personal.

(4) It must be written with full knowledge of and involvement of programme visuals.

(5) It should constantly pick up, stress and reinforce its educational points using different resources.

(6) It should involve the audience, as far as possible, actively.

(7) The commentary should be informal and not book type.

(8) It should not attempt to say too much in limited time and space.

(9) It should end with a simple summary of the main programme points, with a different visual presentation.

(10) It should have a variety of pace and rhythm and must give breathing space occasionally.

(11) Above all, it should attempt to take its viewers/audience on a journey of discovery and not merely give information.

Television or video is primarily a visual medium. Naturally, therefore, the quality of any video programme will be determined by the quality and variety of visual and other resources that have gone into its making. A scriptwriter must, therefore, have a thorough knowledge of different visual and other resources of television which may be available to him to evolve a programme.

For purposes of convenience, the resources for video production can be classified into the following major categories:

Pictures: By pictures, here, we mean any kind of visuals that can be put in front of a video camera. These may include still photographs, slides, filmstrips, overhead transparencies, especially prepared graphics such as charts, diagrams, maps, outlines, summaries, pictures from books, cartoons, captions' with lettering on them. We call all such pictures or photographs as captions or photo-captions. Sometimes, we can prepare special captions in which things and words can be made to move, appear and disappear. These are known as animated captions. All drawn pictures and photo-captions are usually made in a standard size of 12" x 9", unless the camera is required to move about for showing different parts of the picture.

People: Most television is about people, people telling us things, people being interviewed, people acting, people laughing, people weeping, people playing instruments and dancing, people singing, people playing games, people doing all kinds of things from mending bicycles to telling jokes, and people trying to persuade us to take to their point of view. They also include presenters, demonstrators, guests, teachers and class children.

Things: The range of things shown on television is infinite, elephants, puppets, models, machines of all kinds, toys, furniture, bridges, buildings, aeroplanes, the sun, the moon and so on. Television provides a unique opportunity to bring together a huge variety of things, new and old, mundane and unusual.

Drama: Drama is also classified by many as one of the important resources for television. It may be very simple with no studio set or very complex ones using several settings. Drama does have elements of people, things and sound included in it, yet it may be classified as a separate resource.

Film: Films constitute a very important resource for television. The film can be put on a projector and beamed straight at a television camera. Things that are impossible or impracticable to shoot on television-such as under-water photography and complicated cartoon work which we call Film Animation-can be shot on film. Films can also be used to slow down or speed up actions, as you might have seen in programmes shown on games, sports and races. All such specially prepared films can be fed into a TV programme. (The technique of making films and television programmes are in themselves very different, of course).

Set & Lighting: It is also an important resource of TV which gives it reality.

Sound: Sound is an important resource for television though it is often under-utilised. Imaginative use of music and appropriate sound effects can certainly go a long way in making a good TV programme.

This classification of resources into Pictures, People, Things, Drama, Film, Set, Lighting and Sound, is particularly useful and convenient for beginners who, while trying to evolve ideas for video programmes, can refer to this broad classification.

Pictures are of paramount importance in video programmes. The Central Institute of Educational Technology, NCERT has identified the following, mostly related to pictures.

A video programme consists of a series of pictures, i.e., the pictures keep changing in quick succession. This change is not just for variety, but each picture has its own message. All the pictures must synchronise with sound.

Photograph's Utility : Types of pictures (shots) depend on the focal length of the lens and the distance between the camera and the subject. Following types of shots are used commonly:

1. Single Shot-a shot including one person
2. Two Shot-a shot including two persons

3. Three Shot-a shot including three persons
4. Crowd Shot-a shot including a number of people
5. Wide Shot or Very Long Shot (VLS)-a shot which includes along with the principal subject, a large amount of the background in the picture.
6. Full Length Shot or Long Shot (LS)-a shot in which the subject occupies about 3/4 of the vertical height of the picture frame.
7. Medium Long Shot (MLS) or Knee Shot-a shot in which the subject is seen from the knee upwards.
8. Medium Shot or Mid Shot-a shot in which the subject is seen from the waist upwards.
9. Medium Close Shot (MCS) or Medium Close Up (MCU)-a shot which includes the subject's head and shoulders. It is also called the chest or Bust Shot.
10. Close Shot (CS) or Close Up (CU)-a shot which includes the subject's head and neck only
11. Big Close Shot (BCS) or Big Close Up (BCU)-a shot which includes only a section of the subject's head from chin to forehead.
12. Over-Shoulder Shot (OSS)-a shot of a subject or subject taken over the shoulder of person in the foreground.

For maximum effects, the change of pictures must be brought about in the right manner. The following are certain conventional methods of changing the shots.

The Cut: This is an instant change form one picture to another. It is used when the action is continuous in time. A cut should be motivated by an action, by the dialogue or both.

The Dissolve or Mix: This is a gradual change from one picture to another. While the first picture is vanishing slowly, the second one is gradually appearing on the screen. At a point both pictures are visible on the screen simultaneously. It is used when a lapse of time is to be indicated, when there is a change of screen, and in getting to and from captions or telecine.

The Superimposition: This is the imposition of one picture over another one which is already on the screen. It is used for showing written captions over persons or objects in order to identify them, in teaching to reinforce the visual with the verbal, and for special effects, e.g., to show a person dreaming or thinking.

The Fade In and Out: These are the gradual appearance of a picture on a blank screen and the gradual disappearance of a picture from the screen. These are used at the beginning and the end of a programme and instead of a mix when there is longer lapse of time to be indicated.

The Pan: Here the change of picture is brought about by panning i.e., moving the camera head left or right in the horizontal plane while the base of the camera remains static. It is used when following a moving person or thing and for moving from object to object in order to build up a particular effect or to provide background for a series of captions.

The Tilt: Here the change of picture is brought about by swinging the camera head up or down in the vertical plane without moving the base of the camera.

The Crab: Crabbing is like panning except that here the whole camera is moved left or right from the base.

The Zoom In: Using a zoom lens, a wide shot of an object or person is changed to a closer shot. This is used for focusing attention on a particular part of the whole picture and for special effects (horror, surprise, excitement, etc).

The Zoom Out: Using a zoom lens, a close shot of a person or object is changed to a wider shot. It is used for establishing the relationship between the object or person with the surroundings, when a person in close-up moves or is joined by someone else or is going to talk about something next to him but not visible at the moment.

The Track In Out: This has the same effect as the zoom in and out except that here in the absence of a zoom lens the whole camera is moved forward or backward from the base. This not only requires great skill on the part of the cameraman but a very smooth studio floor. It cannot be used for a quick change of shot and the range between the two shots would be limited.

Writing of Script

1. Use active voice as far as possible.
2. Use specific words and examples, wherever possible, to establish specific relationships.
3. Try not to start with a negative sentence.
4. Sometimes, we may write just one sentence as commentary and then change three/four similar slides/shots in succession.
5. There is no need to describe pictures which must speak for themselves.
6. Words should coincide with pictures where they make sense.
7. If you have a marvellous speaker in your programme, let him do the job. It will give your programme some "credibility." So, let it come from horse's mouth.
8. Make your audience see the 'pictures' you want them to see in a long snot.
9. Use just one line of commentary and let the noises take over. Avoid too much use of words. Try to forget your bombastic vocabulary and get rid of words only.
10. In general, the less you write, the better it is. So, learn to get rid of your vocabulary and use simple words only.
11. Never cover all the really dull stuff like facts, figures etc., in commentary. These can be really handled much more amusingly when they are presented graphically.

Software is more important than hardware and is very local specific, objective based and academic in nature. It must be relevant to the curricular needs and is developed with the knowledge and skills based on pedagogy, psychology and content subject. The objectives of software are to impart knowledge, inform, entertain, and so on and learners' experience and interest are taken into account for suitable software development.

Script writing for video production is of paramount importance and is evolved through the efforts of the writer, producer and other associated personnel. In view of the limitations of the video programme, better visualisation and imagination, careful selection of content, appropriate format and language, etc., are used for script writing. A well integrated and inter-dependent process is adopted for developing suitable script and video production.

Various resources like pictures, content about people, things, drama, film, set, lighting, sound, etc., are utilised for video production. Since visuals are of crucial importance, great caution is taken for selecting spots and taking shots relevant to the content. Besides, producers and scriptwriters need to be acquainted with various technicalities including production strategies, terms and techniques used in video production. To write suitable scripts, particularly as regards language, teaching points, visuals, and so on, we need to follow several guidelines.

Designs as Tools

Teaching broadly consists of designs of instructions. The development of educational engineering has provided the scientific basis of instructional system. Educational technology has the main assumption that teaching is not only an art but also a science : teachers are not only effective by birth but they can be mode effective through training institutions.

Glaser (1968) states that professional skill and efficiency can be developed with its help of instructional designs. The expert's and specialists are, attempting to investigated the level of professional skill to be developed. L Carter (1966) found in his investigation that instructional designs were effective for developing group professional efficiency than individual. Glaser has enumerated the following functions of instructional designs:

(1) It emphasizes on structure of the task. The content is analysed for its structure and ascertaining its characteristics.

(2) The learner's responses are analysed in view of objectives and levels of learning. The entering behaviour is considered for providing new stimuli to have desired responses of the learner.

(3) The appropriate teaching strategies, techniques and tactics are selected for presenting, content so that desired learning

structure may be generated. The techniques of motivation are employed for leading the teaching.

(4) The measuring instrument is constructed for evaluating the performance level of the students and decision may be taken about the objectives of learning.

The desired objectives could not achieved on the basis of learning theories therefore, teaching learning structure, teaching theories and structure of the content have been developed. Instructional designs are the sum of these things.

Fundamental Concept

The term 'Science' and 'technology' are very confusing when these are used simultaneously. These are two distinctive terms and have different meanings, though these are closely related to each other. The term 'Science is theoretical in nature while technology is an application to practical task for specific purpose.

The term 'Science' concerns with empirical knowledge based on experiences and observations. A micro-approach is used in science. An element is divided in molecules and atoms. An atom is further divided into electron, protons and neutrons. An experimental method is used in science. An experiment means to control to observe, and to measure. The cause-effect relationship is established in formulating theories and developing principles. The science means advancement of knowledge. It has the following characteristics:

(1) Science is an empirical knowledge based on experiences and observations.

(2) It is based on experimentation-control observe and measure.

(3) Science is based on objectivity.

(4) Science employs micro-approach to study the structure of a phenomenon.

(5) It establishes, cause-effect relationship among the variables or elements of a phenomena.

(6) Theories, principles, laws, postulates and hypothesis are the main content of science.

(7) Science is an edifice of knowledge and advance'men't of human awareness.

Technology is an application of scientific principles to practical task for specific purpose. Technology means engineering or use of machines. It has three aspects—input, process and output. The process is based on feedback theory (cybernetics). It has three functions- initiate., regulate and control. All the -machines are based on feedback system it is an hardware approach of technology. If the scientific principles applied to teaching, training and instruction for specific purpose or specific objective. It is known as software approach of technology.

The word 'technology' is derived from the Greek work technie, meaning art or skill and logia, meaning science or study. A wide definition of technology is the science of study of an art or skill. This work, technology, is differently interpreted in different contexts. Professional engineers, doctors and scientists, economists and politicians, whether they are practitioners or academicians, have their own usage. It is not surprising that teachers have difficulty in understanding the concept of technology and its place in college curriculum.

Technology is more than the academic study of materials and resources. Its importance centres around the practical application of materials - and ' resources, especially in the service of man. Technology is the purposeful use of man's knowledge of materials of different resources, sources of energy And other natural happenings. There is a close relationship between technology and society. Technology is for the benefit of the society in general or a neighbouring community. The interaction of technology and society is one of ends and means. The society opts for certain ends for which, the, technology provides the means. Conversely, technology influences the selection of inputs resulting in the outputs society needs and requires.

Teaching is an art as well as a science. As an art, it portrays the imaginative and artistic abilities of the teacher in creating a worthwhile situation in the classroom in which the learners learn and achieve the immediate and ultimate goal of education. As a science, it points to the logical, mechanical and procedural steps to scientific consideration of teaching has led to the evolution of a concept of teaching technology. Davies, Gage, Britner and Gagne have contributed significantly in this led to the evolution of a have contributed significantly in this area of teaching technology.

Teaching technology has certain fundamental principles on which it is based. Some of these are as follows :

1. Teaching is a scientific process and its major components are content, communication and feedback.
2. There is a close relationship between teaching and learning.
3. It is possible to modify, improve and develop the teaching learning activities.
4. The terminal behaviours of the learner in terms of learning structures can be established, by appropriate teaching environments.
5. Teaching skills can be developed and strengthened by means of feedback devices with or without sophisticated techniques.
6. Pre-determined learning objectives can be achieved by designing suitable teaching activities.
7. Use of achievement motivation techniques enhances the output of the teacher and the learner.

Davies and Glaser (1962), studied what the content of teaching technology should be and Davies presented the structure of content in four steps. The first step is planning of teaching which includes content analysis, identification of objectives and writing these in behavioural terms. Organisation of teaching comes next and it indicates the teaching strategies for achieving the objectives of teaching. In the third step, leading of teaching is mentioned whereby the communication strategies are identified in relation to teacher and student. The last one is controlling/managing of teaching, whereby the focus is placed on the assessment of the learning objectives in terms of student performance and this forms the feedback to teacher and students.

Methods of Teaching

Unwin (1968) has given a comprehensive definition of instructional design: "Instructional design is concerned with an application of modern skills and techniques for the requirements of education and training. This includes facilitation of learning by manipulation of media, methods and the control of environment so far as this reflects on learning."

Such type of thinking was introduced in 1950 and the different approach have been evolved for the problems of education and training but the following three approaches are most popular:

(1) Training Psychology,

(2) Cybernetic Psychology, and

(3) System Analysis.

The three approaches of Instructional Designs are not contradictory but supplementary to one another in solving the problems of education and training. They are closely related to deal with the input, output and process aspects of educational technology.

Training Psychology emphasizes on task analysis and design of interrelated training components. Cybernetic Psychology focuses on dynamic feedback and self-regulation. System Analysis focuses on system.

Training psychology concerns with input aspect and its main function is task analysis. It evolves the structure of teaching and learning. The second approach cybernetic deals with the process aspect of education and its major function is to provide reinforcement for leading the teaching. The third approach system analysis concerns with the development of organization and administration on the basis of output aspect of education. The meaning, principles, procedure and application of these approaches are being described in detailed in the following paragraphs.

Basic Assumptions : In planning, and designing instruction, there are certain factors which should be indicated as these are the fundamentals for proceeding with the task for designing instruction., The following are the basic assumptions:

1. Instructional design, must aim at aiding the learning of the individual. The instruction may be oriented to the individual in spite of the fact that learners may be in large or small groups.

2. Instructional design has phases that are both immediate and long range. Design in the immediate sense relates to the preparation of the design a few hours before the instruction is given. The longer range approach takes time to plan and prepare not only the design of a particular topic but the whole course itself or the entire instructional system. This approach involves more complex and varied designs. Such designs are undertaken by individual teachers, a team of teachers, curriculum planners and textbook writers.
3. Systematically designed instruction can greatly affect individual human development. A nurturing environ-ment is not adequate to develop an individual. Planning and directing are essential aspects of learning. An instructional design should ensure that no one is educationally disadvantaged.
4. Instructional design should be conducted by means of a systems approach. Briefly, systems approach in instruction means planned and organized use of all available learning aids including instructional media, in order to achieve the desirable learning objectives by the most efficient possible way. It focuses on the learner and his performances first and then decisions are made regarding content, learning experiences, instructional media and instructional strategies for realising the objectives.
5. Designed instruction must be based on knowledge of how human beings learn. Consideration should be given not only to what the students should learn but how they should learn. -Instructional design must taken into account learning conditions.

The Functions : Instructional designs provide the scientific basis for the instructional system. It develops the professional skill and efficiency of the teachers. The sequence of teaching acts or events that a teacher plans, organises and carries out, in order to create a learning- environment for the college students is called the instructional design. Glaser (1968) has enumerated the functions of instructional designs:

1. The instructional task is analysed for the structure of the content.
2. Learner's responses are analysed in terms of objectives and levels of learning. The entering behaviours of the students are studied appropriate stimuli for better performance.
3. Teaching strategies, techniques and approaches are selected by the teachers for presenting the content so that the desired learning structures result.
4. The performance of students is assessed in order to find out if the objectives of learning have been realised.

Instructional design is, therefore, concerned with the structuring of the content to create a suitable learning' environment, the selection of appropriate teaching strategies and methods, and the assessment of the performance level of students. The different phases in instructional design are listed below:

1. Stimulating motivation.
2. Informing the learner, the objectives of learning.
3. Gaining and directing attention.
4. Activating recall.
5. Enhancing retention and transfer.
6. Providing learning guidance.
7. Eliciting performance.
8. Providing feedback.
9. Assessing performance.
10. Reviewing the process on the basis of assessment.

When a college teacher designs his instructional hours, he should be conscious of the need to motivate the students not only at the beginning of the class but right through, whenever the opportunity arises. Through motivation, attention is sought and the teacher adopts several ways to maintain it. Some of these steps may include listing the objectives of learning for the particular class or topic, enhancing retention of material learnt during the class by active questioning and providing feedback on the responses given by the students. The questions should not only aim at recall responses but also include reflective thinking, reviewing, generalising and reasoning. Selected instructional aids and media can also be used for better learning outcomes. The learning experiences thus provided may be assessed for replanning the instructional design.

Various Types : Instructional designs can be classified by viewing teaching-learning process as related to teaching skills, instructional objectives, competencies or performances, teaching strategies, teaching models, specific technology, and learning styles.

Instructional Designs : The following are classified in five categories:

1. Objective-based
2. Skill-based
3. Competency-based
4. Model-based and
5. Learning style-based

Competency based education, also known as performance based education is a new approach to teaching having as its core, the ideas of accountability mid competencies. With regard to accountability it is argued that teachers should be held 'accountable' for their products. This accountability is accomplished by breaking teaching into discrete competencies or behaviours which can be stated as objectives competencies or behaviours which can be stated as objectives. Mastery of these competencies, is then possible (Unwin and McAllese 1978).

Competency-based education rests upon few assumptions which are generally shared by educationists. They are of six types as follows:

1. Learning takes place through changes in the behaviour of learners and that teaching aims at facilitating these changes.
2. Individuals achieve similar objectives but at different rates.
3. Teachers should be accountable for the learning that takes place in their students.
4. Continuous evaluation of teaching is used as a feedback for revising the instructional programme and this in turn promotes effective teaching.

5. The objectives of any educational programme bears close relationship to the educational goal.
6. Systems approach can be applied to education, especially to instructional planning and designing.

In competency-based education, competencies are spelled out so that it is possible to assess student learning through direct observation of student behaviour. The student knows in advance the extent and level of competencies to be mastered by him. The accomplishment of the learning objective can be observed mid measured in the form of specified learner behaviours. In order to facilitate this, performance goals are specified and agreed to in great detail much in advance of instruction. The teacher is held accountable, not for his students 'obtaining a passing grade' but for attaining a given level of competency in performing the essential tasks of learning. Student's progress rate depends on demonstrated competencies. The emphasis is laid on exit and not on entrance requirements. Further the focus is, being on acquisition of specific competencies by all the students. Time-becomes, variable and depending on the needs and capabilities of the learner, he is allowed to attain the competencies at his own rate and space.

Elam (1971) explains five basic features of competency-based programme:

1. Competencies to be demonstrated by the students are derived from explicit conceptions of teachers' roles and are publically stated in such a manner that students learned behaviours are related to specified competencies.
2. Criteria are to be employed in assessing competencies are stated in terms of expected levels of mastery under specified conditions.
3. Assessment of competency depends on students performance as the primary source of evidence and strives for objectivity.
4. Student's rate of progress is determined by demonstrated competencies rather than time or course completion.
5. Instructional programme is intended to facilitate the development of specified competencies.

Competency-based education is, therefore, unique in the sense that it focuses on the student's acquisition of pre-specified, agreed-upon competencies and demonstration of these specified competencies through objective assessment.

Modules Concept

Instruction is presented in modules, a module being a set of learning activities with objectives, per-requirements, per-assessment, instructional activities, post assessment and remediation. Modularization helps in self-pacing, individualisation, and independent study. The use of modules allows a much greater variety of experience than standard courses and provides a far better basis for personalised construction. Many competency-based education programmes make use of self instructional modules.

Critetion-referenced testing is an integral part of competency-based teacher-education. Criterion-referenced tests are those kinds of tests that indicate whether the learner has achieved the goal specified for the learning tasks. They do not make a reference in comparison to the performance of other learners. It is considered that the criterion-referenced tests are more sensitive than norm-referenced test for the purposes of detecting instructional efforts. They can provide the only relevant information on student's learning excellence or deficiency.

Competency-based education is unique in the sense that it shifts the emphasis from testing the memory to the demonstration of required competencies and thereby emphasizes outputs. They are not teacher-oriented but student-oriented. The principal, staff member of a concerned discipline at a particular level, under-graduate or post-graduate should evolve the academic scheme. The first step is the preparation of instructional modules suited to the level of a target group. Time is not a factor but the possibility of attaining the competencies specified by the working term, be all students at that level is more important. The prepared modules can be tried out with a small group of students. Implementation of the modules with supporting materials such as books, booklets, and cassette, slides and film strips, if necessary, will form the second stage. Students will not be permitted to proceed to the next unit of a module unless they master the competencies in that unit.

A criterion-referenced test based on the pre-specified competencies should be conducted to ascertain the proficiency of the students. If the performance of the student is satisfactory they are allowed to proceed to the next lesson unit. When it is found that some of the students are lagging behind in mastering the competencies time may be given for attaining the competencies. In some cases a different set of instructional package is needed as students have different patterns of learning and communicating. In case the instructional objectives or the competencies based on them are found to be unsuitable for that particular group the whole programme needs recasting. There may be non-academic reasons such as emotional and personal problems of students that could hinder the mastery of the competencies. The different competencies that students acquire, can be more accurately reflected by a well-defined criterion-referenced test in contrast to its counterpart, the norm referenced tests.

The difficulties experienced by such students can be identified and referred to a teacher or some other qualified person for guidance and counselling. Since the personal and academic problems are intertwined and mutually interacting, cooperation between the class teacher and the counsellor when the help of such a person is requisitioned, is essential for redressing the problems the student faces.

Realising the vital role that the competency-based education could play in cognitive development of college students, teachers could make a modest beginning in preparing competency-based modules on specific topics and try them out on small groups. The instructional design based on competency-based education is yet another approach to efficient learning at college level.

Of recent origin is the research study on the styles of learning adopted by the learners. Students use different approaches when faced with learning tasks and problems. The way in which the students approach the learning tasks, and the, behaviour in learning situations determine their learning style, Rosenberg (1968) defines learning style as referring to an individual's characteristic pattern of behaviour when confronted with a problem. It is pointed out that the learning style of an individual has relation to factors such as prior learning experiences, openness to interpersonal and extra-personal information, physical facilities, and learning environment.

On the basis of the work of researches on learning, Rosenberg has arrived at four general learning- patterns which are rigid-inhibited style, indisciplined style, acceptance-anxious style and creative style. It should be noted that when categorizing an individual as belonging to a given learning style because he exhibits the characteristic of that style, he should be considered first and foremost as an individual person rather than a member of a particular category.

Learners with a rigid inhibited style of learning require constant supervision as they get confused easily. They tend to give unrelated response to questions put forward. Changes in the class routine easily upsets them and they also exhibit signs of nervousness. They depend on the support given to them by the teacher. The behaviour of the rigid-inhibited learner is, therefore, a problem to himself and his teacher.

The indiscipline learner exhibits characteristics such as refusal to obey commands, showing disrespect to teachers, deceiving, stealing, bullying, etc. Such learners invariable leave their learning task unfinished due to lack of tolerance. They concentrated on what gives them pleasure at the moment.

The fourth type of learning style according to Rosenberg is creative style. Learners of creative style are self-confident, and able to evaluate their own performance with objectivity. They are prepared to learn from their mistakes and show divergent thinking ability. Anxiety stimulates their functioning, specialty during the learning process rather than impair it. A creative learner continues with the learning task until he completes it, which gives him satisfaction. He performs well on a divergently and therefore, also prefers to work independently,

There are several other approaches to classifications of learning styles, depending on how a person looks at the whole problem. Kagan (1965) discusses about impulsive-reflective dimensions of learning style. Teachers tend to group students as obedient or disobedient, timid or outgoing, bright or dull rather than as reflective or impulsive. A reflective individual may be categorised as a dull student and impulsive quick individual as bright. Both reflectiveness and impulsiveness are related to the individual's conceptual thinking. Impulsiveness may lead to meeting with difficulties such as proceeding to work out a problem without understanding it, starting an experiment without following the instructions properly, completing a reading passage without understanding the major concepts, etc. Reflectiveness is indicated in trying to comprehend material that has a variety of complex concepts in a passage above the level of students or in going over remedial work. Impassivity can result in developing anxiety and consequently being punished and ridiculed by teachers and classmates, specially when it is associated with the speed of response.

There are also learning styles characterised as dependent-independent, co-operative-non-cooperative, anxiety free-anxiety prone, competitive, non-competitive; study habits oriented-trial students learning styles by probing into their learning patterns some-of which can be indicated indirectly in the classroom through teacher-student's learning styles by probing into their learning patterns some of which can be indicated indirectly in the classroom through teacher-student interactions in the evaluation of academic performances and in the specific behaviour patterns.

Form the above classifications, the college teachers surmise first, the existence of different styles of learning adopted by students and secondly, the effect of these styles on the learning process. Consequently the instructional design could be based on learning styles, where the planning, preparation and conduct of a lesson emphasizes learning styles of the students. The teacher's design of instruction should provide opportunities to the students who use different learning patterns. Teachers should also make an attempt to reduce the factors that do not encourage good learning styles such as anxiety, frustration and emotional instability, dependence on teachers and parents, rote memory and convergent thinking.

Teaching Art

Teacher strategies aim at establishing relationship between teaching inputs and learning outcomes, mainly in terms of realising the learning outcomes. Teaching strategies include teaching methods, approaches and techniques such as lecture method, tutorial approach, case study technique demonstration method, term-teaching approach, programmed instruction,) etc. In planning and instructional design, the teacher selects a particular essential factor to base he design such as objectives, skills, competencies, models or learning styles. In doing so, he focuses attention to the type of design he is going to prepare. The teaching strategies used to elaborate the content or subject-matter of that unit or topic have to be spelled out in that particular design. Teaching strategies have been introduced in this book for large groups, small groups and individual instruction.

Teaching strategies when designed with clearly spelt-out objectives, and effective means of, achieving them with in built evaluation techniques is known as educational technology. Application of technology will ensure the achievement of objectives with the minimum effort and time required. When teaching result in effective learning of all the students taught, then any strategy that is applied to achieve this can be called educational technology. Educational technology is not deterministic, in the sense that if 'x' is done, 'y' will certainly happen. It only says that the probability of 'y' happening is very high if 'x' is done. The teaching strategies suggested have the high probability of effecting effective learning in students. Practising teachers may have to bring about some modifications, minor changes and adapt them to further increase the probability of their success in helping students learn more and better. And that is what educational technology and for the reason, and technology is for.

Training psychology is mainly concerned with the problems of teaching learning and training. This has come up through investigation on complex problems of training. Its origin is taken from military training. The main objective of training psychology is to improve the activities in which learner performs function. The learning outcome could not be improved by learning theories, therefore, training psychology prepares an outline for task by analysing its components. The task components are organized in such a way that desired objectives may be achieved. The crucial aspect of training psychology is the Task Analysis.

It is an approach to teaching and training. It employs learning conditions in teaching learning process rather than learning theories. The main assumption of this approach is that learning is dependent variable where as teaching is the independent variable. The learning can only be improved by developing teaching tasks.

Our training institutions can not produce effective teacher with help of learning theories. Moreover, they have failed to provide substantial solution for teaching and training problems. Training psychology is an approach for these problems.

The Principles : The principles of stimulus-response of military psychology have failed to give the solution for the complex problems of training then the task analysis approach has been followed for the development of training. Robert Gagne has explained the principles of training psychology:

(1) The human task can be analysed in its elements. He further assumed that these elements are quite different from one another. The task elements can be performed by employing different tactics.

(2) The task-elements function as a mediator for last task. The functions of an element are helpful in the transfer of learning and training. The shortage of task elements reduce the transfer to zero.

Training psychology is based on three principles:

(i) The elements are identified and analysed for the performance last task.

(ii) It is assured that every task elements can be performance effectively.

(iii) The elements are organised in such a sequence which may generate appropriate learning conditions.

These statements convey the meaning to the principles of training psychology. These principles are broadly associated with task analysis.

The teachers are prepared by determining the nature of training tasks which they perform in classroom teaching. The development of teaching concept is based on teacher-education model. The large amount of work -has been done in this area during 1960's. The number of teacher-education models have been developed and these models are based on the principles of training psychology.

The teacher-education models can be classified in three groups because B. 0. Smith and Clark have given three types of teaching tasks. On the basis of teaching tasks, the following classification of teacher-education models has been made :

Presage Factors Models

(1) Michigan State Model of Teacher-education

(2) Florida Model of Teacher-education.

(3) Syracuse Model of Teacher-education.

(4) The Wisconssin Model of Teacher-education.

Process Factors Models

(1) Teacher College Model of TEACHERS TRAINING

(2) The Goregia Model of TEACHERS TRAINING

(3) Regional Laboratory Model of TEACHERS TRAINING.

(4) The Toledo Model of TEACHERS TRAINING

Product Factors Models

(1) Teacher for the Real World Model

(2) The North-West Regional Laboratory Model.

The presage factors models training tasks are organized in such a way that their focus is on the development of the internal abilities and efficiency of teachers. The main emphasis is given on the mastery of content and development of right-type of attitude of teaching.

The second type of teacher-education models orient the training for developing teaching skills or teacher-behaviour in the classroom interaction. The Georgia and Toledo models are the examples of this type of model. Pre-service and in-service programmes are organized in Indian conditions for developing process factor.

The third type of teacher-education models are based on out put system. These models are used for improving the outcome of learning. The Real World and -Regional laboratory models are the main examples of product factors. Such type of teacher-education internship in teacher-education programme may be employed for this purpose.

Psychological Education

The principles of training psychology are not only useful for developing teacher-education models but also for developing instruction. Norman A. Crowder has propounded branching programme main stress is given on task analysis and difficulty of the elements is identified.

The diagnosis done for the difficulty of elements and remedial instruction is designed for such difficult elements.

The branching programme is originated from human training and from psychology principles. The task-elements are performed by each learner according to his own needs. This strategy their own requirements for each and every learner.

The training psychology has been developed for the practical problems of training and training. It has a great scope of application in the area of education and training . The principles of training psychology are being used for improving present training programme by developing models of teacher-educational in our country. The principles of training psychology may be helpful for student-teachers—

(1) To analyse the teaching task and developing competency.

(2) To identify the goal of training programme and specify learning objectives.

(3) To plan and prepare educational programmes for actual teaching.

This lesson-planning and presentation in the classroom may be greatly improved by using the spirit of training psychology.

The principles of training psychology can provide scientific basis for designing individualized or remedial instructions and development of curriculum. The curriculum and instructional material cannot be made specific and relevant to the objectives to the competence and skill to be developed in the learner.

The second approach of instructional designs was evolved in second world war. The term cybernetic has come to denote discipline which is associated 'with the research of communication and control'. It suggests concern with component elements of a system and they may function together to produce the most effective integrated system. The term cybernetic is used by Norbest Wiener (1948) associated with the physical system and physics.

The term cybernetic has been coined from the Greek word for steerman and thus, calls to mind and first importance cybernetic concept is that of feedback.

Cybernetic is defined by W. Wiener as the science of control and communication in the animal and the machine.

Cybernetic is the sciences communication and control. In any system control is basic and key element. Control here means connectiveness, and regulation and system is a dynamic state.

Consider our school system, when the error between what the parents want their children to learn in school and they actually receive to become too great, the school policies are changed by the force of public opinions. In this way, the school systems are regulated by the modes of community. All regulatory bodies throughout of our entire society are the feedback control system.

Cybernetic Theory : Cybernetic can be considered as a branch of training psychology. It conceptualizes human beings in engineering terms considering him like an electric machine which used the process of sensory feedback to control and modify its behaviour.

Cybernetic theory views an individual as a feedback system which generates its activities in order to detect and control specific characteristics of the environment. It analyses intrinsic mechanism by which control is established an maintained of sensory feedback mechanism. The focus of the whole theory is the dynamic feedback and self-regulation.

All system include at least three basic elements : Input process and output.

The process unit acts on the material or information to modify it in any way.

The output unit consists of some techniques for discharging the results of process from the system.

The output from a system, which returned as input to control future output, is called feedback.

The system can be of two types-an open loop system and a closed loop system. The closed loop system is often referred to cybernetic system. In the open loop system the output is returned to the system and consequently affects future output of the system is one which places a boundary around the system.

The essence, then, of Cybernetic psychology rests principles of sensory-oriented feedback which are intrinsic for the individual (he 'feels' the effect of his decision) and are the basis of self corrective devices.

Instruction also can be considered as a cybernetic system. The instructional system also has three major elements. A cybernetic instructional system would also include knowledge of results to the learner and some record of students responses. Its input also consists of library material, subject matter content, learner characteristics mid objectives. Students responses function as feedback for input. The procedure controls the presentation and modifies the presentation of display and knowledge of results on the basis of students responses correspondence to the objectives. In the cybernetic system of instruction, following is the order of input, output and procedure.

The first essential input is the content or material to be presented i.e. library material or library input which is inclusive of any written material or audiovisual material programmed instruction, diagrams, charts' etc.

The most important input for an instructional system are the objectives (performance standard) by which the system is designed to accomplish.

A third input for a cybernetic instructional system is the formation concerning with the individual characteristics of the students.

Because this is a cybernetic system so the fourth type of input consists of the feedback for the learner in the form of his responses. This is an important per-without this an instructional system is not able to adjust the presentation and to produce the change in behaviour' specified by the objective input. It may be noted here that in most of the instructions in schools the input of students responses is ignored.

The first essential output for 'an instructional system is the display of the learner, which may be oral such as lecture explanation, visual, written, and so on. A display is any stimulus situation structured and presented to the learner for the purpose of establishing some responses.

In a cybernetic system, a second output presented to learner is in form of knowledge of results.

If student's response is input to the system, a third type of output which may or may not be used in a particular instructional situation will be the record of each student's response.

The procedure is the selection mechanism which presents and displays in a linear fashion, one following the other. Movie or filmstrip presentation are good examples of such a system.

Feedback theory evaluates the techniques of self instruction according to how well they conform to principles of cybernetic design. In order to optimize feedback control of symbolic knowledge and skills original presentation should be more varied and flexible than a permitted by most of the teaching machines and programmes. Specially organized systems of reference are also important. However self instructions is useful for drill and review in specific details.

The mechanism of feedback devices are most effective for the modification of teacher-behaviour. These mechanisms are based on the principles of cybernetic.

Application of Cybernetic : Most useful concept in the cybernetic is that of feedback which has far reaching implications for teaching, learning and training. The following are the major implications of cybernetic:

(1) The principles of cybernetic are applied for classroom instruction, group as well as individual learning.

(2) It enables the teacher to understand some of the fundamental mechanism That control learning.

(3) It provides the basis for self-education. The feedback control is used to develop programmed instructional material.

(4) Cybernetic principles are used for developing remedial instruction or individualized instructional material.

(5) Teacher-education programme can be improved by employing the mechanism of feedback devices for the modification of teacher-behaviour.

(6) The innovative practices in teacher-education programme such as micro teaching, stimulated social skill and interactional analysis are based on the theory of feedback.

(7) The input, output and process units of teaching enable the teacher to understand and analyse teaching in more scientific manner.

(8) The teaching activities can be made highly structured and well organized in view of learning objectives.

The classroom instruction, a school or the programme of teaching, can be considered as a dynamic system. This stresses on the principle that teaching is a resultant activity of the combination or forces, factor and conditions. The teacher has to take in consideration all these factors to generated appropriate teaching situation. Thus, cybernetic concept is most useful for developing design of training programmes for complex behaviour.

The third approach of instructional designs which is closely related to both training psychology and cybernetic, is known as 'System Analysis'. It has emerged during second world war. It has greatly influenced management decision making 'in business, 'industry, government and military. This new technology is known by serval terms, but one term that has gained considerable standardization is, 'System Analysis.'

The word system has been derived from the field or engineering. A system is the sum total of agents working independently and decpendently together to achieve the required goals. The term system conveys the meaning of analysis and development. The term system from the scientific management concept. In general system analysis involves utilization of scientific mathematical techniques applied to organizational operation as' a part of management decision making activities. It has the assumption that no comprehensive system development can take place without prior system analysis. It enables the administrators to use more scientific and quantitative methods for analysing management problems.

The field of educational administration is becoming with the set quantitative-scientific techniques that helps the educational administrators in the decision-making process. System technology brings to educational management a scientific-quantitative approach fur solving complex educational administrative problems. -It is based essentially on mathematics.

A number of steps are followed to accomplish a System Analysis. The following steps must be utilized for conducting system analysis study—

First Step : Formulation of objectives.

The most important and difficult aspect of the entire system analysis study is to formulate the specific objectives to be achieved. To state objectives in general terms is totally inadequate. An objective may be written in behavioural terms or fiscal functions.

Second Step : Review of systems operation.,

The second step in system analysis includes a comprehensive review of the systems operation. System analysis is a problem oriented and it is necessary to understand completely the systems operation. The administrators fell in some problems but these do not always turn out to be the main problem.

Under any circumstance a comprehensive review of the whole system is necessary to isolated the main problem to the solved.

Third Step : Collection of data.

The review of system for identifying the main problem yields the data within the problem area. The collection of data involves basically the statistical techniques and procedure.. In many situations the aspects as system analysis are the applications of classical statistical procedure.

Fourth Step : Analysis of data.

Analysis of data is done to make it meaningful. The analysis of data is employed to experimental paradigms to study the effect of independent variable upon dependent variable. In system analysis study, an objective analysis is made for determining the influence of variables. The investigator is concerned with the influence of variables. The investigator is concerned is to be obtain with interaction of many variables. The primary concern is to be obtain correlation not to establish cause and effect.

Fifth Step : Isolation of the problem.

The administrator does not always know, accurately the main problem therefore, it is necessary to follow earlier steps in order to isolate specific problem of the system. The collection and analysis of data helps in identifying and defining the problem.

Sixth Step : Specify operations in the problem.

After identifying specific problem, it is necessary to review the operations within problem area. It is much more comprehensive than the original review of the total operations. It helps to understand quickly the relationship of all facts of the problem to the total operating system.

Seventh Step : Block Diagram.

The problem area is a final step in the analytical stage of the system analysis. A block diagram is prepared for all functions of the subsystem that make up problem area. It denotes logical structure of the sub-system operations and similar to the block diagram.

Design : After the system analysis, the investigator attempts to design and tentative solution of the problem. A new solution of the problem is subjected to testing. A tentative solution and retesting the tentative solution continues until on analyst reaches to an optimal solution. Once optimal solution is obtained the analyst departs that loop.

Evaluation : The formal evaluation of the new solution is done for checking its work ability. It involves implementation of tentative solution in some aspect of the system. The analyst proceeds through the same steps of loop as mentioned earlier. It is advisable to evaluate all new system solutions in small scale of the required operations.

System Operations : The formal evaluation and acceptance for the solution of the problem, the new design has been implemented within the system. It involves two aspects:

(1) It concerns with implementation of new system operation.

(2) It requires the maintenance of the system where a new system is designed. It continues as monitory of the system in order to check the effectiveness of the system.

General criteria are included in any evaluation system performance, cost, utility and time. A general criterion is that the total system should operate in an optimal fashion. These criteria are discussed here:

Performance : The effectiveness of a system is evaluated on die basis of performance. The design of the problem solution ascertains how will the new system be effective in achieving the objectives. The performance criterion is the concept of validity of the new system. The system is valid if it does what is it supposed to do. Thus, much of the evaluation of the performance is quantitative.

Cost : Analysis of system is influenced by cost function to a major extent. The amount of resources is being put into the system function in terms of money, staff and facilities comparison are made regarding the investment of resources in the new system and old system of education. This is extremely valuable criterion for evaluation system analysis projects.

Utility : The ultimate criterion for evaluating system' project is utility of the system. The return on investment represents the utility of a given function. Many education functions require an assignment of a numerical utility.

Time : Time factors as an evaluate criterion is closely associated with effectiveness. It is particularly relevant criterion in evaluating system projects. There is high correlation between time and cost. Much of the contribution of modern electronic data processing involves time.

Application of System Analysis : The system analysis has greatly influenced the educational administration and organisation. It provides scientific and quantitative basis for studying the problems of educational system. The educational implication of system analysis have been enumerated in the following areas of education.

(1) It brings to educational management a scientific-quantitative approach for solving complex education administrative problems.

(2) It enables educational administrator to identify the actual problem and abstains a verified solution of the problem.

(3) The training programmes can also be improved with the help of system analysis. The new concept of manage-ment may be implemented in training programmes.

(4) The sub-system of eduction is analysed to understand the actual problem and tentative solutions can be verified or tested on a segment of the system.

(5) Any change in the educational system can be brought objectively, empirically and economically with great utility with the help of System Analysis.

System Approach: System approach is a rational, problem-solving method of analysing, the educational process and making it more effective. System is the process taken as a whole incorporating of all its aspects and parts, namely pupils, teachers, curriculum content, instructional materials, instructional strategies, physical environment and the evaluation of instructional objectives.

The purpose of the system analysis is to get the "Best environment in the best place for the best people at the best time and in the best price."

"The system approach in instruction is an integrated, programmed complex of instructional media, hardware and personal whose components are structured as single unit with a schedule of time and sequential phasing."

The instructional process has become complex these days because of the shift in technological focus for the classroom to curriculum planning.

The curriculum should not only specify student behavioural objectives but also suggest the strategies for helping the student to reach the objectives and evaluation instruments to measure the success. It is called the system approach.

Keshaw and Michean (1959) have defined-

"System approach is one of the techniques which aims at finding the most efficient and economically intelligent methods for solving the problems of education scientifically."

The system concept provides a framework for visualizing internal and external environmental factors as an integrated whole. This concept factors are a way of thinking which helps us to recognize the nature of the complex problems and there by provides insight which enables us to operate within the received environment.

System analysis is a systematic way of identifying goals of any system and scientifically working out different steps to more towards these goals.

The approach in general includes the following steps:

1. To analyse the existing situation.
2. To set up the goal for the desired situation.
3. To define the mechanisms to evaluate the achievement of goals.
4. To create alternative situation.
5. To select the most appropriate solution through cost benefit analysis.
6. To work out the layout of the system.
7. To design the monitory mechanisms for the system.
8. To plan for introducing the new solution.

The Components : It is a systematic attempt to coordinate all aspects of a problem toward specific objectives in education. This means planned, organized use of all available learning resources, including audiovisual media, to achieve the desirable learning objectives by the most efficient means possible. The system approach focuses first upon learner and the performance, required of him. Only then, it makes decisions regarding course content, learning experiences and the most effective media and instructional strategies for realizing the objectives.

The Instructional System employs the following steps:

1. Defining instructional objectives in behaviour terms or measurable terms.

2. Determining functions related to the achievement of the objectives by appropriate multimedia approach.
3. Defining learner's characteristics or entering behaviour.
4. Selecting appropriate instructional strategies for effective learning.
5. Selecting suitable learning experiences for available alternatives.
6. Choosing appropriate instructional aids, -resources to facilitate students learning.
7. Defining and assigning appropriate personal roles: teachers of term teaching members and supporting personal students.
8. Implementing the programme : Try out with a small group of pupils in appropriate conditions.
9. Evaluating the pupils learning outcome in terms of learning objectives.
10. Revising if necessary to improve the efficiency of the system to improve student learning.

The system approach applied to educational situations includes: input, process, output and feedback. These are inter linked and interdependent stages and can be described as :

(a) Planned input and process involving learning materials and strategies suitable organised to cater the needs of a particular group of students.
(b) Explicitly stated standard of outcome performances, including sequenced behavioural objectives.
(c) Monitoring output which is used to revise, improve and evaluate the instructional system, providing feedback to the learner and teacher.
(d) A degree of inbuilt flexibility to adjust the individual situation.

The system approach can be effectively used for studying the problems of the following areas of education:

1. Instructional system or procedure.
2. School administration and supervision.

3. Examination and Evaluation system.
4. Non-formal and adult education.
5. Educational guidance system.

An example demonstrating an application of system approach is discussed in the following paragraph in an instructional system.

Robb (1974) has analysed an instructional system and suggested that an instructional system can be employed into three phases : Planning, Execution and Evaluation. These phases involve eight steps and indicate the development of instructional system.

Phase First: Planning instructional system:

Step 1. Defining objective

Step 2. Pre-assessment or determining entering behaviour.

Step 3. Specifying appropriate strategies.

Step 4. Selecting materials, facilities, aids and media.

Phase Second: Execution of instruction:

Step 5. Defining and assigning personnel roles.

Step 6. Synthesising, and implementing the system of instruction.

Phase Third: Evaluation of instruction:

Step 7. Evaluation and outcome.

Step 8. Analysing, result and modifying the system.

The problem is that the development of an instructional system is for a given target population or class of students. The instructional system can be used by the following eight steps:

Defining Objectives : The objectives for the instruction are identical and written in the behavioural terms which the learners are, required to demonstrate.

Determining the Entering Behaviour : The students entry level is determined by the pre-assessment. The knowledge and skills which the learners are already equipped with, are processed.

Specifying Appropriate Method and Strategies : In this step appropriate method and strategies are specified which can suit to the nature of the students and are helpful to achieve the objectives.

Selecting Materials, Aids and Media: The learning expe-riences are provided with the help of appropriate material and media. The instructional strategies require the appropriate material and media to generate academic environment. Therefore, appropriate material and media are selected for providing learning experiences.

Defining and Assigning Personnel Roles : In using instructional procedure effectively, the teacher has to play various roles to assist the learner 'to achieve the objectives.'

Synthesizing and Implementing the Instructional System : This is a step of execution phase of instructional system. The-system approach, strategies, material, media and roles of teachers are integrated in such way so that specified objectives may be achieved. Under this step learning experiences are provided to the learners.

Evaluation of Learning Outcome : The effectiveness of instruction is examined on the basis of post-test scores of the students. The performance of the students indicate the validity of instruction and fulfilment of the objectives.

Analysing the Result and Modifying the System : The learning outcome is analysed to ascertain die inability of the earlier steps. It provides the feedback to the designer and suggests modification and improvement in the different aspects of instructional system. It ensures the effectiveness of planning, and execution phase of the system.

Thus, system analysis or approach can be applied for the development of educational administration and organisation, examination system, Instructional system, models of teacher-education, models of curriculum and educational and vocational guidance system. These three approaches can be applied simultaneously for education and training.

11

Role of Computers

Assuming that the societal changes wrought, by microelectronic technologies would have greater implications for changes in educational programs than would the instructional potential of these technologies. Second, since future scenarios about life in the developing computer culture will, in the final analysis, be written by individuals, the capacities of schools to enhance self-realization will become increasingly significant. Third, all of the important issues related to uses of microcomputers ultimately reside beyond technology in human and social domains. Finally, the objectives of computer literacy programs cannot be permanently fixed; they change as societal values and technology change.

Diverse Knowledge

At a general level, differences in the conceptual and practical meanings of computer literacy exist within and across nations, at a specific level, they are found in the multiple programs offered in given school. Diversity expresses itself through the scope and depth of computer literacy programs, the objectives they seek, the outcomes they produce, and the places they occupy in curricula. Computer literacy programs now found in schools are not easy to classify, in part because they are usually defined in general terms. In addition, those describing programs often fail to distinguish clearly between concepts and their uses, and the resulting obscurities make classification difficult. Nevertheless, the categories of literacy elaborated below do help document and clarify the diverse expressions of current programs.

Those who have acquired "operational" literacy can define the basic components of hardware and software and can demonstrate the machine-related skills needed to make computers work. Designed to introduce students to the computer, this approach is often implemented through daily exercises during a period of several weeks. When the exercises are effective, students understand such concepts as "monitor", "keyboard," and "central processing unit" and how the components labeled by such concepts work together with other parts to make computers function.

Students are also able to turn a computer on and off, load software, show proficiency at the keyboard, demonstrate the use of storage devices, and acquire "minimal" troubleshooting techniques. Operational literacy, then, emphasizes "hands-on" experiences and simple concepts. Directed at elementary understandings and skills, the approach demands neither extensive teacher training nor substantial amounts of instructional time. Nor does it require much change in existing curricula or major investments beyond those made in hardware and software.

The minimal demands of the approach may account for the fact that many school districts have opted for it in their initial literacy efforts. The approach, while limited, provides an entry into the world of the computer and a potential bridge to more significant learning experiences; more easily than other literacy alternatives; operational literacy can be made available equitably to all students. Learning produced through operational literacy, critics argue, are both trivial and subject to quick obsolescence. They might contend, for example, that teaching students how to turn computers on and off is just as trivial as teaching them how to turn television sets on and off. Both activities squander valuable time. Critics also argue that operational literacy outcomes are immediately out of date, hardware and software are changing so fast, they say, that today's operations are obsolescent tomorrow.

In addition, future computers, with their enhanced "friendliness," intelligence, and simplicity, will require only the most elementary skills. Why waste students' and teachers' time, critics ask, by providing trivial and obsolescent learnings? Is the assumption about obsolescence as sound one? Since students of technology typically underestimate, often substantially, the time required to realize new developments, a note of skepticism is in order. Put differently, projections made about impending achievements in intelligent and friendly computers by critics of operational literacy, especially the highly optimistic ones, are likely to be in error. If the new technologies have potential for enhancing learning, then a pertinent question arises—why wait years for more powerful computers while immediately closing the door on opportunities for all students to acquire potentially useful entry skills and concepts?

Is the "triviality" argument sound? If the learnings acquired through operational literacy offer no foundation for new learnings, they can be classed as trivial. However, if the elementary and first-stage learnings facilitate the attainment of more advanced ones, they are not necessarily trivial. To be sure, research is needed to determine if the "operational" learnings acquired in fact enable students to realize more sophisticated learnings. Further, do students from diverse backgrounds actually use the initial learnings to acquire more advanced ones?

Instrumental literacy approach to literacy computers are used as instruments for acquiring stipulated learnings or bodies of subject-matter. In Sweden, for example, leaders have used computers in high schools to teach mathematics and civics. They chose these subjects in parts because they "are taken by all compulsory school pupils, and they are included in most lines of upper secondary school". The approach enables all enrolled students to learn to use computers as they acquire content or skills; in addition, the computer can be used as an instrument for "modernizing" subject-matter teaching.

In the Swedish plan, for example, computer-supported projects produced, according to one observer, a variety of subject-related outcomes among which were new insights by students into mathematical relationships, into "connections" among subject matters, and into the analytical aspects of mathematics. In addition, teachers coordinated instruction in physics and mathematics more effectively. The Swedish approach reflects the instrumental use of computers in selected subjects. Some high school leaders have aspired to use computers in all subjects taught. Those taking clerical courses, for example, might acquire word processing skills; some social studies students, insights into environmental problems through simulations; science students, understandings of physics from computer-based demonstrations; language arts students, enhanced vocabulary and spelling skills, and so forth. In each subject, in other words, the computer would provide a tool for advancing learning.

Descriptive Stand Point

The instrumental concept of computer literacy is not without its critics. Some detractors maintain that this alternative provides "low level" types of learning only. Others are skeptical about whether the quality of future software will exceed significantly that currently available in today's drill and practice programs. On the one hand, school systems do not have the material and human resources to develop effective software, they maintain; on the other, the private sector, with its press to produce programs for mass markets, will continue its "least common denominator" stance toward software. In describing the low state of software development, critics pinpoint a major difficulty.

However, the conditions they describe are not sufficiently compelling to justify the elimination of the instrumental approach to computer literacy. Information presented in this volume suggests that computer-assisted instruction, when compared to other approaches to the improvement of student learning, already offers one viable option to educators. Undoubtedly, future improvements in software will come slowly and incrementally, and the cost of hardware will diminish less rapidly than in the past; nevertheless, comparisons of CAI with competing strategies of instruction are likely to become more rather than less favourable over time. In the meantime, CAI provides students some computer skills and provides staff a stimulus and a medium for assessing traditional modes of instruction.

Algorithmic reasoning, perhaps the most controversial concept of computer literacy, is acquired through computer programming. A.P. Ershov, a member of the USSR Academy of Science, has called programming the "second literacy". Literacy in reading and literacy in programming both have their origins in technologies-the printing press and the computer. Both support basic functions; "communications work, the contemplation of nature and the struggle against it", and they "supplement each other, forming a new harmony of human mind". Ershov suggests that the "acceptance of books blew up the integrity of word and action; it separated the process of knowledge accumulation from its application." Programming, with its emphasis on problem solving and on the clear comprehension of how to carry out what is to be done, helps rejoin, at least in certain types of tasks, what the book rent as under. To become programmers, students must make effective use of algorithmic reasoning, Kemeny writes:

> We have to learn to think in terms of algorithms, which are precise recipes for solving problems or for accomplishing a task. A computer program describes an algorithm; it tells us "how to get there." Although algorithms were used and studied in mathematics in the past, there is today a strong prejudice in favour of formulae-that is, achieved results. But computers are forcing us all, even mathematicians, to readjust our thinking.

Algorithmic reasoning skills, Kemeny admits, are not easily articulated. Nevertheless, he suggests that programmers need—(a) to be able to express thought in very simple language (the small number of concepts available in a language like BASIC makes the task a demanding one); (b) to explain to the computer how to solve the problem (c) to divide complex tasks into small, clearly understood components; (d) to break down a procedure into simple steps and seek the logical relations among them; and (e) to find programming malfunctions and "debug" them. While recognizing that programming can teach "procedural" thinking, Seymour Papert has stressed its potential for providing fundamental insights into mathematical and related abstractions.

By using algorithmic reasoning to make the computer do their bidding, students can gain special insights into thinking and into the nature of knowledge. Put another way, learnings gained from programming can help students become their own "epistemologists". Not only can programming develop generic reasoning skills, it can, its advocates contend, improve the quality of learning. Students, as programmers, are active and involved-preconditions for significant learning. Papert has also suggested that computers can bring constructive change to "sluggish and conservative" school systems. When teachers and students become skillful programmers, they move the posits, beyond passive contexts to richer and more self-actualizing ones. Some advocates of programming cast a critical eye on instrumental literacy because it places students in a passive role. As programmers, students can use computers in the active pursuit of their own learning objectives. If their responses are limited to those in programs developed by others, their imagination and learning are sharply constrained.

Papert and Kemeny, as advocates of programming, speak and write as trained mathematicians. Algorithmic reasoning, an offspring of mathematics, can resolve precisely defined problems. It has repeatedly demonstrated its capacities to resolve technical problems associated with the development and use of microelectronic technologies. In fact, the expansive array of digital artifacts that lies at the heart of the computer culture is in one sense the product of algorithmic thinking. However, the task teaching students computer programming differs markedly from that of teaching them to address effectively the human, social, occupational, and civic problems created by microelectronic technologies. These latter problems lie outside the rational world of computer programming and in the emotion-laden contexts of political organizations, work settings, family milieus, and other locales.

Surrounded by conflicts, these formidably complex problems cannot be fully resolved through algorithmic reasoning. The contentions that all students should acquire computer programming skills, then, should be viewed critically. To make computer programming a literacy standard for all students reflects a questionable strategy. Even if the standard is one which can feasibly be met by all students-a proposition that is far from self-evident-major investments in time and resources would be required to produce a narrowly based set of skills.

Different Approaches

Noble has identified "consumer literacy" "worker literacy," and "citizen literacy" as the major role-related concepts. Although writers do not always define these terms in the same way, the concepts do accurately reflect prevailing views about which roles are being altered by computers and which ones can serve as foci for developing computer literacy. Consumer literacy carries two meanings, one linked more to hardware and the other more to software. The first stresses that individuals should be effective acquirers and users of computers and associated hardware.

Since almost all families will eventually spend large sums of money on home computers and peripheral equipment, advocates of consumer literacy reason that schools should teach all individuals how to handle such expenditure wisely. The second meaning of consumer literacy centres upon the "applications" individuals will be making "as part of their strategies for information retrieval, communication and problem solving". Advocates of this view optimistically project rapidly increasing flows of information out of, into, and through home computers. Individuals using the expanding sources of information will need requisite knowledge and skills. They will need to learn, for example, how to enhance their education through electronic media, exchange ideas through computer networks, and use shared databases to solve individual and community problems. Schools, then, should provide students with the literacy skills required to function in tomorrow's microelectronic environments.

Worker literacy is defined, on the one hand, as the skills needed to perform specific jobs and, on the other, as generic cognitive and information skills. The first definition presumes that the trend away from industrial jobs and toward information jobs will continue and, further, that career and vocational programs should teach individuals to perform such specific information jobs as computer repairing, systems design, and data processing.

The second definition of literacy presumes that future job requirements will always be changing and that schools, more than ever before, should provide students basic skills which they can apply as their jobs undergo change or as they move into new ones.

Workers in information-related jobs, in other words, need higher-level mental skills than industrial workers traditionally have had. During the last decade, the impact of computer technologies on political environments is so far-reaching, some argue, that new approaches to citizen literacy are sorely needed. Today space and time no longer constitute barriers to national and international communication.

However, television and satellites are increasingly communicating political events through images, leaving it to citizens to search for the deeper political meanings behind appearances. Further, as the new technologies take over an ever-expanding number of government and business functions, they are posing far-reaching questions related to the privacy of individuals, equity of citizen access to the new media, and the role of computers in politics. All of these conditions, proponents of computer literacy argue, highlight the need for citizen literacy. Actual descriptions of well-developed programs directed at consumer, worker, or citizen literacy are not as prevalent as are descriptions of other types of computer literacy programs.

For one thing, they are more difficult to design and implement than are operational, instrumental, or algorithmic reasoning programs. Since the definitions of role-related needs are still ambiguous, organized content to support instruction is not yet widely or conveniently available. Finally, support for the idea that schools should provide students generic or higher-order learnings for use in consumer, worker, citizen, and other roles is growing. Role-related literacy has not escaped criticism.

Modern Technological Application

Computer enthusiasts, some contend, have exaggerated the impact of the new technologies on job requirements, consumer demands, and citizen responsibilities. Levin and Rumberger, for example, suggest that the number of "information" workers required will be relatively small as compared to the number of janitors, cashiers, secretaries, and other service, workers needed. Others contend that school and community leaders have launched literacy programs without adequate reflection. Some have blamed an "uncritical press" not only for exaggerating the need for literacy programs but also for providing "free advertising in the guise of objective reporting".

Many educators have tended to accept the claims of computer enthusiasts uncritically. Thus, criticism is needed to develop more realistic views about the educational significance of the new technologies. However, the claims of the critics can be accepted as uncritically as those of enthusiasts. Stated another way, criticisms that lack logical or evidential support need to be viewed skeptically.

Critics of role-related literacy may be correct within an immediate time frame and incorrect within a longer-range time frame. Expanding computerization is changing consumer, worker, and citizen functions, even if slowly. Thus, today's critical messages about role related literacy not only may prove to be errant; even worse, they may reinforce outmoded patterns and stifle the creation of needed new ones.

Advocates of computer literacy, then, have stimulated considerable thought about the concept during the last decade. Witness, for example, the analyses that increasingly dot the educational literature. By aggressively defining and diffusing multiple definitions of literacy and by skillfully linking them to diverse learning objectives, they have contributed significantly to the development and diffusion of literacy programs. However, the mixed messages elicited by computers have slowed the diffusion of the concepts.

Some, seeing nothing new in computer technologies, indifferently dismiss them; in so doing, they rule out the "Whither" question. Others, sensing a computer-created "revolution," urgently call for major adaptations in school programs and a thorough answer to the "whither" question. Given such disparate views, the first question facing those studying computer literacy is whether or not computer uses in schools indeed reflect another passing fad.

The indifferent, who "have seen it all before," believe firmly that the microcomputer is just another in a series of technologies without impact. They point to the high but disappointed hopes past educational leaders have had for programmed texts, televisions, and related innovations. They conclude that after a period of uncritical use the microcomputer will have an uninfluential ending as have past instructional technologies. Since it is only one more in a long series, they ask why one should assume that it has more than passing significance. The "passing fad" argument is erroneous because it is based upon a false assumption, namely, that the capacities and effects of microcomputers are similar to those of previous technologies.

Microcomputers in fact differ substantially from past technologies. Because of their greater versatility and flexibility, they can be put to many more instructional uses. In additions, they can help manage instructional processes; versatility access subject-matter from libraries, information utilities, and other electronic sources; and facilitate the development of programs by students to meet their own objectives-feats that past technologies could not perform.

Computers differ from past technologies in a more fundamental way, namely, in their far-reaching effects on society. The impacts of programmed texts, for example, were confined to educational contexts. Even television, with its widespread influence, has not moved as deeply into society's institutions as has the computer. Microcomputers populate homes. work places, business enterprises, government agencies, social agencies, and other non-school organizations. Having spawned a powerful array of novel industries, computers are now stimulating new dreams and aspirations, redefining human-_machine relationships, shaping cognitive psychology, and altering modes of thinking.

As computers change society, they create new educational needs, as already noted. Microelectronic technologies, then, represent much more than new educational means, they are surfacing profound questions about the ends of education. Therefore, they cannot be blithely dismissed. The conclusion that the computer is not another passing fad does not imply that school purposes and programs will change rapidly. Powerful barriers constrain technological change. The new technologies do demand much more learning and change on the part of school personnel than have past technologies.

The high costs of implementing literacy programs will slow diffusions processes. The clashing tides of positive and negative opinion, which surround decisions about computer uses, will complicate adoption decisions. Finally, it is significant that much larger private-sector investments are currently being directed at 'offices of the future' than at 'schools of the future', and 'at functions performed in business, military, telecommunication and government agencies in contrast to educational ones."

The new technologies have evoked both dark and bright scenarios. Optimists, emphasizing effective uses, see computers producing beneficial outcomes; pessimists, emphasizing misuses, see destructive and even dire consequences. While enthusiasts make expansive claims, skeptics decry these claims and cast them aside. Hope, optimism, and enthusiasm clash with fear, pessimism, and skepticism. The result is bifurcated views. That these views impinge directly upon the 'whither' question can be shown with some specific examples. The first set of examples is linked to current computer uses; the second, to presumed future impacts of computers.

Sherry Turkle has referred to the "Computer as Rorschach." The phrase is an apt one; computers do tap deep human emotions and elicit contrasting perceptions about their meaning and significance. Applications of computers in the political arena, for example, bring dissonant views. Some examples relevant to citizen literacy can help clarify the point. Some have probed the impacts of the new technologies on individual liberty and privacy and have discovered an "electronic nightmare." Others, after studying national experiments in "teledemocracy," have concluded that the new technologies can help citizens influence public policy decisions.

In a similar view, some have observed that the power of "technological elites" constitutes a threat to democratic decision making; others see in the diffusion and use of microcomputers a new means for advancing decentralized communication and democratic action. Or while some argue that linear thinking can be effectively applied to political problems, others contend that intuitive thinking will be required to solve these problems. Some believe that expanding international databases will enable leaders to address worldwide political problems more effectively; others contend that leaders from developing nations will suffer even greater inequalities in political opportunities because they will be unable to access the data.

While the less sanguine stress that large technological systems, with "lives" of their own, cannot be controlled through political processes, the more cheerful contend that humans, as creators and users of these systems, can control their effects. Contrasting positive and negative views, such as those just noted, have implications for research. Inquiry is needed to shed light on actual in contrast to presumed outcomes of computer uses.

Some of the differences in view can be explained by the fact that scholars, in drawing their conclusions, use data about different but related phenomena as, for example, the computer's impact on a process (learning) in contrast to its impact on a value (privacy). However, a more fundamental problem is that the factual premises to support generalizations tend to be weak; effective research could uncover unreliable findings and false conclusions.

Perceptions about future consequences differ just as much as do those about immediate results. Thinkers often hold antithetical views, for example, about the long-range impacts of computers on the economic sector views which have implications for "worker literacy" programs. Some, looking at the steady infiltration of robots into industrial settings, conclude that the result will be a permanently unemployed "underclass"; others, examining the impacts of past technologies on unemployment, assert that the new technologies will create at least as many jobs as they eliminate.

Some contend that the new machines will inevitably dehumanize work; others argue that computers, by taking over the routine, will bring shorter work weeks and that this, in turn, will lead to more educational, social and other humanistic activities. While the optimists believe that ongoing research will make it possible for robots to perform increasingly "intelligent" functions, the least hopeful maintain that research break-throughs in artificial intelligence will be extremely limited. The act that leaders and scholars hold such sharply divided views about the immediate and long-range significance of new technologies signals in still another way the powerful forces unleashed by computers. By surfacing conflictive and vital issues, the forces are stimulating and encouraging proactive throughout.

The precious discussion has stressed that computer literacy is a young concept, that educational leaders have defined and implemented it in diverse ways, and that sharply clashing views surround its uses. At this point an important issue arises, namely, what framework can be used to analyze the newborn, diversely, interpreted, sharply contested and complicated concept of computer literacy? Since the history of the concept is short and relevant research is scarce, analogies offer one framework. Thus, acquiring computer literacy can be compared with the learning of a foreign language or the attainment of "book" literacy. Book literacy offers one fruitful analogy for probing the "whither" question.

Notably, book literacy and computer literacy are both similar and interdependent. The various symbols on the keyboard used to write this chapter are immediate indicators of the reciprocal relationships between written literacy and computer literacy. Other symbols, which appear from time to time on the screen are additional reminders of the interdependencies between books and computers. These linkages underline a significant fact, namely, that individuals cannot acquire computer literacy without literacy in written language. Since one-fifth of the population of the United States is illiterate in written language, when more demanding measures are used, millions are locked out of computer literacy.

The linkages between computers and books, then, suggest an important policy generalization, namely, that when school leaders make commitments to computer literacy they should not do so at the expense of traditional literacy programs. Those comprising today's large illiterate population tend to be members of disadvantaged social, economic, racial and other groups. Since as a rule they have had limited access to written materials in their homes, they have long experienced unequal learning opportunities. Such inequalities, which still persist 500 years after the invention of the printing press, offer another lesson to those concerned with policy related to computer literacy.

The opportunities available to students pursuing computer literacy will undoubtedly be more inequitable, at least for the foreseeable future, than will those available to students pursuing book literacy. Since computers and associated peripherals are much more expensive than books, educational agencies and parents will find it more difficult to provide children and youth the equipment needed to ensure equal opportunities. In addition, there are already public institutions that can diminish inequities in reading opportunities; however, public institutions to nurture computer literacy are not yet widespread.

If support for the concept of computer literacy continues, equity issues will increasingly find their way onto the agenda of school boards. Some educational leaders are already addressing the issues. Affirmative programs directed at computer literacy during the summer, after-school scheduling to expand computer learning opportunities, and the use of such concepts as "student-access ratios" all reflect responses more random than widespread and more inchoate than well developed. The concept of "public information utilities" highlights the access question in the larger context of society. According enable all interested individuals to use large electronic databases to pursue educational, citizenship, and related purposes.

The implementation of this idea is at best a long-range possibility. It could not be realized until more advanced technologies are achieved, new information norms and habits are developed, and the transmission of computer-based information becomes much less expensive, nevertheless, the adjective "public" that stands before "information utilities" denotes an already emergent sensitivity is society to the equity issue. Given the very slow diffusion of reading skills during the last 500 years, public funds to support electronic information exchange will likely come slowly, if at all.

The first to achieve new skills are usually not eager to transfer them to others. Thus, when individuals, centuries ago, acquired written language skills, they became members of an elite group; as elites, they opposed the broad sharing of literacy skills. For example, the reading elite in England in the nineteenth century "viciously criticized" the idea of free libraries for the common people. Arguing that such libraries would cater to the "popular passion for light reading, above all for light fiction," the elite contended that the mass reading of such books would deter human progress, the common people would simply read the wrong things.

It is possible that even today those who have acquired highly sophisticated computer skills tend to look down upon the use of games and drill and practice routines in schools..

Those opposing and those supporting the mass diffusion of literacy skills have confronted one another for centuries. Leaders on the side of the people, including the most disadvantaged, have prevailed, even though their struggle is not yet ended. Aided by powerful institutions, especially governmental agencies, they have repeated and acted upon a simple message, namely, that if individuals are to be enlightened and effective, they must be literate. If computers fulfil their educational promises, the struggle to eradicate inequitable learning opportunities will continue. As computer-utilities, and international promises, the struggle to eradicate inequitable learning opportunities will continue.

As computer-driven interactive cable, electronic universities, information utilities, and international networks are increasingly used, equity issues will become more salient. Since microelectronic technologies are more complex, expensive, and mutable than books, the equity issues they raise will likely be even more difficult to resolve than those associated with written language.

The five-century story about book literacy is broader than that of ever-expanding learning opportunities; it also encompasses a long struggle to define and redefine the goals of literacy in ways that reflect changing societal values. Thus, Patricia Graham, writing about literacy skills in the early 1980s, observed: "literacy... is what everyone needs in late twentieth-century America, both for their own good and for society's good." However, Horrace Mann argued, from a nineteenth-century perspective, that if students acquired literacy, vice would be reduced and morality would be improved a view that in today's climate would strike many citizens as incredible. In Mann's time, however, morality was such a salient value that school leaders could not easily ignore it. Given the secularized public schools of today, Mann's definition of literacy is no longer highly relevant. Definitions of computer literacy will probably follow in the footsteps of traditional literacy; they will, in other words, be temporary and impermanent.

Rather than, policy makers will need to seek definitions and objectives that mesh with the needs, of their time. Since the information society is much more mutable than previous societies, computer literacy objective will likely undergo more frequent changes. Given the many fearful messages about robots and related machines and their deep cultural roots, computer literacy decisions will also likely be more controversial. Witness, for example, the currency of the dark omens expressed a century and a half ago in Shelley's Frankenstein.

Given the long evolution of book literacy, what features best describe its patterns of growth? For one thing, literacy definitions over time have become more complex—a pattern already reflected in computer literacy. For example, the simpler concepts of operational and instrumental literacy are associated more with the 1970s while the more complex concepts of computer programming and role-related literacy are linked more to the 1980s while the more complex concepts of computer programming and role-related literacy are linked more to the 1980s.

The move from the uncomplicated to the more complex can be seen as follows: operational literacy requires minimal machine skills; instrumental literacy requires minimal machine skills; instrumental literacy, the skills to learn from programs developed by others; algorithmic reasoning, the skills to create one's own programs; and role-related literacy, the skills to perform as competent consumers, workers, and citizens in the developing information society. Given the pattern just noted, another question arises: What features best denote literacy's developing complexities? For one thing, more varieties of radiant skill are now assembled under the literacy tent; for another, the functions served by literacy have multiplied.

Why are the meanings of literacy more encompassing today than they were earlier? Today's meanings stem from a multicentury trend toward an ever more varied content disseminated in a widening array of books, monographs, newspapers, magazines, and journals. When Martin Luther translated the Bible into the German language in the sixteenth century, he provided a powerful new stimulus and a popular means for the citizens of his nation to acquire literacy. At that time, however, literacy was by necessity defined largely in relation to one book.

With the spread of the printing press and the growth and popularization of diverse types of knowledge, literacy expanded to include the skills needed to read more diverse materials. In the nineteenth century, when individuals were pressed to understand the world around them by reading the newly invented newspaper, they had to expand their literacy skills. As reading skills have expanded, literacy functions have become more differentiated. "Scientific", "mathematical," "esthetic," "technological," and "language" denote some of these literacy functions. They also symbolize bodies of knowledge that go substantially beyond those in Luther's day or, for that matter, in Horace Mann's time. Significantly, they imply high expectations for schools, and they help to explain the emergence of compulsory education.

Computer literacy has already undergone considerable differentiation. Inherent in Previous descriptions of operational, instrumental, programmatic, and role-related concepts of literacy are such functions as word processing, computing; programming, information processing, and participation in teledemocratic arrangements. On the other hand, Marvin and Winther, through a study of computer specialists, have arrived at a different set of functions. Employing an electronic mail questionnaire sent to users of the Advanced Research Projects Agency Network (ARPANET), a large computer network, they obtained perceptual data from respondents about "the major types of skills and levels of knowledge that organize computer users into major classes." After analyzing their data, Marvin and Winther posited five levels of users. These classes of users, along with pertinent functions and skills, are described here:

1. Many individuals each day come in contact with microwave ovens, candy machines, cash registers, and related devices; since they perform passive rather than active functions, they do not require particular skills.
2. Members of the next group are called "tourists" or casual end-users. Professors, who rely upon experts for data analysis, fall into this category. The skills "tourists" need are very limited.
3. Programmers constitute the next group. They range from those who have written one workable program to those

who have written model programs. The skills required by programmers, as already noted, are specialized ones.

4. Near the top of the hierarchy is the fourth group, called "hackers," who deal effectively with computer "logiams" and "bottlenecks." Their skills, which they express inventively, are, highly technical.
5. At the top of the pyramid are "wizards." Noted for their capacity to perform "amazing feats," they can effect results seemingly by "passing their hands over circuit boards." Their skills are of the highest order.

Marvin and Winther concluded that "the definition of literacy and its proper objects is at any time not only a standard of skillful performance but also a social sorting procedure for labeling certain tasks and domains of knowledge as worthy of social attention and effort."

If computer users at IBM, the New York City public Schools, and the Pentagon had filled in the electronic questionnaire, their lists of functions and skills would likely have differed from one another and from those identified by ARPANET users. Given the diversity of their missions and "social sorting" procedures, they would, in other words, have arrived at different skills. Obviously, schools cannot prepare individuals to perform all computer functions; rather, they must concentrate on basic skills relevant to many differentiated functions.

If computer literacy skills are arrived at through processes of social construction which go on in highly specialized organizations such as ARPANET, the following question becomes pertinent: How are current definitions of literacy, as described above, likely to be reconstructed in the decades ahead? the expanded and interrelated uses of micro-technologies provided one context for examining this question. Since the microcomputer is the most visible of all microelectronic technologies, thinkers have understandably concentrated on computer literacy during the last decade. This approach to literacy has provided a useful focus for designing new learning experiences. However, "computer," as the modifier of literacy, may prove to be an impermanent concept. To be sure, microcomputers are pivotal points in the processing of information; however, they are only part of a much larger and more extended communication complex. The microcomputer is, to use concepts from gestalt psychology, a small "figure" against a more encompassing and expanding "ground."

Computer Literacy

Ministry of Education under the Government of India has launched a pilot project for introducing Computer Literacy and Studies in Schools (CLASS) in collaboration with the Department of Electronics. At the first instance, 250 schools all over the country were brought under the purview of this project and training courses were organised for teachers in the selected Resource Centres. Gradually all the schools would be covered in a phased manner. This has raised a wave of discussion in the country: Why computer in the field of education also? There has very often been hue and cry when computer has entered into the arena of industry, business, banking, examination, and so on. It is usually complained that computer will replace the man and unemployment will be rampant as a result of this.

Computer's Use

Computers in spite of strong opposition are now extensively used in various fields of human activity. Application of the computer in industry and business is considerable. It is used in traffic control and in police investigation. But for its help, space journey would be impossible. It is utilised for student guidance as well as for marriage counselling. It assists the universities and Boards of Secondary Education in tabulating scores and grading students. Now it is also useful in sports and games at the national and international levels.

In data-processing, efficiency of the computer cannot be overestimated. It can make very complicated calculations in a split second. It has proved its wonderful capabilities and is regarded as the most important invention after the birth of the printing process. It may be said that as the printing machine has enlarged the scope of communication, the computer has broadened the field of information and data processing. Its impact on food and material production, defence and remote sensing, scientific research and education is enormous in most of the advanced countries. The scientists and researchers having confidence in computers claim that no teacher ever born, no method ever adopted and no media ever utilised, can match the computer's efficiency.

In view of such increasing importance of the computer, students, the future citizens and employees in various walks of life, cannot afford to keep themselves aloof from this potential medium. Education even at the school stage has to provide for computer instruction. Profound technical knowledge and positive attitude as well as interest in the computer are essential prerequisites for the successful citizens of the coming decades. Besides, some of the challenging job opportunities will be available to the young in near future.

Idea of Computer

The computer is an electronic machine working on the principles of prolonged learning that aim at individualised instruction to meet the special needs of individual learners. The computer is a flexible as well as powerful devise which can cater to these needs by storing, processing and retrieving information.

The computer is equipped with electronic circuits, keyboards recording and storage facilities. Although it is called "a dignified calculating machine", or a "glorified calculator", it has a unique capability of "memorising heaps of information and reproducing or retrieving" them whenever necessary. The procedures and languages used for recording and retrieving information are specific and peculiar. Hence, programming involves great knowledge and skills which call for training and experience for manipulation and translation of the information.

Way of Working

The computer usually has five important components:

(i) in-put system,

(ii) output system,

(iii) a memory storage,

(iv) pro-cessing equipment, and

(v) a control system.

The input system converts our information into computer's language form and the output system retrieves the information into our language. The memory storage retains all the information that is fed into it through the input system. The processing system processes the data through manipulation and selects the information as required. All these functions are controlled and co-ordinated by the control system as per a particular programme.

Two kinds of information are normally fed into the computer and a programme consists of a set of instructions and an amount of information. Both sets of information are preserved in the memory storage.

Educational Utility

The computer is now regarded as a super teaching machine. Its use in education has been tried as an innovation and it has proved its teaching efficiency in many developed countries. The computer has been helping the teacher in the following areas:

(i) Evaluation of students performance and classification of children according to abilities;

(ii) Preparation of timetable and schedules;

(iii) Allocation of learning materials according to individual needs and interests.

(iv) Maintenance of progress cards efficiently and confidentially.

(v) Providing information/data for guidance and reference.

(vi) Provision of direct interaction between pupils and subject-matter.

(vii) Engaging students in tutorial work;

(viii) Providing immediate feedback to students for better interaction and motivation.

Role of Computer

Computer Assisted Instruction or briefly known as CAI is an interesting innovation in educational technology. Its marvels have been demonstrated and seem to revolutionise the whole spectrum of education. It has better flexibility and more versatility than any of the teaching machine. It can cater to the individual needs of many students at a time and record all the responses of all the pupils with reliability. The time taken by individual student in responding to a question and extent of correctness in the same are also recorded by the computer. All this helps the educator in planning instruction and providing relevant materials.

The CAI can deal the problem of quality in education more effectively and more flexible kind of branching is possible on the part of the computer according to the student's performance. A learner can make progress at one's pace, receive and choose the material, sequencing and level of instruction freely. Since each learner's performance is automatically recorded and can be fed back to the teacher, learner's performance can be evaluated and education be provided according to the strategy that is best suited to the individual. The teacher can be relieved from the daily routine and monotonous drilling activities. It has been experimentally proved that any lesson in any subject can be programmed for CAI if the objective is clearly defined and learning materials are represented in words, visuals and experiments.

The CAI installation usually consists of individual learning booths each with a console. Every student sits in front of the console with a television screen displaying information, etc. A complete learning package suiting to his individual needs is presented, sequentially. This package may consist of video as well as audio tape-recordings, films, slides, film strips, and so on. The student may make queries to the computer by means of a type-writer key-board and get answers in printed forms. The student may write the answers directly on the cathode ray tube display screen with a "light-pen" which can be evaluated by the computer. On completion of a programme, the computer records his progress and prints out a report for the teacher.

Although CAI is developed on the principles of programmed learning, it also utilises the concepts of audio-visual education, communication theory, system analysis, data processing and learning theory. CAI produces learning experience effectively and efficiently. A good amount of information stored in the computer is made available to the learner more readily than by any other media. The interaction between the student and instructional programme is made more dynamic and more individualised in CAI than in any other system. But judicious pre-planning and careful programming are essential for this.

CAI is, however, extremely expensive. It is also mostly mechanical and deprived of human touch. Therefore, it is criticised on the ground that this innovation will dehumanise the educational system and the teaching-learning process will be lifeless and mechanised.

Educational technologists, therefore, suggest system approach representing an integrated, sequential and multimedia learning package. This systems approach should also consist of all relevant media, material and methods. It will not replace the teacher, but will relieve him of drudgery and dreariness. The Computer Assisted Instruction will rather bank upon the teacher heavily for constant analysis, curricular revision, better planning human guidance and counselling. A creative and committed teacher is more in demand than anything else when computer is available in education.

The provisions under the NPE, 1986 and POA, 1986 remained intact in the NPE, 1992 but more emphasis was given in the latter on Computer Education. In the beginning the coverage of schools under the CLASS Project was modest. But with a view to increase awareness of computer literacy among students, teachers and parents, more schools were taken up and more agencies were involved in the process. A notable initiative was triggered by the CLASS Project as private schools were allowed to charge fees for the said facility and professional agencies were contracted for providing the hardware and teaching inputs. The CBSE pioneered Computer Science Programme at higher secondary stage and some State Boards followed this lead. The UGC also started the Computer Education Programme by providing PCs, starting certificate, diploma and degree courses in universities and by giving computers for Central Institutions for research and higher studies. IITs and engineering colleges acquired computers and started computer science programmes in many institutions. The World Bank assisted the project for strengthening and modernising polytechnics and giving other facilities.

The CLASS Project expanded and covered many thousands

of senior secondary schools and many advanced schools which implemented the CLASS Project effectively. Computer education with adequate facilities was encouraged in secondary and higher secondary schools. Access of students to computer facilities in universities, colleges and technical institutions was encouraged and computer facility was made available to students and researchers round the clock. With the resources available, computer platforms for MCA students and researchers were upgraded. The polytechnics and professional bodies were accredited by the Departments of Electronics. UGC formulated a concrete programme for motivating and encouraging teachers of Computer Science to commercially link up with the professional agencies for mutual benefit. The UGC set up effective training arrangements for college teachers and initiated the programme for starting a support paper at Master's level.

The MHRD worked with the Ministry of Information & Broadcasting, Department of Space, Department of Electronics, and Finance Ministry for augmentation of transmission facilities for educational programmes and opened a new educational channel. The CIET & UGC continued a co-ordinating role and assisted the State agencies more meaningfully both financially and academically.

As reported earlier, computer education has assumed immense significance in the education system of the country. But it is found that people are more interested in acquiring hardware, particularly computer sets and not in developing and utilizing software suitable for the various groups of clientele. The MHRD, UGC and even the foreign agencies have come forward to finance the projects relating to computer education. But necessary steps need to be taken for giving training and providing necessary facilities for developing and using software in the teaching-learning process. Many educational institutions at school and higher education stages are now equipped with computers. Prof. S. K. Khanna, Vice-Chairman UGC rightly pointed out that there is need to look at computer education in its totality starting from school education to higher education keeping pace with changing technology. He stressed that for imparting proper training, the educational institutions must posse necessary hardware and software.

Prof. M. Mukhopadhya has aptly observed that in the CLASS Project computers were provided with a few CAI software, while colleges were provided with computers without any software. The CAI software is almost absent, and lack of provision of suitable software has led to gross under-utilisation or no utilisation of computers.

The manpower requirement in computer education is wide ranging i. e. from data entry operator and technician to designer and engineer of computer configuration and programmes. It goes without saying that computers can be used effectively for providing good quality education and for removing disparities between slow and bright learners as far as possible. Besides teaching various subjects, there can be versatile use of computers in research experiments and innovations for enriching curricula and improving the standard of education. Unfortunately there is lack of imagination and co-ordination in the planning, management and utilisation of computer education and unless this is removed there would be huge wastage of resources both material and human and instead of computers becoming functional and useful would be ornamental and great wastage. Therefore, the need of the hour is to take concrete steps and utilise all available resources and equipment to greatly improve our education system.

Computer, at Hand

The computer should be used as a learning tool within the student's college classes. Students need to experience how one learn via computer. At WOSC we are in our third year of a National Science Foundation Comprehensive Assistance to Undergraduate Science Education grant titled, "Infusion of Computer Science into Liberal Arts, and teacher faculty member per year concerning the potential of the computer as an educational tool. This is accomplished through a two week summer workshop during which time the faculty member defines a project to be implemented during the course of the following year with grant support. Through these activities we have begun to incorporate the computer as a teaching tool in several courses in various departments on campus. The most successful applications to-date have been in the Music, Dance, English Composition, Biology, Mathematics, Education, and Psychology areas.

Special Education/Psychology-computer-aided testing, software programmes for lab experiences, and student scoring of their own personality inventories.

Music : Pitch and interval ear raining and multi-voice score training.

Physics : Wave motion demonstration programme.

Mathematics : Intermediate Algebra competencies and data research on testing.

Chemistry : Organic compounds nomenclature practice.

English : Composition editing using word, processing.

Education : Application of on-line computer-administered testing.

Psychology /Special Education : Statistical teaching packaged.

Economics /Business : Record keeping system, simulations of running a profitable business, and fiscal management.

Biology : Use of pre-packaged programmes in General Biology and demonstration of various programmes to elementary teachers.

Mathematics : Graphing programmes for trigonometry and vocabulary.

Education : Collection and analysis of student data and transfer of that data to a statistical package.

For the education majors, additional training is required to lay the foundation for using computers as an instructional tool. Very few instructors write primary textbook materials, yet almost all instructors create supplementary materials.

The typical classroom instructor will not be writing computer programmes, but will be creating or managing supplementary materials. The focus is on helping the instructors learn to choose and use good application software in their classroom and to use the computer as a management tool. The following topics are covered in the foundation block for elementary and secondary educational:

1. Computer managed records—
   (a) Grade book;

(b) Test banks of questions;

(c) Achievement records.

2. Drill and practice material—
3. Tutorials.
4. Entire curriculum packages.
5. Video/computer interface.
6. The computer as an exploratory tool.
7. Software evaluation and selection.

For students who wish to develop a computer science emphasis the following courses are available at WOSC.

First Year

CS 101 Computers and Society 4 credits.

CS 133 Computer Coding-BASIC 4 credits.

Second Year

Cs 211 Introduction to Computer Science 4 credits

CS 212 Techniques of Programming-PASCAL 4 credits

CS 215 Computer Organization 4 credits

CS 213 Symbolic Language-FORTRAN 4 credits

CS 217 Into to Data Processing-COBOL 4 credits

Third Year

CS 311 Symbolic Language Programming 3 credits

CS 371 Applications Programming 1 3 credits

CS 372 Application Programming II 3 credits

Fourth Year

CS 430 Data Structures and Management 3 credits

CS 406g Special Topics 3 to 4 credits

MTH 406g Extended BASIC 4 credits

Students who wish to become the managers and area specialists on computers within speed need to have much of the same basic training as any other computer science person on the lower division level. Their upper division work should be directed toward the area of teaching about computers or the development of instructional material. To provide for this need WOSC offers the following courses—

ED 451g Microcomputer Systems 3 Credits

— The building of a working vocabulary dealing with microcomputers. Essential hardware and software components and their functions are studied. Applications of microcomputer systems within the classroom are investigated.

ED 452g Computer Based Education 3 Credits

— Characteristics of computer-based education illustrating the advantages to be derived from using computer-managed and computer-assisted interactive systems. Most of the work in the class will be focused on the microcomputer. Prior classwork in ED 4518 and/or CS 133 is required.

ED 461g Computer-Assisted Instruction 3 credits

— The design of computer-assisted instruction lessons and interactive systems will be studied. Students will be asked to design a set of computer-assisted lessons for classroom use.

ED 466g Computer-Managed Instruction 3 credits

— This course is designed to introduce students to a computerized method of testing, record keeping, and decision making that will assist administrative, classroom, and individual learner management. The student examines how computer-managed instruction can solve the management problems of individualized instruction.

A revised education technology masters degree programming incorporating up to 18 credit hours in computer application courses has received committee approval and is in the process of being implemented. Supporting our underlying philosophy that the computer is an instructional medium available to all students, WOSC has one central facility consisting of 13 APPLE II micro-computers, 10 of which are connected to two CORVUS hard disk drives.

Two of the systems have printers attached to them. In addition there are three free standing units, one of which has a video interface. This facility is located in the college library providing, access to all. There are also six microcomputers located around campus for faculty development of programmes and classroom demonstration. During the course of the school year over 50 per cent of the college population interacts with these computers.

The CAUSE Grant has allowed us, as Western Oregon State College, to begin acquainting faculty and administrators with microcomputers. The faculty has begun to examine the curriculum to see how to make use of computers as a teaching tool and to determine the degree of exposure a beginning teacher needs to be prepared for tomorrow's classroom.

Public education is in a period of dramatic change; we believe that all aspects of teacher-education must be examined to insure that we can help future teachers not only gain skills in working with people but also gain the skills needed to use the developing educational technology. Curriculum must be continually examined and adjusted or teacher education risks being out of phase with both students and society itself.

Before listing some of the things being done for teachers using the resources of the School of Education at the University of Michigan, we should describe the basis for our interest in and approach to serving education through computers. In general, we strive for balance among teaching, research and service' we hope to develop, apply and share knowledge about the use of computers at all levels of education, elementary school through college. We choose to give special attention to school and community resources, and then make the most of the special resources of the University of Michigan and the School of Education.

Focus on School and Community Resources: The things most important to effective learning with computers are happening today in schools and homes, not in universities and the colleges. What we do for teachers using the resources of the School of Education must serve them well in their own schools and communities. Therefore the pre-service training, as well as in-service programmes and consolation, is carried out with an eye for the facilities and situations which will be found in the local schools.

Computers, Education and Teachers: Inexpensive computing facilities that are easy to use will be one of the more important things to happen to education in this century. We believe that she experience of teachers and the availability of technical support will be the most important factor in determining how well computers are used in schools. The need is now, and growing more rapidly than institutions are professional organizations can respond.

A Role for School of Education: Colleges and universities can translate interest in computers and education into actions to meet the needs of students, teachers and administrators by going out into the schools and communities to assist with operational programmes, by maintaining high standards for professional development and practice, and by nurturing appropriate interest in research, e.g., to increase knowledge about teaching and learning processes. More specifically, we recommend that schools of education provide practitioners with skills in teaching and administration of computer-related curriculum as well as information about computers, and arrange for continuing support of on-going programmes as well as one-shot training to get them started. Action-oriented research is appropriately included in all training and support activities, that is, professionals should get involved in planning for, collecting and interpreting data to aid in decisions in their schools.

Resource of the Colleges and Universities: Training and support offered to teachers through colleges and universities should take advantage of the special resources available there. Micro-computers are used throughout the University in many different ways—information systems, process control, laboratory equipment, specialized graphics, etc.

Students have a unique opportunity to learn about current and future uses of microcomputers, and as teachers they need to know about computing in their areas, in jobs, and in society, not just in the classroom. Exploration of microcomputer applications opens doorways onto the entire world of computing. The university of Michigan has been a leader in computers and education since a Food Foundation grant in 1956 for curriculum development in engineering education. Nearly all parts of the University have been involved, humanities and the arts as well as sciences and professions.

Various units provide courses as well as software and applications, Research and development throughout the University contributes to the quality of the programme in the School of Education, and education faculty help other units using computers in teaching give appropriate attention to matters of leaning and teaching. We believe the most effective uses of computers in education today are well based in the subjects taught and in supporting disciplines, so we do not treat "Computers in education" as a separate discipline.

Overview of this Report: The first section describes the academic programmes in the School of Education—degree programmes, courses, independent work, and cooperation with other teaching units. The second and third sections summarize service and research activities. The facilities for educational computing are describeb briefly in the last section, and we close with a brief statement about future directions.

The University of Michigan School of Education is organized in five large units: administration and policy planning; development, learning and teaching; higher science. Computers are used in all the programmes, but they get particular attention in "development, learning and teaching" as part of literacy. Special topic such as problem solving, learning strategies and social relations are considered in all four areas of literacy. Computing in education is not treated as a separate degree programme because the University gives only one masters degree or doctorate in education, and more importantly, because computing in education is considered in context rather than as a separate subject.

Microcomputers and Education provides an overview of computers in education with special attention to instructional design, testing and evaluation. Microcomputer Programming for Educators serves as an introduction as well but leads to specific skills is one or more languages and the development of specific programmes for use in ones teaching. These two courses are offered every term and enroll about 30 students each time. Microcomputers in the classroom integrates programming, instructional design and classroom management. Seminar in the Use of Microcomputers in Education provides for advance project work. These two courses are scheduled once each year and are restricted to graduate students; typical enrollment is 20.

Because the field is growing and changing more rapidly that a school of education can respond with new courses, and because the student learning about computers in education come from varying backgrounds and situations, the College offers many opportunities for study of special topics by individuals and small groups in addition to regular courses. Typically students will define topics for independent reading or research, often derived from questions raided during one of the regular courses, and sometimes based on experiences in their own teaching, research of administration.

One or more faculty members will assist in redefining the topic and identifying resources for independent work. The results often are reported through informal seminars as well as in publishable reports. About ten students use this option each year. These opportunities for independent work provide some of the flexibility needed in a new area of study, and help determine what topics later students should study as a more formal programming is developed. That is, some of the following topics may become regular courses:

- — Computer use in science, match, social studies, etc.
- — Planning and administration of computer labs and programmes.
- — Curriculum science and education.
- — Information sciences and education.
- — Social amplifications of technology.
- — State and regional programmes for computers in education.
- — Learning theories and technology.
- — Research and evaluation.

Various Facilities

The need for practitioners helping with computer applications and studies in schools is considerable and immediate. The linkage between research and practice is of immediate benefit to operational programmes as well as long-term research. Therefore, practical experience is very appropriate in a graduate study of computers in education. We encourage practicums and project experience, either in association with on-going projects in the School of Education or elsewhere in the University, or in the schools in which the candidates presently work. We know no better "examination" than that provided by experience in the field—managing a microcomputer lab, developing instructional applications in one's discipline, or helping teachers to use computers more effectively in their classrooms. We expect about ten students a year to enroll for credit in a practicum; presently the only students in this category are working on doctoral dissertations.

Undergraduates in our teacher preparation programme have ample opportunity to use computers in their regular classes or independent work. In addition to trying computer applications in the relevant discipline, students are likely to be signed other interesting activities, such as using a microcomputer to carry out a readability analysis of text materials and designing a computer-based learning activity. A microcomputer resource center provides machines, software, publications, and other materials for individual work, as well an opportunity to observe learners from pre-school to adult working with computers individually or in classes

Diffusion of computing through methods classes began with a grant from the "faculty development fund" at the Center for Research on Learning and Teaching. We went to the instructors with suggestions for computer use in the various disciplines, demonstrated the applications, and offered to assist. Virtually all methods courses now include computing activity directed by the individual instructors, with technical assistance form the staff of the resources center. Students can go on to teach themselves more about computers; some enroll in the undergraduate classes.

The School of Education draws on the resources of other units that work with computers and information systems, and also coordinates its efforts with others interested in computers in schools. The School of Library Science shares resources for demonstration and research; working together, education and library science prepare students for serving a support function in the schools. The College of Engineering has set up microcomputer classrooms for undergraduate courses in programming and applications. At scheduled times these classrooms are available for demonstrations, workshops and special classes.

The PET shop is available for other uses, especially for summer institutes since only a few chemistry lab sections are scheduled in the summer. The Department of Computer and Communications Sciences helps staff several courses off campus for teachers needing a sound basis in computer science. The Department of Psychology has several laboratories working on learning and instruction using computers, providing graduate students in education access to a wider variety of research opportunities.

The Center for Research on Learning and Teaching helps provide the resources for demons-tration and research, and in return, the School of Education helps faculty elsewhere in the University explore computer applications in their own teaching and scholarly work, a task beyond the resources of the Center. The communication among faculty using computers began with a series of workshops and "faculty seminars" organized by the Center for Research on Learning and Teaching. Later the same series was offered on the site of the resource center in the School of Education, establishing it as the new site of information and advice. The Apple users group meets regularly at the School of Education, further identifying the resource center as a focal point for communication.

The School of Education offers many lectures, demonstrations and consultation on the use of microcomputers for schools. These include;

— faculty orientation sessions;

— intermediate district or country school board sessions; and community meetings.

— At times faculty members help the staff in the planning of computer systems and curriculum to be used throughout a school or district. We are always conscious of helping share experience among organizations and agencies. For example, we helped establish a state task force on computers in schools, we work with regional resource centers in the public schools systems throughout the state, and, of course, we share software through professional associations and user groups.

The University also offers specific in-service programmes for schools system.

Researchers at the University are active in a variety of studies and plan a comprehensive research programme on the use of computers in education. A microcomputer research collaborative established in the summer of 1979 has encouraged and participated in research on attitudes and values; learning with computer assistance; social structures; and futures. CAI, per se is not given much attention, but the researchers focus instead on aspects of learning, procedures for curriculum design, social context for learning, or other disciplines which contribute to effective use of computers in education.

The realities of computer-use in schools for the next few years dominate research planning. For example, attention is being given to conceptualizing how a single microcomputer is best used with a group of students where the institution cannot afford enough machines for everyone individually or in pairs. The programme of research assumes more computers will be purchased for homes that for schools and so explores ways to exploit home computing for education. Research is encouraged in many innovative uses of computers in education. Such uses include but are not limited to attitudes that those using computers in education have towards:

— learning;

— careers;

— educational institutions;

— technology in education;

— lifelong learning;

— creative activities supported by technology;
— family activities.
— efficiency;
— effectiveness;
— long-term effects;
— thinking and problem solving;
— learning skills;
— skills for handling information.
— classroom structure and activities;
— friendships;
— interpersonal relations;
— teacher-student relationships;
— teacher role;
— parent role;
— implications for family.
— anticipating new technology and its impacts;
— assessing social implications;
— shaping alternative futures.

Sources of Material

The computer education resource center is housed in the Instructional Strategy Services unit of the School of Education, providing an appropriate context, technical support, and ready access for students, faculty and the teaching support, and ready access for students, faculty and the teaching community to explore a new technology in education. Other programmes of the Service unit provide links with graphics, video, curriculum review, information services, and the like. Of course, other units in the schools of Education also use microcomputers in their work; students use machines in the Statistical Laboratory, the Center for Evaluation Research Training, and a special programme in education and psychology. Botl the manager and assistant manager of the resource center know the computer field well, along with their own specialities in library science. Workshops, demonstrations, and open access fit well within its domain, and the unit provides the larger context of teaching and learning.

The lab includes at least one of each common microcomputer along with documentation and a library of applications. About seven Pets, ten Apples, and a dozen Atari's can be assembled so that workshops and classes have one computer station for each of two terminals on time sharing systems, and one additional terminal is dedicated to special uses in graphics. Typically half of the machines are out in faculty offices or field research. The equipment kept in the resource center is arranged about the periphery of the space for individual work but it can easily be shifted for group use of classroom demonstration.

A second classroom is used when we call in extra machines. Group viewing is accommodated through use of large monitors: black and white monitors for applications which are primarily text, and colour where that is helpful to the demonstration. The same monitors are used for viewing material from videotape for more convenient use in group demonstrations as well as easy access by individuals. The resource center also has two vediodisc players, one consumer model and one industrial for experiments with computer-controlled videodisc.

The staff person who handles other equipment for the Resource Centre also takes care of computer connectors, cables, and the like. Some time is required for the cleaning and repair of disk and cassette media, the diagnosis of equipment problems, and minor repairs. This person also makes arrangements for outside repair as needed.

The computer lab maintains a large set of materials in cooperation with the Center for Research on Learning and Teaching. The center manages to maintain:

— a comprehensive programme library;

— a substantial reference library;

— most of the relevant periodicals;

— manuals for each of the machines;

— most of the recent textbooks;

— media materials:
  - video tape,
  - tape-slide,
  - computer programmes.

— annotations on programmes and applications;

— self-help posters.

The resources center is supervised by experienced library and media staff. The manager, assistant manager and laboratory aides together provide service to both faculty and students, comparison of equipment options, such identification and review of software, advice on development of applications—and assistance with preparation of graphics for use in papers and other presentations. That is, the resource center provides computer resources for any scholarly work by students, as well as a site for study of computers in education. In addition to the regular staff and faculty, undergraduates are hired as aides and programmers to extend the support staff to serve more people at modest cost.

The students use their work as a learning experience. About twenty undergraduate students benefit from this opportunity each term. Graduate students help with review application programmes and publications. Workshops, short courses and programme review are carried on by faculty members on a regular basis.

Service to other units, organizations and informal groups have proved mutually beneficial. For example, the University of Michigan Apple users group meets regularly, and typically some education students who happened by, get "hooked" and leave with some new ideas of software for innovation or use.

Graduate students have gained excellent experience staffing special courses for the University Children Center, and education classes have observed young children exploring computers. The resource center is a resource for local teachers, providing the full tango of information and examples maintained for University students and faculty, and offering demonstrations in an "open house" format and instruction through institutes and workshops. In addition, and academic programme for talented students offered by the Gifted Students Institute each summer since 1978 provides one example of the "computer camp" idea that has becomes so popular recently. "Properly designed, can allow students to formulate hypotheses, test them, analyze results, and refine their conceptions.

Moreover, they can provide the student with a record of the course of his or her investigations, permitting greater self-awareness of thinking and, learning." There are, however, many barriers to realizing this potential, among them a lack of consensus on the definition of higher-order thinking and an incomplete understanding about the use of technology to promote it. We explore both issues in this chapter.

There are diverse views about the components of higher-order thinking and no adequate and agreed upon theory from which to derive a definition that would elicit consensus. Although a number of researchers have developed theories, definitions, and criteria for higher order thinking, a consensus remains elusive. For instance, Feurstein emphasizes "autonomous learning" and the importance of logical reasoning, recognizing relationships, classifying and comparing concepts.

Foshay stresses the importance of learning to learn, which he labels the "pursuit of meaning," and includes such components as learning facts and findings, learning techniques, learning sources and processes interpreting information. Zacharias is more practical, emphasizing heuristics such as determining whether a problem can be solved, pushing possibilities to the limit, even to absurdity, asking for help, changing scale to achieve a different perspective, and bringing in outside information. Each perspective is valid, but they do not combine to provide a consensus.

For the purpose of this chapter, we suggest that higher order thinking occurs when a person is engaged in active and sustained cognitive effort directed of solving a complex problem and when the person makes effective use of prior knowledge and experience in addressing the problem. The problem must be complex for the person; many problems will meet this criterion for some people but not for others. Problems may be well-structured with clear definition, rules, and goals or ill-structured with unclear definition, ambiguous rules, and subjective goals. By sustained effort we mean engagements requiring anywhere from ten minutes to many hours or longer.

Cognitive effort includes activities generally identified in the literature on problem solving, such as integrating and synthesizing different bodies of information, making critical judgments, and developing and testing hypotheses. We include the concept of effectiveness in our definition because an important overall pedagogical goal is to improve the student's capacity to succeed in solving increasingly complex problems. We believe that a novice problem solver, although engaged in active and sustained cognitive effort, may not use strategies of the same efficiency as those used by an expert.

On the other hand, an expert who very quickly reaches the correct solution to a problem that to other might be complex would not be engaged in higher-order thinking. We believe that effectiveness in higher-order thinking necessarily involves making appropriate use of prior knowledge and experience relating to the problem. This conception of higher-order thinking enables us to think about ways of realistically challenging students of different ages and with different levels of knowledge as they deal with problems they perceive to be intellectually complex.

Although we can not precisely specify the components of higher-order thinking, we have a good idea of what such thinking is not. While higher-order thinking may be involved, it usually is not evident when the central activities of students are—

(a) memo-rizing,

(b) learning isolated facts and findings

(c) using algorithms rigidly or automatically, or

(d) answering problems with solutions already known to them. Such activities do not involve higher-order thinking because they do not represent "complex" problems nor do they require sustained cognitive effort for most students.

Our definition of higher-order thinking suggests that much of what goes on in schools bears only an indirect relationship to higher-order thinking. Evidence of lack of instruction in higher-order skills comes from a variety of places. Studies of reading instruction find that 90 percent of instruction is directed at the learning of isolated words and only 5 percent is focused on understanding text. Surveys of textbooks indicate the tremendous emphasis on vocabulary learning and the superficial and fragmented nature of the material. Studies of mathematics instruction report that early instruction in arithmetic may even drive our some of the effective problem-solving strategies that students bring to school.

The nature of standardized achievement tests discourages teachers from focusing on higher-order skills. Items on such tests typically require responding with discrete bits of information in a multiple-choice format. Domains for these tests are often rigidly defined and rarely require students to synthesize information across defined domains. Recent work by a small group of educators and cognitive psychologists has resulted in school-based curricula designed to improve thinking skills. Like others, Sternberg has argued for the necessity for training students to think: Each program should provide explicit training both in the mental processes used in task performance and in self-management strategies.

Techniques for teaching these skills cover a wide range of options and philosophies. Glaser and Sternberg have described and analyzed several of the more touted instructional programs and their reported successes. These programs range from teaching ways to structure problems and generalizable heuristics in a nearly content-free environment to training strategies within a specific content domain.

Generally, computer software for the schools is similar to other instructional material in its focus on imparting factual information and on low-level algorithmic skills. There is evidence that students can learn factual information effectively by using computers in academic subject areas. For instance, the effectiveness of computer-aided instruction has been consistently demonstrated in foreign language and in science.

Across subject areas, computerized instruction is associated with greater or equal gains in learning when compared with traditional instruction. Furthermore, this achievement is obtained in equal or less time than is needed for regular classroom learning.

An experiment carried out in the Los Angeles Unified School District shows some of the potential for computer-assisted instruction.

In conjunction with the Educational Testing Service, the district conducted a five-years longitudinal experiment using the Computer curriculum Corporation's drill and practice software that was originally developed by Patrick Suppes. The purpose was to determine whether these computer programs could improve performance of students in compensatory education programs in mathematics, reading and language arts. Compared to a control group, students using the CAI materials showed large and significant gains.

The use of CAI curricula helped students to improve standardized test scores significantly. Nearly all the research on effects of computer-assisted instruction in schools focuses on knowledge development programs similar to the programs in the Los Angeles schools. Such programs account for the greatest use of computers in elementary schools. There is little evidence however that computer software stimulates higher-level thinking. This lack of evidence is one of the reasons that software to promote higher-order thinking is used in schools only to a very limited degree. Another reason is that few programs are available, even though the quality of such programs is beginning to improve.

Programs of Software

Software programs which attempt to provide challenges to solve complex problems are (a) apt to require a longer a longer time for the student to complete, (b) difficult to integrate with the curriculum, (c) difficult for the teacher to master, and (d) difficult to evaluate. Nonetheless, there are computer programs and programming languages that, according to authors' claims, can improve problem-solving skills. Data assessing these claims, however, are scarce. Programming languages that allow the student to control the computer and provide an inherently rich problem-solving environment have attracted much attention. One such programming language is Logo, developed explicitly for young children. It includes an interactive component that allows students to give directions to the computer by informing a "turtle" what to draw. The computer draws what the child has directed. This process allows for immediate feedback. Part of the advocacy for teaching even young children how to direct or program a computer results from a belief that learning to think like a computer makes a better thinker. The argument is not that thinking like a computer is somehow better than human thought, but that the consideration of thinking makes humans more thoughtful.

Researchers have compared the problem-solving performance of subjects who used such programs with the performance of those who did not, but no conclusive results have emerged. Some data suggest that learning the Logo programming language is significantly different from learning other languages because of its interactive nature. Scattered and sparse evidence indicates that Logo instruction may have a positive influence on much things as fluency, originality, and divergent thinking. Some have hypothesized that increased facility with Logo provides the potential for improved thinking to the extent that it acts as a tool for expressing powerful ideas.

By using Logo, children have the opportunity to gain a personal understanding of abstract ideas they are unlikely to encounter until a much higher level of schooling, if at all. Evaluating claims about computer programs or language designed to improve higher-order thinking skills is a more complex process than evaluating knowledge-building programs. Definitions are not as precise and, as we have indicated, there are no agreed upon outcome measures. It is only recently that researchers have begun to prove the claims of developers for programs to improve higher-order thinking.

One of the ways in which computer programs may possibly help in developing the skills of higher-order thinking is through instruction in the use of heuristics, that is, instruction in particular strategies of problem solving. Before considering this matter, we found it useful to look into such questions as (a) Can heuristic strategies be taught and do they actually help students solve problems? and (b) Does training in such strategies transfer across various domains of content?

One of the most popular views is that a way to teach higher-order thinking skills is to instruct students in particular strategies to solve problems. Simon has pointed out that "powerful general methods exist and... they can be taught in such a way that they can be used in new domains whether they are relevant." Perhaps the best known set of problem-solving heuristics is included in Polya's classic work *How to Solve it.* He developed four categories of heuristics: figuring out the problem, devising a plan, carrying out the plan and looking back. Feuerstein's instructional techniques to improve problem-solving skills include such activities as classifying and comparing attributes, recognizing relationships, planning, synthesizing, and logical reasoning.

It is important for students to monitor their own thinking by suing such strategies as identifying underlying assumptions, grasping whole-part and part-whole relationships, and applying principles to real-life situations. Newell, Shaw, and Simon argued in 1960 that "heuristics are...things that aid discovery. Heuristics seldom provide infallible guidance.... Often they 'work', but the results are variable and success is seldom guaranteed." Suydam, on the other hand, found that "research evidence strongly concurs that problem-solving performance is strongly enhanced by teaching students to use a wide variety of strategies of heuristics, both general and specific." The twenty years that separate these assessments account in part for the disagreement, but good data are still scarce, and the methods advocated for teaching heuristics are mainly based on common sense and intuitive understandings. As early as 1950, researchers explored the hypothesis that students who use explicit problem-solving strategies are better problem solvers than those who do not and that such strategies can be taught so that skills are improved.

Bloom and Broder investigated the problem-solving skills of college students across a variety of subject areas. They found that bright students who were poor problem solvers could be trained to improve their problem-solving skills using the strategies employed by peers who were successful problem solvers. These, who participated in the training tended to score 49 to 68 grade levels higher than matched groups with no training they also expressed confidence and optimism about their newly learned problem-solving abilities. More recently, Pet found that specific instruction that followed the four-step heuristics of Polya's model was effective in improving fifth graders' use of the strategies, but he did not find significant differences in success in solving problems between the experimental group and a control group that had no training.

Since the period of treatment was only four weeks; it is not surprising that problem-solving outcomes were not dramatically influenced. In another study, fourth graders who were taught to develop pictorial aids, such as tables and diagrams, could solve more problems than others who did not receive such instruction. Within the area of mathematics, instruction in problem solving heuristics is generally supplied to clearly structured problems. Schoenfeld successfully trained college-level students to use specific techniques to improve their strategic for solving work problems in algebra. In a follow-up project, Schoenfeld reported that not only did college level students increase their use of particular strategies, but those who used the heuristics effectively were also more successful at solving algebra problems. Perhaps as a result of this success, the students' self-reports of their problem-solving skills were more favourable. In another study on solving word problems in algebra, Mayer, and Bovenmeyer found that performance was predicted by ability to understand the problem and plan the solution.

Some researchers believe that effective problem-solving strategies are specific to particular domains. The argument is that a student gets deeper into a content domain the problem solving skills become more and more specific to that domain and therefore may not transfer to other domains. Studies of expert and novice problem solvers are particularly salient here. These studies have found that when novices and experts are faced with a problem in the experts' domain, they approach the problem in different ways. Novices tend to focus on the literal objects defined in the statement of the problem.

The possible strategies for solution seen by experts are expanded by their understanding of the relationships among concepts and procedures specific to that domain. How are we to reconcile the findings of these expert-novice studies with the views of those who see the value of generalized problem-solving heuristics across different subject matters? One line of argument is simply that increased knowledge of a content domain makes possible a more efficient and precise application of general heuristic procedures.

Greater knowledge of a domain should increase the chances for a person to define a problem accurately, allow on to decide more easily among possible strategies for solution and facilitate resting the validity of possible solutions. In this argument, procedural problem-solving skills interact with the knowledge base to increase the abilities of the student to solve the problem. We might imagine a model with three significant effects: two main effects and an interaction effect of the two.

Drawing from observational studies of students, recent researchers have considered this issue. In a detailed analysis of problem solving in geometry, Greeno argued that three kinds of knowledge are critical for success:

(a) heuristic knowledge necessary for carrying out proofs, such as setting goals, forming plans, and generally organizing the problem-solving process;

(b) knowledge of specific geometric facts, such as the definition of lines and angles;

(c) geometric concepts essential to making inferences and proving theorems. Similarly, Glaser and Pellegrino concluded that two critical and inter-releated components are necessary for higher-order thinking to occur:

    (i) thoughtful consideration of procedural constraints of a particular problem area, such as inductive or analogical reasoning as problem-solving tools and

    (ii) subject area knowledge.

Recent theoretical work in cognitive sciences has used the notion of knowledge structure or schema to help explain the way people remember, comprehend, and solve problems. Schema theory attempts to describe the relationships between knowledge previously acquired, the way it is organized in the mind, and the ease with which new knowledge is acquired and used. Experts re-viewed as hav:.g rich and complex schema that facilitate the acquisition of new information and the rapid solution of many problems.

The prior knowledge base and schema of the expert in physics is sufficiently rich so that many high school physics problems can be solved algorithmically. The expert "knows" the way to define the problem, "knows" the right strategy to solve it, and "knows" how to evaluate the solution. He may apply Polya's steps but he will do so unconsciously and rapidly; for him this is routine processing, not higher-order thinking. To a high school student with a less complete knowledge schema in physics, however, the same problem may pose a complex task requiring higher-order thinking. Although the student may have a solid base of facts and an understanding of the basic rules of physics, the problem may require combining the facts and rule in novel ways.

The student may have to examine multiple ways of representing the problem and explore a variety of possible will be engaged in higher-order thinking only when they are stretched beyond situations where they already know how to find the solution. It also implies that constant deepening of a subject area to include increasingly complex material is critical for either students of experts as they deal with tasks that require higher-order thinking. Psychologists investigating metacognition suggest that students who self-consciously consider their own cognitive processing can enhance their thinking. Much recent research indicates that the student is very active in selecting, interpreting, and even altering the content of instruction. The key processes seen as integral to effective monitoring of cognition are (a) planning activities prior to undertaking a problem (b) monitoring activities during learning and checking outcomes. These activities are remarkably similar to Polya's heuristics and they also reflect Papert's argument for teaching children to program computer.

Controlled use of Polya's heuristic strategies may be viewed as an example of the regulation of cognition. Brown postulated that individuals have a central processing unit, much like a computer, that controls heuristic routines for problem-solving, planning and scheduling appropriate strategies, and monitoring and evaluating the effects of strategies. The complex operations performed by the executive control component take one of two approaches automotive or controlled. Automatic strategies are quickly retrieved, make little demand on the cognitive system, require minimal conscious learner control, and are not dependent on short-term memory.

Controlled strategies are more slowly retrieved, executed in a deliberate, purposeful way, and thus require a great deal of learner effort and control. Controlled strategies can evolve into automatic operations. For example, if Polya's heuristics are practiced in a controlled, conscious way across a number of problem areas, there is reason to believe that their application will become automatic. This discussion has implications for school curricula intended to encourage higher-order thinking. First, for students to find new ways of interrelating knowledge and algorithms they must have a firm grasp of the knowledge needed to solve the problem. If they cannot retrieve this information automatically, they will be distracted from the problem-solving task. Second, if students are to be challenge with higher-order problems at various stages of their knowledge development in a field, then the curriculum should not be organized hierarchically to focus initially only on learning facts and formulas. Instead, students should be challenged to solve problems early, in their exposure to a field-problem based on the knowledge they have already acquired.

Considerable attention should be given early in the curriculum to the interrelationship among facts and rules in order to develop schema that are sufficiently rich to enable students to deal with problems that require organizing information in ways new to them. The selection of content for early problem-solving activities is therefore particularly important. In addition to depth in a single content area, repeated successful experience in using problem-solving strategies across a variety of content areas reinforces learners' use of them in new situations they recognize as resembling the ones in which they succeeded. Psychologists endorse training in multiple contexts because it "decreases the likelihood that a particular piece of information will be wedded to a particular context."

If students assume that solving a problem requires the use of a formula or algorithm applicable only in a single subject area, then they will use these strategies only within that domain. But, if they see problems requiring heuristic strategies and other substrative concepts across a number of domains, it is likely that they will become more fluid thinkers and, ultimately, more successful in solving problems. Our brief literature review suggests the importance of teaching heuristic strategies, that using these strategies in a rich context enhances their effectiveness, and that there is some evidence that strategies may be transferable across content domains. The analysis indicates that students can learn problems-solving heuristics and that, if they use these strategies, they are more effective problem solvers.

The instructional emphasis should be on the process of solving problems and not on the problem solution. One implication of this focus on process is the need for students to practice using heuristic strategies across a variety of content domains and with different types of problems. The depth of the content appears to be a critical component in improving higher-order thought. Research on expert and novice problem-solvers show the importance of a solid information base that is easily retrieved in a problem-solving environment. The problem-solver should be able to retrieve facts and algorithms automatically, but should also be able to perceive the interrelationships among various concepts within a domain.

There are conflicting opinions about the use in schools of computer programs which "only" provided drill and practice or tutorial instruction. One view is that these activities can be carried out by teachers or aids effectively and cheaply and that we use such programs limits students' and teachers' various on the power of computers and reinforces the already strong emphasis in schools on knowledge development to the exclusion of problem-solving activities.

Another view is that such programs can be easily integrated into the curriculum, that they can free the teacher for more demanding activities, that they have been shown to be effective, that they often command the attention of some students more than does conventional teaching and that they offer a convenient way to introduce computers into the classroom. We favour the latter view, though we quickly concede that many existing programs in these categories are not worth students' time and effort. Moreover, the attention in the early part of this chapter to the need for exposure to content depth and for facility of retrieval of knowledge and algorithms as prerequisites for solving complex problems reinforces our view that the knowledge development programs can serve a very useful purpose.

Drill and Practice Software: It focuses on previously learned factual knowledge and skills, in contrast, the other two types of knowledge development software focus on learning new knowledge or skills. Drill and practice software is used with greater frequency in schools than any other type of programs, other than programming languages. Over the past few years the aesthetic quality and the motivational attributes of these programs have improved greatly as program developers have acquired sophistication in the use of graphics and have learned something about how to design programs that sustain the attention of young people.

Properly constructed drill and practice programs should enhance cognitive processing by requiring students to increase speed in retrieving information and in carrying out skill activities to the point where these activities become automatic. This automatic processing, in turn, should assist higher-order thinking by reducing certain cognitive demands on students when they are faced with a problem-solving situation.

The goal is to get students to the point where they can focus on the dimensions of the problem rather than on the heuristics to solve it. One approach is to have the software deliberately focused on increasing student's speed in processing information. Unlike drill and practice activities that require only paper and pencil, a computer program can record the time it takes a student to carry out a problem or to remember or recognize certain information. In addition, it can adjust the amount of time required to present a problem, based on its record of how quickly similar tasks were complete. Finally, criterion levels can be developed experimentally to assess whether students have achieved the skills to carry out the task automatically.

A second approach would be to design programs to increase the student's capacity to chunk together related pieces of information. The ability to solve problems is partially constrained by the amount of information a person can manipulate in short-term or immediate memory. The capacity of human short-term memory is limited to a small and finite number of independent pieces of information-in the neighborhood of seven. If students could automatically chunk together pieces of information so that the pieces are no longer independent, they might be able to increase their ability to solve complicated problems. Based on some assumption about the structure and extent of students' knowledge schema, drill and practice programs might be designed to help them bring together or "chunk" related information.

Content Tutorial Programs: These differ from drill and practice programs by focusing on new facts and skills rather than on going over material already learned or partially learned. Typical software resembles some of the early teaching matching programs with dry presentation of desecrate information and only a limited branching capacity.

Many of the early tutorial programs developed by the Minnesota Education Computing Consortium are of this sort. More interesting tutorial performance could challenge the student to become involved through game-like situations. The tole of these programs in enhancing problem solving is to provide sufficient grounding in content and skill areas so that complex problems can be presented. The ETS-LAUSD study and other reports indicate that programs in this category can be very successful in teaching information and skills.

The quality and sophistication of this type of program have also increased dramatically over the years. Their demonstrated ability to engage students, particularly low-achieving students, is a good reason to make them available in more schools. Nonetheless, or earlier review of the literature suggests a variety of ways to improve the usefulness of content tutorial programs for preparing a student to solve complex problems. As in the case of drill and practice programs, the concept of chunking has been neglected and might be used to enhance effectiveness. Two strategies that could aid in chunking are (a) the use of mnemonic devices, and (b) semantic mapping. The first strategy is often used to facilitate the learning of lists of apparently unrelated objects. Pictures as well as key words can be useful. Semantic mapping is closer theoretically to the notions of cognitive scientists who perceive the ability to chunk as characteristic of "expert" thinking. It is designed to aid the individual to develop cognitive structures or schema, to organize new knowledge. In semantic mapping, new concepts are systematically related to already known concepts in order to place the new information into a familiar structure or context.

Using semantic mapping as a model for teaching new content would require that the computer program acquire information about the prior knowledge of students in order to relate new information to familiar concepts. Here the computer is at a distance disadvantage when compared to a human teacher; not even the most powerful electronic brains comes close to the capacity of the human brain to make judgments about students' previous experience and to tailor information to meet special group and individual needs. Nonetheless, we can imagine tutorial programs that initially interrogate a student to determine a general level of prior knowledge and then use the results of the interrogation to tailor the tutorial to student needs. Where schools knowledge is ordinarily learned in a hierarchical manner as in mathematics, the computer could pretest and then use responses to place students at the appropriate level in the tutorial.

In areas where knowledge is not clearly hierarchical, the initial assessment would be complicated and require greater teacher involvement. A related way to improve tutorial programs is through the use of diagnostic routines that identify the type of errors that students make and then coach or instruct them in ways to avoid making such errors. This strategy appears to be particularly useful for learning skills such as arithmetic operations. The classing example of such a program is BUGGY, a diagnostic program to detect the nature of errors made by students doing subtraction problems. In its original form it identified a very large number of possible independent error patterns, though the actual errors that students made tended to cluster in far fewer patterns. This software was initially written for a large computer but it being modified for microcomputers.

The small amount of quickly accessed memory is still a general problem for developing effective instructional software for microcomputers. But the BUGGY experience suggests that programs containing a diagnostic and coaching component may need to include only the most frequently occurring errors. Ideally, the program would instruct a student to request teacher assistance if it could not determine the student's error. This would free teachers to focus on the most comply instructional problems. Cognitive scientists have recently observed the phenomenon of systematic misconceptions in the areas of science and mathematics. In the early grades these misconception have only minor consequences for "getting the answer right" and therefore persist into later education, where they could have considerable influence on the problem-solving abilities of students.

Heuristic Tutorial: These programs are specifically designed to teach problem-solving strategies. These computer programs use a well-structured and circumscribed, often game-lime environment for training and practice in the use of specific heuristics. The classic computer programs in this area is the game of "Wumpus", which was designed to teach basic knowledge of logic, probability, decision analysis, and geometry to a wide range of learners, from young children to adults. The game logic resolves around a set of five' basic rules of reasoning. The player is placed randomly in a connected web of waves and is told the neighbors of his current location. The goal is to locate the horrible Wumpus and kill it by shooting an arrow into its lair. Moving from one cave to another produces information on the new neighbors. Players can minimize dangers and make progress in finding the Wumpus by using the warning signals to make appropriate ligistc and probalistics inferences. If the players exhaust their supply of five arrows before killing the Wumpus, the game is lost.

We believe schools and most program-developers are missing major opportunity by not developing and using programs like "Wumpus". Properly developed programs could be used on a regular basis in schools with students of widely varying background to provide them with systematic exposure to problem-solving situations. For instance, the Sunburst Corporation has published a problem-solving skill matrix that is included with software packages designed to teach complex thinking skills such as discrimination, looking for a pattern, and information gathering. Generally, these computer programs are open-ended and create a fantasy environment. For instance, in "Memory Castle" students learn mnemonic systems by playing an adventure game that leads them through a castle, and they must use a special code to find the way out. In another program, "The pond", a small green frog, lost in a pond of lily pads, teaches students to recognize an articulate patterns and generalize from raw data. The student chooses from six ponds, or levels of difficulty, in which lily pads are displayed in increasingly complex patterns.

The objective is to determine which pattern can get the frog across the pond. A second level of the game encourages students to collect points by directing frogs through as many points as possible in the fewest number of moves. There is little question in our minds that these programs areas successful in teaching students to use specific problem-solving heuristics within the limited program environments, but we know of no quantitative evaluations, and whether the strategies learned from these programs have effects that generalize to other settings, particularly those where the problems are more complex or less well-structured, in another matter. Improvements in these programs might proceed along some of the same lines that we have suggested for content tutorial and drill and practice programs.

The use of error diagnosis and coaching routines seems especially promising. Burton and Brown used this strategy in a modification of a well-known arithmetic game programs, "WEST", originally developed for the PLATO system. They included routines which contrast the player's moves with optional strategies and which occasionally suggest alternative moves to the player. Once again, however, we know of no systematic, controlled evaluation.

Specific Strategy

The task of problem-solving simulation programs is to pose complex problems for solution. Unlike knowledge-building programs, which provide practice in sing knowledge and skills and which teach students facts and how to use certain heuristics, simulation programs present situations where the problem itself needs to be identified, where there may be a large variety of possible heuristics to use, and where there may indeed be a number of acceptable solutions. To present such a situation, the computer simulation must assume or create an environment with a sufficiently rich knowledge base and structure so that complex problems can be posed. Paper has labelled this idea "microworld" and defended it as a subset of reality or constructed reality that allows learners to exercise powerful ideas and intellectual skills.

The use of a microworld is based on a learning theory that promotes active exploration in an environment that is sufficiently limited and thus conductive to constructure exploration and at the same time rich enough for discovery. Such a requirement creates a very difficult problem for computer programs because of the difficulties in assessing sufficient levels of students' prior knowledge and the limited memory of the microcomputer.

The limitation on memory, for example, reduces the computer's capacity to communicate easily with students, for only a small vocabulary and a simplified syntax can be stored in a microcomputer. One approach is for the program to build an environment based directly on the curriculum or the common real-life experiences of students, thereby reducing the effects of difference in prior knowledge. A second option is a computer-created artificial environment where the effects of the prior knowledge of the student are minimized. Both of these approaches are described here.

Content Simulation Programs: These are designed to provide environments as lifelike as possible for students to use in problem-solving activities. A substantial number of existing computer programs do this in a sophisticated way. Programs that pose diagnostic problems in medicine, automobile care, or business management are widely used outside precollegiate education.

Much of the content would be inappropriate for elementary and secondary schools, and many of these programs are on large computers rather than on microcomputers and therefore not generally accessible to schools. But they can serve as a vision of what is possible. One prototype is the "MYCIN" system, an interactive program that simulates a medical consultant who specializes in infectious diseases. For approximately twenty minutes, the program questions and responds to doctors seeking the help of a specialist. They may ask "MYCIN" for advice on identifying organisms and prescribing drugs and, further, to explain that advice. This program strikes us as particularly salient in at least three ways. First, it allows the physicians to learn more about the complexities of diseases and treatments outside their specialities. Second, the encyclopedic function embedded in explaining treatments in an option and not a necessary step in using the program. Third, it allows for improvements in the system as new information becomes available, it can always be current. It is not difficult to see how this model might be followed in training students in a variety of content domains.

There are, however, few good examples in education and little use of content simulation programs in schools. Two classic simulations for use in elementary schools have been developed by MECC: "Lemonade", where the students manage a lemonade stand and earn or lose money based on their decisions; and "Oregon Trail," where a student acts as the head of a wagon train in the middle 1800s. These simulations are popular as demonstration devices but typically are not integrated into the curriculum. At the high school level there have been some interesting new programs, but they only scratch the surface. For instance, "Revolutions: Past, Present and Future," developed by Focus Media, was designed to teach high school students a model for understanding the development of revolutionary movements.

Students build their own model of events leading to a revolution following a computer comparison of the American, French, and Russian revolutions. This program is particularly appealing because the objectives include both process and content variables. Another example is "South Dakota", an economics simulation developed by Educational Activities. It is designed to give students an understanding of variables affecting a framer's success. As a grain farmer, the student has a farm of 150 acres on which to survive for ten years and, ideally, make a profit. The student must make decisions in choosing the kind of grain to plant, hiring help to plant and harvest the crop, providing for family needs, paying taxes, and keeping the bank satisfied. In attractive feature of this program is that it can be used individually or in groups. If used in groups, the program requires students to pool their information to succeed.

The limitation on memory is one reason for the lack of useful software in this area. The program needs to be fast and rich enough in content to overcome major differences in the prior knowledge of different students in the classroom. One approach to the memory limitation problem would be to build into the simulation itself tutorial software that could be interrogated by students seeking data or other information, such as the technical terms needed to solve some of the problems posed in the simulation.

Drill and practice programs could be embedded in the simulation program. Error detection and coaching routines could be part of the simulation programs and could, in face, trigger the programs to indicate to the student the need for a tutorial or for a drill and practice experience. These "helping" programs could be designed as part of the simulation "game" though every student need not use them. Designed in this way, they would not have to be carried permanently in immediate memory. This use should reduce the effects of students' prior knowledge. Other strategies to overcome school-based problems seem plausible. It is not entirely possible to control time demands, for the very task of solving a complex problem may require considerable time, but it is possible for the computer to save a simulation until later, and advantage that could help fit higher-order thinking tasks into fifty minutes, time slots.

The biggest problem is to integrate simulations into the curriculum; it's solution would require the acceptance and use of both the computer and problem-solving activities in the classroom. We actually feel quite pessimistic about whether this will occur to a substantial degree in the next ten to twenty years; the conservative nature of the major textbook publishers and the tremendous inertia inside classroom work directly against it.

Nonetheless we have a number of suggestions about approaches that might be taken. One strategy would be to create first-class simulations that focus on content in areas outside the mainstream of academic life in schools.

The vocational education is a prime example; programs that pose problems in aircraft and automobile mechanics, in structural design, and in business management already exist and could be used in many schools. Art, music, health, and the chess club are other areas for which simulation programs are either already developed and used or easily could be. These areas may be able to respond to the new technology more creatively than academic areas in part because their knowledge domains are better defined and in part because they are less bound by tradition. This tactic might also enliven the curriculum in these areas.

If we continue the logic about well-defined knowledge domains, the first academic areas to tackle would be mathematics and science. In both of these areas the national concern over the quality of the curriculum, pedagogy, and the teachers could work in favor of using some high quality programs. Mathematics, for example, will be a fertile field for simulation programs that pose problems in statistics, probability, and data analysis, if the recommendation of a number of the national mathematics groups are adopted. In science, the potentially useful simulation situations seem limitless.

Artificial environment simulations generate a make-believe world with a sufficiently rich knowledge base and set of rules of that complex problems can be posed by the programs. Their capacity both to tutor and to pose problems in an integrated fashion allow them to control the influence of prior knowledge; this control enables the computer to provide successively deeper information and more complex problems. A wide variety of types of programs fits out general conception of this category. These include fantasy adventure games such as the "ZORK" series, science fiction games such as "World Builders", and complex artificial problem settings such as "Rocky's Boots". One such program, "Robot Odyssey I" is both a simulation and an adventure game.

Students can either construct a simulated robot or work through and adventure game that teaches the basic of digital electronic. Players design, build and test robots in a parts laboratory and tutorials assist students in all stages of the game. The problems posed by these programs, in our view, often are of equal or greater complexity and take more ingenuity and perseverance to solve than the most difficult problems posed in schools. Programs like these could present problems of varying complexity, designed to build on themselves in a regular fashion, and include systematic tutorial, diagnostic, and coaching systems to help students.

Teaching Programs

The task of designing effective programs, however, is probably minor compared to the challenge of convincing schools and the general public that problem-solving activities in artificial domains have merit and that time could be allocated for student use of these programs. The best of these programs are immensely popular in the home computing market and used almost not at all in schools. The reasons for the lack of use in schools are clear-they do not fit into the curriculum, they take a long time to run, and they seem frivolous since they are not based on real-life circumstances and are often advertised as games. In particular, adventure games seem most likely to be overlooked. We have observed student pursuing these programs and we have little doubt that such games motivate students and engage them in sustained cognitive activity, whether they are working individually or cooperatively. We have seen students with serious reading difficulties, who rarely read printed material, spend extended periods working on adventure games that interact with users only in a narrative format.

The knowledge development and problem-solving simulation programs exert considerable control over the activities of the student using he program. Problem-solving aids, on the other hand, contain programs that require the student to use them in ways and will help solve problems which may be either self-defined or externally assigned. These programs, moreover, can be embedded in problem-simulation programs to help students to obtain information or to analyze data. We have included a large variety of programs in this category and have divided them into two general types: (a) tools for obtaining information or structural problems situations, and (b) programming languages.

Problem-solving aids are widely used in homes and schools, often for obtaining and structuring information for presentation or for aiding in solving relatively *ell-structured* problems. In our experience it is rare that tools are used in schools to aid in solving ill-defined problems. Thus, for example, a data management system will be used in a school setting to display some data on a chart rather analysis. Or students will be given very highly structured problems in a programming course rather than be asked to design and program solutions to problems of their own choosing or that are deliberately ill-defined. The exception may be when the aids are used deliberately to facilitate complex problem solving in advanced placement course for high school mathematics and computer programming.

Tools for Aiding Problem Solving: These include some of the most imaginative, interesting, and well-developed programs now available for the microcomputer. One reason is that many of them are simply elegant extensions on the microcomputer of tools that already exist in many schools, homes, and businesses; for example, world processing programs function as sophisticated typewriters.

Another reason is that these programs are usable over and over by the same person and therefore are cost-effective. In contrast, an adventure program, upon being solved, loses its usefulness to the solver. One class of these programs, which might deserve a separate category, is designed to facilitate writing. In terms of frequency of use in schools and homes, word processing programs, such as "Bank Street Writer", outstrip just about all other classes of programs.

The growing group of ideas or outline processors is also becoming very popular; they contain a variety of routines to help a writer organize and reorganize textual information. The use of these programs in schools parallels both the emerging literature on the close relationship between writing and higher-order thinking and the recent emphasis on the need to improve writing in the schools. As these programs become familiar to classroom teachers as writing aids, additional features can be added. For example, it should be possible in the future to combine the organizational aids of idea processes with routines which prompt students with question and information on topics related to he curriculum to encourage their writing.

Other tools in this category include dictionaries, information retrieval systems, and data management systems. In the context of our general discussion of software for problem solving, each of these tools could be viewed as standing along to provide information or assistance in carrying our analysis or could be embedded into problem-solving simulation programs. We might imagine a workstation of the future similar to "Dynabank" developed at 'Xerox Parc' several years ago. As student would sit at a computer terminal and have control over an information retrieval system containing as much information as the Library of Congress and the data-analysis power of any modern mainframe computer. It included capabilities for music composition and graphic arts.

The computer could pose a variety of types of problems for the student, provide diagnosis and coaching, encourage the student to enter into a drill and practice or tutorial mode, and keep continuous track of student progress. All of the components of such workstation exist.

Programming Languages: These are essential programs that require their operators to define and solve their own problems within the specific constraints of the language and the general constraints of a computer. Although we have classified programming languages as an aid for solving problems, learning to use the programming language is itself a form of problem solving. Without question, the act of solving programming problem often meets our definition of higher-programming problem often meets our definition of higher-order thinking. But, whether learning to program enhances a child's general facility in solving problems in other issues. Perhaps the view which links learning to programming with the development of higher-order thinking will wither away in the same way that the theories linking the leaning of Latin with complex reasoning have not survived. Computer programming languages, like playing chess, may be too highly stylized and structured to provide training that can be generalized to very different domains, especially those domains with more complex and ambiguous rules.

On the other hand, programming provides the opportunity for combining discrete elements to equal a whole concept, a gestalt. And this is a necessary skills for solving some problems. We indicated earlier that this literature is very thin and inconclusive. The most widespread use of programming languages in the content areas in mathematics, where languages such as FORTRAN aid students in learning how to formulate and solve problems. This is just the beginning of content-based programming languages.

12

The Network

Way of Teaching

A front-end analysis (FEA) was performed to ensure the course would meet training objectives that are validated against real job requirements. The approach was eclectic, based on the experiences of the team doing FEA. Initial contacts with domain experts (DEs) was by phone. Requests for documents, and clarifications over the phone, gave the team the first overview of the training requirements, target population description, and course objectives. Course materials for MDMP-training were gathered and evaluated. This evaluation guided the selection of instructional strategies, the media selection, and the advanced technology selection. The materials were considered up-to-date and suitable to create the interactive courseware for this project. New measurable objectives were created for the course based on the materials and discussions with the DEs.

The team travelled to Fort Knox and observed an ongoing class. This allowed the team to:

- observe the communication between the seven functional positions that the small groups (SG) of students role play;

- broaden our understanding of the tasks of the seven positions;
- observe students creating overlays/MDMP products;
- observe how the small group instructor (SGI) prompted and advised students;
- observe the Comrnander's briefing;
- gain a further understanding of the Armor School's expectations for the courseware;
- observe the creation of maps;
- observe the SGI prompting and advising students;
- observe the commander's briefing/presentations of each position and meet with domain experts (DEs).

The team met with a contractor building courseware that is prerequisite to the MDMP course. The team:

- delineated responsibilities,
- reviewed flowchart; discussed standards and level of interactivity; viewed a demonstration of a small sample of the course; and
- discussed standards and level of interactivity and fidelity.

Area Experts

The team met with DEs to gather information. They:

- met with representatives of four of the seven positions the SG represents when doing the MDMP;
- discussed objectives previously defined with DEs and the Government PM;
- built a list of information students must reference to support the learning tasks;
- delivered a form to assist DEs to collect data for the courseware; and
- completed the information collection forms.

The meetings with the Army POCs and DEs were essential to determine the courseware design and development. The information helped to:

- create a user environment that simulates the work experience, allowing users to interact to solve a problem;
- develop a graphical interface to allow students to create and edit overlays/MDMP products efficiently;
- develop hints and feedback, possibly some intelligence to emulate the instructor;
- provide a technique to allow the seven staff positions to "look up" information; and
- develop ideas for how to make creating maps more efficient.

The Armor Officer Advanced Course is a 20 week course composed of large group instruction, small group instruction, the JANUS command-level simulator exercises, SIMNET unit-level simulator exercises, and field exercises. Initially, the students attend large group instruction together. Then, the students disperse into groups of 15 for the small group portion; a small group instructor (SGI) is assigned to each group. The MDMP planning exercise reinforces the doctrine, planning, and decision making knowledge/ skills. The JANUS simulator is run at the battalion level, with all students divided into command and support functions. The SIMNET simulator is run at the company level, with all students manning specific tank operation positions. These exercises are planned and executed against an OPFOR composed of the instructor group. Field exercises are restricted to terrain appreciation and leader's reconnaissance of the battlefield.

In the current training, the SGI presents the small group with a situation and commander's guidance. The small group is required to exercise the decision making process and analysis tools detailed in the text, and produce intermediate "products" used as input to the next phase of the process. The final product is a recommended Coarse Of Action (COA) plan, which is briefed to the commander.

The Army has traditionally viewed military decision making as both science and art. Many aspects of combat operations, such as movement rates, fuel consumption, and weapon effects are quantifiable. Therefore, the Army considers them to be part of the "science" of war. However, the Army cannot quantify other aspects-the impact of leadership, the complexity of modern operations, and uncertainty regarding enemy intentions/actions/reactions.

Military Decision Making Process is a systematic approach to decision making, which fosters effective analysis by enhancing application of professional knowledge, logic, and judgment, and consists of six steps:

- Recognize and define problems.
- Gather facts and make assumptions to determine the scope of and the solution to problems.
- Develop possible solutions.
- Analyze each solution.
- Compare the outcome of each solution.
- Select the best solution available.

At the highest level, the actions done in the small group relate to:

- Gathering facts;
- Making assumptions;
- Analyzing higher mission and intent ; and
- Receiving commander's guidance.

The architecture for the application of technology to this training requirement will involve two major efforts:

1. the implementation of computer-based training activities to provide mission guidance, provide detail data for analysis, and to capture small group intermediate and final products; and '
2. the implementation of distance learning technology to link the SGIs with the small groups during and after the construction of the intermediate and final products.

Overlaying the automated instruction and DL technologies to the current course provides an interactive course that covers the same objectives as the current stand-up instruction course. The automated instruction functions provide situation details required for each phase of training action. The small group functions are still completed in small groups. The Distance Learning functions provide the organization and communication methods for the small groups to get help during the small group actions and to receive feedback on the small group products. Gates are closed until the student products are reviewed by the SGI. The SGI grades the products and opens the gate before the group moves to the next MDMP phase.

The MDMP includes Mission analysis; Course of Action (COA) development; COA analysis and comparison, and decision and execution. The architecture was implemented as four major phases:

Phase One, Mission Analysis

Task Description : Derive the essential tasks the unit must perform to accomplish the mission.

Input : Commanders guidance.

Methods : Follow the eleven step process for Mission analysis.

Approach : Using the automated instruction lessons, derive the necessary data to drive the small group interaction in the development of the MCOO, the SITTEMP, and the restated mission products.

Deliverables : The MCOO, the SITTEMP and the Restated mission products in a format for the SGI to access via distance learning technologies.

Phase Two, COA Development

Task Description : Develop multiple COA's that would accomplish the mission assigned by the Commander.

Input : Planning Guidance and Phase One products.

Methods : Follow the six step process answering the what/ when /where /why/how of a possible plan open to the commander that would accomplish the mission assigned.

Approach : Using the automated instruction lessons, derive the necessary data to drive the small group interaction in the development of the COA plans.

Deliverables : Several significantly different COA products in a format for the SGI to access via distance learning technologies.

Phase Three, COA Analysis

Task Description : Utilize appropriate analysis methods to identify the COA with the greatest probability of success.

Input : Multiple COAs from phase two.

Methods : Utilize the appropriate analysis methods, such as feasibility checks, war gaming, risk assessment, and comparison of war game results, to identify the best COA. Note that several different analysis techniques can be applied based on the situation.

Approach : Using the automated instruction lessons, derive the necessary data to drive the small group interaction in the development of the COA plans.

Deliverables : The brief for the Commander on the selected COA.

Phase Four, Execute

Task Description : Review the COA with the SGI to determine the probable outcome of the recommended COA.

Input : Recommended COA from phase three.

Methods : The group will provide the SGI with a written analysis of the probable outcome of the recommended COA. The SGI will review, analyze, and comment on the recommended COA, and the small group's analysis of the recommended COA, in a small group session. Alternately, the SGI can interact with the small group in a conference call.

Approach : SGI and small group interaction on the recommended COA.

Deliverables : Analysis of the recommended COA's probable outcome.

Necessity : Successful completion of the final product for each phase.

Primary Operational Environment : The Fort Knox Campus is the primary operational environment. The campus environment is the local-area network, the available networked computer systems, and the client and server software.

Secondary Operational Environment : Distribution via the

world wide web, WWW, is the secondary operational environment. This will be used to service Reserve and Active Duty forces for refresher and preparatory training.

From a standard SVGA PC connected to the ATM LAN at Ft. Knox, the student will download the Mission Analysis TOOLBOOK automated instruction activity which will be executed locally. Because the courseware is much more than page turner courseware, the courseware was deemed too large and therefore slow to do completely over the Internet, hence the hybrid solution. The TOOLBOOK activity will provide a simulated environment for the request for information by the small group; the feedback of the information; and for the control of simulated time to accomplish the discovery of the information requested. A team of four AOAC students will use Microsoft Word to provide a written text and graphic to communicate the intermediate products in a format for the SGI to review. The Word documents will be filed to a server, organized by an email notes file package. The instructor will comment on the Word document using the Word annotating features, which allows comments to be made without including the comments into the main document. The instructor will annotate the drawings; these comments are included in the original drawing.

Mapping Editor : Using a modified version of TIEPAINT from TIE, (Training Icon Environment,) Global demonstrated the abilities needed to display and edit the "layered" map scheme needed for the Army TDMP project. The modified product, called MAPEDIT, consists of the original TIEPAINT and added pop-up menu, labeled ViewLayers and EditLayers. The ViewLayer menu has eight items, numbered 1 through 8. A student can check any or all of these items, and the corresponding layer(s) will be displayed. The EditLayer menu item allows a student to select which layer he wants to currently edit. The editor is basically the standard TIEPAINT "vector" editor. Each vector object has an extra "tag" on it, which indicates which layer it belongs to. When items are displayed, only those items which are part of the active layer(s) are displayed. The scheme is simple, and works very nicely.

MAPEDIT is a 32 bit Windows application developed using Microsoft Visual C/C++ version 4.0. The source code consists of various c, h, dlg, ico,.bmp, all of which comprise the actual "project" file. There is also a "help" file, which uses Microsoft WordView to display hypertext style help.

Data Flow : Student and instructor workstations exchange data via a shared directory on a network server. We do not want to hard code the path to the shared directory. Instead, the directory path is stored in an INI file on each workstation: $WINDOWS \TDMP.INI. The section is "*Server*" and the entry is "Root."

In keeping with Windows convention, the INI file is stored in the Windows directory of each computer. All programs that refer to this file should use the GetWindowsDirectory function to get the name of the Windows directory rather than hard coding the usual path.

The group file serves as the main repository of information about the group's progress through the TDMP lesson. In a production version of the system, group information would be stored in a full-featured relational database with Internet capability. However, the proof of concept version will use a simple Windows initialization file ("INI" file). The INI file contains a section for each step in the TDMP lesson. The group file contains a summary of the group's progress. Large items, such as justification statements, COA sketches, the Sync Matrix, and the DECMAT, are stored in separate files.

One instructor leads a typical class consisting of 64 students broken up into 16 groups of 4 students each. The primary role of the instructor is to facilitate the tactical decision making process as students try to formulate effective course of actions (COAs). During the decision making process, students are assigned one or two functional roles in which to analyze the information. A total of seven roles are divided among the four students in each group. Students must submit two interim products and one final product. The instructors will review, score, and provide feedback to the group for each submitted product.

Independent Measures : The independent variables to be manipulated include instruction and on-line help. The dependent variables that will be measured include: 1. achievement and efficiency as scored by instructor ratings of the three submitted COA products and the time it took to reach the COA products,

2. subjective workload, 3. the mental model developed during the tactical decision making process as measured by paired concepts, 4. the rate and quality of communications across teams and, 5. affective preferences. Covariates will include individual differences in subject-matter knowledge as scored on a pretest and prior field experience.

Achievement and Instructional Efficiency : Two interim products and one final product will be scored and used as a measure of student achievement. 'The instructors for the course will grade these products. Each instructor will be responsible for scoring half of the products produced by each treatment group. In addition, the products will be submitted to the instructors using codes so that they will be blind as to the source of the product. These methods will be used to prevent bias toward a particular treatment condition.

The amount of time the students took to submit each COA will also be recorded automatically by the system. In the traditional classroom treatments, the instructors will log the time of each lesson taught. Any additional help by the instructor to various students outside the classroom will also be logged.

Collaborative Learning : The issue of collaborative learning is relevant for this project as students in both learning environments will be working together in four person teams. In addition to these four team members collaborating together to meet a mission objective, these teams are encouraged to seek advice and information from the other teams formed within the class.

Interaction Frequencies : Computer mediated learning involves many, sometimes radical changes in communication patterns. Rather than numerous verbal and nonverbal cues available in face to face encounters, distance learning environments constrain contact to primarily text. Typically, user acceptance of distance technology requires changes in how one thinks, composes materials, and communicates. Researchers point out that often new learners appear to experience some form of "culture shock" which dissipates with additional practice and experience with the system. In an attempt to quantify these reactions to the medium of communication, learner discussions will be audiotaped and transcribed verbatim,

From these transcripts, independent raters will classify each recorded learner interaction into one of four categories suggested by Dalton in the measurement of computer-supported collaborative work: management, social, task, or content.

Attitudes Toward Instruction and Content : Learner attitudes toward distance learning can be grouped into four categories:

1. Attitude toward the technology,
2. attitude toward distance education teaching methods,
3. attitude toward student and teacher interaction, and
4. attitude toward being a remote student. Of the research reviewed, only one affective survey has been found that adequately samples learners on all four of these dimensions.

The Teleconference Evaluation Questionnaire was developed by Ball State University to assess students attitudes toward their telecourses. It consists of 33 items by which students rate their degree of satisfaction with various facets of their telecourse on a five point Likert scale ranging from "Very Poor" to "Very Good." Although developed to assist in the evaluation of telecourses, it will be adapted to survey learners' attitudes toward the current TDMP multimedia distance learning course.

Web Culture : Changes in teaching and learning with the new educational technologies indicate changes in design and development of instructional materials. The impact of educational technology and its effects on students learning become even more important issues. Researchers argue that changes of technology attributes may not affect learners' cognitive and information processing. Students may benefit from the new techniques of presenting learning content through current educational technology. The phenomenon of today's technology, especially Internet technology, has changed our daily life. Massive amounts of information can be reviewed through desktop computers. We are able to commu-nicate with others through electronic mail, video conferences, and chat lines without leaving our offices or homes. Recently Deep Blue, a super computer, defeated the world chess champion for the first time in history. Altris, a file management company, stepped forward to build software on the premise that document files have intelligence of their own. It allows users to be recipients of information without requesting it. Can we completely separate what technology can provide to us from what we can do with technology? Compared to the web, limits of each technology, including videotape and CD-ROM, certainly restrain our creative abilities in the design and delivery of our learning materials. We, as humans, have tried very hard to improve modern technology to provide quick connections, materials access, and interaction without boundaries and time constraints. According to Schrage, "The key is to remember that even as we use technology to shape our environment, technology is shaping us. Technology rearranges our perceptual world and subtly redefines our relationship with our environment". In a study by Internet Commerce, it reports that there are 34.6 million web users. We see the fast growing trend of using the web as a vehicle to deliver on-line educational programs. Educators should examine the approaches they choose for enhancing the learning process and make it as good, if not better than conventional teaching methods in the classroom. This article discusses students perception on learning through Web technology, including class syllabus, professor notes, course-packs, projects, tests, and self-paced learning courses.

The web technology permits us to represent the learning materials in any combination of media format, such as text, image, graphics, and animation (no sound and video clips were employed on the web pages during this study). This multimedia information environment can be accessed and displayed simultaneously.

The survey was administered to the students who were taking the self-paced web units as a trial run for the new media. Fortysix participants filled out an on-line survey when they finished the units. Eleven of them were interviewed at the end of their final test for the course. All interviews were recorded and transcribed by the researcher. The interview lasted from thirty minutes to fifty minutes. Qualitative data obtained in the interviews were analyzed using interpretive / descriptive analysis procedure. Both data were employed to assess how students' experience of using new media influenced their attitudes toward their learning performance.

Main Concept : The questionnaire and interviews indicated that using web-based instruction was a positive learning experience for the participants. The study indicated educational technology could offer a rich learning environment if we were able to integrate collaborative on-line environments, proper pedagogical design, and flexible user's interface.

Web-based instruction was designed in such a way that learning materials were arranged into small modules, including presentation, examples, and exercises. Objectives were incorporated into each module so that learners could be aware of the learning expectation. Preview and post-view questions for the learning content allowed students to analyze and evaluate their learning through each module. Students were presented with examples and exercises following reading paragraphs. Once they believed that they mastered the materials, they could move onto the practice test. There were links to an interactive learning environment. For each stage, a student was able to click on a more detailed explanation if he/she had any problems before proceeding. Auto feedbacks and diagnosis messages were incorporated in all parts of exercises. Students could evaluate themselves before they were ready for tests. They were able to communicate with the professor through email, chat room, and/or telephone. Following is a summary of the results—

> All survey questions were on a Liker scale except items one to three. A majority of students (87%) had prior experience in using the web, which made implementation of web-based instruction much easier than what we expected. One-third of students had access to the Internet at home while others still came to use the campus labs. Students spent slightly less time studying a unit on the web (3-6 hours) than they did for the regular class. In general, the students were very positive about their experiences in learning through the web. The results indicated that the web-course not only met their needs but also helped them use time more effectively. However, they were undecided when asked whether they preferred the electronic format or the traditional instructor lecture. Their hesitation and concerns were also echoed during the interview.

The interview data agreed with the results of the survey. The students valued alternative learning styles that technology offered. They praised the potential of technology to establish a feasible learning environment in higher education. However, they also addressed their concerns and limitation of educational technology.

The study indicated that the high level of interactively inherent on the web gave the users dynamic control of information. Interaction with linked information was very structured in terms of proficiency level and direction. The students preferred such full control over their learning situation.

"I enjoyed it for a number of reasons. I could do it in my own schedule.... I could get back to review it which you couldn't do in a classroom."

"I thought that it was helpful to have questions where you got immediate answers and you determined whether you're right or wrong. That helped me for a couple of incidents because I always tested myself and that kind of exercise reinforces what you are looking at."

"I was going more in depth in the stuff that I didn't know. In a class sometimes, the professor has to go over it again if some people don't understand. With a computer, you have the control. It made it more personal for me."

Students also felt that the experience in working with web-based instruction offered the opportunity not only to learn the content but to learn how to use a computer and how to access Internet. The students were encouraged to browse other resources by being provided with course related links. They suggested that such hands-on experience was really beneficial.

"Using the Internet-what a great learning tool! I had some computer experience before coming to this class but had never used the Internet. Having our reading on it made for a great experience for the entire class."

"...for some people in the class it was difficult but they finally caught on. I am lucky to have my fiancé teach me at home. We've had Internet access for some time but I've never been that interested in it until this semester. In another of my classes we get our notes and important material off the Internet. Some of my friends were jealous that we learned this in this class."

" Allowed the students to experience technology. It is a very ingenious way to get people involved with Internet and apply what we learn to technology. "

"It made me use a computer. It was nice not having to use pen and paper."

The Use : In traditional classroom teaching, we focused more on the students' performance based on the selected objectives. Web-based instruction permitted the meaningful learning which allowed students to choose self-exam exercises after the guided practice and to have an opportunity to construct their learning to provide openness to new information and multiple perspectives.

"I think that the program was effective. I like how there are questions throughout the reading because it tests how much I am retaining. The animation entertains me and the graphs help me to understand what is being presented. The test helped a lot because it helped me to feel more comfortable when taking the exam."

"It took me a lot longer than I thought it would because I took so many notes but it was worth it."

"The first thing I did was to take the practice assessment. That was a kind of pre-test for me, which showed me what I needed to study and which behavior objectives that I needed to concentrate on.... So I took extensive notes for the objectives that I needed to work on and I just scanned through the reading, and I did OK."

"I feel that using a computer program helped me have a better understanding of the Epsilon mini-unit. The questions that follow the text really helped me understand the material. It seemed to go into more depth than in the classroom."

As we have learned, the World Wide Web is a universal medium that everyone who has an Internet access can use. It doesn't have problems with different platforms and can be accessed from anywhere in the world. The web is an international information delivery tool. Students' feedback regarding the class syllabus, professor notes, coursepak, and projects was extremely positive. First, students liked to have the convenience in accessing their class information. They valued the opportunity to read and/ or download the syllabus, professor's notes, or coursepak. Deadlines and test schedules through the web could be checked at any time. Instead of worrying about misplacing their hard copy of the syllabus and buying the coursepak, now they could turn to the web. Second, the study showed that students strongly appreciated their capability to obtain actual learning materials from the web without time and location boundaries, especially for people who worked full time. It not only saved them time from traveling to the campus but also offered flexibility for them to choose their own time.

"I like it because I could do it any time I wanted to and it was easy to use."

"I really liked that fact that I could work at my own pace at home. I did not have to worry about my notes not being adequate."

"I work full time and I feel this gives me flexibility."

The web-based course provided non-linear access to resources links on the web which could be obtained rapidly and easily through multiple links and paths. Students could flexibly move among related elements of information and explored many related data and ideas in a non-linear format. Students liked the related links which broadened their learning beyond the classroom and also helped them obtain more information or real data, especially links to professional journals and organizations. The only suggestion from students was to have more meaningful links. Some students actually went out and searched for the links that they would like to have. As one of the students described:

"Internet offers us opportunities for self-direction and exploration. The more varied the cybernetic environment, the more possibilities exist for us to make connections, access materials and develop their own theoretical and practical postures as achievers. We are given opportunities to experiment and grow. We learn not just a few tricks of the keyboard but thinking strategies for connecting with rapidly changing technological landscape."

The learning styles and learners' characteristics have been the central concerns of educators. Each individual has a, perso-nality which affects his/her learning style. Some learning styles and personality needs can be particularly well addressed in a web-based learning environment.

Some students, who were not out-spoken, were more comfortable working on web-based courses while others may have felt less pressure in such a format. Web-based instruction may provide a learning environment which better meets learning needs. One student stated: "I thought the computer course took off a lot of stress because it could be done when we wanted."

However, several disadvantages were identified by students, such as Internet traffic-a long waiting time to log on and/or to load some information, a lack of audio, and no face-to-face communication.

Records of achievement (ROAs) and the use of portfolios as frameworks for the assessment of prior learning from work and other social and vocational experiences (AP(E)L) have become widespread over the past decade. Both potentially lay the basis for recognizing achievements previously beyond the reach of assessment. Both were intended to foster 'learning through success' not failure. Both emphasize the notion of students as active learners responsible for their own development. When first introduced to education, both also emphasized personal achievement and development and centred upon the production of documents which represented not just an end in themselves but also a philosophy of education. This philosophy aims to raise levels of achievement by broadening the range of what is recognized as valuable and emphasizes the value of experiential, student centred approaches to learning. In particular the introduction of both ROAs and AP(E)L initiatives challenged the notion of formal examinations as a useful measure of achievement.

The early focus was on the personal gain to the individual resulting from going through the process of recording achievement. While the main aim was the production of a record detailing a range of achievements and learning, at the same tune the process itself aimed to encourage individuals by building confidence in their achievements, helping them review their experiences, helping to plan and manage future learning, and by providing a basis for viewing learning as something they were a part of rather than something that was done to them. As the use of ROAs and AP(E)L grew more widespread, however, they began to change. In some cases the emphasis shifted from personal to public, from formative to summative. Instead of focusing on an individual's perceptions and personal achievements, some ROAs and AP(E)L portfolios began to contain ever more information about the skills, attainments and personal qualities in a form which aimed to be of use to prospective employers and admissions tutors. From a framework for promoting a developmental process they became almost an alternative 'qualification'.

This shift in emphasis from formative to summative resulted in a confusing (and confused) variety of attitudes towards the production of records and portfolios. In early initiatives the formative process was justification in itself. The shift in emphasis to the summative, however, posed the questions of what was being assessed and how and also potentially devalued the process underpinning the document. Today the development of AP(E)L systems in higher education goes alongside moves towards assisting students to reflect on their learning experiences to enable them to gain formal credit for informal learning experiences. As the process gains recognition nationally and opportunities for crediting a wide range of learning increase, there is also increasing concern that such processes should have a degree of parity. The result has been a requirement that ROAs and AP(E)L portfolios conform to national quality standards. This sounds reasonable but marks a shift in emphasis, indicating that now the benefits of ROAs are for an audience outside the student not for the student themselves.

This paper outlines the background to recording achievement initiatives, summarizes the tension between the benefits of formative assessment and the requirements of summative assessment and identifies the issues which must be addressed if the tension is to be resolved.

The Recording Achievement initiative developed at the same time as the introduction of the assessment and accreditation of prior experiential learning (AP(E)L) to formal education. Both were a response to the social and political context of the 1970s and 1980s. At the time the primary political emphasis in education and training was the reskilling of the workforce in the face of foreign competition and the need to adjust to changes in the way work is organized. The demand for more skilled labour and for skills which are often informally learned, such as personal skills, resulted in an education and training strategy which sought to recognize and accredit the widest possible range of educational achievement in the attempt to raise levels of attainment as a basis for a more highly qualified labour force.

The education system which existed in Britain in the 1970s had been designed to qualify only between 20 and 30% of the population and was equally ill fitted to providing either qualifications or routes to further training for those who had traditionally left school with no qualifications at all. Against this setting, practitioners with a philosophical interest in promoting experiential learning and student centred assessment were able to develop a number of local initiatives. Records of Achievement provided the opportunity to recognize the achievements of young people who had traditionally been out of reach of educational assessment. AP(E)L enabled a similar process for mature learners to progress to further and higher education. Both provided a basis for a fuller account of the range of learner achievement as well as a way to recognize achievement which cannot be assessed with conventional methods of assessment. For a time, at least, policy objectives appeared to accord with the concerns of educationalists who wanted to broaden opportunity and promote experiential learning.

Recognizing a broad range of achievement was, however, only the first step to the policy objective of achieving a more highly qualified workforce. A tension soon developed between the aims of educationalists and the aims of policy makers as individual achievements summarized in ROAs and AP(E)L portfolios were looked at from the standpoint of providing evidence of ability to progress to further education or training, or as a basis for accreditation and formal qualifications. The need to accord with the public, externally defined criteria of higher education gatekeepers and employers was at odds with a focus on personally defined achievement.

The tension between the personal arid the public in recording achievement was played out in the development of the National Record of Achievement (NRA). Local ROA initiatives emphasized formative processes and student centredness. Once local initiatives were officially brought together in the NRA, launched in 1991, the emphasis was on summative documents. The drive to recognize and qualify achievement for a public audience also affected AP(E)L developments. At the same time as ROAs were changing to summative documents, moves to give prior experiential learning a semi-formal status as a basis for progression to higher education began to overshadow formative processes in AP(E)L in favour of satisfying criteria for public recognition and assessment.

The NRA was designed to coordinate, and publicly document, student achievement through school, college, higher education and employment. In 1992 action planning was incorporated into the process. Although inclusion of action plans in the NRA is not mandatory, failure to do so may be interpreted in a negative way, a development which clearly indicates the move towards an emphasis in individual accountability rather than personal discovery.

The NRA is presented as a framework for managing the teaming process. It requires learners to summarize the outcomes of their formal and informal learning and identify actions taken as a result. The underpinning process requires reflecting on past experiences ' reviewing progress and action planning. This ostensibly represents an active learning process in which the young person takes responsibility for their own personal development-but if the document is really about personal development per se why does it have to be public and follow a nationally dictated format? A prescribed format could be seen as being at odds with Kolb's notions of individual learning style.

Producing an ROA, it is argued, provides a framework for developing skills beyond the academic-personal skills and transferable skills can all be included. Such transferable skills are common to all areas of academic study and include outcomes of learning and competences which in the past have been left unrecorded. They include skills associated with both individual and group working and range from the ability to make presentations to the application of computerized materials. In all cases the students are encouraged to focus and reflect on their individual learning experiences in whatever settings they may occur. In doing this, however, and in requiring learner achievement to be summarized in forms which have employer currency, explicitly naming certain 'core' or 'transferable' skills for example, ROAs raise a number of methodological problems. Not only do they pose a tension between the benefits of the formative and the summative processes in ZOAs, they also raise questions about the nature of transferable skills.

The concept of core or transferable skill is a problem. It has dogged developments in the post-16 field for nearly a decade and remains unresolved. There is a continuing debate about the transferability of skills from one situation to another, particularly about problem-solving skills at higher levels. Findings on comparative studies between novices and experts in several fields appear to suggest that many cognitive abilities used in the conscious processing stage are domain specific and not generally transferable.

A related debate about issues in assessing core skills focuses on the problem of level as well as context. Wolf attempts to show that it is not possible to give meaning to a concept independent of the context in which it is practised. She further argues that it is difficult to give any general meaning to levels of problem solving or communication. From this we could argue that attempts to name and assess core skills independently of context, as in the NRA, may be meaningless.

By 1995 a growing number of young people entering higher education had completed an NRA or ROA. Over the last five years increasing numbers of mature students have also gained entry to higher education through AP(E)L and the submission of portfolios summarizing their prior achievements. The idea of a common format for recording achievements for higher education is gaining ground.

The Record of Achievement is also potentially useful for professionals as a framework for Continuous Professional Development. In this case it might be referred to as a portfolio of professional practice rather than a Record of Achievement, but it is still engaged in promoting the same reflective process.

An ROA for higher education could be viewed simply as a logical step to extend what already exists. Some higher education courses have used such frameworks for managing learning for many years-largely BTEC awards and vocational courses such as initial teacher training, occupational therapy or physiotherapy. On such courses the demonstration of active learning takes various forms and may include a daily log or diary of work with school children, patients or clients and includes the assessment of progress made by the individual in their relationship with these groups. In completing the record for assessment the student has the opportunity to demonstrate their 'transferable' skills appropriate to a possible future career.

The establishment of the national Record of Achievement in schools means there is already a proportion of students entering higher education who are used to reflecting on their past learning experiences, whether formal academic studies or informal activities. Such students are able to assess their learning by reviewing their progress over all aspects of their course. They are also able to identify tasks and plan future study. This involvement in decision making enables students to gain confidence and carry over transferable skills gained through recording achievement to future learning. It also builds an expectation that the process will continue. If the student progresses to a vocational course this expectation is usually met in the production of professional portfolios or similar documents. For students embarking on non-vocational degree courses, however, the process may not be available. A range of personal and transferable skills may be lost unless recording achievement can be incorporated, either by integrating recording achievement into the framework for personal tutor systems or subject-based monitoring procedures, or by introducing institution-wide profiling schemes available to all students.

Alternatively the initiative to extend ROAs to higher education can be viewed as inevitably increasing the tensions between the educational aims of student centredness and the normative requirements of policy makers and employers. It has already been noted that the introduction of portfolios and profiling systems as frameworks for assessment in higher education should be based on a clearly identified purpose and the interests and involvement of all parties should be specified. True, a framework for recording achievement in higher education could have many benefits: providing a basis for tutorial work, enhancing student autonomy, promoting learner centredness, and providing a basis for the student to identify and present informally learned skills as well as academic learning to a future employer but the tension between these various aims should be recognised. A formative process-driven document is not necessarily the same as one which presents outcomes in a way that employers can recognize. Moreover, a personal formative document is almost by definition not the same as a summary of achievement which accords with nationally recognized criteria. This contradiction must be consciously managed if an ROA for higher education is, to be either useful or effective.

A number of formats for a higher education Record of Achievement have been proposed. The attached Summary Record of Achievement is based on papers already published by BTEC and UDACE which identify learning outcomes. Many of the learning outcomes are common to more than one subject area and echo the core or transferable skills identified by bodies such as the CBI, FEU and the NCVQ in the debate about developing core skills in the Post-16 curriculum during the late 1980s and early 1990s. Learning outcomes proposed for higher education include the ability to manage and process information, to work cooperatively, to analyse and develop one's personal skills as well as act ethically and possess basic computer skills. BTEC have identified common skills relating to these outcomes which should be developed and assessed at each level in relation to their own qualifications.

The proposed record includes a summary-sheet outlining the student's achievements in a range of skills which all higher education students would be expected to achieve during the course of their studies. This poses problems. First the methodology of recording such information is proving difficult, which is not surprising given the difficulties in defining what we mean by core or transferable skills, or more recently 'key skills'. Second the initiative must be clear about the aims of the record-are they formative or summative? These purposes should be clearly defined and stated in advance. If the aims are summative how do we counter growing criticisms that portfolios and records of achievements are not a basis for rigorous assessment? If the aims are formative how do we justify them?

***The Assessment*:** One solution is to ensure that the credibility of any assessment is seen to be rigorous. Rigorous assessment systems need primarily to be reliable; results need to be replicable irrespective of the assessor or the context. Much of this depends on ensuring there is a focus on moderation, both internal and external, to agree standards and appropriateness of submissions. It also requires internal and external reviews and clearly stated outcomes against which achievement can be measured and assessed by both the students and their assessors. Above all it requires 'socialization' of assessors so that standards and procedures become common currency. Exemplars can assist the moderation process and enable discussion to focus on issues such as the acquisition of personal skills and their summary in reflective diaries or logs. Matching of evidence to outcomes is not an exact science and assessors need to agree on what they see as appropriate and inappropriate forms of evidence of achieving given outcomes.

The SEEC guidelines (SEEC, 1995) are a relevant development. These guidelines are an attempt to ensure that everybody involved in recording prior achievements for assessment and accreditation in a higher education institution is working to similar quality standards. The guidelines have developed to promote rigour and accountability in AP(E)L procedures but, because of the similarity between them, are also equally appropriate for the summative recording of achievement in ROAs. The guidelines require the assessment process to be transparent, with information available at all stages and levels of recording and assessment.

While the guidelines clearly have relevance for the practice of accrediting prior learning and achievement, what the guidelines cannot tackle is the context in which ROAs (and AP(E)L) are developed and used. It. could also be argued that the very emphasis on quality is, by implication, a contradiction of the original aims of AP(E)L. The emphasis on credit and academic quality negates personal development issues and student empowerment. The attempt to get our practices recognized means we conform with the very regulations and assumptions which AP(E)L once sought to challenge.

The Expectation : At present there is debate and concern about the notion of 'graduateness' and about the competence of graduates leaving higher education with degrees or other graduate qualifications. The HEQC is currently preparing its thoughts on the concept of 'graduateness' and how the meaning 'of the idea of a graduate has changed in relation to current employment patterns and policy initiatives. In addition to subject-specific knowledge and skills, new' graduates are also expected to acquire a range of transferable skills which will enable flexibility in a rapidly changing work environment. Such skills, especially at high levels, can only be recognized, recorded and presented when reflection has taken place. There have been fierce criticisms that this is purely an employer-oriented notion of 'graduateness'. On the other hand, it can be argued that the move towards profiling in higher education is a way of providing more effective support to individuals and enabling personal development for students who access HE from a variety of different routes.

Many vocational HE courses such as initial teacher training, occupational therapy, physiotherapy and social work courses already use this approach for assessing skills, although sometimes under a different name. In a number of cases the subject-specific criteria or competences are stipulated by relevant professional bodies, although significant staff development may be needed to enable education staff to understand, recognize and assess them.

Within the current trend towards an emphasis on lifelong teaming and continuous professional development, the recording of personal and professional skills will undoubtedly increasingly extend to all vocational HE courses and across education and training in general. ROAs will become increasingly important. The forms of assessment and the focus on particular skills may change as local and regional employment initiatives vary, but an increasing emphasis is developing on enabling the recording of evidence of an individual's 'employability'.

Utility of Web : The design team begins by meeting with someone who is intimately familiar with the training needs and audience. Instructional designers spend time with that expert, analyzing the current training situation and looking carefully at the role online training might play in meeting long-term training needs. They will work to clarify the training requirements. During this part of the process, clients often become aware of training strategies and methods existing in their companies that were never recognized as such. The design team keeps those strategies in mind while developing the courseware. After the session, the team provides a *Training Assessment Report* containing its findings:

- Where your training is today and where it might go tomorrow.
- A list of "next-step" action items.
- Concrete options for course delivery.
- Price ranges for various platforms and audio/visual treatments.

If your requirements are already clearly defined, a Needs Assessment may not be necessary. In that case, it can be replaced with a shorter meeting or series of conference calls designed to gather information and collect all existing training materials. This process usually occurs if you are ready to proceed with a specific project and are able to provide detailed information on all of the following:

- Project description.
- Project scope.
- Audience profile.
- Current platform deployment.
- Desired delivery environment.
- Desired treatment approach.
- High level content outline.

After the Needs Assessment or meeting/conference calls, the final decisions are made on the delivery method and scope for the course. Armed with this information, the design team will provide a price for the Content and Design phase of the project.

Web Designing : The Content and Design phase results in the delivery of a Course Architecture and Design Blueprint. Together they specify what will be taught and how it should be presented. The Course Architecture is a detailed outline of instructional material that has been sequenced and structured (for example: modules, lessons, and topics). It describes:

1. What you want to teach?
2. What teaching sequence should be used?. What is the best course structure?

The Working : Instructional Designers meet with the Subject Matter Experts (SMEs) to extract all of the course content, existing or new.

The design team puts the information about job tasks and job knowledge gained from these meetings to work to help design the hierarchy of learning objectives.

Before proceeding to the Design Blueprint, it is necessary to be certain that the content is both thorough and accurate. The appropriate manager must provide approval, indicating acceptance of the Course Architecture "as is," or "with changes."

Once the Course Architecture determines what needs to be taught, the Design Blueprint specifies how it will be taught.

- Designers work with the artists and programmers to define the creative treatment (look and feel) and plan the instructional, presentational, and navigational strategies.
- The team prescribes the menu functionality and designs the viewer interface screens based on audience and content needs.

The team selects and define key components and their functionality (such as a mastery test, record keeping, index, and glossary). The team creates flowcharts detailing possible pathways through the course. All of this information is put together in the Design Blueprint. It, along with the Course Architecture, becomes the "blueprint" for the training project. After review and approval of the Design Blueprint, a price for the production and delivery of your product can be determined.

In addition to the instructional design blueprint, the Engineering Design phase specifies the hardware and software delivery systems that will be used to deliver the course.

The engineering team reviews the options of the playback systems for course delivery considering your organization's available multimedia computer systems and online connection speed.

The engineering team defines all the software development tools to be used on the project including specific authoring languages or systems, graphics packages, and audio editing tools.

The engineering team specifies how the course will work at a detailed level. Course navigation, required media elements, and any other technical issues are carefully considered.

All components of the engineering design are clearly articulated. The course is designed to be error free from the start, a much less costly alternative than finding errors later.

The development and delivery of a Rapid Prototype constitutes the third phase. The Rapid Prototype demonstrates the planned look and feel for the course along with expected course navigation functions and sample screens. It is implemented using the software to be used for the final course and is delivered on the actual hardware you plan to use.

The Rapid Prototype allows us to make any necessary changes to the production plans before launching into full-scale production.

In certain circumstances, a more extensive prototype may be needed to fully prove the course concept. In that event, we will story-board and implement in software a complete instructional unit exactly as it will appear in the final product, inclusive of actual, approved course content.

Extra Techniques : Following the Content and Design and Rapid Prototype phases, instructional designers begin story-boarding the course.

A story-board is a written plan for a discrete unit of instruction, usually referred to as a topic. Developed with a special template customized for your project, a story-board is typically 5 to 20 pages in length depending on the duration and complexity of the topic. A typical course may have 30 or more story-boards.

Story-boards include:

- A description of the overall scene and action for the topic.
- Narration scripts for spoken audio voiceover.
- Onscreen text that the viewer will read.
- Quiz/test questions with feedback.
- Descriptions of visuals to be displayed (video, animations, and graphics).
- Descriptions of music and sound effects.
- File names for all multimedia elements.

Story-boards are delivered to you for editing and approval. There are no surprises you will see only content and design treatments that you have previously approved. One way to measure perfection is how closely the final product matches the approved storyboards.

A production pathway, based on the seven production phases, is a definable and repeatable process. With input from the entire project team, the Project Manager customizes this process for each project.

A Pathway Document is created that facilitates the accurate and timely completion of all production tasks. This document reflects adherence to Instructional Systems Development principles. Not coincidentally, this process parallels practices in the best manufacturing plants.

Specifies procedures and standards for each of the production phases relevant to your project. Defines the day-to-day logistics to be used by the team for producing, storing, transferring, archiving, and assembling all of the video and audio elements of the program into a finished product.

Using the Pathway Document, together with the approved storyboards, the project team gets to work. The artists and animators create the visuals; the video producer shoots and/or edits live action footage; the audio engineer records the narration; and the music and sound effects are identified and produced. As the components are finalized, programmers assemble them to create a "beta" or test version of the product.

The Yardstick : The purpose of Usability Testing is to see how representative learners from the target audience interact with the Rapid Prototype.

Testing can be done formally, in a usability lab... or... informally, within your company or training deployment site.

Information from a usability test is invaluable in determining the effectiveness of the proposed training, including instructional strategies, ease of navigation, and user reaction to the overall look and functionality of the product. Usability testing, thought to be superfluous by some, is actually an essential "reality check."

Joy Mountford, interface guru, said it all in an interview in Interactivity Magazine:

"The most important thing to remember is that the user is never wrong. If they feel it's not good, if they feel it's uninteresting, if they feel it's difficult, then they're right."

Using the beta version to identify every possible interaction and pathway through the course, our Quality Assurance and Testing coordinator writes a testing plan for the product. Supervised by the coordinator, the testing team uses a database utility to record and prioritize any bugs they find while following the prescribed testing pathway. After two (2) passes through the program are completed, any bugs are repaired and the program is retested.

After Quality Assurance and Testing, the beta course is delivered for final review (and in some cases, further Usability Testing) and approval before replication takes place.

Basics of ISD: (Instructional Systems Development) ISD is a systematic approach to designing, producing, and evaluating multimedia training programs using a series of logically sequenced steps.

1. Who is the learner? (audience profile)
2. What does the learner need to learn? (objectives)
3. What will enable that learning? (content analysis)

4. What is the best way to teach it? (instructional strategies)
5. How can we be sure it has been learned? (mastery testing)
6. Why use ISD principles as part of the courseware development process?

Practiced effectively, this systematic approach minimizes the time, effort, and money needed for development, and maximizes the usage of these resources. Training projects in trouble can inevitably trace their woes to skipping or shortchanging one of the five key steps listed above.

Programs are produced without using the Instructional Systems Development (ISD) approach (you've probably seen some). It's a sad fact because critical content is often omitted, while irrelevant content is included. When instructional strategies and delivery platforms are chosen by default, the outcome is haphazard at best. It is not a pretty sight.

Without ISD, testing is general rather than measuring specified and needed outcomes. There is a lack of cohesiveness across training curriculums, training goals, and testing. Finally, there is little or no attention given to assessing the effectiveness of the program or providing the means to keep it current.

The Utility : Multimedia training, according to Rockley L. Miller, founder of the Interactive Multimedia Association, is reported by corporate users to have the following benefits:

Reduced Learning Time-Multiple studies have found that interactive technologies reduce learning time by an average of 30 percent.

*Reduced Cost :*The primary costs of interactive instruction lie in design and production not replication, distribution, and delivery. With traditional instructional methods, the costs of training lie primarily in the delivery (instructor salaries, overhead, travel, etc.) and remain constant or even increase as more students place greater demands on fixed resources.

Instructional Consistency : Technology-based instructional systems do not have bad days or forget to cover key points, nor do they cover the same material differently from class to class.

Privacy : With one-on-one systems, students are free to ask questions and explore areas at their own speed, without embarrassment or slowing down an entire class.

Mastery of Learning : Unlike normal classroom situations, an interactive system will not move on to new material until the current material is mastered.

Increased Retention : The process of interaction with material being studied provides strong learning reinforcement that significantly increases content retention over time.

Increased Safety : With interactive systems, students can explore any subject from within the safety of the training environment.

Increased Motivation : Interactive systems provide a level of responsive feedback and individual involvement that has proven to be highly motivating in both individual and classroom learning environments.

Increased Access : Interactive systems can provide greater and more equal access to quality training. They can be used to simulate laboratory equipment that is typically too expensive to make available to each student.

Enjoyment of Interactive Learning-Interactive systems allow learners to take greater control of, and hence, responsibility for, their own learning process. Along the way, they discover that learning can still be enjoyable-even fun!

Training Process : The power of any courseware can be augmented by web based training management. A good web-based training management system launches and works with web-based and CD-ROM-based courses. This tool can be customized for your company to:

- Provide convenient program distribution to multiple locations.
- Accurately manage and measure each stage of the program's execution.
- Broadly support advanced multimedia technologies streaming audio and video, animations.

To be effective, the web based management system must provide fast, easy access to courses for students and accurate, timely reports at a click of the mouse. To be responsive, the web based gaining management system must allow customized curricula, as well as changes and updates to the database from one central location.

Culture of Computer

The school education experts, on one hand have been designing computer literacy programs, the French have coined the term "telematique". The concept, translated into English as "telematics," refers to the growing connections between and among computers and such telecommunication media as modems, information utilities, microwave relays, satellites, and cable TV. As such, telematics reflects a new technological reality that transcends nations and cultures. Rooted in research and development breakthroughs, telematics carries special meanings. it draws attention to the unprecedented scope of current communication networks and to the invisibility of much of their operations. It highlights the connectedness of networks components and their collective and far-reaching potential for influencing local, national and global communication.

Modern Communication

Telematics, as a new symbol of the power of modern communication media, may well foreshadow the need for new literacy concepts. More specifically, children born in the mid-1980s, upon graduation from high school may find that computer literacy is a receding concept and that "telematic literacy" or some similar concept is making its way onto the educational stage. Since the schools today are only beginning to link microcomputers to information utilities and thereby to provide students new sources of knowledge and ideas, the move away from computer literacy will surely be slow. However, even today we can see that the concept of computer literacy sharply constrains our perspective on the new technologies and on our capacities to comprehend their educational possibilities; since "computer literacy" misses many important meanings inherent in today's complex information environments, it is a provincial concept. If future citizens, workers, and thinkers are to come to grips with the needs created by the changing information society, today's ideas about literacy will need to become more telematic. Such an expanded meaning will enable students to confront both the ends and the means of the microelectronic revolution.

By using a telematic perspective, they can probe the promise of micro-technologies and contemplate the dangers that large-scale, rapidly proliferating and smoothly functioning telematic systems present to individuals and society. The acceptance of a broad ended concept of literacy will enable individuals to gain more than basic understandings of telematic systems and of their import for society. Given the remarkable progress already achieved in electronic information transmission, skilled individuals pursuing decision-making, work, educational, or other objectives can even today tap sources of information far beyond those immediately available in their homes and local libraries.

Tens of thousands of adults are already accessing data through CompuServe; The Source, and other information utilities, in addition, through electronic linkages, leading schools are providing some students with the skills needed to use these utilities. As individuals learn to use electronic networks, they will be able to acquire information from new sources related to the solution of self-defined problems; to define, with the aid of other computer network members, technical and social problems and to seek solutions to these problems, and to develop with others new knowledge, products, and proposals. Form today's perspective such projections may seem unrealistic; however, when 1985 enrollees in kindergarten graduate from high school in the twenty-first century, they will step into a society where information is richer, more varied, and more accessible than it is today. The power of computers and of their telematic companions to change society will surely have more far-reaching effects on the purposes of education than on the means of instructions since schools are now "in between" the descendant industrial and the ascendant information society, their purpose need to be reformulated.

Underlying the all significant concepts of literacy and

educational purpose assumptions about desirable qualities of thought. Given the fact that the beliefs about desirable qualities differ, policy makers face a fundamental question: What types of thinking should the schools develop in students? Since the information industries have an insatiable appetite for newly created hardware and software products, their representatives tend to press for means-oriented thinking that can alleviate this appetite. Others, disturbed by the negative impacts of large-scale, computer-based systems on society, see the need for a different type of thinking.

The qualitative and quantitative needs for effective software systems in the future will grow markedly. Programmers responding to this need, as already noted, will apply algorithmic thinking, many other specialists engaged in the development and use of information technologies will be applying similar modes of "instrumental" thinking-modes that are notable for their technical problem-solving capacities, their highly rational expressions, and their effectiveness in dealing with means-oriented questions in here-and-now contexts.

Proficient in procedural analysis, instrumental reasoning can add to an already astounding array of technical solutions and computer artifacts: Significantly, however, more and more critics argue that this type of reasoning cannot resolve the troublesome societal problems which microelectronic technologies are creating. Such reasoning they contend, is too uncritical of the status quo, too constrained by machine requirements, and too blind and indifferent to the negative consequences of large-scale telematic systems to address overriding social problems. Although critics have argued that instrumental reasoning lacks the capacities to deal effectively with a "permanent underclass," structural unemployment, the loss of privacy, clarification of purpose, inequity of access, nuclear warfare, and other problems created or exacerbated by modern technologies, they have not yet provided a clearly defined alternatives. Unless well-defined alternatives are developed, today's literacy programs, which are linked largely to traditional modes of thought, cannot easily be redirected.

One place to look for the salient features of an alternative is in the computer culture itself. Outlined in broad strokes here are features of a type of thought nourished by the problems computerization is creating. Features dealt with include the scope of its perspective, its capacities for critique, the class of problems it addresses, and the outcomes it seeks. How the features depicted are related to the computer culture is also addressed. The computer culture is encouraging thinkers to think more about the future than did members of previous cultures.

Most of the history of book-literacy transpired in rural contexts where tradition was a strong influence on thought. Since past patterns provided reliable standards for the future, rural thinking tended to be oriented toward the past. Those living in the dynamic computer culture, on the other hand, have found that past patterns are very reliable forecasters of, emergent ones; consequently, individuals are pressed to anticipate and to think about the future in uncertain, rapidly changing, and sometimes threatening situations. Masuda has noted that the "purposeful use of future time" is a critical value of the information society. The founding in 1964 of the World Future Society, about the time the integrated circuit began to alter technology radically, is only one of many developments symbolizing the shift towards future's thinking. This thinking has found its way into thousands of publications in many languages; in addition, implementers of future programs in schools are seeking to engender a type of thinking very different from that required to program computers. Another concept of thinking spawned by the computer culture is associated with the term "global." Thinking directed at the development, programming, and operation of computers takes place in relatively bounded environments.

Developers are not pressed to probe the impact of their projected products on society, even though technologies have generated an array of complicated and largely unanticipated societal problems; paradoxically, at the same time technologies have eliminated barriers to worldwide, instantaneous communications and, in the process, have pushed global thinking to the fore. As a result, recognizing that sharply bounded definitions of problems suffer from missing ingredients, leaders are now applying the concept of "world problematique" to such disparate problems as energy and human equity. Expanding international databases are nurturing the budding trend toward global thinking. However, those engaged in such thinking face deeply conflicting national and world interests, as they think within almost unbounded perspective and as they strive to understand the intricacies of global issues.

Instrumental reasoning, by definition, is effective in the logical clarification of steps to be followed and procedures to be used in the attainment of specified objectives. Its mission is limited largely to the elucidation and implementation of efficient means. Users of instrumental reasoning tend to accept uncritically ends specified for them and to ignore the long-range consequences of the developments they achieve.

Pursuing means in contexts where ends are determined by others, instrumental reasoners are not oriented toward larger issues of policy. This condition highlights another feature of needed thought, namely, a capacity to be critical about the ends sought in the information society and how these ends are related to the large-scale technological outcomes that instrumental reasoning helps produce. This feature of thinking transcends narrowly proscribed contexts and concentrates upon purposive issues, strategic questions, and problems that center in public interests. Its target would not be the development and use of technology but the consequences of such development and use. Eschewing the procedural orientation of instrumentally oriented thinkers, it would be more intuitive and eclectic in its methods. Its bias would be toward holistic thinking and against narrower instrumental tendencies in thought.

To return to the "whither" question, even with its impressive accomplishments instrumental reasoning as a mode of thinking is an insufficient guide for those designing computer literacy programs. Thinking that would counter instrumental reasoning, as already implied, would be directed not at technologies but at the attainment of an effective society. Certainly, the ideal of self-realization of, in more specific terms, the fulfillment of the potential of individuals would become prominent in the design of computer literacy programs. To be sure, it is easier to develop machines than to nurture individuals and it is easier to generate information than to use it wisely. However, only developed individuals will be able to achieve an effective society and to fashion a positive story about life and achievements in the computer culture. Literacy programs directed at the self-realization of individuals in the unfolding computer culture will need a base in thinking that reaches beyond instrumental reasoning. Although the press for instrumental reasoning will continue in both society and schools, emergent signs suggest that a different type of thinking is now in the ascendancy—a thinking that is more futuristic, global, critical, holistic, and goal-oriented in its expression. Computer literacy programs based upon the emergency mode of thinking deserve priority; the complicity and the severity of the problems created by micro-electronic technologies require it.

Programs based upon simpler concepts of literacy, while more widespread, are not as well integrated into curricula as are programs based upon more complex concepts. Activities directed at operational literacy, for example, are typically tangential to, if not outside, established courses; on the other hand, more complex concepts such as citizen literacy can be taught in existing courses; since most literacy programs are not integrated into existing course.

Since most literacy programs are not integrated into existing curricula, institutional support for them is likely to be weak. Much controversy surrounds decisions about computer literacy. Computers, as increasingly powerful machines, activate deeply rooted cultural fears; changes now under way in human-machine relationships, the pessimists stress, will surely bring about a dehumanized society. On the other hand, computer also stimulate expansive new dreams for a more effective society in which humans, aided by machines, reach new levels of self-actualization. Leaders who address literacy decisions, then, are faced with two very different messages, one coloured by despair and the other by hope. These inharmonious views about the consequences of computers complicate literacy decisions.

Given the tender age of computer literacy concepts and the paucity of relevant research, the analogy of "book literacy" can shed light on the query: Whither computer literacy? The history of book literacy contains clues about future developments in computer literacy. Thus, if computer literacy follows the pattern of book literacy, it will become increasingly complex, more expansive in its meanings, and more differentiated in the functions it denotes. Advocates of computer literacy will struggle long to realize equal educational opportunities as have advocates of book literacy; for several reasons, the former may face even greater challenges in attaining equity than have the latter.

Paralleling the struggle to achieve equity will be another challenge, namely, that of ever redefining computer literacy objectives to make them consonant with changing standards of knowledge and with altered societal needs. Since the computer is only a small figure in the larger context of electronic communication, it is already a provincial modifier of "literacy." A more fruitful and encompassing concept could be "telematic literacy", the latter provides a larger window for viewing the understandings and skills needed to function in the developing information society.

The Hypothesis

All concepts of literacy contain underlying assumptions about what qualities of thinking schools need to develop in students. The press in the computer culture towards the development and use of hardware and software has required instrumental or means-oriented thinking. The limitations of this emphasis are becoming increasingly apparent; future concepts of computer literacy will need to place greater emphasis upon defining and implementing futuristic, global, intuitive, critical, ends-oriented, and holistic thinking. Most countries have a government body to run the telephones. In the United States a number of private companies are given licences by the Federal Communications Commission (FCC) which oversees the arrangements. Such licensees are known as common carriers in the USA. The effect of the monopoly given to the licensees is that only the licensee can erect systems to carry signals such as telephone conversations or computer data. The licensees are usually called Ms and this reflects the arrangements more common in the rest of the world rather than those in the USA.

The major problem with the PSTN is that it was designed before anyone even thought of computers. The telephone system is ideally suited to carry speech where a human being can concentrate on decoding the received sounds and try to understand them. There are a number of factors contributing to the PSTN being a poor medium for the type of signals. Firstly, the equipment has a frequency range of 3003400 Hz, which is not very wide for high-speed data traffic. Secondly, the frequency range is not continuous; some frequencies may be used to operate equipment at exchanges, which explains how phone freaks in the USA can make calls by whistling into the telephone handset and causing the exchange to set up the call. If a data signal produces the wrong frequency the call may be disconnected. This problem is taken up in the section on modulation.

Finally, to protect the exchange equipment from damage, no DC (direct current) is allowed through the local exchange. By looking at the type of wave produced by speech against a data signal, in figure,. it can be seen that the speech signal never has the same voltage continuously, whereas the data signal consists almost entirely of a continuous voltage at one of two levels. The continuous voltage is the DC part which would be removed by the exchange. Removing the DC part would seriously distort a digital data signal.

The Ms provide four solutions to these problems—

1. Special equipment to convert digital data signals into audio signals which can easily be transmitted through the PSTN.
2. Private four-wire connections to the local exchange, then a fixed circuit to the remote site. This cuts out some parts of the PSTN that cause problems, but not all of them.
3. Direct links of high bandwidth most of the way between sites.
4. More recently, some PTTs now offer digital services directly to the customer, in multiples of 64K bps.

The introduction of digital telephone exchanges will enable the provision of digital circuits direct-to ordinary subscribers in the near future. The major piece of equipment needed to transfer data through the PSTN is the MODEM. Modulation is a technique that can enable information signals to be passed through a medium not really suited to them. The original, and still the major, use of modulation is in radio transmission. By using that analogy it is possible to see how modulation can be used to pass digital data signals, through a medium designed to carry voice signals. The human voice does not travel very far on its own, and if more than one person were to try broadcasting at the same time it would be very difficult to separate out the messages.

The frequency range of an original signal is called the *base band*; for the human voice a base band of 300 to 3300 Hz is used on the telephone though a wider range is possible. When two people talk at once close together, they confuse listeners because they are both using the same frequency range, the base band. To transmit speech over long distances very much higher frequencies have to be used, and care must be taken to ensure that different frequencies are used for each different transmission. The original base band frequencies have to be increased and no two transmissions should use the same frequency range. The only problems now are how to increase the frequency of the base band signal without losing any information in the signal, and then how to recover the original signal so that the transmission can be heard in the base band.

The problems are solved by modulation. Modulation, very simply, involves superimposing the information signal on to a simple carrier signal in such a way that one, or more, components of the carrier are modified to carry the information.

In the technique known as 'differential phase modulation', there are four possible phase changes (0°, 90°, 180°, 270°) so each possibility represents two bits of data. A continuous frequency simple wave is used so that only the phase component changes; figure shows the phase changes. To be able to detect the phase changes a complete wave, or cycle, is used. In any one cycle there are four possible changes that could occur, so each cycle represents two bits of information. For instance, if we use a frequency of 1200 Hz we can have an information rate of 2400 bits per second.

Sometimes a faster rate of data transfer is required, say for printing messages, though the input may still be slow. The bandwidth available on the PSTN is not sufficient, given the noise, to allow a full duplex connection faster than 300 bps. However, research is continuing on modulation techniques to achieve faster data rates. A second type of MODEM is used to provide a higher speed in one direction, but a much lower speed in the other direction. Up to 600 bps can be guaranteed on the PSTN in the UK, passing through the exchange in one direction, whilst the return channel has only 75 bps. The return channel is called a 'supervisory channel' and is not expected to carry much data.

Up to 1200 bps may be obtained using a dial-up connection if the noise is very low, but a 'private circuit' will provide a guaranteed 1200 bps. If a connection of 600/1200 bps is needed in both directions, then two MODEMs are needed at each end. If the PSTN is used 'via a dial-up line only a half duplex connection is possible, because the circuit can only manage 600/1200 bps in one direction at a time. If a private four-wire circuit is used then a full duplex connection is possible. Because the direction of the main data transfer is fixed, one type of MODEM is used for sending on the fast channel (600/1200 bps) and receiving the supervisory channel (75 bps), whilst a different model performs the reverse operation at the other end.

The receiving MODEM can always tell if the sender is using 600 or 1200 bps as the idle frequency is different for the two data rates. Note that the frequency range 13002 100 Hz fills the middle of the available frequencies on the PSTN. This means that the supervisory channel is relegated to using the low frequencies, and therefore has a low data rate.

A popular speed for synchronous transfer is 2400 bps. This is provided by a group of MODEMS that use differential phase encoding to obtain the higher data rate within the frequency range of the PSTN. The connection pattern is the same as for the 600/1200 bps MODEM; a simplex connection is available on the two-wire circuit via the exchange with a sending and receiving MODEM. If sending and receiving MODEM are provided at each end, a half duplex connection can be made by sharing the two-wire circuit.

A full duplex connection can be obtained by using a private four-wire circuit. A 2400 bps MODEM is available for use over the PSTN using a dial-up line, but may be limited to 1200 bps by noise. The 2400 bps main data connection can be augmented by a 75 bps supervisory channel in the reverse direction, as in the 600/1200 MODEM. The differential phase encoding uses four possible phase changes on a 1200 Hz signal to obtain the 2400 bps data rate. MODEM speeds of 4800 bps and 9600 bps are also available, but only using private circuits.

For use in inter-computer communications, an arrangement is available for data rates between 40.8K bps and 50K bps over 48 kHz wide band circuits. Some of the larger exchanges in the PSTN are connected by very wide band circuits. These can be utilised for data transfer, although a private high-speed circuit may have bypassed several exchanges on the way to the large exchange. For the high-speed circuit four MODEMS are used, one pair to reach the large exchange, and another pair at the other end. Between the end pairs of MODEMs the data is passed in the base band frequency of the data signals on a special private circuit.

MODEM's Utility

The main uses of MODEMs are listed below.

1. To connect a teletype or slow VDU (110/300 bps) to any computer in full duplex, by dialing through the PSTN.
2. To connect a faster terminal (600/1200 bps); but to get a full duplex connection a permanent private circuit is needed, so only one computer can be used.
3. To provide a synchronous connection using higher data rates (1200/2400, 4800, 9600 bps); but again a private circuit is needed for full duplex and full speed operation.
4. A very high data rate can be achieved, but at a higher cost, using base band signaling for part of the distance on a special circuit.

In terms of cost the acoustic coupler represents the cheapest modulation equipment. The cost then rises through the four types of MODEM described above. The higher the data rate, the higher the cost; however, the relationship is not linear. A 1200 bps service does not cost four times as much as a 300 bps service: it is more likely to cost only about twice as much to install, especially if a private wire is needed, but the rental may only be half as much again. Thus the problem of obtaining the optimum cost/service is not easy.

The PTTs from all over the world work through a body called the CCITT. The CCITT is a part of the United Nations. It is concerned with enabling the individual PTTs from all over the world to cooperate and provide an international service. The CCITT is one of the most authoritative standards organisations in communications, so any standard adopted by the CCITT is very important. All of the MODEMs discussed in this chapter conform to international, standards for their operation, so it is possible for a terminal user in the UK to use a timesharing computer in Germany by dialing the computer. The German computer uses a German MODEM, while the UK user has a UK MODEM, but because they conform to the same standards they will be able to operate together. The CCITT have had a tremendous impact on computer communications by standardising various interfaces between computing equipment.

The most important interface is that between the MODEM and the user's equipment. For instance, for a synchronous terminals the interface standard is called V24. The V24 standard defines all of the control and data signals used to enable the MODEM and the user's equipment to operate together and pass data, including the signal levels. The result of the standards and their widespread adoption by equipment manufacturers means that any terminal having a V24 interface can be plugged into any MODEM, anywhere. Furthermore computer manufacturers now use the V24 standard for connecting local terminals as well.

This compatibility between equipment is very important in allowing various different types of equipment, from different manufacturers, to be interchangeable. Because the manufacturers in the United States dominate the computer industry the standards adopted by the United States often become the international standards of the CCITT.

One of the US standards called RS232C is in fact the same as the V24 recommendation and preceded it. RS232C was the name given to the standard in the US before it became an international recommendation. Many US manufacturers still refer to it as RS232C rather than V24. The CCITT have defined a standard interface for connecting communications equipment to a digital switched network; this standard is known as X.21. A second interface standard, known as X.21(bis), allows the same mechanisms but over the analogue PSTN, because there are still so few digital services available. The packet switched network access interface, X.25, is defined to used X.21 as its lowest level. However, X.21 (bis), or even V24, may be used where a digital network is not yet available.

13

Communication at Work

Man is a social being and cannot live without communicating. He communicates to express his feelings, needs, ideas and opinions about himself, environment and other people around him. He communicates, because he feels and he feels not only for himself but also for his fellow-beings. Various means are used by man today to communicate. When such communication is meant for the mass, the media used for the purpose is called mass communication media or mass media in brief.

Sphere and Usage

The history of man and the history of communication seem to be synonymous. One cannot be separated from the other. The different types of inventions and discoveries that man has so far made are all to enhance his ability to communicate and to make his work better and easier. Emerson in his famous essay "Works and Days" has aptly said, "All the tools and engines on earth are only extension of its (mankind's) limbs and senses." Samuel Butler in his "Erewhor" (1872) develops the same idea "that machines were to be regarded as a part of man's own physical nature, being really nothing, but extra-corporeal limbs, every past invention being an addition to the resources of the human body." In The Study of Invention" (1928) Hendrik Van Loon has illustrated the tools as the extensions of man - his hand, foot, mouth, skin, eyes and ears (Dale, 1969 p. 612)

The history of man is thus an account of the extension of his powers. Particularly, the invention of alphabets, printing from movable types, invention of radio and television are landmarks not only in the history of mankind, but also in the development of mass communication media. It has therefore been observed by Mohanty: "In this age of science and technology, importance of mass media cannot be over-estimated. It is felt difficult to spend a single day without the use of mass media. Different aspects of our life-social, political, economic and personal, are being influenced by mass media."

Like Industrial Revolution many people call the present day changes "Communication Revolution" James Kinder (1959, p. 2) had pointed out, "Today the mass media of communication reach millions of people scattered over the face of the earth. Through the mass media, every working hour of everyday, modern man is entertained, is informed, is urged to act this way or that way, and to spend money on an infinite variety of goods and services."

Mass media of communication are the results of the modern age of science and technology. Previously, there were traditional modes of communication like meetings, conferences, fairs, yatras, beating the drums, blowing the trumpets, and so on. Then the manuscripts with many limitations acted as a medium of communication. But printing of the book with movable types brought about a significant change in the communication system. Lately, electricity and electronics started a revolution in the communications. Radio, television, films and newspapers acted as the effective mass media of communication. Mass media are many and to describe their development here is far more difficult. However, attempts will be made to discuss briefly the development of some important mass media like folk art and music, printed materials, including newspapers, radio in the political and economic life of the people.

Traditional arts and music dominated the scene of mass

communication in India. They were, of course, associated with the cultural festivals and religious rituals. Folk songs, folk dance, folk drama, puppet shows, *kirtans, palas, daskathias, yatras,* etc., were used both as the media of information as well as entertainment. These were of universal appeal, crossing the barriers of religious and economic backgrounds. These folk arts and music were quite indigenous and appealing to all sections of the society.

During the freedom struggle also these art forms were utilised for creating patriotism and nationalism among the people. The poets, dramatists and writers also contributed their mite to this noble cause through their creative activities. Folk musical forms were found effective for fostering heroic spirit and sacrifice in the hearts of the people. These were oral and aural mass media of communication. Although entertainment is emphasised, education is also promoted by the use of folk art and music.

Books, journals and newspapers constitute the whole gamut of printing materials. These are comparatively less expensive and more popular. Prior to this, there were manuscripts namely "Pothis" in palm-leaves or Bhurja leaves which were very limited in number as well as in use. At first the European Missionaries brought printing technology to India, two centuries ago. The first newspaper was published in Calcutta in 1780. Indian newspapers with Indian editorship and proprietorship started during the period of renaissance under the inspiration of Raja Ram Mohun Roy. The first Indian newspaper in English was the Bengal Gazette (weekly) published in 1816. Although it died after a year, the era of Indian journalism was opened and by 1823 the country had atleast three newspapers published in Bengali, three in Persian and one in Gujarati.

During the struggle for freedom the press restrictions were harsher and the Anglo-Indian press defended the government by belittling the people's fight and aspiration for freedom. On the other hand, the Indian leaders like Aurobindo, Annie Besant, Lajpat Rai, Bipin Behari Pal, Surendranath Banerjee, Tilak, Gandhi and Gopabandhu were the shining luminaries not only in politics but also in journalism. Mahatma Gandhi launched his Non-cooperation Movement soon after the First World War and demanded fearless criticism from the press. This led to the enactment of the Press (Emergency Powers) Act of 1931 for dealing with the terrorist activities and crushing the Civil Disobedience Movement.

After Independence the "freedom of speech and expression" was recognised as a fundamental right under Article 19 (1 a) of the Constitution. Although there is no special provision on the freedom of press as such, it is covered under this fundamental right.

The Registrar of Newspapers was appointed in 1956 for regulation and collection of authentic statistics regarding all aspects of the press. Some other Acts and amendments were also passed for controlling the press and during the Emergency of 1975. Severe restrictions were imposed for curbing freedom of the press. Most of these restrictions have been removed by the amendments to the Constitution.

Printed materials made education available to a vast population. In place of "class education" it became - "mass education."

Printed materials in fact became the most popular means of education. Textbooks, handbooks, guide books and journals are used as very useful teaching-learning materials. In-spite of electronic advancements, printed materials are felt indispensable.

Since 1924, the era of radio broadcasting began in our country as a Radio Club at Madras which started a broadcasting service. In 1926 Government granted a license to the Indian Broadcasting Company to establish broadcasting stations in the country. The company got the monopoly of broadcasting earning revenues through licences. The first station was set up at Bombay on July 23, 1927 and the second one at Calcutta on August 26, 1927. The Broadcasting Company was, however, liquidated in 1930 and the Government of India took over the broadcasting service. Originally, it was called the Indian States Broadcasting Service and in 1936 it was re-designated as the All India Radio.

Liene! Fielden took over the office of the Controller of Broadcasting from the beginning and Government of India provided a sum of Rs. 40 lakhs for development of the service initially. With an impetus from the World War, broadcasting developed considerably. The AIR, however, had to face a lot of administrative problems on account of foreign rule, multiplicity of languages and economic backwardness. Menon (1976) has rightly pointed out, "It was only after Independence that broadcasting was organised as a national service. In the last twenty years the growth has been both in quantity and quality, steady, if not spectacular. The orientation in outlook, the shift in emphasis of values, the transformation of an existing set-up into a national service, these take time. And the wheels of Government grind slowly."

With a view to formulating programme policies, advisory committees were attached to the radio stations from the very beginning of the service and such committees are still continuing with every station. The AIR always functions under a code of conduct. News involving sex, crime, religious fanaticism, communalism, personal attacks, threats to public place are generally avoided.

Television service was inaugurated in Delhi on September 15, 1959 and was operated from a small improvised studio. It was telecasting programmes twice a week for a duration of one hour each. Only 21 TV sets were installed for community viewing and a UNESCO assisted project was implemented to assess the effectiveness of social education programmes. Since the report was quite encouraging the Government of India started telecasting educational programmes since 1964 with the Ford Foundation assistance.

An innovative project in television was the SITE (Satellite Instructional Television Project Experiment) during the year 1975-76. The international communication experts like Wilbur Schramm pleaded for mass medium like satellite for India and the Indian scientists with vision and zeal like Vikram Sarabhai made the project of satellite communication a success. The SITE was inaugurated on Aug. 1, 1975 and TV programmes produced by the Doordarshan and ISRO (Indian Space Research Organisation) were telecast to 2400 selected villages of 6 states - Andhra Pradesh, Bihar, Karnataka, Madhya Pradesh, Orissa and Rajasthan. The satellite which was loaned by NASA of USA to India for a year was called ATS-6 (Applications Technology Satellite-6).

After the SITE, the Government of India decided to provide TV viewing facility in 40 per cent of the SITE served villages by setting up terrestrial transmitters in the six SITE States. The project called Community Viewing Scheme was implemented in these States at different times during the years 1977-80. Then detailed planning was made for another ambitious project named INSAT (Indian National Satellite) which is an experiment of great national importance in the field of multipurpose communication system. The INSAT-IA was launched on April 10, 1982 in order to provide TV service in the states of Andhra Pradesh, Orissa, Bihar, Maharashtra, Gujarat and Uttar Pradesh.

After its mechanical failure in September '82, INSAT-IB was launched in August 30, 1983 and was made operative from October 15, 1983. It is successfully providing facilities of nationwide coverage by direct telecast to low-cost community receivers, television and radio programme distribution, disaster warning, and relay of meteorological data. About 4000 community viewing TV sets have been installed in these States and television programmes were being broadcast daily for two hours and forty-five minutes in the morning for Primary schools and two hours in the evening for adults.

TV is now the magic carpet being used as a means of exploring the mysteries of the universe and a magic box for providing education and entertainment simultaneously. It is now a window to the world and a very potential and pragmatic medium of education catching the attention of all-high and low, rural and urban, students and teachers.

Films are a very effective mass media of communication and provide education as well as entertainment. India entered into the era of film production in 1912 with "Pundalik" a silent film produced by R.G. Torney. The age of silent films came to an end in 1931 when the talkies began to be produced. Over these years thousands of films have been produced and the majority of them in a few important centres of film production like Bombay, Madras and Calcutta.

Documentary films are useful for mass communication and most of these films are produced by the Film Division of the

Government of India. Its headquarters is at Bombay and branch offices in different States for distribution of such films. Films are produced almost on all subjects of national interest and include documentaries, cartoons and TV films in almost all important languages of the country.

Educational films are a very interesting medium of education. On a wide canvas we can see the real world or imaginary world with keen interest and rapt attention. Educational films produced with specific academic theme and suitable methods as well as techniques, are helpful in imparting instruction and happiness. They provide reality and imagination, variety and novelty, motion and animation by making instruction interesting. Students learn from educational films without tears, without boredom and without any strain. They enjoy and get themselves enlightened. Children are quite sensitive and creative. They are to be "warmed up" or motivated to get information, develop positive interests and attitudes so that their education becomes effective.

Mass Media in Operation

Impact of mass media is felt on every aspect of the modern life-social, economic, political, and so on. A man in the society is a man in communication with others - his kith and kin, his friends and fellows. He is always exposed to the lifestyle of others, ideas and opinions of others, news and views conveyed through all kinds of media—newspapers, radio, television, films, etc. He is influenced by them and cannot keep himself aloof from the effects of mass media. The entire people, and the whole mankind is shaped according to the mass media that are available at the time. R. K. Chatterjee (1979) has rightly remarked, "The activities of the mass media follow closely the development in various fields, informing people, reacting to policies and creating the social climate in which development and nation-building programmes can take place. They cannot operate in a social and political vacuum, nor do they deal with outdated philosophies. Mass media are every day dealing with problems that affect the destiny of the nation and in the wider context, of humanity as a whole. Mass media not only inform, but also entertain. They promote cognitive as well as affective development of students. They transmit knowledge and understanding very economically and interestingly. That is why, they are very cost-effective and impact-effective. Today, mass media is regarded the most effective tool of education. These media cater to the education needs of all age groups, all kinds of branches of education in both formal and non formal education systems.

Significant Factors

In this age of revolution of information technology there has been explosion of knowledge in almost all fields, but man is still discovering, classifying and recording new information at a phenomenal rate starting from the minutest particle of the atom to the farthest body of the universe. Application of this new knowledge in various disciplines has minimised the problems of time and space and facilitated the discovery of still newer knowledge in an endless cycle. Therefore it has been felt imperative on the part of teachers, to keep themselves abreast with the latest developments in their subjects and develop skills in applying criteria to assess the accuracy and validity. The development of new knowledge has resulted in the constant expansion of the school curriculum. As the curriculum expands, not only teachers fail to do justice to teach, but students too get very few opportunities and too little time to learn all objects in depth.

On the other hand, student population is amazingly increasing year by year due to population growth and democratisation of education. Students come from varying experience, backgrounds and differing facilities. Their levels of motivation and aspiration are quite different from one group to another. Even in the developing countries like India a large percentage of students are first generation learners who are deficient in background as well as motivation. Such heterogeneity and diversity among the pupils pose great problems in teaching as well as learning. In view of such problems and developments, special attempts are to be made for two types of instructional media, methods and materials: (i) those which are likely to prove effective for use with groups consisting of individuals of widely varying backgrounds and abilities and (ii) those which can be used advantageously for individualised instruction with only a minimum of teacher assistance.

Fortunately, educational technology has come to our rescue with wide a range of hardware as well as software for tackling these problems. It is the development, application and evaluation of systems, techniques and aids in the field of human learning. The main objective of its use is to optimise learning processes and experience. Technology of education is intended to make learning effective as well as efficient. It facilitates learning through the systematic identification, development, organisation and utilization of a full range of learning resources, and through management of these processes. In brief, students are to be enabled to "learn more in less time" meaningfully and to remember longer what they learn without "watering down" or sacrificing quality.

Learning Facilities

According to Wilbur Schramm (1954, p. I) the world famous expert in mass media and communication, there are at least four elements of communication (1) the source (2) the message (3) the channel and (4) the destination. This applies to both human and mechanical communication. But education is mainly concerned with personal or human communication. In this context either an organisation or a person can transmit a message which may be received by an individual or many. The message may be conveyed by verbal expressions, gestures, spoken or written symbols or by hand drawn or photographed pictures. The source is also called an encoder, the message a signal and destination a decoder. These terms indicate the need for common understanding of language and word-meanings based on similar experience background for making communication a success.

Mere presentation of a message or a lesson by the teacher may be a communication, but cannot be effective unless it leads to true learning. For example, a teacher teaches a new word. The child can repeat the spelling of the word correctly, but he should be able to use the word rightly on subsequent occasions. True learning has not taken place unless the teaching as an act of communication has succeeded in making a permanent and meaningful addition to the student's own communication skills. Brown (1964, p. 9) and others have therefore observed that classroom communication involves far more than the unilateral presentation by the teacher of new words or new facts or new ideas; it requires intercommunication between students and teachers, a mutual sharing of experiences and a continual feedback process.

Principles for Learning

Learning means modification of behaviour. Change in response or behaviour is caused partly or wholly by experience. Munn (1954) has rightly defined learning as "the process of being modified, more or less permanently, by what happens in the world around us, by what we do, or by what we observe." Geoch instead of giving a rigid definition of the learning process has made a general statement as following, "Learning, as we measure, is a change in performance which occurs under the conditions of practice." Thus learning depends on the following:

i. Experience of the learner.
ii. Capacity and motivation of the learner.
iii. Methods in which the learning materials are presented to the learner.
iv. Meaningful or difficulty of learning task; and
v. Interaction between the above variables.

Sunitee Dutt (1960, pp11-12) has enunciated the characteristics of learning as follows:

1. Learning is purposive or goal-oriented. Human beings always learn to achieve something. Purposeless learning may not be effective. But when the goal is fixed and clear, the learning becomes more meaningful and effective.
2. Learning is an active process. There is no learning without self-activity. That is why, it is said, "whether or not you learn and what you learn depends upon what you yourself do, for learning an activity."
3. Learning is individual. Each learner has his own needs and interests, abilities and attitudes, hopes and aspirations. Some may learn quickly and some slowly. Thus the pace and depth of learning depends on that individual.
4. Learning is socially conditioned. It is not only individual

but also social. It occurs in relation to social environment of the learner and a teacher has to take this into account.

5. Learning is the response of the whole individual to the total situation. It is unitary as man learns as a whole being. So for effective teaching and learning, the physical, mental, social and emotional aspects of his whole being are to be taken note of and setting up the environment is very important.
6. Learning is creative. It is not just an addition to the previous knowledge and experience of the learner. It is a creative synthesis of all the new and old knowledge and experience. True human learning aims at creative and critical thinking.
7. Learning is transferable. It is transferred to new tasks and the learner establishes relationship of the previous learning experiences with the new ones. Of course it is possible when there is identity of context, procedures and ideals and such transfer is necessary for economy as well as efficiency of learning.

Concept of Communication

There are different principles of learning like readiness, exercise, effect and insight which are useful for success of communication. Again there are various approaches to learning. The association theories of learning lay stress on the responses of the learner and bonds with stimuli and the behavioural changes of the learner. The field theories emphasize the learner's perception of the whole field of events. Skinner, Thorndike, Guthrie and Hall are the proponents of association theories. Lewin, Tolman and the gestalt psychologists are the advocates of the field theories. The association theories put emphasis on the stimulus - response, environment and previous experiences and part elements in learning. On the contrary, field theories emphasise on perception and cognition of the learner, the whole rather than the parts and the relationship between parts.

Again, learning processes are classified into three: (i) enactive or learning by doing (ii) iconic learning by organisation of perception and (iii) symbolic, learning through symbols and language representations.

All these learning theories, principles and processes are of vital importance for successful communication which is equivalent to active learning. Participation, interaction, cooperation and different skills promote such lively learning experiences. Various media, materials and methods capitalise such principles and approaches for providing better learning experiences. That is why, educational technology consisting of all means, media and materials based on the psychological principles and precepts helps promoting learning as well as teaching.

The Report of the Meeting of Chief Technical Advisers, National Directors and UNESCO specialists in Methods and Techniques, Paris, December, 1979 has said that, Educational Technology is a communication process resulting from the adaptation of the scientific method to the behavioural science of teaching/learning. It is a communication process which may or may not require the use of extending media (i. e., radio, television, film and other audio-visual media). The process contains essentially the following components.

1. Specification of goals and behavioural objectives.
2. Analysis of the characteristics of the learners.
3. Selection and organisation of the content or subject matter to be learned.
4. Presentation of the content.
5. Evaluation of the results.
6. Feedback. Feedback must be continuously interacting among all of the preceding five components. It is not just a final component, but it provides essential linkages among all the components.

All these components are also essential elements in learning. Unless all these points are taken into consideration, learning cannot be made effective. These are the basic needs for organisation of suitable media and materials in order to optimise learning outcomes. Modern communication methods, visual arts, classroom organisation and teaching techniques are to be made use of and geared to achieve the instructional objectives. Communication processes supported by technology of education intend to bring about effective and efficient learning.

Role of Teacher

Pedagogy, the science of teachers' behaviour, has now given place to mathetics, the science of learners' behaviour, that is there has been a shift in focus from the teacher to the pupil and learners' behaviour has been given more emphasis than teachers' behaviour. In other words, the learning process is replacing the teaching process. Learning to learn is essential and learning is more important than teaching.

Learning is also a continuous process. It is lifelong. It is apt to be equivalent with education. Through education students learn how to learn, learn how to keep on learning, learn how to be creative and innovative, and learn how to contribute meaningfully and significantly to solving the new problems that are encountered in day to day world.

If learning is so important, what is the role of a teacher? Faure and others (1982 pp 77-78) have rightly replied, "the teachers' duty is less and less to inculcate knowledge and more and more to encourage thinking; his formal functions apart, he will have to become more and more an adviser; a partner to talk to, someone who helps seek out conflicting arguments rather than reading out readymade truths. He will have to devote more time and energy to productive and creative activities such as interaction, discussion, stimulation, understanding and encouragement."

The teacher is no longer the monopolistic purveyor of information and authoritative transmitter of knowledge. He is to inspire, motivate, guide and stimulate. His role is not merely to communicate the new knowledge, understanding and skills but to identify the pupils needs and provide facilities for their allround development.

Organs and Theories : Communication and its advancement is vital to modern civilization. It has affected the entire world immensely as well as wonderfully. The whole world has been reduced to a close neighbourhood. The distance of time and space has been almost removed and all barriers of castes, communities, creeds and colours have given place to mutual fellow-feeling, interrelationships and cooperative ventures. Robert M-Hutchines, a distinguished educationist has named it "a communication revolution." In fact, today it has exerted inevitable influence on millions and billions of people all over the globe through various means and media. It is informing, entertaining and inspiring individuals in many ways.

Area of Communication : The term "Communication" has been derived from the Latin word "Communis" meaning "Common." It implies common experiences, mutual sharing or give and take. It gives different meanings to different people.

Communication is defined as the sharing of ideas and feelings in a mood of mutuality. It involves interaction which encourages give and take. This provides feedback to individuals involved in the exchange of ideas. Effective communication is, therefore, a two-way process.

Communication assumes a democratic philosophy of life which implies the dignity and respect of all persons who enter into communication. It also assumes freedom to learn and criticize. John Dewey, an exponent of democracy has emphasized shared experience as a key element in communication and pointed out, "communication is a process of sharing experience till it becomes a common possession. It modifies the disposition of both the parties who partake of it."

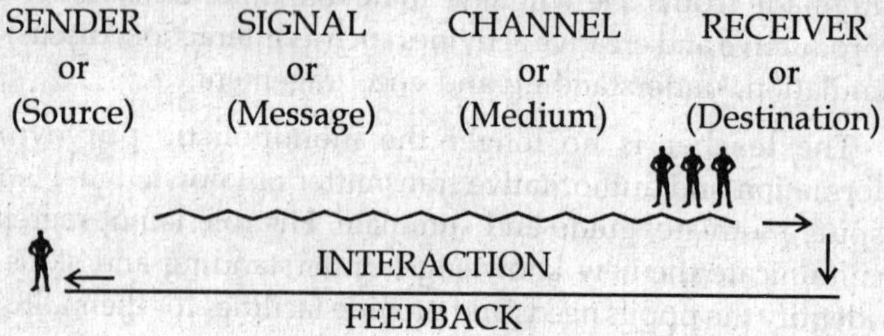

Wilbur Schramm, an outstanding communication expert has said that it "is concerned with all the ways in which information and ideas are exchanged and shared. Thus we are talking about both mass and interpersonal communication. We are talking about the spoken word, signal, gesture, picture, visual display, print, broadcast, film-all the signs and symbols by which humans try to convey meaning and value to another."

Organs of Communication : There are mainly four components of communication. They are (i) source or sender which is technically called "encoder", (ii) message or signal, (iii) channel or medium, and (iv) destination or receiver which is technically known as "decoder."

In the communication process, the source or the sender has the correct information and transmits the same as accurately, clearly and speedily as possible. The content of transmission is called the message. It should be conveyed through the medium of words both written and verbal, gestures, pictures, and so on. Thus the medium or channel may be either audio or visual or both. Every medium has its peculiar influence on the message to a great extent. That is why, it becomes, in a sense, an integral part of the message and it is aptly called "medium is the message." The sender encodes the ideas or information as the message and channelises the same upto the receiver through medium or media. The receiver decodes or understands the message or interprets the information according to his background.

Since communication involves at least two or more persons, interaction is a "must" in order to make it effective. This ensures the mutual sharing or give and take of ideas and experiences. Such communication must also have a desired reaction called "feedback". Thus in any effective communication, in addition to the original four components, two more (i) interaction and (ii) feedback are also essential. Thus the process of communication can be represented by the following diagram:

But interaction is so much inter-mingled with feedback that many communication experts like Harold D. Lasswell take both as one-feedback. The five essential elements of communication are: "who, says what, in which channel, to whom, with what effect?"

Diverse Way of Communication : There are mainly three modes of communication. They are (i) Speaking ⟷ Listening, (ii) Visualising ⟷ Observing (iii) Writing ⟷ Reading. They may briefly be discussed as follows:

Speaking ⟷ ***Listening*** : In this type of communication one speaks and another listens. This is mainly face-to-face as in the case of conversation or listening to a speech. In some cases, there may be gap or distance in between the sender and the receiver or the source and the destination like in radio broadcasting. But both the sender and the receiver of messages share the feelings and may interact with each other if they are in eye to eye contact.

Visualising ⟷ ***Observing*** : In this type of communication one visualises and another observes. There is usually a physical separation between the producer of the message and the audience to whom the message is conveyed as in the case of a television programme or a film. Dramatisation may also be included under this category in which facial expression and gestures produce an effective communication.

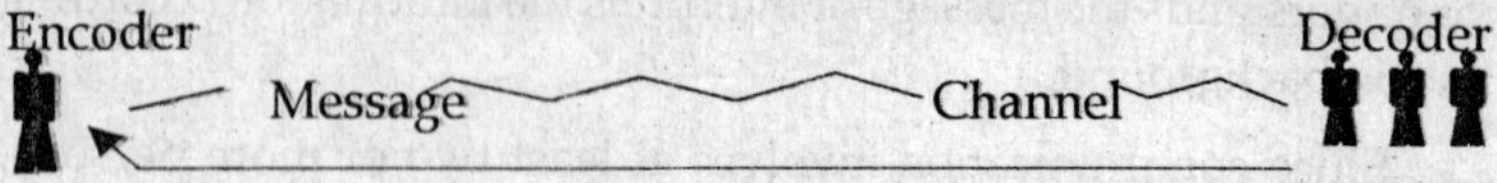

Feedback

Writing ⟷ ***Reading*** : In this model of communication, the sender and the receiver are physically separated all the time, but both are able to share the experiences and feelings. An example of this model is the writing of a book by an author and reading of the same by a reader or a group of readers who can enjoy and appreciate the feelings and ideas of the writer properly.

The arrows moving both ways indicate that in all three kinds of communication, interaction and feedback are essential features in effective communication.

Communication Theories : The basic communication theory indicates that there must be four elements - source, message, channel and destination, in the communication process. Any communicator sends message through a channel to the audience. In the technical jargon, the communicator is known as the encoder, the message whether words, pictures or signs is called symbol, the channel may be one of the media or means and the audience is called decoder. The diagram of this basic theory is as simple as this:

In this process, an adept communicator knows what he wants to communicate as message, understands the characteristics of the channel and the social as well as psychological background of individuals constituting the audience.

Then it was found that feedback is essential for making communication effective. The communicator should know the reaction or response of the audience, so that it will be possible on his part to modify his message as well as the channel. There must be interaction between both the communicator and the audience. Thus the second model may be represented like this:

Everybody has his own background physical, social, psychological and sociological. He sends or understands a message from his own background. The physical and emotional conditions like health, mood, attitude and ego involvement influence his understanding or reception of the message. The audience provide their reaction to the message and the communicator modifies or revises his message and media according to such feedback effects. This classic model is again modified by some communication specialists like Wilbur Schramm who advocated a circular diagram to represent the communication process. According to them both the parties - communicator as well as audience - should play the ideal roles as senders and receivers. This diagram is as follows:

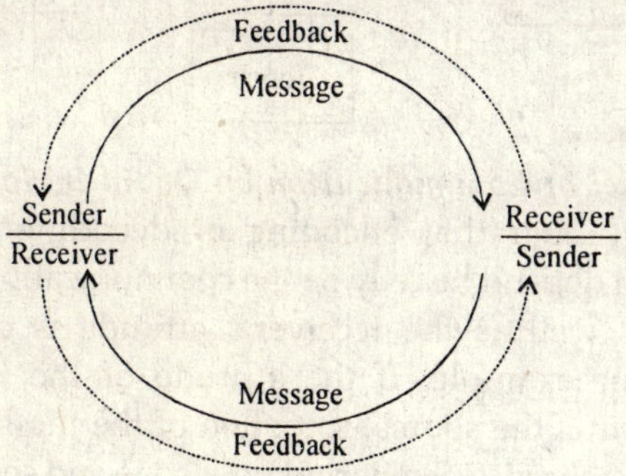

This is a kind of communication that occurs normally in conversation between two persons. But in order to ensure effectiveness in communication, it is felt imperative that there must be interaction and feedback continuously and mutual sharing or give and take of experiences and ideas.

Another theory or model of communication is known as SMCR developed by David K. Berlo. This model emphasizes the psychological nature of communication and provides an analysis of messages and of sensory channels of communication. In this model, source is considered along with communication skills, attitudes, knowledge and socio-cultural context; message includes content, treatment and code; channel consists of eyes, ears, taste, nose and touch and receiver comprises communication skills, attitudes, knowledge and socio-cultural context. The model is represented in the following diagram.

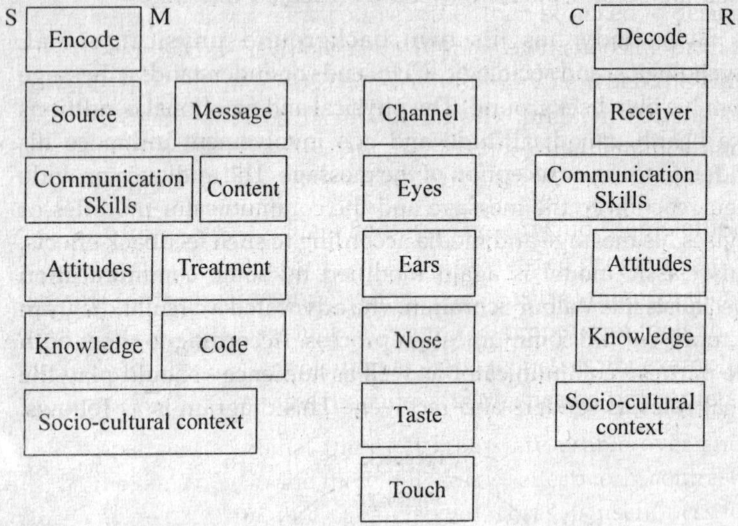

SMCR Model of Communication by David Berlo : Berlo has rightly made it clear that encoding or decoding a message successfully will depend heavily on the communication skills. But the sender's as well as the receiver's attitude is of immense significance. For example, if the attitude of the recipient is favourable towards the source, reception of the message will be different, if it is otherwise. Similarly, knowledge and socio-cultural background of the source as well as of the receiver are equally significant for successful transmission and reception of the message. It is a fact that the message actually does not convey the meaning. The meaning is grasped according to the psychological, emotional and sociological background of the receiver. Berlo has aptly said,

"Communication does not consist of the transmission of meaning. Meanings are not transmittable, not transferable, only messages are transmittable, and meanings are not in the message, they are in message - users."

Communication and Decisive Questions : It is said that beauty lies in the eyes of receiver. Similarly, meaning lies with the listener. Edgar Dale has corroborated Berlo's statement very strongly and clearly, when he observed that you can present stimuli to an individual, but his needs and background determine whether it will be accurately interpreted, and create the intended meanings. Furthermore, messages are also distorted by the receiver. They see what they want to see, hear what they want to hear, and distort messages unintentionally. Even there is selective perception; for example, heavy cigarette smokers do not quit smoking when they read about the harmful effects noted in research, rather they quit reading about cancer studies.

Even today the experience of Galileo about refusal of persons to see the truth holds good to a very great extent. Galileo wrote to his friend Kepler, "Here at Padua is the principal professor of philosophy, whom 1 have repeatedly and urgently requested to look at the moon and planets through my glass, which he perniciously refused to do... what glorious folly!". In this context what can the communicator do? He may take the horse to the water, how can he make it drink? If the meaning lies with the receiver, neither with the message nor with the channel, what can the sender do to make the communication effective? The next chapter looks to answer these questions.

Communication as Equipment of Social Transformation : Change in the human society is continuous, perennial and pervading. Change takes place always, everywhere and in all aspects of the society. It may, therefore, be said that the only 'changeless' element in the society is the 'change' itself. That is why *Democritus*, the Greek philosopher has said that you cannot live in the same society a second time.

It is only through change that progress in the society is brought about. More are the changes, greater is the progress. Human civilisation has reached the present stage only due to social changes.

The primitive society was comparatively less prone to change than the modern one and the lethargic, dull and backward people are more averse to changes than the energetic, ebullient and advanced persons. Thus the social change is the key to social progress.

Sorts of Social Change

Social changes are mainly of two kinds. One is structural and the other is functional. When the entire structure of the society is changed by means of a political movement or national struggle, it is a structural social change and when a change take place in man's behaviour, ways of living, dress and food habits through education and culture, it is functional. The American War of Independence, the French Revolution, the Russian Revolution and the Struggle of Indian Independence come under the first category and change over from wearing the untailored dhoti to putting on a pair of suit, from using the bullock-drawn plough to a power driven tractor, from squatting on a mat for eating to dining at a table are the examples of the latter. Both structural and functional changes have almost the same degree of difference as between the major and minor operations. Thus in the struggle parlance 'operation' and in the social science "social change" have both the broad and narrow connotations and have immense significance for physiological and sociological life.

Communications Dynamics of Social Transformation : According to Ottaway (1962) social change is the result of interaction of both techniques and values. It is of little use to desire social change either in terms of technical progress or in terms of a change in values when one is considered independently of the other. The state of society depends on both and they are inseparable. It is also not easy to say which influence is dominant or takes the lead in any particular social change.

It is said by some social scientists that new inventions and discoveries are a primary cause of social change. But any invention or discovery alone is not adequate to explain the social change. Its use depends on the prevailing set of values in the society. The aims and objectives, lifestyles and philosophy of a community determine how its techniques will be used. The same technical invention can be used differently in different societies or its use may be delayed if the existing conditions of the society are not favourable or it may be accelerated if the society is amply prepared for the same.

On the other hand, some sociologists believe that the value-systems, ideas and aspirations play a dominant part in changing the society. We must, of course, recognize the force of technology, which brings about changes in our habits of work, thought and belief. Thus we have to deal with the problems of social change by considering a number of variables, each influencing the other.

Maciver and Page (1950) in their important work "Society" have distinguished between the technological factors and the cultural factors in bringing about social change. These two factors may be compared with techniques and values given by Ottaway. All these three authors also equally believe in interaction between the two sets of factors and reject all theories which place the technical and cultural factors in opposition to each other and stress the dominance of the one or the other in determining social change.

Ogburn (1947) has also used the terms material culture and non-material culture and described the "cultural lag". When the former comes first, it is more rapid and more effective in determining the social change. That is, non-material factors likes values lag behind the material factors or conditions like techniques. Marx and Engels had earlier put forth their extreme views of economic or material determinism in the change. Recently, Thorstein Veblin has developed a thesis that the kind of work and leisure which men do determine the social structure. Here he has stressed the importance of adjustment to changing techniques.

It may thus be concluded that both material and non-material aspects of culture are simultaneously involved in any social change and that neither is necessarily dominant. The relative significance of these factors will be different on different occasions. The cultural lag or social leeway however often comes into being when a man's values cannot keep pace with his technical development and a cycle of interaction always revolves involving both techniques and values simultaneously, but not equally.

Social Change by Communication

Communication is the powerful means of bringing about social change. Mac Luhan has developed a thesis of technological determinism which says that changes in the technology of communication brings about social changes. The revolution in the media of communication has helped accelerate the pace of social change during these few decades. Radio, television, newspapers and other mass-media have not only made this world "shrunk" but also have revolutionised the values, attitudes, interests and social milieus.

An important task of communication is to promote development and without its support no project can be made successful. Balcomb (1975) has aptly mentioned that many ambitions projects have failed because of poor all round communications. From his own experience he has clearly pointed out that the UNICEF and other agencies had supplied a considerable amount of audio-visual equipment to various projects but much of this equipment was being poorly used. The hardware was there, but the software had very often been left to take care of itself. That is, proper dovetailing and adequate coordination as well as integration of the technical equipments used for communication purposes and the messages or information that are to be transmitted through these mechanisms are essential for effective communication. Thus for implementing projects in every field whether health or agriculture or education, the building of such overall communication systems is technically called the "Project Support Communication."

It may be mentioned in this connection that at least four elements are required for communication: (I) a source (II) message (III) channel and (IV) destination, (Schramm, 1954). These involve both human and mechanical segments of communication. There must be person (s) to initiate at one end and receive at the other end and a message to be conveyed by expressions, gestures, spoken or written symbols or by drama or photographed pictures. This process emphasizes the need for common understanding of language and word meaning based on similarity of experience background for effective communication.

The source must have the correct message to be transmitted clearly to the receiver. It is also to be ensured that the receiver is understanding the message accurately and producing a desired response. Thus the communication must be a two way process resulting in intercommunication and based on mutual sharing of experiences and a continual feedback.

Idea of Making Communication Function : With a view to making communication effective, motivation of the persons concerned is to be generated. The people should think for themselves and on their own initiative. They must do whatever they think right and desirable for them, not as they are told to do. They are to function as project participants, not merely as project's beneficiaries.

Without the needs being felt by the beneficiaries themselves the project howsoever need based and useful, cannot be implemented successfully. A small example may be cited here. In a tribal village women had to go to distant hilltops to fetch drinking water. Under the Community Development Project in that village a well was sunk and sweet water was also available. But alas! the tribal women were so much used to bringing water from a high altitude and not oriented to draw water from a well nearby that the well turned to be a big dustbin!

Another interesting incident of this nature has been narrated by Matheson (1975). Many years back a big project was started in the vicinity of Rome to clear the Pontine Marshes for eliminating mosquitoes and the diseases from the city and at the same time to create more arable land for cultivation of vegetables and fruits. But fishermen living in the swampy places and earning their livelihood from fishing grew irate at the prospect of swamps being drained. As a matter of fact they broke the walls of the water tanks that had been created to lead off the water and soon the ambitious drainage project was completely wrecked.

These phenomena clearly indicate the communication gap as the tribals and fishermen were not explained about these projects which were meant for a better and happier life. Matheson has therefore remarked that unfortunately although the tools of technology are available today to help improve the lives of people throughout the developing world, too many projects are failing to achieve their goals because communication experts and development planners often do not communicate effectively with each other or with the people they are trying to help. Unless the people themselves are made ready for the changes and feel the needs, no project can be a success.

We may use various kinds of mass media and audio-visual aids but our message must be clear at first and communicated as effectively as possible. In order to facilitate this, audience have to be motivated through various means, most important of which is felt to be interpersonal communication. Matheson has again hammered this point when he says that finding the right message for the right medium for a specific audience is a constant challenge to communication experts and development planners and workers. Much has been claimed for the power of the mass media and it has certainly achieved wonders in bringing people instant information and in shaping lifestyles and beliefs. But when it comes to rural societies especially where literacy levels are low and traditions deep-rooted, the effectiveness of mass media in bringing about change is very limited. Experience has shown that probably the single most effective means of communication is the interpersonal one - dialogue between two or more people.

Every medium of communication has its own limitations. So it has to be selected according to the socio-cultural conditions of the clientele and be used in appropriate time and place with much caution. Nevertheless communication elements should be built into a project in the initial planning stage. They must be integrated with the whole system and not just tagged on as an after thought. Moreover adequate awareness of the target population should be generated, their needs felt by themselves, their motivations created and attitude changed so that communication is made effective to achieve the desired kind of social change.

Bibliography

Apter, Michel : *The New Technology of Education*, Macmillan, London, 1968.

Awasthy, G.C. : *Broadcasting in India*, Allied Publishers Private Ltd., Bombay, 1965

Bloom, B.S. : *Taxonomy of Educational Objectives: The Classification of Educational Goals. Handbook Cognitive Domain and Affective Domain*, Oxford, New York, 1965.

———, *Human Characteristics and School Learning*, Harper, New York, 1976.

Beiggs L.S. : *Instruction Media*, Fitteburgh American Institute for Research, 1966.

Brown, J.W. Lewis, R.B. & Hercleread. A.V. : *Instruction: Materials and Methods*, Mc Graw Hill Book Co., New York, 1964.

Chauhan, S.S. : *A Textbook of Programmed Instruction*, Sterling Publishers, New Delhi.

Chatterjee, R.K. : *Mass Communication*, National Book Trust, New Delhi, 1993.

Dhinnie, Dinald Mc and Dutt Sunitee : *The Art of Radio*, Faber & Faber, London, 1961.

Dale, Edgare : *Audio Visual Method in Teaching*, Dryden Rinehart and Winston, New York. 1969.

Das, R.C. : *Educational Technology*, Sterling Publishers, New Delhi.

Gagne, R.M. : *The Conditions of Learning*, Holt Binsort and Winston, New York, 1965.

Goodman, Loster : *Educational Radio*, CET, NCERT, 1977.

Haban, Charles, F. : *Movies that Teach*, New York, Dryden Press, 1945.

Hancock, Alan : *Planning for Educational Mass-Media*, Longmans, London, 1977.

Kinder, James. S. : *Audio-Visual Materials and Techniques*, American Book Company, New York, 1959.

Kulkarni, S.S. : *Teaching Learning Process: A Systems Analysis*, UNESCO Regional Office for Education in Asia, Bangkok, 1975.

Kaul, B.N. & Others : *Studies in Distance Education*, Association of Indian Universities, IGNOU, New Delhi, 1988.

Lowman, J. : *Mastering Techniques of Teaching*, Prentice Hall India, New Delhi, 1987.

Matheson, Alastair : *The Communication Materials and Methods*, Mc Graw Hill Book Company, New Delhi, 1964.

Mc Luhan : *Understanding Media*, Routludge, London, 1964.

Mohanty, J. : *Educational Broadcasting: Radio & Television in Education*, Sterling Publishers, New Delhi, 1984.

———, *Educational Administration, Management & School Organisation*, Meneka Prakashan, Sambalpur, 1996.

———, *Indian Education in the Emerging Society*, Sterling Publishers, New Delhi, 1982.

———, *Studies in Educational Broadcasting*, Deep & Deep Publications, New Delhi.

———, *Dynamics of Higher Education in India*, Deep & Deep Publications, New Delhi.

———, *Current Trends in Higher Education*, Deep & Deep Publications, New Delhi.

Menon, Narayan : *The Communication Revolution*, National Book Trust, New Delhi, 1976.

Mukhopadhyay, M. : *Educational Technology Year Book*, 1988, AIAET, New Delhi, 1989.

Munn, Norman L. : *The Fundamentals of Human Adjustment*, Houghter Miffin Co., Boston, 1965.

Ottaway A.K.C. : *Education and Society*, Routldge and Kegan Paul, London, 1962.

Rahman, S.A. : *Study in Educational Television*, Royal Pub., Orissa, 1972.

Rewntreu, Desk : *Educational Technology in Curriculum Development*, Harper and Row Publishers, London, 1990.

Sampath, K. : *Introduction to Educational Technology*, Sterling, New Delhi, 1981.

Schramm, Wilbur : *The Process and Effects of Mass Communication*, Uni of Illinois, Urbane, 1993.

———, *Programmes Instruction: Today and Tomorrow*, The Funds of Advancement of Education, New York, 1962.

Sharma, G.D. & Ahmed, S.R. : *Methodologies of Teaching in Colleges*, UNESCO UGC & NIEPA, New Delhi, 1994.

Singh, Bakshish : *Correspondence Education in India*, National Council for Correspondence Education, India, 1978.

Vedanayagam, G. : *Teaching Technology for College Teachers*, Sterling Publishers, New Delhi, 1989.

Index